Study Guide

Study Guide

Richard O. Straub
University of Michigan, Dearborn

Joan Winer Brown

to accompany

BERGER / THOMPSON

The Developing Person
Through Childhood and Adolescence
Fourth Edition

WORTH PUBLISHERS

Study Guide
by Richard O. Straub and Joan Winer Brown
to accompany
Berger/Thompson: The Developing Person Through Childhood
and Adolescence, Fourth Edition

ISBN: 1-57259-009-2

Printing: 2 3 4 5 — 99 98 97 96

Cover: Maurice Brazil Prendergast, *Low Tide*, ca. 1895-1897. Oil
on panel. Height: 13 1/2 in. Width: 18 in. Williams College
Museum of Art, Williamstown, Massachusetts. Gift of Mrs.
Charles Prendergast.

Worth Publishers
33 Irving Place
New York, New York 10003

Contents

Preface

This Study Guide is designed for use with *The Developing Person Through Childhood and Adolescence,* Fourth Edition, by Kathleen Stassen Berger and Ross Thompson. It is intended to help you to evaluate your understanding of that material, and then to review any problem areas. "How to Manage Your Time Efficiently, Study More Effectively, and Think Critically" provides detailed instructions on how to use the textbook and this Study Guide for maximum benefit. It also offers additional study suggestions based on principles of time management, effective note-taking, evaluation of exam performance, and an effective program for improving your comprehension while studying from textbooks.

Each chapter of the Study Guide includes a Chapter Overview, a set of Guided Study questions to pace your reading of the text chapter, a Chapter Review section to be completed after you have read the text chapter, and three review tests. The review tests are of two types: Progress Tests that consist of questions focusing on facts and definitions and a Thinking Critically Test that evaluates your understanding of the text chapter's broader conceptual material and its application to real-world situations. For all three review tests, the correct answers are given, followed by textbook page references (so you can easily go back and reread the material), and complete explanations not only of why the answer is correct but also of why the other choices are incorrect.

I would like to thank Joan Winer Brown for use of some of her excellent material from the first three editions of this Study Guide. Thanks, too, to Laura Rubin for keeping us all on schedule, and especially to Betty and Don Probert of The Special Projects Group for their exceptional work in all phases of this project.

Those at Worth Publishers who assisted in the preparation of this Study Guide join me in hoping that our work will help you to achieve your highest level of academic performance in this course and to acquire a keen appreciation of human development.

Richard O. Straub
February 1995

How to Manage Your Time Efficiently, Study More Effectively, and Think Critically

How effectively do you study? Good study habits make the job of being a college student much easier. Many students, who *could* succeed in college, fail or drop out because they have never learned to manage their time efficiently. Even the best students can usually benefit from an in-depth evaluation of their current study habits.

There are many ways to achieve academic success, of course, but your approach may not be the most effective or efficient. Are you sacrificing your social life or your physical or mental health in order to get A's on your exams? Good study habits result in better grades *and* more time for other activities.

Evaluate Your Current Study Habits

To improve your study habits, you must first have an accurate picture of how you currently spend your time. Begin by putting together a profile of your present living and studying habits. Answer the following questions by writing *yes* or *no* on each line.

_____ 1. Do you usually set up a schedule to budget your time for studying, recreation, and other activities?

_____ 2. Do you often put off studying until time pressures force you to cram?

_____ 3. Do other students seem to study less than you do, but get better grades?

_____ 4. Do you usually spend hours at a time studying one subject, rather than dividing that time between several subjects?

_____ 5. Do you often have trouble remembering what you have just read in a textbook?

_____ 6. Before reading a chapter in a textbook, do you skim through it and read the section headings?

_____ 7. Do you try to predict exam questions from your lecture notes and reading?

_____ 8. Do you usually attempt to paraphrase or summarize what you have just finished reading?

_____ 9. Do you find it difficult to concentrate very long when you study?

_____ 10. Do you often feel that you studied the wrong material for an exam?

Thousands of college students have participated in similar surveys. Students who are fully realizing their academic potential usually respond as follows: (1) yes, (2) no, (3) no, (4) no, (5) no, (6) yes, (7) yes, (8) yes, (9) no, (10) no.

Compare your responses to those of successful students. The greater the discrepancy, the more you could benefit from a program to improve your study habits. The questions are designed to identify areas of weakness. Once you have identified your weaknesses, you will be able to set specific goals for improvement and implement a program for reaching them.

Manage Your Time

Do you often feel frustrated because there isn't enough time to do all the things you must and want to do? Take heart. Even the most productive and successful people feel this way at times. But they establish priorities for their activities and they learn to budget time for each of them. There's much in the saying "If you want something done, ask a busy person to do it." A busy person knows how to get things done.

If you don't now have a system for budgeting your time, develop one. Not only will your academic accomplishments increase, but you will actually find more time in your schedule for other activities. And you won't have to feel guilty about "taking time off," because all your obligations will be covered.

Establish a Baseline

As a first step in preparing to budget your time, keep a diary for a few days to establish a summary, or baseline, of the time you spend in studying, socializing, working, and so on. If you are like many students, much of your "study" time is nonproductive; you may sit at your desk and leaf through a book, but the time is actually wasted. Or you may procrastinate. You are always getting ready to study, but you rarely do.

Besides revealing where you waste time, your diary will give you a realistic picture of how much time you need to allot for meals, commuting, and other fixed activities. In addition, careful records should indicate the times of the day when you are consistently most productive. A sample time-management diary is shown in Table 1.

Plan the Term

Having established and evaluated your baseline, you are ready to devise a more efficient schedule. Buy a calendar that covers the entire school term and has ample space for each day. Using the course outlines provided by your instructors, enter the dates of all exams, term paper deadlines, and other important academic obligations. If you have any long-range personal plans (concerts, weekend trips, etc.), enter the dates on the calendar as well. Keep your calendar up to date and refer to it often. I recommend carrying it with you at all times.

Develop a Weekly Calendar

Now that you have a general picture of the school term, develop a weekly schedule that includes all of your activities. Aim for a schedule that you can live with for the entire school term. A sample weekly schedule, incorporating the following guidelines, is shown in Table 2.

1. Enter your class times, work hours, and any other fixed obligations first. *Be thorough.* Using information from your time-management diary, allow plenty of time for such things as commuting, meals, laundry, and the like.

Table 1   Sample Time-Management Diary

Monday		
Activity	Time Completed	Duration Hours: Minutes
Sleep	7:00	7:30
Dressing	7:25	:25
Breakfast	7:45	:20
Commute	8:20	:35
Coffee	9:00	:40
French	10:00	1:00
Socialize	10:15	:15
Videogame	10:35	:20
Coffee	11:00	:25
Psychology	12:00	1:00
Lunch	12:25	:25
Study Lab	1:00	:35
Psych. Lab	4:00	3:00
Work	5:30	1:30
Commute	6:10	:40
Dinner	6:45	:35
TV	7:30	:45
Study Psych.	10:00	2:30
Socialize	11:30	1:30
Sleep		

Prepare a similar chart for each day of the week. When you finish an activity, note it on the chart and write down the time it was completed. Then determine its duration by subtracting the time the previous activity was finished from the newly entered time.

2. Set up a study schedule for each of your courses. The study habits survey and your time-management diary will direct you. The following guidelines should also be useful.

(a) Establish regular study times for each course. The 4 hours needed to study one subject, for example, are most profitable when divided into shorter periods spaced over several days. If you cram your studying into one 4-hour block, what you attempt to learn in the third or fourth hour will interfere with what you studied in the first 2 hours. Newly acquired knowledge is like wet cement. It needs some time to "harden" to become memory.

(b) Alternate subjects. The type of interference just mentioned is greatest between similar topics. Set up a schedule in which you spend time on several *different* courses during each study session. Besides reducing the potential for interference, alternating subjects will help to prevent mental fatigue with one topic.

(c) Set weekly goals to determine the amount of study time you need to do well in each course. This will

Table 2   Sample Weekly Schedule

Time	Mon.	Tues.	Wed.	Thurs.	Fri.	Sat.
7–8	Dress Eat	Dress Eat	Dress Eat	Dress Eat	Dress Eat	
8–9	Psych.	Study Psych.	Psych.	Study Psych.	Psych.	Dress Eat
9–10	Eng.	Study Eng.	Eng.	Study Eng.	Eng.	Study Eng.
10–11	Study French	Free	Study French	Open Study	Study French	Study Stats.
11–12	French	Study Psych. Lab	French	Open Study	French	Study Stats.
12–1	Lunch	Lunch	Lunch	Lunch	Lunch	Lunch
1–2	Stats.	Psych. Lab	Stats.	Study or Free	Stats.	Free
2–3	Bio.	Psych. Lab	Bio.	Free	Bio.	Free
3–4	Free	Psych.	Free	Free	Free	Free
4–5	Job	Job	Job	Job	Job	Free
5–6	Job	Job	Job	Job	Job	Free
6–7	Dinner	Dinner	Dinner	Dinner	Dinner	Dinner
7–8	Study Bio.	Study Bio.	Study Bio.	Study Bio.	Free	Free
8–9	Study Eng.	Study Stats.	Study Psych.	Open Study	Open Study	Free
9–10	Open Study	Open Study	Open Study	Open Study	Free	Free

This is a sample schedule for a student with a 16-credit load and a 10-hour-per-week part-time job. Using this chart as an illustration, make up a weekly schedule, following the guidelines outlined here.

depend on, among other things, the difficulty of your courses and the effectiveness of your methods. Many professors recommend studying at least 1 to 2 hours for each hour in class. If your time-management diary indicates that you presently study less time than that, do not plan to jump immediately to a much higher level. Increase study time from your baseline by setting weekly goals [see (4)] that will gradually bring you up to the desired level. As an initial schedule, for example, you might set aside an amount of study time for each course that matches class time.

(d) Schedule for maximum effectiveness. Tailor your schedule to meet the demands of each course. For the course that emphasizes lecture notes, schedule time for a daily review soon after the class. This will give you a chance to revise your notes and clean up any hard-to-decipher shorthand while the material is still fresh in your mind. If you are evaluated for class participation (for example, in a language course), allow time for a review just before the class meets. Schedule study time for your most difficult (or least motivat-

ing) courses during hours when you are the most alert and distractions are fewest.

(e) Schedule open study time. Emergencies, additional obligations, and the like could throw off your schedule. And you may simply need some extra time periodically for a project or for review in one of your courses. Schedule several hours each week for such purposes.

3. After you have budgeted time for studying, fill in slots for recreation, hobbies, relaxation, household errands, and the like.

4. Set specific goals. Before each study session, make a list of specific goals. The simple note "7–8 PM: study psychology" is too broad to ensure the most effective use of the time. Formulate your daily goals according to what you know you must accomplish during the term. If you have course outlines with advance assignments, set systematic daily goals that will allow you, for example, to cover fifteen chapters before the exam. And be realistic: Can you actually

expect to cover a 78-page chapter in one session? Divide large tasks into smaller units; stop at the most logical resting points. When you complete a specific goal, take a 5- or 10-minute break before tackling the next goal.

5. Evaluate how successful or unsuccessful your studying has been on a daily or weekly basis. Did you reach most of your goals? If so, reward yourself immediately. You might even make a list of five to ten rewards to choose from. If you have trouble studying regularly, you may be able to motivate yourself by making such rewards contingent on completing specific goals.

6. Finally, until you have lived with your schedule for several weeks, don't hesitate to revise it. You may need to allow more time for chemistry, for example, and less for some other course. If you are trying to study regularly for the first time and are feeling burned out, you probably have set your initial goals too high. Don't let failure cause you to despair and abandon the program. Accept your limitations and revise your schedule so that you are studying only 15 to 20 minutes more each evening than you are used to. The point is to identify a regular schedule with which you can achieve some success. Time management, like any skill, must be practiced to become effective.

Techniques for Effective Study

Knowing how to put study time to best use is, of course, as important as finding a place for it in your schedule. Here are some suggestions that should enable you to increase your reading comprehension and improve your note-taking. A few study tips are included as well.

Using SQ3R to Increase Reading Comprehension

How do you study from a textbook? If you are like many students, you simply read and reread in a *passive* manner. Studies have shown, however, that most students who simply read a textbook cannot remember more than half the material ten minutes after they have finished. Often, what is retained is the unessential material rather than the important points upon which exam questions will be based.

This *Study Guide* employs a program known as SQ3R (*S*urvey, *Q*uestion, *R*ead, *R*ecite, and *R*eview) to facilitate, and allow you to assess, your comprehension of the important facts and concepts in *The Developing Person Through Childhood and Adolescence*, Fourth Edition, by Kathleen Stassen Berger and Ross Thompson.

Research has shown that students using SQ3R achieve significantly greater comprehension of textbooks than students reading in the more traditional passive manner. Once you have learned this program, you can improve your comprehension of any textbook.

Survey Before reading a chapter, determine whether the text or the study guide has an outline or list of objectives. Read this material and the summary at the end of the chapter. Next, read the textbook chapter fairly quickly, paying special attention to the major headings and subheadings. This survey will give you an idea of the chapter's contents and organization. You will then be able to divide the chapter into logical sections in order to formulate specific goals for a more careful reading of the chapter.

In this Study Guide, the *Chapter Overview* summarizes the major topics of the textbook chapter. This section also provides a few suggestions for approaching topics you may find difficult.

Question You will retain material longer when you have a use for it. If you look up a word's definition in order to solve a crossword puzzle, for example, you will remember it longer than if you merely fill in the letters as a result of putting other words in. Surveying the chapter will allow you to generate important questions that the chapter will proceed to answer. These question correspond to "mental files" into which knowledge will be sorted for easy access.

As you survey, jot down several questions for each chapter section. One simple technique is to generate questions by rephrasing a section heading. For example, the "Preoperational Thought" head could be turned into "What is preoperational thought?" Good questions will allow you to focus on the important points in the text. Examples of good questions are those that begin as follows: "List two examples of . . .." "What is the function of . . .?" "What is the significance of . . .?" Such questions give a purpose to your reading. Similarly, you can formulate questions based on the chapter outline.

The *Guided Study* section of this Study Guide provides the types of questions you might formulate while surveying each chapter. This section is a detailed set of objectives covering the points made in the text.

Read When you have established "files" for each section of the chapter, review your first question, begin reading, and continue until you have discovered its answer. If you come to material that seems to answer an important question you don't have a file for, stop and write down the question.

Using this Study Guide, read the chapter one section at a time. First, preview the section by skimming it, noting headings and boldface items. Next, study the appropriate section objectives in the *Guided Study*. Then, as you read the chapter section, search for the answer to each objective.

Be sure to read everything. Don't skip photo or art captions, graphs, marginal notes. In some cases, what may seem vague in reading will be made clear by a simple graph. Keep in mind that test questions are sometimes drawn from illustrations and charts.

Recite When you have found the answer to a question, close your eyes and mentally recite the question and its answer. Then *write* the answer next to the question. It is important that you recite an answer in your own words rather than the author's. Don't rely on your short-term memory to repeat the author's words verbatim.

In responding to the objectives, pay close attention to what is called for. If you are asked to identify or list, do just that. If asked to compare, contrast, or do both, you should focus on the similarities (compare) and differences (contrast) between the concepts or theories. Answering the objectives carefully will not only help you to focus your attention on the important concepts of the text, but it will also provide excellent practice for essay exams.

Recitation is an extremely effective study technique, recommended by many learning experts. In addition to increasing reading comprehension, it is useful for review. Trying to explain something in your own words clarifies your knowledge, often by revealing aspects of your answer that are vague or incomplete. If you repeatedly rely upon "I know" in recitation, you really may not know.

Recitation has the additional advantage of simulating an exam, especially an essay exam; the same skills are required in both cases. Too often students study without ever putting the book and notes aside, which makes it easy for them to develop false confidence in their knowledge. When the material is in front of you, you may be able to recognize an answer, but will you be able to recall it later, when you take an exam that does not provide these retrieval cues?

After you have recited and written your answer, continue with your next question. Read, recite, and so on.

Review When you have answered the last question on the material you have designated as a study goal, go back and review. Read over each question and your written answer to it. Your review might also include a brief written summary that integrates all of your questions and answers. This review need not take longer than a few minutes, but it is important. It will help you retain the material longer and will greatly facilitate a final review of each chapter before the exam.

In this Study Guide, the *Chapter Review* section contains fill-in and one- or two-sentence essay questions for you to complete after you have finished reading the text and have written answers to the objectives. The correct answers are given at the end of the chapter. Generally, your answer to a fill-in question should match exactly (as in the case of important terms, theories, or people). In some cases, the answer is not a term or name, so a word close in meaning will suffice. You should go through the Chapter Review several times before taking an exam, so it is a good idea to mentally fill in the answers until you are ready for a final pretest review. Textbook page references are provided with each section title, in case you need to reread any of the material.

Also provided to facilitate your review are two *Progress Tests* that include multiple-choice questions and, where appropriate, matching or true–false questions. These tests are not to be taken until you have read the chapter, written answers to the objectives, and completed the *Chapter Review*. Correct answers, along with explanations of why each alternative is correct or incorrect, are provided at the end of the chapter. The relevant text page numbers for each question are also given. If you miss a question, read these explanations and, if necessary, review the text pages to further understand why. The *Progress Tests* do not test every aspect of a concept, so you should treat an incorrect answer as an indication that you need to review the concept.

Following the two Progress Tests is a *Thinking Critically Test*, which should be taken just prior to an exam. It includes questions that test your ability to analyze, integrate, and apply the concepts in the chapter. As with the *Progress Tests*, answers for the *Thinking Critically Test* are provided at the end of each chapter, along with relevant page numbers.

The chapter concludes with a list of *Key Terms*; definitions are to be written on a separate piece of paper. As with the *Guided Study* objectives, it is important that these answers be written from memory, and in your own words. The *Answers* section at the end of the chapter gives a definition of each term, sometimes along with an example of its usage and/or a tip to help you remember its meaning.

One final suggestion: Incorporate SQ3R into your time-management calendar. Set specific goals for completing SQ3R with each assigned chapter. Keep a record of chapters completed, and reward yourself for being conscientious. Initially, it takes more time and effort to "read" using SQ3R, but with practice, the steps will become automatic. More important, you will comprehend significantly more material and retain what you have learned longer than passive readers do.

Taking Lecture Notes

Are your class notes as useful as they might be? One way to determine their worth is to compare them with those taken by other good students. Are yours as thorough? Do they provide you with a comprehensible outline of each lecture? If not, then the following suggestions might increase the effectiveness of your note-taking.

1. Keep a separate notebook for each course. Use 8 1/2 ¥ 11-inch pages. Consider using a ring binder, which would allow you to revise and insert notes while still preserving lecture order.

2. Take notes in the format of a lecture outline. Use roman numerals for major points, letters for supporting arguments, and so on. Some instructors will make this easy by delivering organized lectures and, in some cases, by outlining their lectures on the board. If a lecture is disorganized, you will probably want to reorganize your notes soon after the class.

3. As you take notes in class, leave a wide margin on one side of each page. After the lecture, expand or clarify any shorthand notes while the material is fresh in your mind. Use this time to write important questions in the margin next to notes that answer them. This will facilitate later review and will allow you to anticipate similar exam questions.

Evaluate Your Exam Performance

How often have you received a grade on an exam that did not do justice to the effort you spent preparing for the exam? This is a common experience that can leave one feeling bewildered and abused. "What do I have to do to get an A?" "The test was unfair!" "I studied the wrong material!"

The chances of this happening are greatly reduced if you have an effective time-management schedule and use the study techniques described here. But it can happen to the best-prepared student and is most likely to occur on your first exam with a new professor.

Remember that there are two main reasons for studying. One is to learn for your own general academic development. Many people believe that such knowledge is all that really matters. Of course, it is possible, though unlikely, to be an expert on a topic without achieving commensurate grades, just as one can, occasionally, earn an excellent grade without truly mastering the course material. During a job interview or in the workplace, however, your A in Cobol won't mean much if you can't actually program a computer.

In order to keep career options open after you graduate, you must know the material and maintain competitive grades. In the short run, this means performing well on exams, which is the second main objective in studying.

Probably the single best piece of advice to keep in mind when studying for exams is to *try to predict exam questions*. This means ignoring the trivia and focusing on the important questions and their answers (with your instructor's emphasis in mind).

A second point is obvious. How well you do on exams is determined by your mastery of both lecture and textbook material. Many students (partly because of poor time management) concentrate too much on one at the expense of the other.

To evaluate how well you are learning lecture and textbook material, analyze the questions you missed on the first exam. If your instructor does not review exams during class, you can easily do it yourself. Divide the questions into two categories: those drawn primarily from lectures and those drawn primarily from the textbook. Determine the percentage of questions you missed in each category. If your errors are evenly distributed and you are satisfied with your grade, you have no problem. If you are weaker in one area, you will need to set future goals for increasing and/or improving your study of that area.

Similarly, note the percentage of test questions drawn from each category. Although exams in most courses cover both lecture notes and the textbook, the relative emphasis of each may vary from instructor to instructor. While your instructors may not be entirely consistent in making up future exams, you may be able to tailor your studying for each course by placing additional emphasis on the appropriate area.

Exam evaluation will also point out the types of questions your instructor prefers. Does the exam consist primarily of multiple-choice, true–false, or essay questions? You may also discover that an instructor is fond of wording questions in certain ways. For example, an instructor may rely heavily on questions that require you to draw an analogy between a theory or concept and a real-world example. Evaluate both your instructor's style and how well you do with each format. Use this information to guide your future exam preparation.

Important aids, not only in studying for exams but also in determining how well prepared you are, are the Progress and Thinking Critically Tests provided in this Study Guide. If these tests don't include all of the types of questions your instructor typically writes, make up your own practice exam questions. Spend extra time testing yourself with question formats that are most difficult for you. There is no better way to evaluate your preparation for an upcoming exam than by testing yourself under the conditions most likely to be in effect during the actual test.

A Few Practical Tips

Even the best intentions for studying sometimes fail. Some of these failures occur because students attempt to work under conditions that are simply not conducive to concentrated study. To help ensure the success of your time-management program, here are a few suggestions that should assist you in reducing the possibility of procrastination or distraction.

1. If you have set up a schedule for studying, make your roommate, family, and friends aware of this commitment, and ask them to honor your quiet study time. Close your door and post a "Do Not Disturb" sign.

2. Set up a place to study that minimizes potential distractions. Use a desk or table, not your bed or an extremely comfortable chair. Keep your desk and the walls around it free from clutter. If you need a place other than your room, find one that meets as many of the above requirements as possible—for example, in the library stacks.

3. Do nothing but study in this place. It should become associated with studying so that it "triggers" this activity, just as a mouth-watering aroma elicits an appetite.

4. Never study with the television on or with other distracting noises present. If you must have music in the background in order to mask outside noise, for example, play soft instrumental music. Don't pick vocal selections; your mind will be drawn to the lyrics.

5. Study by yourself. Other students can be distracting or can break the pace at which your learning is most efficient. In addition, there is always the possibility that group studying will become a social gathering. Reserve that for its own place in your schedule.

If you continue to have difficulty concentrating for very long, try the following suggestions.

6. Study your most difficult or most challenging subjects first, when you are most alert.

7. Start with relatively short periods of concentrated study, with breaks in between. If your attention starts to wander, get up immediately and take a break. It is better to study effectively for 15 minutes and then take a break than to fritter away 45 minutes out of an hour. Gradually increase the length of study periods, using your attention span as an indicator of successful pacing.

Critical Thinking

Having discussed a number of specific techniques for managing your time efficiently and studying effectively, let us now turn to a much broader topic: What exactly should you expect to learn as a student of developmental psychology?

Most developmental psychology courses have two major goals: (1) to help you acquire a basic understanding of the discipline's knowledge base, and (2) to help you learn to think like a psychologist. Many students devote all of their efforts to the first of these goals, concentrating on memorizing as much of the course's material as possible.

The second goal—learning to think like a psychologist—has to do with critical thinking. Critical thinking has many meanings. On one level, it refers to an attitude of healthy skepticism that should guide your study of psychology. As a critical thinker, you learn not to accept any explanation or conclusion about behavior as true until you have evaluated the evidence. On another level, critical thinking refers to a systematic process for examining the conclusions and arguments presented by others. In this regard, many of the features of the SQ3R technique for improving reading comprehension can be incorporated into an effective critical thinking system.

To learn to think critically, you must first recognize that psychological information is transmitted through the construction of persuasive arguments. An argument consists of three parts: an assertion, evidence, and an explanation (Mayer and Goodchild, 1990).

An assertion is a statement of relationship between some aspect of behavior, such as intelligence, and another factor, such as age. Learn to identify and evaluate the assertions about behavior and mental processes that you encounter as you read your textbook, listen to lectures, and engage in discussions with classmates. A good test of your understanding of an assertion is to try to restate it in your own words. As you do so, pay close attention to how important terms and concepts are defined. When a researcher asserts that "intelligence declines with age," for example, what does he or she mean by

xvi   How to Manage Your Time Efficiently, Study More Effectively, and Think Critically

"intelligence"? Assertions such as this one may be true when a critical term ("intelligence") is defined one way (for example, "speed of thinking"), but not when defined in another way (for example, "general knowledge"). One of the strengths of psychology is the use of *operational* definitions that specify how key terms and concepts are measured, thus eliminating any ambiguity about their meaning. "Intelligence," for example, is often operationally defined as performance on a test measuring various cognitive skills. Whenever you encounter an assertion that is ambiguous, be skeptical of its accuracy.

When you have a clear understanding of an argument's assertion, evaluate its supporting evidence, the second component of an argument. Is it *empirical*? Does it, in fact, support the assertion? Psychologists accept only *empirical (observable) evidence* that is based on direct measurement of behavior. Hearsay, intuition, and personal experiences are not acceptable evidence. Chapter 1 discusses the various research methods used by developmental psychologists to gather empirical evidence. Some examples include surveys, observations of behavior in natural settings, and experiments.

As you study developmental psychology, you will become aware of another important issue in evaluating evidence—determining whether or not the research on which it is based is faulty. Research can be faulty for many reasons, including the use of an unrepresentative sample of subjects, experimenter bias, and inadequate control of unanticipated factors that might influence results. Evidence based on faulty research should be discounted.

The third component of an argument is the explanation provided for an assertion, which is based on the evidence that has been presented. While the argument's assertion merely *describes* how two things (such as intelligence and age) are related, the explanation tells *why*, often by proposing some theoretical mechanism that causes the relationship. Empirical evidence that thinking speed slows with age (the assertion), for example, may be explained as being caused by age-related changes in the activity of brain cells (a physiological explanation).

Be cautious in accepting explanations. In order to think critically about an argument's explanation, ask yourself three questions: (1) Can I restate the explanation in my own words?; (2) Does the explanation make sense based on the stated evidence?; and (3) Are there alternative explanations that adequately

explain the assertion? Consider this last point in relation to our sample assertion: It is possible that the slower thinking speed of older adults is due to their having less recent experience than younger people with tasks that require quick thinking (a disuse explanation).

Because psychology is a relatively young science, its theoretical explanations are still emerging, and often change. For this reason, not all psychological arguments will offer explanations. Many arguments will only raise additional questions for further research to address.

Some Suggestions for Becoming a Critical Thinker

1. Adopt an attitude of healthy skepticism in evaluating psychological arguments.

2. Insist on unambiguous operational definitions of an argument's important concepts and terms.

3. Be cautious in accepting supporting evidence for an argument's assertion.

4. Refuse to accept evidence for an argument if it is based on faulty research.

5. Ask yourself if the theoretical explanation provided for an argument "makes sense" based on the empirical evidence.

6. Determine whether there are alternative explanations that adequately explain an assertion.

7. Use critical thinking to construct your own effective arguments when writing term papers, answering essay questions, and speaking.

8. Polish your critical-thinking skills by applying them to each of your college courses, and to other areas of life as well. Learn to think critically about advertising, political speeches, and the material presented in popular periodicals.

Some Closing Thoughts

I hope that these suggestions help make you more successful academically, and that they enhance the quality of your college life in general. Having the necessary skills makes any job a lot easier and more pleasant. Let me repeat my warning not to attempt to make too drastic a change in your life-style immediately. Good habits require time and self-discipline to develop. Once established they can last a lifetime.

Study Guide

Introduction

Chapter Overview

The first chapter introduces the study of human development. In the first section, a definition of development is provided and the three domains into which it is often divided are described.

The second section makes clear that development is influenced as much by external factors as by internal factors. Beginning with a discussion of the ecological perspective—Bronfenbrenner's model of how the individual is affected by, and affects, many other individuals, groups of individuals, and larger systems in the environment—this section describes different aspects of the social context in which people develop. The story of David illustrates the effects of this context.

The third section focuses on three important controversies that have evolved among developmentalists: (1) how much of any given characteristic or behavior is due to nature, or heredity, and how much is due to nurture, or environmental influences; (2) whether development is best described as a gradual, continuous process, or as occurring in identifiable stages; and (3) the extent to which development during the first few years influences later development.

The fourth section discusses the ways in which developmentalists work, beginning with a description of the scientific method. Several specific techniques for testing hypotheses are discussed, including observation, experiments, interviews or surveys, and case studies. Also described are the research designs that developmentalists have created to study people over time: cross-sectional research (the comparison of people of different ages) and longitudinal research (the study of the same people over a period of time).

The chapter concludes by noting that the study of human development involves values and goals—including those of you, the student.

NOTE: Answer guidelines for all Chapter 1 questions begin on page 10.

Guided Study

The text chapter should be studied one section at a time. Before you read, preview each section by skimming it, noting headings and boldface items. Then read the appropriate section objectives from the following outline. Keep these objectives in mind and, as you read the chapter section, search for the information that will enable you to meet each objective. Once you have finished a section, write out answers for its objectives.

The Study of Human Development (pp. 2–4)

1. Define the study of human development.

2. Identify and describe the three domains into which human development is often separated.

The Many Contexts of Development (pp. 4–17)

3. Describe the ecological approach to human development and explain how this approach leads to an understanding of contextual influences on development.

4. Identify the four major contextual influences and explain how, together, they play a role in development.

Three Controversies (pp. 17–23)

5. Explain and discuss the nature-nurture controversy.

6. Explain and discuss the continuity-discontinuity controversy.

7. Discuss the controversy regarding the degree to which early experiences influence later development.

The Scientific Method (pp. 23–37)

8. List the basic steps of the scientific method.

9. (Research Report) List six steps scientists often take to ensure that their research is as valid as possible.

10. Describe four research methods psychologists commonly use to test hypotheses, noting at least one advantage (or strength) and one disadvantage (or weakness) for each.

11. (text and A Closer Look) Define correlation and give at least one example of a positive correlation, a negative correlation, and a correlation of zero.

12. Describe the two basic research designs used by developmental psychologists.

13. (Public Policy) Discuss the most important ethical concerns of developmental psychologists.

Chapter Review

When you have finished reading the chapter, work through the material that follows to review it. Complete the sentences and answer the questions. As you proceed, evaluate your performance for each section by consulting the answers on page 10. Do not continue with the next section until you understand each answer. If you need to, review or reread the appropriate section in the textbook before continuing.

The Study of Human Development (pp. 2–4)

1. The study of human development can be defined as the study of _____

_____ .

2. The study of human development involves many academic disciplines, especially

_____ , _____ , and

_____ .

3. Developmentalists study two different types of changes: _____-

_____ developments and

_____ developments.

4. The study of human development can be separated into three domains: _____ ,

_____ , and _____ .

5. The study of brain and body changes and the social influences that guide them falls within the _____ domain.

6. Thinking, perception, and language learning fall mainly in the _____ domain of development.

7. The study of emotions, personality, and interpersonal relationships falls within the

_____ domain.

8. Each of the domains _____ (is/is not) affected by the other two.

The Many Contexts of Development (pp. 4–17)

9. Forces outside the individual that influence development make up the

_____ of development.

10. The approach that emphasizes the influence of the systems, or contexts, that support the developing person is called the _____ approach to development.

11. According to this model, the family, the peer group, and other aspects of the immediate social setting constitute the _____ .

12. Systems that link one microsystem to another constitute the _____ .

13. Economic, political, educational, and religious institutions and practices make up the

_____ .

14. The overarching traditions, beliefs, and values of the society make up the _____ .

15. The ecological perspective emphasizes the

_____ (unidirectional/multidirectional) and _____ nature of social influences.

Give an example of how the ecological approach provides a larger perspective on development.

16. Taken together, all the ecosystems that influence development make up the _____

_____ of the individual.

17. When considering development within the family setting, the contextual approach considers each family member as both a "_____" and "_____" of whatever problems the family might have.

18. The ecological approach emphasizes that human development must be understood not only in the context of the family, but also in its

    _____ , _____ ,

    _____ , and _____

    contexts.

19. The idea that women should be docile house-wives while men should be strong and independent is an example of a _____

    _____ . An important point about such ideas is that they _____

    (often change/are very stable) over time.

20. The life stages of _____ and

    _____ are also examples of social constructions.

21. A group of people born within a few years of each other is called a _____ .

22. The values, assumptions, and customs that a group of people have adopted as a design for living constitute a _____ .

23. A collection of people who share certain attributes, such as ancestry, national origin, religion, and language and, as a result, tend to have similar beliefs, values, and experiences is called a(n)

    _____ _____ .

24. A contextual influence that is determined by a person's income, education, residence, and occupation, is called _____

    _____ , which is often abbreviated _____ .

25. Because his mother contracted the disease _____ during her pregnancy, David was born with a heart defect and cataracts over both eyes. Thus, his immediate problems centered on the _____ domain.

Three Controversies (pp. 17–23)

26. In the nature-nurture controversy, traits inherited at conception give evidence of the influence of _____ ; those that emerge in response to learning and environmental influences give evidence of the effect of

    _____ .

27. Developmentalists agree that, at every point, the _____ between nature and nurture is the crucial influence on any particular aspect of development.

28. Theorists who see a slow, steady, and gradual progression from the beginning of life to the end emphasize the _____ of development.

29. Theorists who see growth as occurring in identifiable stages emphasize the _____ of development.

30. In the twentieth century, the _____ view of development has been dominant. Developmentalists such as _____ have cautioned against overemphasizing this viewpoint. In predicting the abilities of a particular child, for example, it is sometimes more useful to know the child's _____ ,

    _____ , or _____

    background than the child's age.

31. A third controversy concerns the extent to which

    _____ .

32. For much of its history, developmental psychology endorsed the view that the first years of life _____ (do/do not) provide the basic structure for later personality development.

33. Increasingly, developmental psychologists are coming to agree with the view that the first years of life _____ , but rarely _____ , later personality.

The Scientific Method (pp. 23–37)

34. In order, the basic steps of the scientific method are:

    a. _____

    b. _____

    c. _____

    d. _____

    e. _____

35. To repeat an experimental test procedure and obtain the same results is to _____ the test of the hypothesis.

36. Psychologists may test a scientific hypothesis by observing people in either a _____ or a _____ setting.
Identify the chief limitation of observation.

37. (Research Report) The researcher who carefully selects a sample population that is large enough to prevent his or her results from being unduly affected by extreme individual cases is aware of the importance of sample _____ .

38. (Research Report) When a sample population is typical of the group under study—in gender, ethnic background, and other important variables—the sample is called a(n) _____ sample.

39. (Research Report) When the person carrying out research is unaware of the purpose of the research, that person is said to be a(n) _____ _____ .

40. (Research Report) Researchers use _____ _____ to define variables in terms of specific, observable behavior that can be measured precisely.

41. (Research Report) To test a hypothesis, researchers often compare a(n) _____ group, which receives some special treatment, with a(n) _____ group, which does not.

42. (Research Report) To determine whether or not experimental results are merely the result of chance, researchers use a statistical test, called a test of statistical _____ .

43. (text and A Closer Look) A statistic that indicates whether two variables are related to each other is _____ . To say that two variables are related in this way _____ (does/does not) necessarily imply that one caused the other.

44. (A Closer Look) When one variable changes in the same direction as another variable, the corre-

lation is said to be _____ . When one variable increases while the other decreases, the correlation is said to be _____ .

45. (A Closer Look) Correlations range from _____ , the highest positive correlation, to _____ , the most negative correlation. A value of _____ indicates no correlation between two variables.

46. The method that allows a scientist to test a hypothesis in a controlled environment, in which the variables can be manipulated, is the _____ .

47. This research method is sometimes criticized for studying behavior in a situation that is _____ .

48. In a(n) _____ , scientists ask people a series of questions in order to determine their knowledge, opinions, or personal characteristics. Sometimes, it consists of a _____ measure that is designed to reveal specific personal characteristics.

49. An intensive study of one individual is called a(n) _____ _____ .

50. When researchers obtain information about people from others who know them well, they are using _____ _____ _____ .

51. Research that involves the comparison of people of different ages is called a(n) _____-_____ research design.

52. Research that follows the same people over a relatively long period of time is called a(n) _____ research design.

53. Psychologists using either research design must always bear in mind _____ effects. In societies that are characterized by rapid _____ change, research on people developing in one era may not be _____ for people developing in an earlier or later generation.

54. (Public Policy) Guidelines established by the _____

_____

help ensure that researchers pursue their studies in an ethical manner.

Progress Test 1

Multiple-Choice Questions

Circle your answers to the following questions and check them against the answers on page 11. If your answer is incorrect, read the explanation for why it is incorrect and then consult the appropriate pages of the text (in parentheses following the correct answer).

1. The study of human development is defined as the study of:
   a. how and why people change or remain the same over time.
   b. psychosocial influences on aging.
   c. individual differences in learning over the life span.
   d. all of the above.

2. The cognitive domain of development includes:
   a. perception.   c. imagination.
   b. memory.   d. all of the above.

3. Changes in height, weight, and bone thickness are part of the _____ domain.
   a. cognitive
   b. biosocial
   c. psychosocial
   d. physical

4. Psychosocial development focuses primarily on personality, emotions, and:
   a. intellectual development.
   b. sexual maturation.
   c. relationships with others.
   d. perception.

5. The ecological approach to developmental psychology focuses on the:
   a. biochemistry of the body systems.
   b. cognitive domain only.
   c. nature-nurture controversy.
   d. overall environment of development.

6. The nature-nurture controversy considers the degree to which traits, characteristics, and behaviors are the result of:
   a. continuity or discontinuity.
   b. genes or heredity.
   c. heredity or experience.
   d. different historical concepts of childhood.

7. The stage view of development emphasizes:
   a. the continuity of development.
   b. the discontinuity of development.
   c. enduring personality characteristics.
   d. the effects of ecosystems.

8. A hypothesis is a:
   a. conclusion.
   b. prediction to be tested.
   c. statistical test.
   d. correlation.

9. A scientist can manipulate the environment to provide a precise test of a hypothesis:
   a. by using statistics.
   b. in an experiment.
   c. in interviews with representative population samples.
   d. by using reports from secondary sources.

10. A disadvantage of experiments is that:
    a. people may behave differently in the artificial environment of the laboratory.
    b. control groups are too large to be accommodated in most laboratories.
    c. it is the method most vulnerable to bias on the part of the researcher.
    d. proponents of the ecological approach overuse them.

11. (Research Report) For a psychologist's generalization to be valid, the population sample must be representative of the group under study and:
    a. significant.   c. all the same age.
    b. large enough.   d. none of the above.

12. (A Closer Look) When two variables are entirely unrelated, the correlation is:
    a. positive.   c. inverse.
    b. negative.   d. zero.

13. To study how behavior changes over time, scientists:
    a. study more than one control group.
    b. use longitudinal studies.
    c. present their interpretations before reporting on the behavior studied.
    d. employ only the case study.

14. A developmentalist who is interested in studying the influences of a person's immediate environment on his or her behavior is focusing on which system?

a. mesosystem
b. macrosystem
c. microsystem
d. exosystem

15. Socioeconomic status is determined by a combination of variables, including:
a. age, education, and income.
b. income, ethnicity, and occupation.
c. income, education, and occupation.
d. age, ethnicity, and occupation.

True or False Items

Write *true* or *false* on the line in front of each statement.

_____ 1. Psychologists separate human development into three domains, or areas of study.

_____ 2. The case study of David clearly demonstrates that for some children only nature (or heredity) is important.

_____ 3. "Nurture" can refer to environmental influences that come into play before a person is born.

_____ 4. Theorists who emphasize the discontinuity of development maintain that growth occurs in distinct stages.

_____ 5. Some researchers see development as a continuous gradual progression without identifiable stages.

_____ 6. A study of history suggests that particular well-defined periods of child and adult development have always existed.

_____ 7. Observation usually indicates a clear relationship between cause and effect.

_____ 8. The case-study method of research involves studying a number of people.

_____ 9. A "blind" experimenter is one who is not sufficiently objective.

_____ 10. To eliminate the possibility that their results are due to chance, scientists test for significance.

Progress Test 2

Progress Test 2 should be completed during a final chapter review. Answer the following questions after you thoroughly understand the correct answers for the Chapter Review and Progress Test 1.

Multiple-Choice Questions

1. An individual's social context refers to his or her:
a. microsystem and mesosystem.

b. exosystem.
c. macrosystem.
d. microsystem, mesosystem, exosystem, and macrosystem.

2. The three domains of developmental psychology are:
a. physical, cognitive, psychosocial.
b. physical, biosocial, cognitive.
c. biosocial, cognitive, psychosocial.
d. biosocial, cognitive, emotional.

3. Which of the following is true of the three domains of development?
a. They are important at every age.
b. They interact in influencing development.
c. They are more influential in some cultures than in others.
d. a. and b. are true.

4. People often mistakenly believe that most developmental changes:
a. originate within each individual.
b. take place in a larger social context.
c. are temporary.
d. occur in the same way in all people.

5. According to the ecological perspective, the macrosystem would include:
a. the peer group.   c. values.
b. the community.   d. the family.

6. The effects of a person's family life on his or her development would be classified as part of the:
a. microsystem.   c. exosystem.
b. mesosystem.   d. macrosystem.

7. According to the ecological perspective:
a. developmental influences are multidirectional.
b. actions in any one part of the system affect all the other parts.
c. human development must be understood in terms of its cultural, historical, ethnic, and socioeconomic context.
d. all of the above are true.

8. A cohort is defined as a group of people:
a. of similar national origin.
b. who share a common language.
c. born within a few years of each other.
d. who share the same religion.

9. According to developmentalists who believe in continuity, development proceeds:

a. in a gradual progression from the beginning of life to the end.
b. in identifiable stages.
c. in a series of abrupt transitions.
d. according to a biologically determined timetable.

10. Recent studies of infant-mother attachment have found that the security of this first human bond:
a. rarely has long-term consequences.
b. can have long-term consequences for the child's future relationships.
c. can have long-term consequences for the child's self-esteem.
d. can do both b. and c.

11. Nature is to nurture as _____ is to _____ .
a. environment; heredity
b. heredity; environment
c. gradual development; sudden development
d. sudden development; gradual development

12. The dominant view of developmental psychologists in the present century has been that development is:
a. continuous.
b. discontinuous.

c. more a product of nurture than nature.
d. both a. and c.

13. (Research Report) In order to ensure that their research is as valid as possible, researchers:
a. study a large sample population.
b. select a representative sample population.
c. remain "blind" to the hypothesis being tested.
d. take all of the above steps.

14. (Research Report) The control group in an experiment:
a. receives the treatment of interest.
b. does not receive the treatment of interest.
c. is always drawn from a different population than the experimental group.
d. must be larger in size than the experimental group.

15. (A Closer Look) To say that two variables are positively correlated means that:
a. one causes the other.
b. as one increases, the other decreases.
c. as one increases, the other increases.
d. a. and c. are true.

Matching Items

Match each definition or description with its corresponding term.

Terms

_____ 1. operational definition
_____ 2. test of statistical significance
_____ 3. experiment
_____ 4. replicate
_____ 5. survey
_____ 6. case study
_____ 7. cross-sectional research
_____ 8. longitudinal research
_____ 9. cohort
_____ 10. ethnic group

Definitions or Descriptions

a. group of people born within a few years of each other
b. follows the same group of people over a period of time
c. series of questions designed to determine people's knowledge, experiences, or opinions.
d. studies one person in great detail
e. collection of people who share certain attributes, such as national origin
f. compares groups of people who are different in age but similar in other ways
g. specifies precisely how variables are measured
h. determines whether the results of a study are simply the result of chance
i. tests a hypothesis in a controlled manner
j. to repeat a study and obtain the same findings

Thinking Critically About Chapter 1

Answer these questions the day before an exam as a final check on your understanding of the chapter's terms and concepts.

1. A developmental psychologist interviews a large sample of young people to learn about their sexual experiences and values. The psychologist is using:
    a. an unrepresentative population sample.
    b. the case study.
    c. the survey.
    d. observation.

2. A team of psychologists observes the play patterns of groups of 12-month-old, 18-month-old, and 24-month-old infants. The team is conducting:
    a. a longitudinal study.
    b. research of questionable ethics and worth.
    c. research concerning only one of the three domains.
    d. a cross-sectional study.

3. (A Closer Look) Snow and summer:
    a. are negatively correlated.
    b. have zero correlation.
    c. are positively correlated.
    d. are unrelated.

4. Dr. Ramirez looks at human development in terms of the individual's supporting ecosystems. Evidently, Dr. Ramirez subscribes to the _____ perspective.
    a. psychosocial
    b. ecological
    c. biosocial
    d. cognitive

5. For her class project, Shelly decides to write a paper on how neighborhood and community structures influence development. She cleverly titles her paper:
    a. "The Microsystem in Action."
    b. "The Mesosystem in Action."
    c. "The Exosystem in Action."
    d. "The Macrosystem in Action."

6. In concluding his presentation, "The Nature-Nurture Controversy Today," Enrique states that:
    a. "Developmentalists increasingly acknowledge the greater influence of heredity in directing the course of development."
    b. "Developmentalists today agree that nurture, rather than nature, is the more potent influence on development."
    c. "The debate has been abandoned as unproductive."
    d. "Developmentalists agree that the interaction between nature and nurture is the crucial influence on any particular aspect of development."

7. Dr. Jenkins's class on life-span development was organized around the concept of age-related crises, such as the "midlife crisis." Evidently, Dr. Jenkins is working from the _____ perspective on development.
    a. nature
    b. nurture
    c. continuity
    d. discontinuity

8. A psychologist who watches the behaviors of people in their usual surroundings is using which research method?
    a. survey
    b. experiment
    c. naturalistic observation
    d. case study

9. In explaining why some psychologists prefer the experiment to other research methods, Dr. Nash notes that:
    a. its results are usually more applicable to everyday life.
    b. it may uncover cause-and-effect relationships.
    c. it eliminates the need for statistical analysis.
    d. all of the above are true.

10. Which of the following is an example of longitudinal research?
    a. An investigator compares the performance of several different age groups on a test of memory.
    b. An investigator compares the performance of the same group of people, at several different ages, on a test of memory.
    c. An investigator compares the performance of an experimental group and a control group of subjects on a test of memory.
    d. An investigator compares the performance of several different age groups on a test of memory as each group is tested repeatedly over a period of years.

11. A developmentalist who studies early temperament by interviewing children's parents is using:
    a. reports from secondary sources.
    b. cross-sectional research.
    c. longitudinal research.
    d. correlational reports.

12. Karen's mother is puzzled by the numerous discrepancies between the developmental psychology textbook she used in 1976 and her daughter's contemporary text. Karen explains that the differences are the result of:
    a. the lack of regard by earlier researchers for the scientific method.
    b. changing social conditions and cohort effects.
    c. the widespread use of cross-sectional research today.
    d. the widespread use of longitudinal research today.

13. (A Closer Look) If height and body weight are positively correlated, which of the following is true?
    a. There is a cause-and-effect relationship between height and weight.
    b. Knowing a person's height, one can predict his or her weight.
    c. As height increases, weight decreases.
    d. All of the above are true.

14. "It is difficult to get valid data with this research method because it is particularly vulnerable to bias on the part of the researcher and the subjects." The person who made this statement is *most likely* referring to which research method?
    a. case study
    b. experiment
    c. observation
    d. survey

15. (Research Report) When researchers find that the results of a study are significant, this means that:
    a. they may have been caused purely by chance.
    b. it is unlikely they could be replicated.
    c. it is unlikely they could have occurred by chance.
    d. the sample population was representative of the general population.

Key Terms

Using your own words, write a brief definition or explanation of each of the following terms on a separate piece of paper.

1. biosocial domain
2. cognitive domain
3. psychosocial domain
4. ecological approach
5. social context
6. cohort
7. culture
8. ethnic group
9. socioeconomic status (SES)
10. nature
11. nurture
12. continuity
13. discontinuity
14. scientific method
15. replicate
16. observation
17. sample size
18. representative sample
19. blind
20. operational definition
21. experimental group
22. control group
23. statistical significance
24. variable
25. correlation
26. experiment
27. interview or survey
28. case study
29. reports from secondary sources
30. cross-sectional research
31. longitudinal research

ANSWERS
CHAPTER REVIEW

1. how and why people change as they grow older, as well as how and why they remain the same
2. biology; education; psychology
3. age-typical; individual
4. biosocial; cognitive; psychosocial
5. biosocial
6. cognitive
7. psychosocial
8. is
9. context
10. ecological
11. microsystem
12. mesosystem
13. exosystem
14. macrosystem
15. multidirectional; interactive

Research has shown that the quality of life in the family microsystem directly affects a worker's productivity on the job. At the same time, the microsystem of the workplace affects the quality of life at home.

16. social context

17. victim; architect

18. historical; cultural; ethnic; socioeconomic

19. social construction; often change

20. childhood; adolescence

21. cohort

22. culture

23. ethnic group

24. socioeconomic status; SES

25. rubella; biosocial

26. nature; nurture

27. interaction

28. continuity

29. discontinuity

30. stage (or discontinuity); Flavell; cultural; ethnic; family

31. early experiences affect later development

32. do

33. influence; determine

34. a.   formulate a research question;

    b.   develop a hypothesis;

    c.   test the hypothesis;

    d.   draw conclusions;

    e.   make the findings available

35. replicate

36. naturalistic; laboratory

Observation does not pinpoint the direct cause of the behaviors being observed.

37. size

38. representative

39. blind experimenter

40. operational definitions

41. experimental; control

42. significance

43. correlation; does not

44. positive; negative

45. +1.0; -1.0; 0

46. experiment

47. artificial

48. survey (or interview); performance

49. case study

50. reports from secondary sources

51. cross-sectional

52. longitudinal

53. cohort; social; valid

54. Society for Research in Child Development

PROGRESS TEST 1

Multiple-Choice Questions

1. **a.** is the answer. (p. 2)

   b. & c. The study of development is concerned with a broader range of phenomena, including biosocial aspects of development, than these answers specify.

2. **d.** is the answer. (p. 3)

3. **b.** is the answer. (p. 3)

   a. This domain is concerned with thought processes.

   c. This domain is concerned with emotions, personality, and interpersonal relationships.

   d. This is not a domain of development.

4. **c.** is the answer. (p. 3)

   a. This falls within the cognitive and biosocial domains.

   b. This falls within the biosocial domain.

   d. This falls within the cognitive domain.

5. **d.** is the answer. This approach sees development as occurring within four interacting levels, or environments. (pp. 4–5)

6. **c.** is the answer. (p. 17)

   a. This controversy is concerned with the issue of whether development is gradual and continuous, or abrupt and stagelike.

   b. Genes and heredity refer to the same thing.

   d. This is not an aspect of the nature-nurture controversy.

7. **b.** is the answer. (p. 20)

   a. Researchers who emphasize this view see development as occurring in gradual increments rather than abrupt transitions.

   c. & d. The stage view of development is not concerned with either of these issues.

8. **b.** is the answer. (p. 23)

9. **b.** is the answer. (p. 30)

   a. Statistics are used *after* research has been conducted, in order to summarize data and determine whether results are significant or due to chance.

c. & d. Only in experiments can researchers directly manipulate environmental variables.

10. **a.** is the answer. (pp. 30–31)

11. **b.** is the answer. (p. 26)

    a. Significance refers to whether or not research results are due to chance factors.

    c. This is not a requirement of a valid population sample.

12. **d.** is the answer. (p. 29)

13. **b.** is the answer. (p. 35)

    a. & c. These are irrelevant in studying how behavior changes over time.

    d. The case study *can* be used to study how behavior changes over time; it is not the only method that serves this purpose, however.

14. **c.** is the answer. (p. 5)

    a. This refers to systems that link one microsystem to another.

    b. This refers to the overarching traditions, beliefs, and values of the society.

    d. This includes the community structures that affect the functioning of smaller systems.

15. **c.** is the answer. (pp. 11–12)

True or False Items

1. T (p. 3)
2. F   The case study of David shows that both nature and nurture are important in affecting outcome. (pp. 13–17)
3. T (p. 17)
4. T (p. 20)
5. T (p. 20)
6. F   Our ideas about the stages of childhood and adulthood are historical creations that have varied over the centuries. (p. 9)
7. F   A disadvantage of observation is that the variables are numerous and uncontrolled, and therefore cause-and-effect relationships are difficult to pinpoint. (p. 28)
8. F   The case-study method is an intensive study of one individual. (p. 32)
9. F   A "blind" experimenter is one who is unaware of the purpose of an experiment, and can therefore be objective in reporting results. (p. 26)
10. T (p. 27)

PROGRESS TEST 2

Multiple-Choice Questions

1. **d.** is the answer. (p. 6)

2. **c.** is the answer. (p. 3)

3. **d.** is the answer. (p. 3)

    c. Research has not revealed cultural variations in the overall developmental influence of the three domains.

4. **a.** is the answer. (p. 4)

    b. This is the emphasis of the newer, ecological perspective.

    c. & d. The text does not suggest that people commonly make these assumptions.

5. **c.** is the answer. (p. 5)

    a. & d. These are part of the microsystem.

    b. This is part of the exosystem.

6. **a.** is the answer. (p. 5)

    b. This refers to systems that link one microsystem to another.

    c. This refers to the community structures that affect the functioning of smaller systems.

    d. This refers to the overarching traditions, beliefs, and values of the society.

7. **d.** is the answer. (pp. 5–6)

8. **c.** is the answer. (p. 9)

    a., b., & d. These are attributes of an ethnic group.

9. **a.** is the answer. (p. 20)

    b., c., & d. These are viewpoints of developmentalists who believe in discontinuity.

10. **d.** is the answer. (p. 21)

11. **b.** is the answer. (p. 17)

    c. & d. These are concerned with the continuity-discontinuity issue.

12. **b.** is the answer. (p. 20)

13. **d.** is the answer. (p. 26)

14. **b.** is the answer. (p. 27)

    a. This is true of the experimental group.

    c. The control group must be similar to the experimental group (and therefore drawn from the same population).

    d. The control group is usually the same size as the experimental group.

15. **c.** is the answer. (p. 29)

    a. Correlation does not imply cause and effect.

    b. This describes a negative correlation.

Matching Items

1. g (p. 26)
2. h (p. 27)
3. i (p. 30)
4. j (p. 24)
5. c (p. 31)
6. d (p. 32)
7. f (p. 33)
8. b (p. 35)
9. a (p. 9)
10. e (p. 11)

THINKING CRITICALLY ABOUT CHAPTER 1

1. **c.** is the answer. (p. 31)

   a. It is impossible to determine from the information provided whether the population sample is representative or unrepresentative.

   b. In this method, one person is studied intensively.

   d. In this method, subjects are observed unobtrusively.

2. **d.** is the answer. (p. 33)

   a. In such a study, a single group is studied over a period of time.

   b. & c. Whether or not these are true of the study described cannot be determined from the information provided.

3. **a.** is the answer. As temperatures warm (summer), snow becomes unlikely. (p. 29)

   b. & d. When the correlation between two events is zero, the events are unrelated. In such an instance, it is impossible to predict one from the other. In this example, it *is* possible to predict that snow will not occur during summer.

   c. When two events are positively correlated, increases in one are accompanied by increases in the other. In this example, increases in temperature are accompanied by decreases in the likelihood of snow.

4. **b.** is the answer. (p. 4)

   a., c., & d. These are the three domains of development.

5. **c.** is the answer. (p. 5)

6. **d.** is the answer. (p. 18)

7. **d.** is the answer. (p. 20)

   a. & b. The nature-nurture issue is separate from the continuity-discontinuity issue.

   c. Continuity theorists see development as gradual, rather than as occurring in abrupt transitions.

8. **c.** is the answer. (p. 25)

   a. These researchers conduct interviews or distribute questionnaires.

   b. Experimenters test hypotheses in a controlled situation.

   d. The case study is an intensive study of one person.

9. **b.** is the answer. (p. 30)

   a. In fact, experiments are often criticized because they occur in artificial settings.

   c. Statistical analysis is needed in virtually every type of research, including the experiment.

10. **b.** is the answer. (pp. 35–36)

    a. This is an example of cross-sectional research.

    c. This is an example of an experiment.

    d. This type of study is not described in the text.

11. **a.** is the answer. (p. 32)

12. **b.** is the answer. (p. 9)

    a. Earlier developmentalists had no less regard for the scientific method.

    c. & d. Both cross-sectional and longitudinal research were widely used in the 1970s.

13. **b.** is the answer. (p. 29)

    a. Correlation does not imply causality.

    c. This would be true if height and body weight were *negatively* correlated.

14. **d.** is the answer. (p. 31)

15. **c.** is the answer. (p. 27)

KEY TERMS

1. The **biosocial domain** is concerned with brain and body changes and the social influences that guide them. (p. 3)

2. The **cognitive domain** is concerned with thought processes, perceptual abilities, and language, and the educational institutions that influence these aspects of development. (p. 3)

3. The **psychosocial domain** is concerned with emotions, personality, interpersonal relationships, and the complex social contexts in which they occur. (p. 3)

4. Developmentalists who take the **ecological approach** take into account the various physical and social settings in which development occurs. (p. 4)

5. The **social context** consists of all the social settings that an individual develops within, is influenced by, and in turn influences. (p. 6)

6. A **cohort** is a group of people born within a few years of each other. (p. 9)

7. **Culture** refers to the set of values, assumptions, and customs, as well as the physical objects, that a group of people have developed over the years as a design for living to structure their life together. (p. 10)

8. An **ethnic group** is a collection of people who share certain attributes, such as national origin, religion, ancestry, and/or language and who, as a result, tend to identify with each other and have similar daily encounters with the social world. (p. 11)

9. An individual's **socioeconomic status (SES)** is determined by his or her income, education, residence, and occupation. (pp. 11–12)

10. **Nature** refers to the range of traits, capacities, and limitations that each person inherits genetically. (p. 17)

11. **Nurture** refers to all the environmental influences that come into play after conception, including the mother's health during pregnancy and all of one's experiences in the outside world. (p. 17)

12. Researchers who emphasize the **continuity** of development believe that there is a continual, gradual progression from the beginning of life to the end. (p. 20)

13. Researchers who emphasize the **discontinuity** of development see growth as occurring in identifiable stages. (p. 20)

14. The **scientific method** is a procedural model that helps researchers remain objective as they study behavior. The five basic steps of the scientific method are: (1) formulate a research question; (2) develop a hypothesis; (3) test the hypothesis; (4) draw conclusions; and (5) make the findings available. (pp. 23–24)

15. To **replicate** a test of a research hypothesis is to repeat it and obtain the same results using a different but related set of subjects or procedures in order to test its validity. (p. 24)

16. **Observation** is the unobtrusive watching and recording of subjects' behavior, either in the laboratory or in natural settings. (p. 24)

17. In order to make research more valid, scientists ensure that **sample size** is sufficiently large so that a few extreme cases will not distort the picture of the group as a whole. (p. 26)

18. A **representative sample** is a group of subjects who are typical of the general population the researchers wish to learn about. (p. 26)

19. A **blind** experimenter is one who is unaware of the purpose of the research and can therefore remain objective in gathering data. (p. 26)

20. **Operational definitions** prevent ambiguity of meaning in research by defining variables in terms of specific, observable behavior that can be measured with precision. (p. 26)

21. In an experiment, the **experimental group** receives some special treatment. (p. 27)

Example: In a study of the effects of a new drug on reaction time, subjects in the **experimental group** would actually receive the drug being tested.

22. The **control group** in an experiment is the one from which the treatment of interest is withheld so that comparison to the experimental group can be made. (p. 27)

23. **Statistical significance** means that an obtained result, such as a difference between two groups, very likely reflects a real difference rather than chance factors. (p. 27)

24. A **variable** is any factor or conditions that can change or vary from one individual or group or situation to another and thus affect behavior. (p. 28)

25. **Correlation** is a statistical term that merely indicates whether two variables are related to each other. (p. 28)

Example: If there is a *positive correlation* between air temperature and ice cream sales, the warmer (higher) it is, the more ice cream is sold. If there is a *negative correlation* between air temperature and sales of cocoa, the cooler (lower) it is, the more cocoa is sold.

26. The **experiment** is the research method in which an investigator tests a hypothesis in a controlled situation in which the relevant variables are limited and can be manipulated by the experimenter. (p. 30)

27. The **interview** or **survey** is the research method in which people are asked specific questions in order to determine their knowledge, opinions, or experiences. (p. 31)

28. The **case study** is the research method involving the intensive study of one person. (p. 32)

29. **Reports from secondary sources** consist of information about research subjects that is provided by others (such as parents) who know them well. (p. 32)

30. In **cross-sectional research**, groups of people of various ages are compared on a characteristic of interest. (p. 33)

31. In **longitudinal research**, the same group of individuals is studied over a period of time. (p. 35)

CHAPTER

2 Theories

Chapter Overview

Developmental theories are systematic statements of principles that explain behavior and development. Many such theories have influenced our understanding of human development. This chapter describes and evaluates the four kinds of theories—psychoanalytic, learning, cognitive, and sociocultural—that will be used throughout the book to present information and to provide a framework for interpreting events and issues in human development. Each of the theories has developed a unique vocabulary with which to describe and explain events as well as to organize ideas into a cohesive system of thought.

Three of the theories presented—Freud and Erikson's psychoanalytic theories and Piaget's cognitive theory—are clearly stage theories. Details of each particular stage will be amplified in subsequent chapters; this chapter provides an overview of the stages and a sense of the theories' perspectives on development. The learning, information-processing, and sociocultural theories, on the other hand, are not stage theories; each, in varying degrees, offers principles of behavior that can be applied to people of all ages.

As you study the chapter, consider what each of the theories has to say about your own development, as well as that of friends and relatives in other age groups. It is also a good idea to keep the following questions in mind as you study each theory: Which of the theory's principles are generally accepted by contemporary developmentalists? How has the theory been criticized? In what ways does this theory agree with the other theories? In what ways does it disagree?

NOTE: Answer guidelines for all Chapter 2 questions begin on page 26.

Guided Study

The text chapter should be studied one section at a time. Before you read, preview each section by skim-

ming it, noting headings and boldface items. Then read the appropriate section objectives from the following outline. Keep these objectives in mind and, as you read the chapter section, search for the information that will enable you to meet each objective. Once you have finished a section, write out answers for its objectives.

What Theories Do (pp. 41–42)

1. Define developmental theory and explain how developmental theories are used to understand human behavior and development.

Psychoanalytic Theories (pp. 43–49)

2. Discuss the major focus of psychoanalytic theories and identify the stages in Freud's theory of childhood sexuality.

3. Identify the components of personality as outlined by Freud and discuss their role in psychological development.

4. Describe Erikson's theory of psychosocial development and contrast it with Freud's theory.

5. Evaluate the psychoanalytic perspective on development.

Learning Theories (pp. 49–57)

6. Discuss the major focus of learning theories and explain the basic principles of classical and operant conditioning.

7. Discuss social learning theory as an extension of learning theory.

8. Evaluate the contributions of learning theory to the understanding of development.

Cognitive Theories (pp. 57–66)

9. Identify the prime focus of cognitive theories and briefly describe Piaget's stages of cognitive development.

10. Discuss the processes that, according to Piaget, underlie cognitive development.

11. Explain how information-processing theorists portray the human mind and identify the steps of the information-processing system.

12. Evaluate the contributions of cognitive theories to developmental psychology.

Sociocultural Theory (pp. 66–69)

13. Discuss the basic ideas of Vygotsky and evaluate the sociocultural perspective on development.

The Theories Compared (pp. 69–72)

14. Summarize the contributions and criticisms of the major developmental theories and explain the eclectic perspective of contemporary developmentalists.

Chapter Review

When you have finished reading the chapter, work through the material that follows to review it. Complete the sentences and answer the questions. As you proceed, evaluate your performance for each section by consulting the answers on page 26. Do not continue with the next section until you understand each answer. If you need to, review or reread the appropriate section in the textbook before continuing.

What Theories Do (pp. 41–42)

1. A systematic statement of principles that explain behavior and development is called a(n) _____ _____.

2. Developmental theories form the basis for educated guesses, or _____ , about behavior.

Psychoanalytic Theories (pp. 43–49)

3. Psychoanalytic theories interpret human development in terms of intrinsic _____ and _____ , many of which are _____ (conscious/ unconscious).

4. The psychoanalytic theory, which was formulated by _____ , challenged many of the ideas that prevailed in Europe in the late 1800s, including that _____ .

5. The medical establishment _____ (supported/did not support) Freud's "talking cure," which was based on the assumption that the origin of many physical disorders was in the _____ .

6. According to Freud's theory of _____ _____ , children experience sexual pleasures and desires long before adolescence as they pass through three _____ . From infancy to early childhood to the preschool years, these stages are the _____ stage, the _____ stage, and the _____ stage. Finally, after a period of sexual _____ , which lasts for about _____ years, the individual enters the _____ stage, which begins during _____ and lasts throughout adulthood.

Specify the focus of sexual pleasure and the major developmental need associated with each psychosexual stage.

oral _____

anal _____

phallic _____

genital _____

_____

7. According to Freud, personality consists of three components: the _____ , the _____ , and the

_____ .

8. The source of unconscious impulses toward gratification of needs is the _____ , which operates according to the

_____ _____ .

9. The ego, which develops _____ (before/after) the id and attempts to satisfy the id's demands in realistic ways, operates according to the _____

_____ .

10. The superego starts to develop at about age _____ , as children begin to identify with their parents' _____ standards and develop their own conscience.

11. According to psychoanalytic theory, the growth of new skills, understanding, and competence is largely an outgrowth of the functioning of the

_____ .

12. In order to cope with internal conflict or challenging environmental demands, the ego may resort to using a _____

_____ , such as

_____ , in which a disturbing memory, idea, or impulse is blocked from consciousness.

13. The theorists who developed their own, modified versions of Freud's psychoanalytic theory are called _____ .

14. Erik Erikson's theory of development, which focuses on social and cultural influences, is called a(n) _____ theory. In this theory, there are _____ (number) developmental stages, each characterized by a particular developmental _____ related to the person's relationship to the social environment. Unlike Freud, Erikson proposed stages of development that _____ (span/do not span) a person's lifetime. Central to

Erikson's theory is the conviction that different cultures _____ (promote/do not promote) different paths of development.

Complete the following chart regarding Erikson's stages of psychosocial development.

Age Period	Stage
Birth to 1 yr.	trust vs. _____
1–3 yrs.	autonomy vs. _____
3–6 yrs.	initiative vs. _____
7–11 yrs.	_____ vs. inferiority
Adolescence	identity vs. _____
Young adulthood	_____ vs. isolation
Middle adulthood	_____ vs. stagnation
Older adulthood	_____ vs. despair

15. Identify three psychoanalytic ideas that are widely accepted.

a. _____

b. _____

c. _____

16. Identify two psychoanalytic ideas that are not widely accepted by contemporary developmentalists.

a. _____

b. _____

Learning Theories (pp. 49–57)

17. A major theory in American psychology is _____ , which forms the basis for a variety of contemporary _____ theories because of its emphasis on how we learn specific behaviors. This theory emerged early in the present century under the influence of _____ .

18. Learning theorists have formulated laws of behavior that are believed to apply _____ (only at certain ages/at all ages). The basic principles of learning theory explore the relationship between an experience or event (called the _____) and the behavioral reaction associated with it (called the _____). The learning process, which is called _____ , takes two forms: _____

_____ and

_____ .

19. In classical conditioning, which was discovered by the Russian scientist _____ and is also called _____ conditioning, a person or an animal learns to associate a(n) _____ stimulus with a meaningful one. Many human _____ responses are susceptible to classical conditioning, particularly in childhood.

20. According to _____ , the learning of more complex responses is the result of _____ conditioning, in which a person learns that a particular behavior produces a particular _____ , such as a reward. This type of learning is also called _____ conditioning.

21. A stimulus that increases the likelihood that a behavior will be repeated is called a(n) _____ . A stimulus that strengthens the behavior that leads to its presentation is a(n) _____ . A stimulus that strengthens the behavior that leads to its removal is called a(n) _____ , whereas a stimulus that makes behavior less likely to be repeated is referred to as _____ . In the latter case, the individual _____ (is/is not) taught a desirable alternative behavior; furthermore, there may be _____ side effects.

22. Reinforcers that come from the environment are _____ ; those that come from within are _____ . With external reinforcers, the _____ and _____ of reinforcement are important.

23. The extension of learning theory that emphasizes the ways that people learn new behaviors by observing others is called _____ theory. The process whereby a child patterns his or her behavior after a parent or teacher, for example, is called _____ .

24. Children's susceptibility to modeling _____ (does/does not) change as they mature. This indicates that cognitive and motivational processes _____ (are/are not) important factors in modeling.

25. Also important in social learning is a person's sense of his or her own aspirations and capabilities, or the person's perceptions of _____ .

26. Social learning theorists find that behavior is the outcome of the mutual interaction of the person's internal characteristics, the environment, and the behavior itself; this interaction is called _____ _____ .

Identify two ways in which the study of human development has benefited from learning theory.

Identify one common criticism of learning theories.

Cognitive Theories (pp. 57–66)

27. Theories that focus on the structure and development of the individual's thought processes and the way those thought processes affect the person's understanding of the world are called _____ theories. A major pioneer of these theories is _____ .

28. In Piaget's first stage of development, the _____ stage, children experience the world through their senses and motor abilities. This stage occurs between infancy and age _____ .

29. According to Piaget, during the preschool years

(up to age _____), children are in the _____ stage. A hallmark of this stage is that children begin to think

_____ .

30. Piaget believed that children begin to think logically in a consistent way at about _____ years of age. At this time, they enter the _____ _____ stage.

31. In Piaget's final stage, the _____ _____ stage, reasoning expands from the purely concrete to encompass _____ thinking. Piaget believed most children enter this stage by age

_____ .

32. According to Piaget, cognitive development is guided by the need to maintain a state of mental balance, called _____ .

33. A mental concept that helps one think about or interact with ideas and objects in the environment is a(n) _____ . When new experiences challenge existing schemes, creating a kind of imbalance, the individual experiences _____ , which eventually leads to mental growth.

34. According to Piaget, this mental growth is achieved through two innate, interrelated processes: _____ and _____ .

35. People adapt their thinking to include new ideas by simply adding new information to existing schemes (a process called _____) and by changing schemes to adjust to the new information (a process called _____). An example of these processes at work is mastery of the principle that the amount of a liquid does not change even when the appearance of its container changes; this is called _____ of liquids.

36. The recent view of cognitive development that takes the computer as a model for the human mind is _____ - _____ theory.

37. In the information-processing system, incoming sensory information is first stored, for a split second, in the _____ _____ . Meaningful material that is currently receiving attention is held in short-term memory, which is also called _____ memory. Some of that information is transferred to long-term memory, or the _____ _____ , where it is stored for months, weeks, or years.

38. According to information-processing theory, a person's reactions to the environment are organized by the _____ _____ .

39. Throughout childhood and adolescence, the _____ _____ expands. The most significant developmental changes occur in the individual's _____ _____ , as the child acquires more sophisticated memory, attention, and retrieval strategies. These processes regulate the analysis and flow of _____ .

40. Unlike Piaget, information-processing theorists view cognitive development as a _____ (more/less) gradual process involving the acquisition of skills and strategies that affect memory, learning, and _____ _____ .

Cite several contributions, and several criticisms, of cognitive theories of development.

Sociocultural Theory (pp. 66–69)

41. Sociocultural theory seeks to explain development in terms of the broad _____ _____ in which it occurs. A major pioneer of this perspective was _____ , who was primarily interested in the development of _____ competencies.

42. Vygotsky believed that these competencies result from the interaction between children and _____ , in what has been called an _____ _____ .

43. Vygotsky believed that the specific _____ of a society is the most important of all learning tools.

44. According to Vygotsky, a mentor draws a child into the _____ _____ _____ , which is defined as the range of skills that the child can exercise with _____ but cannot perform independently.

Cite several contributions, and several criticisms, of sociocultural theory.

The Theories Compared (pp. 69–72)

45. Which major theory of development emphasizes:
    a. the importance of social interaction in fostering development? _____
    b. the ways in which thought processes affect actions? _____
    c. environmental influences? _____
    d. the impact of "hidden dramas" on development? _____

46. Which major theory of development has been criticized for:
    a. being too mechanistic? _____
    b. overlooking developmental processes that are not primarily social? _____
    c. being too subjective? _____
    d. overemphasizing rational, logical thought? _____

47. Because no one theory can encompass all of human behavior, most developmentalists have a(n) _____ perspective, which capitalizes on the strengths of all the theories.

Progress Test 1

Multiple-Choice Questions

Circle your answers to the following questions and check them with the answers on page 27. If your answer is incorrect, read the explanation for why it is incorrect and then consult the appropriate pages of the text (in parentheses following the correct answer).

1. The purpose of a developmental theory is to:
   a. provide a broad and coherent view of the complex influences on human development.
   b. offer guidance for practical issues encountered by parents, teachers, and therapists.
   c. generate testable hypotheses about development.
   d. do all of the above.

2. Which developmental theory emphasizes the influence of unconscious drives and motives on behavior?
   a. psychoanalytic
   b. learning
   c. cognitive
   d. sociocultural

3. Which of the following is the correct order of the psychosexual stages proposed by Freud?
   a. oral stage; anal stage; phallic stage; latency period; genital stage
   b. anal stage; oral stage; phallic stage; latency period; genital stage
   c. oral stage; anal stage; genital stage; latency period; phallic stage
   d. anal stage; oral stage; genital stage; latency period; phallic stage

4. Erikson's psychosocial theory of human development describes:
   a. eight crises all people are thought to face.
   b. four psychosocial stages and a latency period.
   c. the same number of stages as Freud's, but with different names.
   d. a stage theory that is not psychoanalytic.

5. The learning process whereby new behaviors emerge in response to new stimuli, while old, unproductive responses fade away is called:
   a. negative reinforcement.
   b. conditioning.
   c. stimulation.
   d. social modeling.

6. An American psychologist who explained complex human behaviors in terms of operant conditioning was:
   a. Lev Vygotsky.   c. B. F. Skinner.
   b. Ivan Pavlov.   d. Jean Piaget.

7. Pavlov's dogs learned to salivate at the sound of a bell because they associated the bell with food. This experiment was an early demonstration of:
   a. classical conditioning.
   b. operant conditioning.
   c. positive reinforcement.
   d. social learning.

8. A reinforcer can be the removal of something unpleasant when a person or animal responds in a particular way. Such a reinforcer is called:
   a. punishment.
   b. a negative reinforcer.
   c. a positive reinforcer.
   d. a physiological response.

9. Social learning is sometimes called modeling because it:
   a. follows the scientific model of learning.
   b. molds character.
   c. follows the immediate reinforcement model.
   d. involves people's patterning their behavior after that of others.

10. Cognitive theories focus most closely on the individual's:
    a. observable behaviors.
    b. correct answers and perceptions.
    c. emotional development.
    d. thought processes.

11. Working memory includes current, conscious mental activity—such as your reading of this question. Another name for working memory is:
    a. the sensory register.
    b. the response generator.
    c. short-term memory.
    d. the knowledge base.

12. Which is the correct sequence of stages in Piaget's theory of cognitive development?
    a. sensorimotor, preoperational, concrete operational, formal operational
    b. sensorimotor, preoperational, formal operational, concrete operational
    c. preoperational, sensorimotor, concrete operational, formal operational
    d. preoperational, sensorimotor, formal operational, concrete operational

13. When an individual's existing schemes no longer fit his or her present experiences, the result is called:
    a. assimilation.   c. disequilibrium.
    b. equilibrium.   d. repression.

14. Intelligence, in Piaget's view, consists of two interrelated processes—organization and:
    a. cognition.   c. assimilation.
    b. adaptation.   d. accommodation.

15. The zone of proximal development refers to:
    a. the control process by which information is transferred from the sensory register to working memory.
    b. the influence of a pleasurable stimulus on behavior.
    c. the range of skills that a child can exercise with assistance but cannot perform independently.
    d. the mutual interaction of a person's internal characteristics, the environment, and behavior.

True or False Items

Write *true* or *false* on the line in front of each statement.

_____ 1. Learning theorists study what people actually do, not what they might be thinking.

_____ 2. Erikson's eight developmental stages are centered not on a body part but on each person's relationship to the social environment.

_____ 3. A stage view of human development is held by most learning theorists.

_____ 4. A reinforcer is always pleasant and takes the form of a reward, such as candy or a pat on the back.

____ 5. The term *reciprocal determinism* describes behavior that is determined mostly by the environment.

____ 6. The finding that some adults are very inconsistent in using the skills of abstract thinking has led some researchers to conclude that Piaget's stages are not universal.

____ 7. The sensory register stores incoming stimulus information for approximately three minutes.

____ 8. In part, cognitive theories examine how an individual's understandings and expectations affect his or her behavior.

____ 9. According to Piaget, children begin to think only when they reach preschool age.

____ 10. Most contemporary researchers have adopted an eclectic perspective on development.

Progress Test 2

Progress Test 2 should be completed during a final chapter review. Answer the following questions after you thoroughly understand the correct answers for the Chapter Review and Progress Test 1.

Multiple-Choice Questions

1. Sigmund Freud began his career as a(n):
   a. medical doctor working in Europe during the 1870s.
   b. widely traveled American psychologist.
   c. student of Erik Erikson in the 1950s.
   d. advocate of extrinsic reinforcement.

2. Of the following terms, the one that does *not* describe a stage of Freud's theory of childhood sexuality is:
   a. phallic.   c. anal.
   b. oral.   d. sensorimotor.

3. We are more likely to imitate the behavior of others if we particularly admire and identify with them. This belief finds expression in:
   a. stage theory.
   b. sociocultural theory.
   c. social learning theory.
   d. Pavlov's experiments.

4. The id can best be described as:
   a. a relentless moral conscience.
   b. one of Erikson's stages of psychosocial development.

   c. a defense mechanism that entails banishing a threatening impulse from consciousness.
   d. the source of unconscious impulses toward gratification of needs.

5. Children and adults are drawn to certain models more than to others, based in part on their perceptions of self-efficacy. *Self-efficacy* is best defined as a(n):
   a. kind of reciprocal determinism.
   b. person's sense of his or her own goals and capabilities.
   c. person's expectancies about the likely responses to a given behavior.
   d. individual's academic or athletic potential.

6. Defense mechanisms are best described as:
   a. evidence of mental illness.
   b. infantile sexual behavior.
   c. a means of avoiding unbearable inner conflict.
   d. smoking and other ways of gaining oral gratification.

7. When a disturbing idea is blocked from consciousness, the defense mechanism that is operating is:
   a. assimilation.   c. accommodation.
   b. repression.   d. adaptation.

8. Learning theorists have found that they can often solve a person's seemingly complex psychological problem by:
   a. analyzing the patient.
   b. admitting the existence of the unconscious.
   c. altering the environment.
   d. administering well-designed punishments.

9. According to Piaget, an infant first comes to know the world through:
   a. sucking and grasping schemes.
   b. naming and counting schemes.
   c. preoperational thought.
   d. instruction from parents.

10. According to Piaget, the stage of cognitive development that generally characterizes preschool children (2 to 6 years old) is the:
    a. preoperational stage. c. oral stage.
    b. sensorimotor stage.   d. psychosocial stage.

11. People organize their thoughts so that they make sense. When they encounter new ideas and experiences, they adapt their thinking by means of assimilation and:
    a. equilibrium.   c. conservation.
    b. organization.   d. accommodation.

12. Information-processing theory is an example of a:
    a. learning theory.
    b. social learning theory.
    c. cognitive theory.
    d. psychoanalytic theory.

13. Selective attention, rehearsal, rules of thumb, and other strategies for regulating and retrieving information are called:
    a. control processes.   c. working memory.
    b. sensory registers.   d. knowledge bases.

14. Which of the following is a common criticism of sociocultural theory?
    a. It places too great an emphasis on unconscious motives and childhood sexuality.
    b. Its mechanistic approach fails to explain many complex human behaviors.
    c. Development is more gradual than its stages imply.
    d. It neglects developmental processes that are not primarily social.

15. A major pioneer of the sociocultural perspective was:
    a. Jean Piaget.
    b. Albert Bandura.
    c. Lev Vygotsky.
    d. Ivan Pavlov.

Matching Items

Match each theory or term with its corresponding description or definition.

Theories or Terms

_____   1. psychoanalytic theory
_____   2. psychosocial theory
_____   3. learning theories
_____   4. social learning theory
_____   5. cognitive theories
_____   6. information-processing theory
_____   7. sociocultural theory
_____   8. negative reinforcer
_____   9. punishment
_____ 10. self-efficacy
_____ 11. reciprocal determinism

Descriptions or Definitions

a. emphasize the impact of the immediate environment on behavior
b. a stimulus that makes behavior less likely to be repeated
c. proposes stages of development centered around developmental crises
d. the removal of an unpleasant stimulus as the result of a particular behavior
e. a person's sense of his or her own capabilities
f. emphasizes the "hidden dramas" that influence behavior
g. emphasizes the cultural context in development
h. emphasize how our thoughts shape our actions
i. the mutual interaction of a person's internal characteristics, the environment, and behavior itself
j. uses the computer as a metaphor for the human mind
k. emphasizes that people learn by observing others

Thinking Critically About Chapter 2

Answer these questions the day before an exam as a final check on your understanding of the chapter's terms and concepts.

1. Psychoanalytic theories are difficult to test in a laboratory, under controlled conditions, because:
   a. attempting to manipulate the id, ego, and superego could cause permanent psychological damage.
   b. the sexual emphasis of its perspective would make testing unethical.
   c. its concepts are subjective and cannot be experimentally manipulated.
   d. the variables cannot be introduced before a child reaches the phallic stage.

2. When a pigeon is rewarded for producing a particular response, and so learns to produce that response to obtain rewards, psychologists describe this chain of events as:

a. operant conditioning.
b. classical conditioning.
c. modeling.
d. reflexive actions.

3. At every age, a word of praise can have a powerful effect. Praise is a(n):

a. negative reinforcer.   c. intrinsic reinforcer.
b. extrinsic reinforcer.   d. modeling device.

4. A reinforcer is something that makes it more likely that a behavior will be repeated. Which of the following would *not* be considered a reinforcer?

a. a reward such as a piece of candy
b. a kind word or a pat on the back
c. a spanking or a slap
d. a smile

5. A child who thinks that only old people die is forced to acknowledge the death of a young friend. The child must therefore rearrange his or her thinking, a kind of adaptation called:

a. accommodation.   c. organization.
b. assimilation.   d. equilibrium.

6. Piaget's four major stages of cognitive development describe:

a. different bodies of knowledge.
b. different ways of thinking.
c. conservation of intelligence.
d. conservation of liquids.

7. Which of Freud's ideas would *not* be accepted by most psychologists today?

a. Sexuality is a potent drive in humans.
b. People are often unaware of their deep needs, wishes, and fears.
c. The child's experiences during the first two psychosexual stages form the basis for character structure and personality problems in adulthood.
d. Human thoughts and actions are probably far more complicated than is at first apparent.

8. After watching several older children climbing around a new junglegym, 5-year-old Jennie decides to try it herself. Which of the following best accounts for her behavior?

a. classical conditioning
b. modeling
c. information-processing theory
d. working memory

9. Carl cannot remember the details of the torture he experienced as a prisoner of war. According to

Freud, Carl's failure to remember these painful memories is an example of:

a. a crisis.
b. the reality principle.
c. the pleasure principle.
d. a defense mechanism.

10. Two-year-old Jamail has a simple scheme for "dad," and so each time he encounters a man with a child, he calls him "dad." Jamail is demonstrating Piaget's process of:

a. conservation.   c. accommodation.
b. cognition.   d. assimilation.

11. Sixty-five-year-old Betty can't memorize new information as quickly as she could when she was younger. Evidently, Betty's _____ has declined.

a. sensory register   c. knowledge base
b. working memory   d. response generator

12. The school psychologist believes that each child's developmental needs can only be understood by taking into consideration the child's broader social and cultural background. Evidently, the school psychologist is working within the _____ perspective.

a. psychoanalytic   c. social learning
b. information-processing d. sociocultural

13. Four-year-old Bjorn takes great pride in successfully undertaking new activities. Erikson would probably say that Bjorn is capably meeting the psychosocial challenge of:

a. trust vs. mistrust.
b. initiative vs. guilt.
c. industry vs. inferiority.
d. identity vs. role confusion.

14. Dr. Cleaver's developmental research draws upon insights from several theoretical perspectives. Evidently, Dr. Cleaver is working from a(n) _____ perspective.

a. cognitive
b. learning
c. eclectic
d. reciprocal determinism

15. Dr. Bazzi believes that development is a lifelong process of gradual and continuous growth. Based on this information, with which of the following theories would Professor Bazzi most likely agree?

a. Piaget's cognitive theory
b. Erikson's psychosocial theory
c. Freud's psychoanalytic theory
d. learning theory

Key Terms

Using your own words, write a brief definition or explanation of each of the following terms on a separate piece of paper.

1. developmental theory
2. psychoanalytic theories
3. childhood sexuality
4. psychosexual stages
5. oral stage
6. anal stage
7. phallic stage
8. latency
9. genital stage
10. id
11. ego
12. superego
13. repression
14. psychosocial theory
15. crisis
16. behaviorism
17. learning theories
18. stimulus and response
19. conditioning
20. classical conditioning
21. operant conditioning
22. reinforcement/reinforcer
23. positive reinforcer
24. negative reinforcer
25. punishment
26. extrinsic reinforcers
27. intrinsic reinforcers
28. social learning theory
29. modeling
30. self-efficacy
31. reciprocal determinism
32. cognitive theories
33. sensorimotor stage
34. preoperational stage
35. concrete operational stage
36. formal operational stage
37. equilibrium
38. scheme
39. disequilibrium
40. organization and adaptation
41. assimilation
42. accommodation
43. conservation of liquids
44. information-processing theory
45. sensory register
46. working memory
47. knowledge base
48. response generator
49. control processes
50. sociocultural theory
51. zone of proximal development
52. eclectic perspective

ANSWERS
CHAPTER REVIEW

1. developmental theory
2. hypotheses
3. motives; drives; unconscious
4. Sigmund Freud; behavior is governed by rational thought and mature judgment, and that children are "innocent" and devoid of sexual feelings
5. did not support; mind (unconscious)
6. childhood sexuality; psychosexual stages; oral; anal; phallic; latency; 5 or 6; genital; adolescence

Oral stage: The mouth is the focus of pleasurable sensations as the baby becomes emotionally attached to the person who provides the oral gratifications derived from sucking and biting.

Anal stage: Pleasures related to control and self-control, initially in connection with defecation and toilet training, are paramount.

Phallic stage: Pleasure is derived from genital stimulation; interest in physical differences between the sexes leads to the development of gender identity and to the child's identification with the moral standards of the same-sex parent.

Genital stage: Mature sexual interests that last throughout adulthood emerge.

7. id; ego; superego
8. id; pleasure principle
9. after; reality principle
10. 4 or 5; moral
11. ego
12. defense mechanism; repression
13. neo-Freudians
14. psychosocial; 8; crisis (challenge); span; promote

Age Period	Stage
Birth to 1 yr.	trust vs. **mistrust**
1–3 yrs.	autonomy vs. **shame and doubt**
3–6 yrs.	initiative vs. **guilt**
7–11 yrs.	**industry** vs. inferiority
Adolescence	identity vs. **role confusion**
Young adulthood	**intimacy** vs. isolation
Middle adulthood	**generativity** vs. stagnation
Older adulthood	**integrity** vs. despair

15. **a.** development occurs in a series of stages
    b. unconscious motives affect behavior
    c. the early years are a formative period of personality development

16. **a.** Freud's emphasis on experiences during the earliest psychosexual stages as the basis for character structure and personality problems in adulthood
    b. Freud's depiction of the struggle between the impulsiveness of the id and the relentless morality of the superego

17. behaviorism; learning; John B. Watson

18. at all ages; stimulus; response; conditioning; classical conditioning; operant conditioning

19. Ivan Pavlov; respondent; neutral; emotional

20. B. F. Skinner; operant; consequence; instrumental

21. reinforcer; positive reinforcer; negative reinforcer; punishment; is not; destructive

22. extrinsic; intrinsic; timing; consistency

23. social learning; modeling

24. does; are

25. self-efficacy

26. reciprocal determinism

First, learning theory's emphasis on the causes and consequences of behavior has led researchers to see that many seemingly inborn problem behaviors may be the result of the environment. Second, learning theory's emphasis on scientific rigor has challenged researchers to define terms precisely, to test hypotheses critically, to explore alternative explanations for research findings, and to avoid reliance on theoretical concepts that cannot be tested.

Learning theorists are criticized for providing an incomplete explanation for complex behaviors and developmental changes that ignores biological and maturational influences.

27. cognitive; Jean Piaget

28. sensorimotor; 2

29. 6; preoperational; symbolically

30. 7; concrete operational

31. formal operational; abstract (hypothetical); 12

32. equilibrium

33. scheme; disequilibrium

34. organization; adaptation

35. assimilation; accommodation; conservation

36. information-processing

37. sensory register; working; knowledge base

38. response generator

39. knowledge base; control processes; information

40. more; problem solving

By focusing attention on active mental processes, cognitive theories have given developmentalists a greater appreciation of the different ways in which each age knows the world and of the ways these capacities and limitations affect behavior. Critics have found fault with Piaget's depiction of cognitive stages as consistent and comprehensive and with his lack of emphasis on the role of culture and education in development, and with information-processing theory's use of the computer as a metaphor for the mind and preoccupation with the development of specific skills and abilities.

41. cultural context; Lev Vygotsky; cognitive

42. more mature members of the society; apprenticeship in thinking

43. language

44. zone of proximal development; assistance

Sociocultural theory has deepened our understanding of the diversity in the pathways of development. It has also emphasized the need to study development in the specific cultural context in which it occurs. The theory has been criticized for neglecting the importance of developmental processes that are not primarily social, such as the role of biological maturation in development.

45. **a.** sociocultural
    b. cognitive
    c. learning
    d. psychoanalytic

46. **a.** learning
    b. sociocultural
    c. psychoanalytic
    d. cognitive

47. eclectic

PROGRESS TEST 1

Multiple-Choice Questions

1. **d.** is the answer (pp. 41–42)

2. **a.** is the answer. (p. 43)

   b. Learning theory emphasizes the influence of the immediate environment on behavior.

   c. Cognitive theory emphasizes the impact of *conscious* thought processes on behavior.

   d. Sociocultural theory emphasizes the influence on development of social interaction in a specific cultural context.

3. **a.** is the answer. (pp. 44–45)

4. **a.** is the answer. (pp. 46–47)

   b. & c. Whereas Freud identified four stages of psychosexual development, Erikson proposed eight psychosocial stages.

   d. Although his theory places greater emphasis on social and cultural forces than Freud's, Erikson's theory is nevertheless classified as a psychoanalytic theory.

5. **b.** is the answer. (p. 50)

   a. Negative reinforcement is the response-strengthening influence of the removal of an unpleasant stimulus. Although negative reinforcement is one means by which new behaviors are conditioned, it does not account for the elimination of unproductive responses.

   c. Although stimulation per se was not presented as a term in the text, a stimulus refers to an event, rather than a learning process.

   d. Social modeling refers to learning that results from the imitation of other people's behavior.

6. **c.** is the answer. (p. 50)

7. **a.** is the answer. In classical conditioning, a neutral stimulus—in this case, the bell—is paired with a meaningful stimulus—in this case, food. (p. 50)

   b. In operant conditioning, the consequences of a voluntary response determine the likelihood of its being repeated. Salivation is an involuntary response.

   c. & d. Positive reinforcement and social learning pertain to voluntary, or operant, responses.

8. **b.** is the answer. (p. 51)

   a. Punishment is an unpleasant event that makes behavior *less* likely to be repeated.

   c. Positive reinforcement is the *presentation* of a *pleasant* stimulus following a desired response.

   d. Reinforcers are stimuli, not responses.

9. **d.** is the answer. (p. 53)

   a. & c. These are true of all types of learning.

   b. This was not discussed as an aspect of developmental theory.

10. **d.** is the answer. (p. 57)

    a. This describes learning theory.

    b. & c. Neither of these was discussed in association with any particular developmental theory.

11. **c.** is the answer. (p. 62)

    a. & d. We are not directly conscious of material in either of these storage mechanisms.

    b. The response generator is a network of mental processes that organize behavior.

12. **a.** is the answer. (p. 58)

13. **c.** is the answer. (p. 59)

    a. & b. Assimilation and equilibrium occur when existing schemes *do* fit a person's current experiences.

    d. Repression is a Freudian defense mechanism.

14. **b.** is the answer. (p. 60)

    a. Cognition refers to all ongoing thought processes.

    c. In the process of assimilation, new information is incorporated into an existing scheme.

    d. In the process of accommodation, existing scheme are modified to incorporate new experiences.

15. **c.** is the answer. (p. 68)

    a. This describes attention.

    b. This describes positive reinforcement.

    d. This describes reciprocal determinism.

True or False Items

1. T (p. 49)

2. T (p. 47)

3. F Learning theorists see development as a gradual and continuous process based on principles of conditioning that operate throughout the life span. (p. 49)

4. F Reinforcement can entail the removal of an unpleasant stimulus (negative reinforcement). (p. 51)

5. F Reciprocal determinism refers to the mutual interaction of the individual's internal characteristics, the environment, and the behavior itself. (p. 56)

6. T (p. 65)

7. F This describes working memory; the sensory register lasts for only a split second. (p. 62)

8. T (p. 57)

9. F The hallmark of Piaget's theory is that, at every age, individuals think about the world in unique ways. (p. 58)

10. T (p. 71)

PROGRESS TEST 2

Multiple-Choice Questions

1. **a.** is the answer. (p. 44)

2. **d.** is the answer. This is one of Piaget's stages of cognitive development. (pp. 44–45, 58)

3. **c.** is the answer. (p. 53)

4. **d.** is the answer. (p. 45)

   a. This describes the superego.

   b. The id is a concept described by Freud; it is not a stage and is not part of Erikson's theory.

   c. This describes repression.

5. **b.** is the answer. (p. 55)

   a. Reciprocal determinism refers to the mutual interaction of a person's internal characteristics, the environment, and the behavior itself.

   c. This aspect of social learning theory addresses a different cognitive issue in learning; it does not pertain to self-efficacy.

   d. These were not discussed in association with any developmental theory.

6. **c.** is the answer. (p. 46)

7. **b.** is the answer. (p. 46)

   a., c., & d. These are aspects of Piaget's theory of cognitive development, not defense mechanisms.

8. **c.** is the answer. (p. 57)

   a. & b. These are psychoanalytic approaches to treating psychological problems.

   d. Learning theorists generally do not recommend the use of punishment.

9. **a.** is the answer. These behaviors are typical of infants in the sensorimotor stage. (p. 58)

   b., c., & d. These are typical of older children.

10. **a.** is the answer. (p. 58)

    b. The sensorimotor stage describes development from birth until 2 years of age.

    c. This is a psychoanalytic stage described by Freud.

    d. This is not the name of a stage; "psychosocial" refers to Erikson's stage theory.

11. **d.** is the answer. (p. 60)

    a. Equilibrium refers to a state of mental balance between a person's schemes and experiences.

    b. Organization refers to the general cognitive process by which people integrate their knowledge in systematic and cohesive ways.

    c. Conservation is the awareness that a substance does not change simply because its appearance changes.

12. **c.** is the answer. (p. 61)

    a. & b. These theories are concerned with the effect of environmental factors on behavior and development.

    d. Unlike information-processing theory, which is concerned with the processing of conscious experiences, psychoanalytic theory emphasizes unconscious thought processes.

13. **a.** is the answer. (p. 63)

    b. The sensory register is a memory system that stores incoming stimulus information for a split second.

    c. Working memory, which is also called short-term memory, refers to a person's current, conscious memory.

    d. The knowledge base, or long-term memory, stores information for days, months, or years.

14. **d.** is the answer. (p. 69)

    a. This is a common criticism of psychoanalytic theory.

    b. This is a common criticism of learning theory.

    c. This is a common criticism of psychoanalytic and cognitive theories that describe development as occurring in a sequence of stages.

15. **c.** is the answer. (p. 67)

Matching Items

1. f (p. 43)   5. h (p. 57)   9. b (p. 52)
2. c (p. 47)   6. j (p. 61)   10. e (p. 55)
3. a (p. 49)   7. g (p. 66)   11. i (p. 56)
4. k (p. 53)   8. d (p. 51)

THINKING CRITICALLY ABOUT CHAPTER 2

1. **c.** is the answer. (p. 49)

2. **a.** is the answer. This is an example of operant conditioning because (a) a voluntary, rather than involuntary, response is involved, and (b) positive reinforcement is described. (pp. 50–51)

   b. & d. Classical conditioning, which entails reflexive responses, is a form of learning in which the individual learns to associate a neutral stimulus with a meaningful stimulus.

   c. In modeling, learning occurs through the observation of others, rather than through direct exposure to reinforcing or punishing consequences, as in this example.

3. **b.** is the answer. (p. 52)

   a. Negative reinforcement is the removal of an unpleasant stimulus following a particular behavior.

   c. Intrinsic reinforcers, such as a feeling of satisfaction in a job well done, come from within the individual.

d. This concept was not introduced in the text.

4. c. is the answer. These are examples of punishment. (pp. 51–52)

5. a. is the answer. (p. 60)

b. Assimilation entails incorporating new experiences *without* modifying existing schemes.

c. Organization refers to the general process by which individuals integrate their thought processes; it is not a kind of adaptation.

d. Equilibrium is a state of mental balance in which new experiences are fully consistent with existing schemes.

6. b. is the answer. (pp. 58–59)

a. Piaget's theory does not concern specific bodies of knowledge.

c. No such phenomenon is described in Piaget's theory.

d. Conservation of liquids is a cognitive *concept* that children acquire during the stage of concrete operations.

7. c. is the answer. Although the early years are an important formative age, most developmentalists agree that development is lifelong. (p. 48)

8. b. is the answer. Evidently, Jennie has learned by observing the other children at play. (p. 53)

a. Classical conditioning is concerned with reflexive responses and the association of stimuli, not with complex, voluntary responses, as in this example.

c. Information-processing theory is concerned with the ways in which the mind analyzes and processes information.

d. Working memory is a stage in information processing.

9. d. is the answer. Carl has evidently banished his painful memories from conscious awareness; this is an example of the defense mechanism called repression. (p. 46)

a. According to Erikson, each of eight psychosocial stages is characterized by a specific crisis.

b. & c. According to Freud, the reality and pleasure principles are the bases by which the ego and id, respectively, operate.

10. d. is the answer. Jamail is assimilating each encounter with a new man into his existing scheme. (p. 60)

a. Conservation is the ability to recognize that objects do not change when their appearances change.

b. Cognition refers to all mental activities associated with thinking.

c. Jamail is not accommodating because he is not adjusting his scheme to fit his new experiences.

11. b. is the answer. In late adulthood, limitations in the speed and efficiency of working memory may restrict how easily adults can recall information. (p. 62)

a., c., & d. These components of the information-processing system do not usually decline with advancing age.

12. d. is the answer. (p. 66)

13. b. is the answer. (p. 47)

a. According to Erikson, this crisis concerns younger children.

c. & d. In Erikson's theory, these crises concern older children.

14. c. is the answer. (p. 71)

a. & b. These are two of the many theoretical perspectives upon which someone working from an eclectic perspective might draw.

d. Reciprocal determinism is a social learning process that refers to the mutual interaction among an individual's internal characteristics, the environment, and behavior itself.

15. d. is the answer. (pp. 49–50)

a., b., & c. Each of these theories emphasizes that development is a discontinuous process that occurs in stages.

KEY TERMS

1. A **developmental theory** is a systematic statement of principles that explains behavior and development and provides a framework for future research. (p. 41)

2. **Psychoanalytic theories** interpret human development in terms of intrinsic drives and motives, many of which are hidden from awareness. (p. 43)

3. Freud's theory of **childhood sexuality** views development in the first six years as occurring in three psychosexual stages, during which infants and children experience sexual fantasies and erotic pleasures. (p. 44)

4. In each of Freud's four **psychosexual stages**, sexual urges and pleasures are focused on a particular part of the body. (p. 44)

5. In the **oral stage**, which occurs during infancy, the mouth is the focus of pleasurable sensations as the baby becomes emotionally attached to the

person who provides oral gratification of its needs. (p. 44)

6. In the **anal stage**, which occurs during early childhood, pleasures related to control and self-control, initially in connection with defecation and toilet training, are paramount. (p. 44)

7. In the **phallic stage**, which occurs during the preschool years, pleasure is derived from genital stimulation, and interest in physical differences between the sexes leads to the development of gender identity and to the child's identification with the moral standards of the same-sex parent. (p. 44)

8. During sexual **latency**, which occurs in children from 7 to 11 years of age, sexual needs are quiet and psychic energy is invested in other activities. (p. 45)

   Memory aid: Something that is *latent* exists but is not manifesting itself.

9. During the **genital stage**, which begins during adolescence, mature sexual interests that last throughout adulthood emerge. (p. 45)

10. In Freud's theory, the **id** is the source of our unconscious sexual and aggressive impulses toward fulfillment of our needs. (p. 45)

11. According to Freud, the **ego** is the rational component of personality that develops in order to mediate between the unbridled demands of the id and the limits imposed by the real world. (p. 45)

12. The **superego** is the third component of personality, according to Freud's theory. At age 4 or 5, the superego, which is like a relentless conscience that distinguishes right from wrong in unrealistically moralistic terms, begins to emerge as children identify with their parents' and society's moral standards. (p. 45)

13. **Repression** is a Freudian defense mechanism in which a disturbing memory, idea, or impulse is blocked from consciousness. (p. 46)

14. In his **psychosocial theory**, Erikson proposed that development follows a sequence of eight stages, or crises, that are centered on each person's relationship to the social environment. (pp. 46–47)

    Memory aid: To help differentiate between the theories of Freud and Erikson, remember that the former proposed a sequence of psycho*sexual* stages and the latter a sequence of psycho*social* stages.

15. In Erikson's theory, each developmental stage is characterized by a particular psychosocial con-

flict, or **crisis**, such as becoming self-sufficient in everyday activities (autonomy vs. shame and doubt). (p. 47)

16. **Behaviorism** is a theory that emphasizes the systematic study of observable behavior, especially how it is conditioned. (p. 49)

17. **Learning theories** emphasize the sequences and processes of conditioning that underlie most of human and animal behavior. (p. 49)

18. Learning theorists explore the relationship between a particular experience or event (**stimulus**) and the behavioral reaction (**response**) associated with it. (p. 49)

19. **Conditioning** is the process of learning that occurs either through the association of two stimuli (classical conditioning) or through the use of positive or negative reinforcement or punishment (operant conditioning). (p. 50)

20. In **classical conditioning**, a person or an animal learns to associate a neutral stimulus with a meaningful one. Human emotional responses are susceptible to this type of learning. (p. 50)

    Memory aid: Classical conditioning is also called *respondent* conditioning because, in this case, learning involves involuntary *responses* elicited by specific stimuli.

21. In **operant conditioning**, a person or an animal learns to perform or to refrain from performing particular behaviors because of their consequences. According to B. F. Skinner, this type of learning plays a role in the acquisition of more complex responses. (p. 50)

    Memory aid: In **operant**, or *instrumental*, **conditioning**, voluntary behavior operates on the environment and is *instrumental* in obtaining rewards.

22. **Reinforcement** is the process that makes it more likely that a behavior will recur, and a **reinforcer** is the stimulus that strengthens a behavior or makes it occur more often. (p. 51)

23. A **positive reinforcer** is a pleasant stimulus, such as praise, presented following a desired behavior that increases the likelihood that the behavior will recur. (p. 51)

24. A **negative reinforcer** is the removal of an unpleasant stimulus following a desired behavior that increases the likelihood that the behavior will recur. (p. 51)

    Memory aid: In operant conditioning, "positive" and "negative" do not mean good and bad, but to present or withdraw a stimulus, respectively.

25. **Punishment** is the presentation of an unpleasant stimulus that makes a behavior less likely to be repeated. (p. 52)

26. **Extrinsic reinforcers** are reinforcers that come from the environment and other people—for example, money, praise, and privileges. (p. 52)

27. **Intrinsic reinforcers** are reinforcers that come from within the individual, such as pride in completing a difficult assignment. (p. 52)

    Memory aid: Extrinsic means "from the outside"; *intrinsic* means "from within."

28. An extension of learning theory, **social learning theory** emphasizes that people often learn new behaviors merely by observing others. (p. 53)

29. **Modeling** refers to the process by which we observe other people's behavior and then pattern our own after it. (p. 53)

30. Social learning is affected by perceptions of **self-efficacy**, that is, by a person's sense of his or her own goals and capabilities. (p. 55)

31. **Reciprocal determinism** is a social learning developmental concept that refers to the mutual interaction of a person's internal characteristics, the environment, and his or her behavior. (p. 56)

32. **Cognitive theories** emphasize that individuals think and choose, and that these mental activities have a powerful influence on behavior and personality. (p. 57)

33. According to Piaget, during the **sensorimotor stage** (birth to 2 years) infants think exclusively through their senses and motor abilities. (p. 58)

34. According to Piaget, during the **preoperational stage** (2–6 years) children begin to think symbolically. (p. 58)

35. According to Piaget, during the **concrete operational stage** (7–11 years) children begin to think logically in a consistent way—but only about real and concrete features of their world. (pp. 58–59)

    Memory aid: To help differentiate Piaget's stages, remember that "operations" are mental processes, such as conservation of liquids, that form the basis of logical thinking. *Pre*operational children, who lack these operations, are "before" this developmental milestone. Concrete operational children *can* operate on real, or concrete, objects.

36. In Piaget's final stage of cognitive development, the **formal operational stage** (from 12 years on), adolescents and adults are able, in varying degrees, to think hypothetically and abstractly. (p. 59)

37. In Piaget's theory, **equilibrium** refers to a universal need for mental balance between current experiences and a person's mental concepts (p. 59)

38. In Piaget's theory, a **scheme** is a general way of thinking about, or interacting with, ideas and objects in the environment. (p. 59)

39. According to Piaget, **disequilibrium** is a state of mental imbalance that occurs when existing schemes do not fit present experiences. This imbalance eventually leads to cognitive growth. (p. 59)

    Memory aid: The prefix *dis* means "to cause to be the opposite of." *Disequilibrium* is the opposite of equilibrium.

40. In Piaget's view, cognitive understanding is achieved through two innate, interrelated processes: **organization** and **adaptation**. People *organize* their thoughts so that they make sense, separating important thoughts from those that are less important and connecting one idea to another. People *adapt* their thinking to include new experiences and maintain mental equilibrium. (p. 60)

41. **Assimilation** refers to the addition of new information to existing schemes. (p. 60)

42. **Accommodation** refers to the modification of existing schemes in order to incorporate new, conflicting experiences. (p. 60)

43. **Conservation of liquids** is the realization that the amount of liquid in a container does not change despite changes in the container's appearance. (p. 61)

44. Using the computer as a model for the human mind, **information-processing theory** studies the flow of information within the mind and the way information is handled by different cognitive processes. (p. 61)

45. The first step in the information-processing system occurs in the **sensory register**, where information is stored for a split second after it is received. (p. 62)

46. **Working memory**, also called short-term memory, is the information-processing stage in which current conscious mental activity occurs. (p. 62)

47. The **knowledge base**, or long-term memory, stores information for days, months, or even years. (p. 62)

48. In the information-processing system, the **response generator** is a network of mental processes that organize behavior. (p. 62)

49. According to information-processing theory, **control processes**, such as memorization strategies, regulate the analysis and flow of information within the system. (p. 63)

50. **Sociocultural theory** seeks to explain development as the result of a dynamic interaction between developing persons and their surrounding culture. (p. 66)

51. According to Vygotsky, developmental growth occurs when mentors draw children into the **zone of proximal development**, which is the range of skills the child can exercise with assistance but cannot perform independently. (p. 68)

52. Most contemporary developmentalists have an **eclectic perspective**: rather than adopting any single theory exclusively, they incorporate insights from several perspectives. (p. 71)

CHAPTER 3

Heredity and Environment

Chapter Overview

Conception occurs when the male and female reproductive cells—the sperm and ovum, respectively—come together to create a new, one-celled zygote with its own unique combination of genetic material. The genetic material furnishes the instructions for development—not only for obvious physical characteristics, such as sex, coloring, and body shape, but also for certain psychological characteristics, such as moodiness, intelligence, and verbal fluency.

Every year scientists make new discoveries and reach new understandings about genes and their effects on the development of individuals. This chapter presents some of their findings, including that most human characteristics are polygenic and multifactorial, the result of the interaction of many genetic and environmental influences. Perhaps the most important findings have come from research into the causes of genetic and chromosomal abnormalities. The chapter discusses the most common of these abnormalities and concludes with a section on genetic counseling. Genetic testing before and after conception can help predict whether a couple will have a child with a genetic problem.

Many students find the technical material in this chapter difficult to master, but it *can* be done with a great deal of rehearsal. Working through the Chapter Review several times and mentally reciting terms are both useful techniques for rehearsing this type of material.

NOTE: Answer guidelines for all Chapter 3 questions begin on page 45.

Guided Study

The text chapter should be studied one section at a time. Before you read, preview each section by skimming it, noting headings and boldface items. Then read the appropriate section objectives from the following outline. Keep these objectives in mind and, as you read the chapter section, search for the information that will enable you to meet each objective. Once you have finished a section, write out answers for its objectives.

The Beginning of Development (pp. 78–79)

1. Describe the process of conception and the first hours of development of the zygote.

The Genetic Code (pp. 79–82)

2. Identify the mechanisms of heredity and explain how sex is determined.

3. Discuss genetic uniqueness and distinguish between monozygotic and dizygotic twins.

7. Identify some environmental variables that affect genetic inheritance and describe how a particular trait, such as susceptibility to alcoholism or shyness, might be affected.

From Genotype to Phenotype (pp. 82–92)

4. Differentiate genotype from phenotype and explain the polygenic and multifactorial nature of human traits.

Genetic and Chromosomal Abnormalities (pp. 92–96)

8. Describe the most common chromosomal abnormalities.

9. Identify several common genetic disorders and discuss reasons for their relatively low incidence of occurrence.

5. Explain the additive and nonadditive patterns of genetic interaction. Give examples of the traits that result from each type of interaction.

Genetic Counseling (pp. 96–106)

6. Explain how scientists distinguish the effects of genes and environment on development.

10. Describe six situations in which couples should seek genetic testing and counseling.

11. (text and Research Report) Identify five tests used in prenatal diagnosis and describe their purposes.

12. (Public Policy) Discuss the Human Genome Project, focusing on its goals and potential applications.

Chapter Review

When you have finished reading the chapter, work through the material that follows to review it. Complete the sentences and answer the questions. As you proceed, evaluate your performance for each section by consulting the answers on page 45. Do not continue with the next section until you understand each answer. If you need to, review or reread the appropriate section in the textbook before continuing.

The Beginning of Development (pp. 78–79)

1. The human reproductive cells, which are called _____, include the female's _____ and the male's _____ .

2. When the gametes' genetic material combine, a one-celled organism referred to as a _____ is formed.

3. Before the zygote begins the process of cellular division that starts human development, the combined genetic material from both gametes is _____ to form two complete sets of genetic instructions. Soon after, following a genetic timetable, the cells start to _____ , with various cells beginning to specialize and reproduce at different rates.

4. A complete copy of the genetic instructions inherited by the zygote at the moment of conception is found in _____ (every/most/only a few) cell(s) of the body.

The Genetic Code (pp. 79–82)

5. The basic units of heredity are the _____ , which are discrete segments of a _____ , which is a molecule of _____ .

6. Genetic instructions are "written" in a chemical code, made up of four bases: _____ , _____ , _____ , and _____ . The precise nature of a gene's instructions, called the _____ _____ , is the overall _____ of these bases.

7. These genetic instructions direct the synthesis of hundreds of different kinds of _____ , including _____ , that are the body's building blocks and regulators. Genes direct not only the form and location of cells, but also their specific _____ .

8. Each normal person inherits _____ chromosomes, _____ from each parent.

9. The developing person's sex is determined by the _____ pair of chromosomes. In the female, this pair is composed of two _____-shaped chromosomes and is designated _____ . In the male, this pair includes one _____ and one _____ chromosome and is therefore designated _____ .

10. During cell division, the gametes each receive _____ (one/both) member(s) of each chromosome pair. Thus, in number each gamete has _____ chromosomes.

11. The critical factor in the determination of a zygote's sex is which _____ (sperm/ovum) reaches the other gamete first.

12. Genes ensure both genetic _____

across the species and genetic _____ within it.

13. When the twenty-three chromosome pairs divide up during the formation of gametes, which of the two pair members will end up in a particular gamete is determined by _____. Genetic variability is also affected by the _____-_____ of segments of chromosome pairs, and by the interaction of genetic instructions in ways unique to the individual. This means that any given mother and father can form approximately _____ genetically different offspring.

14. Identical twins, which occur about once in every _____ pregnancies, are called _____ twins because they come from one zygote. Such twins _____ (are/are not) genetically identical.

15. Twins who begin life as two separate zygotes created by the fertilization of two ova, are called _____ twins. Such twins have approximately _____ percent of their genes in common.

From Genotype to Phenotype (pp. 82–92)

16. Most human characteristics are affected by many genes, and so are _____; and by many factors, and so are _____.

17. The total of all the genes a person inherits for a given trait is called the _____. The actual expression of that trait is called the _____.

18. For any given trait, the phenotype arises from the interaction of the proteins synthesized from the specific _____ that make up the genotype, and from the interaction between the genotype and the _____.

19. A phenotype that reflects the sum of the contributions of all the genes involved in its determination illustrates the _____ pattern of genetic interaction. Genes that affect _____ and _____ are of this type.

20. Less often, genes interact in a _____ fashion. In one example of this pattern, some genes are more influential than others; this is called the _____-_____ pattern. In this pattern, the more influential gene is called _____, and the weaker gene is called _____. In one variation of this pattern, called _____, the phenotype is influenced primarily, but not exclusively, by the dominant gene. Hundreds of _____ characteristics follow this basic pattern.

21. A person who has a recessive gene in his or her genotype that is not expressed in the phenotype is said to be a _____ of that gene.

Explain how it is possible for two brown-eyed parents to have a blue-eyed child.

22. Some recessive genes are called _____-_____ because they are located only on the X chromosome. Examples of such genes are the ones that determine _____. Because they have only one X chromosome, _____ (females/males) are more likely to have these characteristics in their phenotype.

23. Recessive genes _____ (are/are not) always completely suppressed by dominant genes.

24. The complexity of genetic interaction is particularly apparent in _____ characteristics.

Explain how social scientists define environment.

25. To identify genetic influences on development, researchers must distinguish genetic effects from _____ effects. To this end, researchers study _____ and _____ children.

26. If _____ (monozygotic/dizygotic) twins are found to be much more similar on a particular trait than _____ (monozygotic/dizygotic) twins are, it is likely that genes play a significant role in the appearance of that trait.

27. Traits that show a strong correlation between adopted children and their _____ (adoptive/biological) parents suggest a genetic basis for those characteristics.

28. The best way to try to separate the effects of genes and environments is to study _____ twins who have been raised in _____ (the same/different) environments.

29. Environment, as broadly defined in the text, affects _____ (most/every/few) human characteristic(s).

30. Throughout the twentieth century, as _____ and _____ improved, each generation grew slightly taller than the previous one. Over the past several decades, this trend has _____ (continued/stopped).

Briefly explain how shyness, which is influenced by genes, is also affected by the social environment.

31. Other psychological traits that have strong genetic influences include _____ , _____ , _____ , and _____ .

32. Genes are _____ (often/rarely/never) the exclusive determinant of any psychological characteristic.

33. If one monozygotic twin becomes schizophrenic, the chances are about _____ percent that the other will too. Environmental influences _____ (do/do not) play an important role in the appearance of schizophrenia.

34. Alcoholism _____ (is/is not) partly genetic; furthermore, its expression _____ (is/is not) affected by the environment. Certain temperamental traits correlate with abusive drinking, including _____ .

Genetic and Chromosomal Abnormalities (pp. 92–96)

Researchers study genetic and chromosomal abnormalities for three major reasons. They are:

35. Chromosomal abnormalities occur during the formation of the _____ , producing a sperm or ovum that does not have the normal complement of chromosomes.

36. An estimated _____ of all zygotes have too few or too many chromosomes. Most of these _____ (do/do not) begin to develop. Nevertheless, about 1 in every _____ newborns has one chromosome too few or one too many.

37. In most cases, the presence of an extra chromosome _____ (is/is not) lethal. Two exceptions are when the extra chromosome

is at the _____ pair or at the
_____ pair. These cases lead to
a recognizable _____ .

38. The most common extra-chromosome syndrome
is _____ _____ ,
which is also called _____-
_____ .

List several of the physical and psychological characteristics associated with Down syndrome.

39. About 1 in every 500 infants has either a missing
_____ chromosome or three or
more such chromosomes.

Look at Table 3.1 on page 94, which lists the most
common sex-linked chromosomal abnormalities. List
at least two characteristics associated with each of the
following syndromes.

Kleinfelter syndrome: _____
XYY: _____
XXX: _____
Turner syndrome: _____

40. A genetic disease that is the result of extra genetic
material on chromosome 17 is called
_____-_____-
_____ syndrome.

41. When genetic material is missing, problems are
usually _____ (more/less)
severe than when additional genetic material is
present. The syndrome in which the newborn's
cry resembles that of a cat, called
_____ _____
_____ syndrome, is caused by
missing material on chromosome
_____ or _____ .

42. In some individuals, part of the X chromosome is
attached by such a thin string of molecules that it

seems about to break off; this abnormality is
called _____-_____
syndrome.

43. Chromosomal abnormalities such as Down and
Kleinfelter syndromes _____
(occur/do not occur) more frequently when the
parents are middle-aged, possibly because of ___
_____ .

44. It is much _____ (more/less)
likely that a person is a carrier of one or more
harmful genes than that he or she has abnormal
chromosomes.

45. Although all of us carry some of the destructive
genes of our parents, most babies have no apparent genetic problems because many such problems are _____ , others are
_____ , and many are
_____ . About one in every
_____ babies is born with a serious genetic problem.

Study Table 3.2 (pp. 98–99). Name two common
genetic diseases or conditions that are multifactorial.

_____
_____

Name two genetic diseases or conditions that are carried by a recessive gene.

_____
_____

Genetic Counseling (pp. 96–106)

46. Through _____
_____ and _____ ,
couples today can learn more about their genes,
and about their chances of conceiving a child
with chromosomal or other genetic abnormalities.

47. List six situations in which genetic counseling is
strongly recommended.
a. _____
b. _____
c. _____

d. _____

e. _____

f. _____

48. A simple blood test is all that is needed for carrier detection of the genes for certain disorders:

_____

_____.

For disorders for which the harmful genes have yet to be located, screening involves identifying the presence of _____ in the person's phenotype or genotype.

49. When two carriers of the same recessive gene for a particular disorder procreate, each of their children has one chance in _____ of having the disease. When genetic diseases are carried by the dominant rather than the recessive gene, the chances are about _____ that a child will inherit the condition.

50. (text and Research Report) Once pregnancy has begun, further tests, such as testing the level of _____ , the _____ , _____ , and _____ _____ _____ , can often reveal whether the fetus has an abnormality.

51. Diseases such as _____ _____ are difficult to predict because there is no single genetic _____ , and because they can arise from a spontaneous _____ .

52. For couples who know their offspring are at risk for a particular genetic disease, the new technique called _____ _____ may soon be available.

53. It is estimated that, within the next decade, researchers will be able to detect elevated genetic vulnerability for many conditions, including ____ _____ .

54. (Public Policy) The worldwide effort to map all the codes of the 100,000 human genes is called the _____ _____ .

Progress Test 1

Circle your answers to the following questions and check them against the answers on page 46. If your answer is incorrect, read the explanation for why it is incorrect and then consult the appropriate pages of the text (in parentheses following the correct answer).

Multiple-Choice Questions

1. When a sperm and an ovum merge, a one-celled _____ is formed.
   a. zygote   c. gamete
   b. reproductive cell   d. monozygote

2. Genes are discrete segments that provide the biochemical instructions that each cell needs to become:
   a. a zygote.
   b. a chromosome.
   c. a specific part of a functioning human body.
   d. deoxyribonucleic acid.

3. In the male, the twenty-third pair of chromosomes is designated _____ ; in the female, this pair is designated _____ .
   a. XX; XY   c. XO; XXY
   b. XY; XX   d. XXY; XO

4. Since the twenty-third pair of chromosomes in females is XX, each ovum carries an:
   a. XX zygote.
   b. X zygote.
   c. XY zygote.
   d. X chromosome.

5. When a zygote splits, the two identical, independent clusters that develop become:
   a. dizygotic twins.
   b. monozygotic twins.
   c. fraternal twins.
   d. trizygotic twins.

6. In scientific research, the *best* way to separate the effects of genes and the environment is to study:
   a. dizygotic twins.
   b. adopted children and their biological parents.
   c. adopted children and their adoptive parents.
   d. monozygotic twins raised in different environments.

7. Which of the following is *not* one of the chemical bases that make up the genetic code?
   a. adenine   c. fluoxine
   b. guanine   d. thymine

8. When we say that a characteristic is multifactorial, we mean that:
   a. many genes are involved.
   b. many environmental factors are involved.
   c. many genetic and environmental factors are involved.
   d. the characteristic is polygenic.

9. Genes are segments of molecules of:
   a. genotype.
   b. deoxyribonucleic acid (DNA).
   c. karyotype.
   d. phenotype.

10. The potential for genetic diversity in humans is so great because:
    a. there are approximately 8 million possible combinations of chromosomes.
    b. when the sperm and ovum unite, genetic combinations not present in either parent can be formed.
    c. just before a chromosome pair divides during the formation of gametes, genes cross over, producing recombinations.
    d. of all the above reasons.

11. A chromosomal abnormality that affects males only involves a(n):
    a. XO chromosomal pattern.
    b. XXX chromosomal pattern.
    c. YY chromosomal pattern.
    d. XXY chromosomal pattern.

12. Polygenic complexity is most apparent in _____ characteristics.
    a. physical
    b. psychological
    c. recessive gene
    d. dominant gene

13. Babies born with trisomy-21 (Down syndrome) are often:
    a. born to older parents.
    b. unusually aggressive.
    c. abnormally tall by adolescence.
    d. blind.

14. Some serious diseases or handicaps are polygenic. This means that:
    a. many genes make it more likely that the individual will inherit the disease or handicap.
    b. several genes must be present in order for the individual to inherit the disease or handicap.
    c. the condition is multifactorial.
    d. most people carry some destructive genes for the disease or handicap.

15. Many genetic diseases are recessive, so the child cannot inherit the condition unless both parents:
    a. have Kleinfelter syndrome.
    b. carry the same recessive gene.
    c. have XO chromosomes.
    d. have the disease.

Matching Items

Match each term with its corresponding description or definition.

Terms

_____ 1. gametes
_____ 2. chromosome
_____ 3. genotype
_____ 4. phenotype
_____ 5. markers
_____ 6. monozygotic
_____ 7. dizygotic
_____ 8. additive
_____ 9. fragile-X syndrome
_____ 10. carrier
_____ 11. zygote

Descriptions or Definitions

a. a person's genetic potential for a particular characteristic
b. identical twins
c. sperm and ovum
d. the first cell of the developing person
e. a person who has a recessive gene in his or her genotype that is not expressed in the phenotype
f. fraternal twins
g. a pattern in which each gene in question makes an active contribution to the final outcome
h. a DNA molecule
i. the behavioral or physical expression of genetic potential
j. indicators of harmful genes
k. a chromosomal abnormality

Progress Test 2

Progress Test 2 should be completed during a final chapter review. Answer the following questions after you thoroughly understand the correct answers for the Chapter Review and Progress Test 1.

1. Which of the following provides the best broad description of the relationship between heredity and environment in determining height?
   a. Heredity is the primary influence, with environment affecting development only in severe situations.
   b. Heredity and environment contribute equally to development.
   c. Environment is the major influence on physical characteristics.
   d. Heredity directs the individual's potential and environment determines whether and to what degree the individual reaches that potential.

2. Research studies of monozygotic twins who were raised apart suggest that:
   a. virtually every human trait is affected by both genes and environment.
   b. only a few psychological traits, such as emotional reactivity, are affected by genes.
   c. most traits are determined by environmental influences.
   d. most traits are determined by genes.

3. Males with fragile-X syndrome are:
   a. feminine in appearance.
   b. less severely affected than females.
   c. frequently retarded intellectually.
   d. unusually tall and aggressive.

4. Which of the following is true regarding genetic diseases that are caused by dominant versus recessive genes?
   a. There are twice as many known recessive-gene disorders.
   b. There are twice as many known dominant-gene disorders.
   c. There is an equal number of dominant- and recessive-gene disorders.
   d. Research has not shown either type of disorder to be more common than the other.

5. The incidences of sickle-cell anemia, phenylketonuria, thalassemia, and Tay-Sachs disease indicate that:
   a. these disorders are more common today than 50 years ago.
   b. these disorders are less common today than 50 years ago.
   c. certain genetic disorders are more common in certain ethnic groups.
   d. both a. and c. are true.

6. Dizygotic twins result when:
   a. a single egg is fertilized by a sperm and then splits.
   b. a single egg is fertilized by two sperm.
   c. two eggs are fertilized by two different sperm.
   d. either a single egg is fertilized by one sperm or two eggs are fertilized by two different sperm.

7. Molecules of DNA that in humans are organized into twenty-three complementary pairs are called:
   a. zygotes.   c. chromosomes.
   b. genes.   d. ova.

8. Shortly after the zygote is formed, it begins the processes of duplication and division. Each resulting new cell has:
   a. the same number of chromosomes as was contained in the zygote.
   b. half the number of chromosomes as was contained in the zygote.
   c. twice, then four times, then eight times the number of chromosomes as was contained in the zygote.
   d. all the chromosomes except those that determine sex.

9. If an ovum is fertilized by a sperm bearing a Y chromosome:
   a. a female will develop.
   b. cell division will result.
   c. a male will develop.
   d. spontaneous abortion will occur.

10. When the male cells in the testes and the female cells in the ovaries divide to produce gametes, the process differs from that in the production of all other cells. As a result of the different process, the gametes have:
    a. one rather than both members of each chromosome pair.
    b. twenty-three chromosome pairs.
    c. X but not Y chromosomes.
    d. chromosomes from both parents.

11. Most human traits are:
    a. polygenic.
    b. multifactorial.
    c. determined by dominant-recessive patterns.
    d. both a. and b.

12. Genotype is to phenotype as _____ is to _____ .
    a. genetic potential; physical expression
    b. physical expression; genetic potential
    c. sperm; ovum
    d. gamete; zygote

13. The genes that influence height and skin color interact according to the _____ pattern.
    a. dominant-recessive   c. additive
    b. X-linked   d. nonadditive

14. X-linked recessive genes explain why some traits seem to be passed from:
    a. father to son.
    b. father to daughter.
    c. mother to daughter.
    d. mother to son.

15. According to the text, the effects of environment on genetic inheritance include:
    a. direct effects, such as nutrition, climate, and medical care.
    b. indirect effects, such as the individual's broad economic, political, and cultural context.
    c. irreversible effects, such as those due to brain injury.
    d. everything that can interact with the person's genetic inheritance at every point of life.

True or False Items

Write *true* or *false* on the line in front of each statement.

_____ 1. Most human characteristics are multifactorial, caused by the interaction of genetic and environmental factors.

_____ 2. Less than 10 percent of all zygotes have harmful genes or an abnormal chromosomal makeup.

_____ 3. Research suggests that susceptibility to alcoholism is at least partly the result of genetic inheritance.

_____ 4. The human reproductive cells (ova and sperm) are called gametes.

_____ 5. Only a very few human traits are polygenic.

_____ 6. The zygote contains all the biologically inherited information—the genes and chromosomes—that a person will have during his or her life.

_____ 7. A couple should probably seek genetic counseling if several earlier pregnancies ended in spontaneous abortion.

_____ 8. Many genetic conditions are recessive; thus a child will have the condition even if only the mother carries the gene.

_____ 9. Two people who have the same phenotype may have a different genotype for a trait such as eye color.

_____ 10. When cells divide to produce reproductive cells (gametes), each sperm or ovum receives only twenty-three chromosomes, half as many as the original cell.

Thinking Critically About Chapter 3

Answer these questions the day before an exam as a final check on your understanding of the chapter's terms and concepts.

1. Each person has two eye-color genes, one from each parent. If one gene is for brown eyes and the other for blue, the person's eye color is:
   a. blue.   c. brown.
   b. recessively   d. impossible to predict.
      produced.

2. If two people have brown eyes, they have the same phenotype with regard to eye color. Their brown eyes may be caused by:
   a. different genotypes.
   b. one brown-eye gene and one blue-eye gene.
   c. two brown-eye genes.
   d. all of the above.

3. Eye color can be hundreds of shades and tones, depending on the genes inherited. This is a result of:
   a. sex-linked chromosomal inheritance.
   b. the influence of the dominant genes only.
   c. the action of the twenty-third chromosome pair.
   d. incomplete dominance.

4. Some men are color-blind because they inherit a particular recessive gene from their mother. That recessive gene is carried on the:
   a. X chromosome.
   b. XX chromosome pair.
   c. Y chromosome.
   d. X or Y chromosome.

5. If your parents are much taller than your grandparents, the explanation probably lies in:
   a. genetics.
   b. environmental factors.

c. better family planning.

d. good genetic counseling.

6. If a dizygotic twin becomes schizophrenic, the likelihood of the other twin experiencing serious mental illness is much lower than is the case with monozygotic twins. This suggests that:

a. schizophrenia is caused by genes.

b. schizophrenia is influenced by genes.

c. environment is unimportant in the development of schizophrenia.

d. monozygotic twins are especially vulnerable to schizophrenia.

7. A person's skin turns yellow-orange as a result of a carrot-juice diet regimen. This is an example of:

a. an environmental influence.

b. an alteration in genotype.

c. polygenic inheritance.

d. incomplete dominance.

8. The personality trait of shyness seems to be partly genetic. A child who inherits the genes for shyness will be shy:

a. under most circumstances.

b. only if shyness is the dominant gene.

c. if the environment does not encourage greater sociability.

d. if he or she is raised by biological rather than adoptive parents.

9. If a man carries the recessive gene for Tay-Sachs disease and his wife does not, the chances of their having a child with Tay-Sachs disease is:

a. one in four.

b. fifty-fifty.

c. zero.

d. dependent upon the wife's ethnic background.

10. One of the best ways to distinguish the relative influence of genetic and environmental factors on behavior is to compare children who have:

a. the same genes and environments.

b. different genes and environments.

c. similar genes and environments.

d. the same genes but different environments.

11. (A Closer Look) Even when identical twins have been reared apart, researchers have generally found strong similarities because:

a. identical twins tend to evoke similar degrees of warmth and encouragement.

b. they are usually raised in families that have a great deal in common culturally.

c. most identical twins reared apart have quite similar home experiences.

d. of all of the above reasons.

12. Laurie and Brad, who both have a history of alcoholism in their families, are concerned that the child they hope to have will inherit a genetic predisposition to alcoholism. Based on information presented in the text, what advice should you offer them?

a. "Stop worrying, alcoholism is only weakly genetic."

b. "It is almost certain that your child will become alcoholic."

c. "Social influences, such as the family and peer environment, play a critical role in determining whether alcoholism is expressed."

d. "Wait to have children until you are both middle-aged, in order to see if the two of you become alcoholic."

13. Sixteen-year-old Joey experiences some mental slowness and hearing and heart problems, yet he is able to care for himself and is unusually sweet-tempered. Joey probably:

a. is mentally retarded.

b. has Alzheimer's disease.

c. has Kleinfelter syndrome.

d. has Down syndrome.

14. Genetically, Claude's potential height is 6'0. Because he did not receive a balanced diet, however, he grew to only 5'9". Claude's actual height is an example of a:

a. recessive gene.

b. dominant gene.

c. genotype.

d. phenotype.

15. Winona inherited a gene from her mother that, regardless of her father's contribution to her genotype, will be expressed in her phenotype. Evidently the gene Winona received from her mother is a(n) _____ gene.

a. polygenic   c. dominant

b. recessive   d. X-linked

Key Terms

Using your own words, write on a separate piece of paper a brief definition or explanation of each of the following terms.

1. gametes

2. ovum

3. sperm
4. zygote
5. genes
6. chromosomes
7. DNA (deoxyribonucleic acid)
8. genetic code
9. twenty-third pair
10. monozygotic twins
11. dizygotic twins
12. polygenic
13. multifactorial
14. genotype
15. phenotype
16. additive pattern
17. nonadditive pattern
18. dominant-recessive pattern
19. carrier
20. X-linked gene
21. environment
22. syndrome
23. Trisomy-21 (Down syndrome)
24. fragile-X syndrome
25. genetic counseling
26. markers
27. alphafetoprotein (AFP)
28. sonogram
29. amniocentesis
30. Human Genome Project

ANSWERS
CHAPTER REVIEW

1. gametes; ova; sperm
2. zygote
3. duplicated; differentiate
4. every
5. genes; chromosome; DNA
6. adenine; guanine; cytosine; thymine; genetic code; sequence
7. proteins; enzymes; function
8. 46; 23
9. twenty-third; X; XX; X; Y; XY
10. one; 23
11. sperm

12. continuity; diversity
13. chance; crossing-over; 64 trillion
14. 270; monozygotic; are
15. dizygotic (or fraternal); 50
16. polygenic; multifactorial
17. genotype; phenotype
18. genes; environment
19. additive; height; skin color
20. nonadditive; dominant-recessive; dominant; recessive; incomplete dominance; physical
21. carrier

Eye color follows the dominant-recessive pattern of genetic interaction. Thus, a person with brown eyes (phenotype) may have two dominant genes for brown eyes (genotype)—or one dominant gene for brown eyes and a recessive gene for blue eyes (genotype). In order for a child to inherit blue eyes from brown-eyed parents, both parents have to be carriers, with each contributing the recessive gene for blue eyes.

22. X-linked; color blindness, certain allergies and diseases, and some learning disabilities; males
23. are not
24. psychological

Social scientists define *environment* broadly to refer to the multitude of variables that can interact with the person's genetic inheritance at every point of life. These variables include direct effects, such as the impact of the immediate cell environment on the genes, nutrition, climate, medical care, and family interaction; indirect effects, such as the broad economic, political, and cultural contexts; irreversible effects, such as the impact of brain injury; and less permanent effects, such as the impact of the immediate social environment on temper.

25. environmental; twins; adopted
26. monozygotic; dizygotic
27. biological
28. identical (or monozygotic); different
29. every
30. nutrition; medical care; stopped

A genetically shy child whose parents are outgoing, for example, would have many more contacts with other people and would observe his or her parents socializing more freely than if this same child's parents were also shy. The child might grow up less timid socially than he or she would have been with more introverted parents, despite the genetic predisposition toward shyness.

31. intelligence; emotionality; activity level; neuroticism

32. never

33. 50; do

34. is; is; a quick temper, a willingness to take risks, and a high level of anxiety

By studying genetic disruptions of normal development, researchers (a) gain a fuller appreciation of the complexities of genetic interaction, (b) reduce misinformation and prejudice directed toward those afflicted by such disorders, and (c) help individuals understand the likelihood of occurrence and to become better prepared to limit their harmful effects.

35. gametes

36. half; do not; 200

37. is; twenty-first; twenty-third; syndrome

38. Down syndrome; trisomy-21

Most people with Down syndrome have certain facial characteristics—a thick tongue, round face, slanted eyes—as well as distinctive hands, feet, and fingerprints. Many also have hearing problems, heart abnormalities, muscle weakness, and short stature. Almost all experience some mental slowness.

39. sex

Kleinfelter syndrome (XXY): undeveloped secondary sex characteristics; learning disabled

XYY: prone to acne, unusually tall; aggressive, mildly retarded

XXX: normal female appearance; retarded in most intellectual skills

Turner syndrome (XO): short in stature, undeveloped secondary sex characteristics; learning disabled

40. Charcot-Marie-Tooth

41. more; cri du chat; 4 or 5

42. fragile-X

43. occur; degeneration of the ova or malformed sperm

44. more

45. recessive; polygenic; multifactorial; thirty

Multifactorial diseases: cleft palate, cleft lip, club foot, diabetes, hydrocephalus, pyloric stenosis, some forms of muscular dystrophy, neural tube defects

Recessive-gene diseases: some forms of muscular dystrophy; thalassemia, Tay-Sachs, sickle-cell anemia, PKU, cystic fibrosis, hemophilia (X-linked)

46. genetic counseling; testing

47. Genetic counseling is recommended for (a) those who already have a child with a genetic disease; (b) those who have relatives with genetic problems; (c) those who have had previous pregnancies that ended in spontaneous abortions; (d) those who have a history of infertility; (e) those in which the woman is over 34 or the man is over 44; and (f) those whose ancestors came from particular regions of the world where matings usually occurred between members of the same small ethnic group.

48. sickle-cell anemia, Tay-Sachs, PKU, hemophilia, and thalassemia; markers

49. four; 50-50

50. AFP; sonogram; amniocentesis; chorionic villi sampling (CVS)

51. cystic fibrosis; marker; mutation

52. implantation testing

53. cancer, heart disease, diabetes, and many types of retardation and psychopathology

54. Human Genome Project

PROGRESS TEST 1

Multiple-Choice Questions

1. **a.** is the answer. (p. 78)

   b. & c. The reproductive cells (sperm and ova), which are also called gametes, are individual entities.

   d. *Monozygote* refers to one member of a pair of identical twins.

2. **c.** is the answer. (p. 79)

   a. The zygote is the first cell of the developing person.

   b. Like genes, chromosomes are units of heredity that are found *within* cells.

   d. DNA molecules contain genes and other materials.

3. **b.** is the answer. (p. 80)

4. **d.** is the answer. When the gametes are formed, one member of each chromosome pair splits off; since in females both are *X* chromosomes, each ovum must carry an *X* chromosome. (p. 80)

   a., b., & c. The zygote refers to the merged sperm and ovum that is the first new cell of the developing individual.

5. **b.** is the answer. *Mono* means "one." Thus, monozygotic twins develop from one zygote. (p. 82)

   a. & c. Dizygotic, or fraternal, twins develop from two (*di*) zygotes.

   d. A trizygotic birth would result in triplets (*tri*), rather than twins.

6. **d.** is the answer. In this situation, one factor (genetic similarity) is held constant while the other factor (environment) is varied. Therefore, any similarity in traits is strong evidence of genetic inheritance. (p. 87)

7. **c.** is the answer. The fourth chemical base is cytosine. (p. 79)

8. **c.** is the answer. (p. 82)

   a., b., & d. *Polygenic* means "many genes"; *multifactorial* means "many factors," which are not limited to either genetic or environmental ones.

9. **b.** is the answer. (p. 79)

   a. Genotype is a person's genetic potential.

   c. A karyotype is a picture of a person's chromosomes.

   d. Phenotype is the actual expression of a genotype.

10. **d.** is the answer. (pp. 81–82)

11. **d.** is the answer. (p. 94)

   a. & b. These chromosomal abnormalities affect females.

   c. There is no such abnormality.

12. **b.** is the answer. (p. 85)

   c. & d. The text does not equate polygenic complexity with either recessive or dominant genes.

13. **a.** is the answer. (p. 96)

14. **b.** is the answer. (p. 96)

   a. It is the combination of several specific genes that makes polygenic diseases somewhat uncommon.

   c. Multifactorial diseases are those that are manifest only if several influences, both genetic and environmental, are present.

   d. Although this is true, it is not the definition of *polygenic*.

15. **b.** is the answer. (p. 96)

   a. & c. These abnormalities involve the sex chromosomes, not genes.

   d. In order for an offspring to inherit a recessive condition, the parents need only be carriers of the recessive gene in their genotypes; they need not actually have the disease.

Matching Items

1. c (p. 78)   5. j (p. 100)   9. k (p. 95)
2. h (p. 79)   6. b (p. 82)   10. e (p. 84)
3. a (p. 82)   7. f (p. 82)   11. d (p. 78)
4. i (p. 82)   8. g (p. 83)

PROGRESS TEST 2

Multiple-Choice Questions

1. **d.** is the answer. (p. 87)

2. **a.** is the answer. (p. 87)

3. **c.** is the answer. (pp. 94, 95)

   a. Physical appearance is usually normal in this syndrome.

   b. Males are more frequently and more severely affected.

   d. This is true of the XYY chromosomal abnormality, but not the fragile-X syndrome.

4. **b.** is the answer. (p. 100)

5. **c.** is the answer. Sickle-cell anemia is more common among African-Americans; phenylketonuria, among those of Norwegian and Irish ancestry; thalassemia, among Greek-, Italian-, Thai-, and Indian-Americans; and Tay-Sachs, among Jews as well as certain French-Canadians. (pp. 97–99)

   a. & b. The text does not present evidence indicating that the incidence of these disorders has changed.

6. **c.** is the answer. (p. 82)

   a. This would result in monozygotic twins.

   b. Only one sperm can fertilize an ovum.

   d. A single egg fertilized by one sperm would produce a single offspring or monozygotic twins.

7. **c.** is the answer. (p. 79)

   a. Zygotes are fertilized ova.

   b. Genes are the smaller units of heredity that are organized into sequences on chromosomes.

   d. Ova are female reproductive cells.

8. **a.** is the answer. (p. 78)

9. **c.** is the answer. The ovum will contain an X chromosome, and with the sperm's Y chromosome, will produce the male XY pattern. (p. 80)

   a. Only if the ovum is fertilized by an X chromosome from the sperm will a female develop.

   b. Cell division will occur regardless of whether the sperm contributes an X or a Y chromosome.

   d. Spontaneous abortions are likely to occur when there are chromosomal or genetic abnormalities; the situation described is perfectly normal.

10. **a.** is the answer. (p. 81)

   b. & d. These are true of all body cells *except* the gametes.

c. Gametes have either *X* or *Y* chromosomes.

11. **d.** is the answer. (p. 82)

12. **a.** is the answer. Genotype refers to the total of all the genes a person inherits for a given characteristic; phenotype refers to the actual expression of that characteristic. (p. 82)

13. **c.** is the answer. (p. 83)

14. **d.** is the answer. X-linked genes are located only on the *X* chromosome. Since males inherit only one *X* chromosome, they are more likely than females to have these characteristics in their phenotype. (pp. 84–85)

15. **d.** is the answer. (p. 86)

True or False Items

1. T (p. 82)

2. F   An estimated half of all zygotes have an odd number of chromosomes. (p. 93)

3. T (p. 91)

4. T (p. 78)

5. F   Most traits are polygenic. (p. 82)

6. T (p. 79)

7. T (p. 97)

8. F   A trait from a recessive gene will be part of the phenotype only when the person has two recessive genes for that trait. (p. 96)

9. T (pp. 82–83)

10. T (p. 81)

THINKING CRITICALLY ABOUT CHAPTER 3

1. **c.** is the answer. If one gene is for brown eyes and the other for blue, the person's eyes will be brown, since the brown-eye gene is dominant. (p. 83)

    b. In this eye-color example, the dominant gene will determine the phenotype.

2. **d.** is the answer. (p. 83)

3. **d.** is the answer. (p. 83)

    a. & c. Eye color is not a sex-linked trait.

    b. Recessive genes are not always completely suppressed by dominant genes.

4. **a.** is the answer. (p. 84)

    b. The male genotype is *XY*, not *XX*.

    c. & d. The mother contributes only an *X* chromosome.

5. **b.** is the answer. This trend in increased height has been attributed to improved nutrition and medical care. (p. 87)

a., c., & d. It is unlikely that these factors account for height differences from one generation to the next.

6. **b.** is the answer. Since monozygotic twins are genetically identical, while dizygotic twins share only 50 percent of their genes, greater similarity of traits between monozygotic twins suggests that genes are an important influence. (pp. 90–91)

    a. & c. Even though schizophrenia has a strong genetic component, it is not the case that if one twin is schizophrenic the other is also automatically. Therefore, the environment, too, is an important influence.

    d. This does not necessarily follow.

7. **a.** is the answer. (p. 86)

    b. Genotype is a person's genetic potential, established at conception.

    c. Polygenic inheritance refers to the influence of many genes on a particular trait.

    d. Incomplete dominance refers to the phenotype being influenced primarily, but not exclusively, by the dominant gene.

8. **c.** is the answer. (p. 90)

    a. & b. Research on adopted children shows that shyness is affected by both genetic inheritance and the social environment. Therefore, if a child's environment promotes socializing outside the immediate family, a genetically shy child might grow up much less timid socially than he or she would have been with less outgoing parents.

    d. Either biological or adoptive parents are capable of nurturing, or not nurturing, shyness in their children.

9. **c.** is the answer. Tay-Sachs is a recessive-gene disorder; therefore, in order for a child to inherit this disease, he or she must receive the recessive gene from both parents. (pp. 96, 99)

10. **d.** is the answer. To separate the influences of genes and environment, one of the two must be held constant. (p. 87)

    a., b., & c. These situations would not allow a researcher to separate the contributions of heredity and environment.

11. **d.** is the answer. (p. 89)

12. **c.** is the answer. (pp. 91–92)

    a. Some people's inherited biochemistry makes them highly susceptible to alcoholism.

    b. Despite a strong genetic influence, the environment plays a critical role in the expression of alcoholism.

d. Not only is this advice unreasonable, but it might increase the likelihood of chromosomal abnormalities in the parents' sperm and ova.

13. **d.** is the answer. (pp. 93–94)

14. **d.** is the answer. (p. 82)

 a. & b. Genes are discrete segments of a chromosome.

 c. Genotype refers to genetic potential.

15. **c.** is the answer. (p. 83)

 a. There is no such thing as a "polygenic gene." *Polygenic* means "many genes."

 b. A recessive gene paired with a dominant gene will not be expressed in the phenotype.

 d. X-linked genes may be dominant or recessive.

KEY TERMS

1. **Gametes** are the human reproductive cells. (p. 78)

2. **Ovum** (the Latin word for "egg") refers to the female reproductive cell, which, if united with a sperm, develops into a new individual. (p. 78)

3. Male gametes are called **sperm**. (p. 78)

4. The **zygote** (a term derived from the Greek word for "joint") is the fertilized egg, that is, the one-celled organism formed during conception by the union of sperm and egg. (p. 78)

5. **Genes** are discrete segments of a chromosome, which is a DNA molecule, that are the basic units of heredity. (p. 79)

6. **Chromosomes** are molecules of DNA that contain the genes organized in precise sequences. (p. 79)

7. **DNA (deoxyribonucleic acid)** is a complex molecule containing genetic information that makes up the chromosomes. (p. 79)

8. The precise nature of a gene's instructions, called the **genetic code**, is determined by the overall sequence of the four chemical bases along a segment of DNA. (p. 79)

9. The **twenty-third pair** of chromosomes determines the individual's sex. (p. 80)

10. **Monozygotic**, or identical, **twins** develop from a single fertilized ovum that splits in two, producing two genetically identical zygotes. (p. 82)

 Memory aid: Mono means "one"; **monozygotic twins** develop from one fertilized ovum.

11. **Dizygotic**, or fraternal, **twins** develop from two separate ova fertilized by different sperm, and therefore are no more genetically similar than ordinary siblings. (p. 82)

 Memory aid: A fraternity is a group of two (*di*) or more nonidentical individuals.

12. Most human traits, especially psychological traits, are **polygenic**, that is, affected by many genes. (p. 82)

13. Most human traits are also **multifactorial**—that is, influenced by many factors, including genetic and environmental factors. (p. 82)

 Memory aid: The roots of the words **polygenic** and **multifactorial** give their meaning: *poly* means "many" and *genic* means "of the genes"; *multi* means "several" and *factorial* obviously refers to factors.

14. The total of all the genes a person inherits for a given trait—his or her genetic potential—is called the **genotype**. (p. 82)

15. The actual physical or behavioral expression of a genotype, the result of the interaction of the genes with each other and with the environment, is called the **phenotype**. (p. 82)

16. In the **additive pattern** of genetic interaction, the phenotype reflects the sum of the contributions of all the genes involved. The genes affecting height, for example, interact in this fashion. (p. 83)

17. When a gene pair acts in a **nonadditive pattern**, the outcome depends much more on the influence of one gene than of the other. (p. 83)

18. In the **dominant-recessive pattern**, a type of nonadditive pattern, some genes are dominant and act in a controlling manner as they hide the influence of the weaker (recessive) genes. (p. 83)

19. A person who has a recessive gene in his or her genotype is called a **carrier** of that gene. (p. 84)

20. **X-linked genes** are genes that are located only on the X chromosome. Since males have only one X chromosome, they are more likely to have the characteristics determined by these genes in their phenotype than are females. (p. 84)

21. When social scientists discuss the effects of the **environment** on genes, they are referring to everything—from the impact of the immediate cell environment on the genes to the multitude of ways elements in the outside world, such as nutrition, climate, and family interactions—that can interact with the person's genetic inheritance at every point of life. (pp. 85–86)

22. A **syndrome** is a cluster of distinct characteristics that tend to occur together in a given disorder. (p. 93)

23. **Trisomy-21 (Down syndrome)** is a chromosomal disorder in which there is an extra chromosome at site 21. Most people with Down syndrome

have distinctive physical and psychological characteristics, including rounded face, short stature, and mental slowness. (pp. 93–94)

24. The **fragile-X syndrome** is a single-gene disorder in which part of the X chromosome is attached by such a thin string of molecules that it seems about to break off. Although the characteristics associated with this syndrome are quite varied, some mental deficiency is relatively common. (p. 95)

25. **Genetic counseling** involves a variety of tests through which couples can learn more about their genes, and can thus make informed decisions about their childbearing future. (p. 97)

26. **Markers** are usually harmless physiological characteristics or gene clusters that suggest that an individual is a carrier of harmful genes. (p. 100)

27. The **alphafetoprotein (AFP) assay** tests the level of AFP in the mother's blood to determine whether a fetus has a neural tube defect or Down syndrome. (pp. 100–101)

28. A **sonogram** uses high-frequency sound waves to outline the shape of the fetus, allowing the detection of abnormalities in body shape or rate of growth. (pp. 100–101)

29. **Amniocentesis** is a genetic test in which amniotic fluid is withdrawn and analyzed for chromosomal abnormalities, as well as other genetic and prenatal problems. (pp. 100–101)

30. The **Human Genome Project** is a worldwide effort to map all 3 billion codes of the 100,000 human genes. (p. 103)

CHAPTER

4

Prenatal Development

Chapter Overview

Prenatal development is complex and startlingly rapid—more rapid than any other period of the life span. During the prenatal period, the individual develops from a one-celled zygote to a complex human baby. This development is outlined in Chapter 4, along with some of the problems that can occur—among them prenatal exposure to disease, drugs, and other environmental hazards—and the factors that moderate the risks of teratogenic exposure.

NOTE: Answer guidelines for all Chapter 4 questions begin on page 61.

Guided Study

The text chapter should be studied one section at a time. Before you read, preview each section by skimming it, noting headings and boldface items. Then read the appropriate section objectives from the following outline. Keep these objectives in mind and, as you read the chapter section, search for the information that will enable you to meet each objective. Once you have finished a section, write out answers for its objectives.

From Zygote to Newborn (pp. 110–118)

1. Describe the significant developments that occur during the germinal period.

2. (A Closer Look) Discuss the causes of infertility and describe alternative approaches to reproduction.

3. Describe the significant developments that occur during the period of the embryo.

4. Describe the significant developments that occur during the period of the fetus.

Preventing Complications (pp. 118–138)

5. Define teratology and discuss several factors that determine whether a specific teratogen will be harmful.

6. Identify at least five teratogens and describe their effects on the developing embryo or fetus, focusing on the effects of the so-called social drugs.

7. Discuss several factors that may moderate the risk of teratogenic exposure.

Chapter Review

When you have finished reading the chapter, work through the material that follows to review it. Complete the sentences and answer the questions. As you proceed, evaluate your performance for each section by consulting the answers on page 61. Do not continue with the next section until you understand each answer. If you need to, review or reread the appropriate section in the textbook before continuing.

From Zygote to Newborn (pp. 110–118)

1. Prenatal development is divided into
_____ main periods. The first
_____ weeks of development
are called the _____ period;
between _____ and
_____ weeks is known as the
period of the _____ ; and from
this point until birth is the period of the
_____ .

2. At least through the _____
(how many?) doubling of cells following conception, each of the zygote's cells is identical. Soon after, clusters of cells begin to take on distinct traits. The first clear sign of this process, called
_____ , occurs about
_____ week(s) after conception,

when the multiplying cells separate into one mass that will become the _____ ,
and another that will become the

_____ .

3. The next significant event is the burrowing of the outer cells of the organism into the lining of the uterus, a process called _____ .
This process _____ (is/is not) automatic.

Describe several physical changes triggered in a woman's body by implantation.

4. The quality of a woman's early interaction with her future child depends on several factors, including the couple's _____ ,
their _____ _____ ,
and the woman's _____ .

5. Almost all pregnancies under age 15 are
_____ , while most pregnancies
of women between ages 30 and 35 are

_____ .

6. (A Closer Look) Approximately _____
percent of all married couples experience
_____ —usually defined as
being unable to conceive a child after
_____ (how long?) of trying.

7. (A Closer Look) About one couple in
_____ (how many?) is infertile
when the woman is in her early twenties, whereas about one couple in _____ is
infertile when the woman is in her early thirties.

8. (A Closer Look) Until middle age, _____
(men/women/neither sex) contribute(s) more
often to a couple's fertility problems.

9. (A Closer Look) In men, infertility can be the
result of inadequate _____
_____ , or the poor functioning
of the _____ .

List several factors that affect sperm production.

10. (A Closer Look) In women, the most common cause of infertility is a difficulty with
_____ or _____
_____ _____ .
Another common cause is _____ ,
a condition in which fragments of the
_____ lining become implanted
and grow on the surface of the ovaries or the
Fallopian tubes. This condition is most likely to
occur between the ages of _____
and _____ , and about
_____ (what proportion?) of
those who have it are infertile.

11. (A Closer Look) One technique for treating infertility is _____ _____ ,
in which the husband's sperm are collected in a
laboratory and injected directly into the woman's
cervix. With _____ _____
_____ , ova are surgically
removed from the ovaries and fertilized by sperm
in the laboratory. Two variations of this latter
technique, called GIFT and ZIFT, involve inserting either _____ or
_____ into a Fallopian tube.

12. (A Closer Look) In one "third-party" solution to
infertility problems, a woman volunteers to
become impregnated by the father-to-be and carries the baby to term. This solution is called
_____ _____ .

(A Closer Look) State several ethical and legal questions raised by infertility solutions such as surrogate motherhood.

13. At the beginning of the period of the embryo, the
_____ (outer/inner) cells of the
developing individual form a structure known as
the _____ _____ ,
which consists of three layers:
   a. the outer layer, or _____ ,
      will become the _____
      _____ ;
   b. the middle layer, or _____ ,
      will become the _____
      _____ ;
   c. the inner layer, or _____ ,
      will become _____
      _____ .

14. The first perceptible sign of body formation is a
fold in the ectoderm, which becomes the
_____ _____
and later becomes the _____
_____ _____ .

15. Growth then proceeds from the head downward,
referred to as _____ -
_____ _____ ,
and from the center outward, referred to as
_____ -_____
_____ . Following this pattern,
the _____ system is the first
organ system to begin to function.

16. Rapid growth also occurs in the
_____ , the life-giving organ
that enables the fetus to obtain nourishment from
the mother's bloodstream and to excrete wastes
back into it.

Briefly describe the major features of development during the second month.

17. Eight weeks after conception, the embryo weighs
about _____ and is about
_____ in length. The organism
now becomes known as the _____ .

18. All the major organs, including the
_____ , _____ ,
_____ , and _____ ,
complete their formation during the
_____ month.

19. The first stage of development of the sex organs is
the appearance in the _____
week of the _____
_____ , a cluster of cells that
can develop into male or female sex organs.

20. If the fetus has a(n) _____ (X/Y)
chromosome, a gene on this chromosome sends a
biochemical signal that triggers the development
of the _____ (male/ female) sex
organs at about seven weeks. Without that gene,
no signal is sent, and the fetus begins to develop
_____ (male/ female) sex
organs at about the
week. Not until the _____ week
are the external male or female genital organs
fully formed.

21. By the end of the _____ month,
the fetus is fully formed, weighs approximately
_____ , and is about
_____ long.

22. Each three-month period of pregnancy is referred
to as a _____ .

23. During the second trimester, weight increases by
a factor of _____ , while the
brain increases in size by a factor of
_____ .

Briefly describe some of the other major developments during the second trimester.

24. The age at which a fetus has at least some chance
of surviving outside the uterus is called the
_____ _____
_____ , which occurs between

_____ and _____
weeks after conception.

25. Two important developments during the third
trimester are the strengthening of the muscles
that enable _____ and a final
maturation of the _____
system. Measurement of the brain's electrical
activity during this trimester reveals distinct
patterns of _____ and
_____ .

26. An important part of the fetus's weight gain is
the formation of body_____ ,
which will provide a layer of insulation to keep
the newborn warm, along with nourishment and
vitamins in the early days after birth.

27. The normal due date is calculated at
_____ weeks after conception.

28. Beginning at about _____
weeks, the fetus becomes very active physically.
At about the _____ week, the
fetus begins to _____ in and
digest amniotic fluid.

29. Toward the end of prenatal development, the
_____ systems begin to func-
tion. The most remarkable of the fetus's responses to the immediate environment involve the
sense of _____ . Recent studies
have revealed that newborns actually
_____ some of what they heard
while in the womb.

Preventing Complications (pp. 118–138)

30. The scientific study of factors that can cause or
prevent birth defects is called _____ .
Harmful agents that can cause birth defects,
called _____ , include _____
_____ .

31. Teratology is a science of _____
_____ , which attempts to evalu-
ate the factors that can make prenatal harm more
or less likely to occur.

32. Three crucial factors that determine whether a
specific teratogen will cause harm, and of what

nature, are the _____ of exposure, the _____ of exposure,
and the developing organism's
_____ _____
to damage from the substance.

33. The time when a particular part of the body is
most susceptible to teratogenic damage is called
its _____ _____ .
However, for _____ teratogens,
which damage the _____ and
_____ _____,
the entire prenatal period is critical.

34. Drugs such as tobacco have a _____
effect on the developing individual. Other drugs
have a _____—that is, the sub-
stances are harmless until exposure reaches a certain frequency or amount. However, the
_____ of some of these drugs
when taken together may make them more harmful at lower dosage levels than when taken sepa-
rately.

35. Because the _____ chromosome carries fewer genes, _____
(male/female) embryos and fetuses are more vulnerable to teratogens. This sex not only has a
higher rate of teratogenic birth defects and later
behavioral problems, but also a higher rate of
_____ _____
and _____ .

36. The health and functioning of the father's
_____ can also be affected by
teratogens.

37. When contracted during the critical period,
German measles, also called _____,
is known to cause structural damage to the heart,
eyes, ears, and brain. This and other teratogenic
diseases, including _____
_____ , are now
curbed by immunization.

38. The most devastating viral teratogen is
_____ _____
_____ , which gradually overwhelms the body's natural immune responses

and leads to a host of diseases that together constitute _____
_____ _____
_____ . About one in every four
infants born to women with this virus will die,
usually before _____ . This dis-
ease's long incubation period—up to
_____ years or more—compli-
cates its prevention.

39. Two other diseases that can harm the fetus are
_____ , a sexually transmitted
disease which can be cured, and
_____ , which is caused by a
parasite in raw meat, cat feces, and yard dirt.

40. In 1960, thousands of women were given the nausea-reducing drug _____ ,
which was found to cause severe physical birth
defects. Other prescription drugs that can be teratogenic include _____ .

41. Social drugs such as the psychoactive agents
_____
_____
have teratogenic effects that are primarily
_____ , producing long-term
_____ _____ ,
impaired _____ , and
_____ . Social drugs inflict their
damage by reducing the _____
and nutrition supplied through the placenta and
by directly impairing growth of the
_____ . The teratogenic effects
of these drugs are _____ (more/
less) variable than those of other teratogens.

42. Prenatal exposure to alcohol may lead to
_____ _____
_____ , which includes such
symptoms as abnormal facial characteristics,
slowed physical growth, behavior problems, and
mental retardation. Likely victims of this syndrome are those who are genetically vulnerable
and whose mothers ingest more than
_____ drinks daily during
pregnancy.

List some of the effects of fetal exposure to tobacco.

43. Infants born to heavy users of marijuana and heroin often show impairment to their

_____ _____

systems. Heroin-exposed infants also have a variety of other problems, including _____

_____ .

List some of the effects of fetal exposure to cocaine.

44. More than any other drug, crack cocaine causes

_____ _____

to virtually disappear.

45. Environmental teratogens known to cause serious damage include _____ .

46. The developing organism may also be at risk if the mother's occupation is unusually

_____ .

Describe two defenses against teratogenic hazards that are "built into" the developmental process.

47. Three important factors that protect the developing individual against teratogenic hazards are adequate _____ ,

_____ _____ ,

and _____ _____ .

48. Optimal weight gain in pregnancy for normal-weight women is between _____

and _____ pounds.

49. Just as inadequate nutrition during pregnancy

can be harmful, a diet that contains excessive _____ supplementation can also lead to complications.

50. One protective nutrient that many women do not get in adequate amounts from the typical diet is

_____ _____ .

Deficiency of this nutrient may lead to

_____ _____

defects.

51. Medical care that begins early in pregnancy and includes prenatal _____ as well as basic _____ tests is one of the best predictors of a healthy pregnancy, an easy birth, and a normal newborn.

52. China has achieved a lower rate of birth defects and complications than many wealthier nations, largely due to efforts of a network of workers in basic medicine, called "_____

_____ ," who provide prenatal care even in the most remote areas.

53. Objective measures of social networks _____ (are/are not) as accurate as subjective indices, such as how helpful the woman feels her friends and relatives are.

Describe several ways in which social support can reduce prenatal complications.

Progress Test 1

Multiple-Choice Questions

Circle your answers to the following questions and check them with the answers on page 63. If your answer is incorrect, read the explanation for why it is incorrect and then consult the appropriate pages of the text (in parentheses following the correct answer).

1. The third through the eighth week after conception is called the:

a. period of the embryo.
b. period of the ovum.
c. period of the fetus.
d. germinal period.

2. Marijuana is a behavioral teratogen whose damage is:
a. related to the timing of exposure.
b. dose-related.
c. related to the socioeconomic status of the mother-to-be.
d. related to both the timing and the amount of exposure.

3. The neural tube develops into the:
a. respiratory system.
b. umbilical cord.
c. brain and spinal column.
d. circulatory system.

4. The embryo's growth from the head downward is called:
a. cephalo-caudal development.
b. fetal development.
c. proximo-distal development.
d. teratogenic development.

5. By the eighth week after conception, the embryo has almost all of the basic organs except the:
a. skeleton.   c. sex organs.
b. elbows and knees. d. fingers and toes.

6. In one study, newborns listened to stories being read by their own mother and by another baby's mother. The babies:
a. paid greater attention to the unfamiliar mother's reading.
b. were more responsive to their own mother, particularly when she read a story to which they had been exposed during prenatal development.
c. were equally responsive to both mothers until about two weeks after birth.
d. paid more attention to their own mother but behaviorally were more responsive to the other baby's mother.

7. The most critical factor in attaining the age of viability is development of the:
a. placenta.   c. brain.
b. eyes.   d. skeleton.

8. During the last trimester, the:
a. fetus gains about 1 pound in weight.
b. lungs and heart become able to sustain life without the placenta.

c. brain's activity reveals distinct patterns of sleeping and waking.
d. the indifferent gonad appears.

9. An important nutrient that many women do not get in adequate amounts from the typical diet is:
a. vitamin A.   c. guanine.
b. zinc.   d. folic acid.

10. An embryo begins to develop male sex organs if _____ , and female sex organs if _____ .
a. genes on the Y chromosome send a biochemical signal; no signal is sent from a Y chromosome.
b. genes on the Y chromosome send a biochemical signal; genes on the X chromosome send a signal.
c. genes on the X chromosome send a biochemical signal; no signal is sent from an X chromosome.
d. genes on the X chromosome send a biochemical signal; genes on the Y chromosome send a signal

11. A teratogen:
a. cannot cross the placenta during the first trimester.
b. is usually inherited from the mother.
c. can be counteracted by good nutrition most of the time.
d. may be a virus, drug, or chemical, or radiation and environmental pollutants.

12. Because most body organs form during the first two months of pregnancy, this period is sometimes called the:
a. period of teratology.
b. genetically dangerous period.
c. proximo-distal period.
d. critical period.

13. Maternal cigarette smoking is most often associated with:
a. nicotine addiction in the newborn.
b. low birth weight and prematurity.
c. serious brain damage.
d. physical deformities of the head and face.

14. Among the characteristics of babies born with fetal alcohol syndrome are:
a. slowed physical growth and behavior problems.
b. addiction to alcohol and methadone.
c. deformed arms and legs.
d. blindness.

15. Several pollutants, when ingested in large doses, have been proven to be teratogenic. Among these are:
    a. dust and silver chloride.
    b. mercury, lead, and PCBs.
    c. carbon dioxide.
    d. salt water.

Matching Items

Match each definition or description with its corresponding term.

Definitions or Descriptions

_____ 1. the prenatal period during which a body part is most susceptible to damage
_____ 2. the scientific study of birth defects
_____ 3. when the age of viability is attained
_____ 4. the precursor of the central nervous system
_____ 5. also called German measles
_____ 6. a disease characterized by abnormal facial characteristics, slowed growth, behavior problems, and mental retardation
_____ 7. a virus that gradually overwhelms the body's immune responses
_____ 8. the life-giving organ that nourishes the embryo and fetus
_____ 9. when implantation occurs
_____ 10. the prenatal period when all major body structures begin to form
_____ 11. a 3-month-long segment of pregnancy

Terms

a. period of the embryo
b. period of the fetus
c. placenta
d. trimester
e. teratology
f. rubella
g. HIV
h. critical period
i. neural tube
j. fetal alcohol syndrome
k. germinal period

Progress Test 2

Progress Test 2 should be completed during a final chapter review. Answer the following questions after you thoroughly understand the correct answers for the Chapter Review and Progress Test 1.

Multiple-Choice Questions

1. During which period does cocaine use affect the fetus and/or newborn?
   a. throughout pregnancy
   b. before birth
   c. after birth
   d. during all of the above periods

2. In order, the correct sequence of prenatal stages of development is:
   a. embryo; germinal; fetus
   b. germinal; fetus; embryo
   c. germinal; embryo; fetus
   d. ovum; fetus; embryo

3. Risk analysis attempts to evaluate what factors make prenatal harm more, or less, likely to occur. The *most* influential factors are:
   a. environment and health care.
   b. timing and amount of exposure.
   c. nutrition and social support.
   d. all of the above.

4. The ectoderm is to the _____ as the _____ is to the muscles of a developing embryo.
   a. skin; embryonic disk
   b. nervous system; endoderm
   c. skin; mesoderm
   d. digestive system; endoderm

5. The first clear sign of differentiation occurs about _____ after conception.
   a. one hour
   b. one day
   c. one week
   d. one month

6. The embryo's growth from the spine outward is called:
   a. cephalo-caudal development.
   b. fetal development.
   c. proximo-distal development.
   d. teratogenic development.

7. The developing organism's sensory systems begin to function during the:
   a. germinal period.
   b. first trimester.
   c. second trimester.
   d. third trimester.

8. Pregnant women who are *not* immune to toxoplasmosis should avoid:
   a. eating raw meat.
   b. handling puppies.
   c. taking multivitamins.
   d. stressful work.

9. Tetracycline, valium, retinoic acid, and most hormones:
   a. can be harmful to the human fetus.
   b. have been proven safe for pregnant women after the second trimester.
   c. will prevent spontaneous abortions.
   d. are safe when used before the third trimester.

10. Babies born to mothers who are addicted to heroin may suffer tremors, sleeplessness, and hyperactive reflexes. These symptoms are best understood as:
    a. evidence of brain damage.
    b. the usual effects of taking heroin.
    c. complications of prematurity.
    d. evidence of an unstable nervous system.

11. (A Closer Look) A common cause of female infertility in which fragments of the uterine lining block the reproductive tract is:
    a. toxoplasmosis.
    b. endometriosis.
    c. FAS.
    d. mesodermititis.

12. One of the most devastating teratogens, possibly causing deafness, blindness, and brain damage if the fetus is exposed during the first trimester, is:
    a. rubella (German measles).
    b. anoxia.
    c. acquired immune deficiency syndrome (AIDS).
    d. neural tube defect.

13. Nourishment is carried to, and waste is removed from, the embryo or fetus through the:
    a. uterus.
    b. placenta.
    c. neural tube.
    d. Fallopian tubes.

14. A pollutant that is teratogenic if a woman is exposed to it in unusually high amounts is:
    a. rubella.
    b. lithium.
    c. mercury.
    d. HIV.

15. The most realistic way for pregnant women to reduce the risk of birth defects in their unborn children is to avoid unnecessary drugs and:
    a. have a diagnostic x-ray or sonogram.
    b. improve their genetic predispositions.
    c. seek early and regular prenatal care.
    d. avoid exposure to any suspected pollutant.

True or False Items

Write *true* or *false* on the line in front of each statement.

_____ 1. Many of the developing organism's sensory systems begin to function during the second trimester.

_____ 2. Recent studies demonstrate that newborns can recognize some of what they heard while in the womb.

_____ 3. Normal-weight women should gain between 15 and 25 pounds during pregnancy.

_____ 4. Once the zygote reaches the uterus, implantation is almost assured.

_____ 5. Eight weeks after conception, the embryo has formed almost all the basic organs.

_____ 6. The embryo develops from the head downward, and from the center outward.

_____ 7. Unless a woman is severely malnourished, the adequacy of her diet is most important in the last months of pregnancy.

_____ 8. In general, behavioral teratogens have the greatest affect during the first trimester.

_____ 9. The effects of cigarette smoking during pregnancy remain highly controversial.

_____ 10. (A Closer Look) Until middle age, fertility problems are more often associated with reproductive malfunctioning in women than in men.

Thinking Critically About Chapter 4

Answer these questions the day before an exam as a final check on your understanding of the chapter's terms and concepts.

1. Concluding her report on the importance of social support for the mother-to-be, Rachel states that:
   a. there is a strong correlation between the size of a woman's social network and the likelihood that she will have a healthy birth.
   b. social support is more important for mothers in industrialized societies than for those in nonindustrialized societies.
   c. social support is more important for second and third births than for first births.
   d. in industrialized countries an important source of social support—the extended kin network—is often absent because of residential mobility.

2. A newborn whose mother has used cocaine during pregnancy is *most* likely to be described as:
   a. shorter than normal.
   b. brain damaged.
   c. sleepy and inattentive.
   d. abnormal in facial appearance.

3. Babies born to mothers who are powerfully addicted to a psychoactive drug are *most* likely to suffer from:
   a. structural problems.   c. both a. and b.
   b. behavioral problems.   d. neither a. nor b.

4. Darlene wants to be sure her unborn baby receives adequate nutrition. You advise her to:
   a. make sure her diet is balanced early in the pregnancy since the first trimester is the most critical time period.
   b. eat a balanced diet supplemented with megadoses of multivitamins.
   c. not worry about her diet, as long as she gains at least 15 pounds during her pregnancy.
   d. eat a balanced diet throughout her pregnancy, making sure she gets sufficient amounts of dark-green leafy vegetables, fruits, and grains.

5. At Carla's first prenatal checkup her doctor cautions her regarding the use of alcohol because of the:
   a. potential for FAS.
   b. potential for HIV.
   c. danger of preterm birth.
   d. danger of brain damage from anoxia.

6. Nadia was treated for rubella during the eighth month of her pregnancy. Her doctor is not overly worried about her child-to-be because this disease has its greatest effect:
   a. during the second trimester of pregnancy.
   b. during the first trimester of pregnancy.
   c. during the last trimester of pregnancy.
   d. in women in developing countries.

7. (Public Policy) The text relates the case of Adam, a young Sioux child adopted by a Native American family. Adam suffered from retarded intellectual development because, in his father's words, he was "conceived and grown in an ethanol bath." Among other things, Adam's story sheds light on:
   a. the effects of maternal crack cocaine addiction.
   b. the importance of early intellectual stimulation.
   c. the critical changes that take place during the germinal period.
   d. community concern for the health of the unborn versus parents' rights to live as they choose.

8. I am about 1 inch long and 1 gram in weight. I have all of the basic organs (except sex organs) and features of a human being. What am I?
   a. a zygote   c. a fetus
   b. an embryo   d. an indifferent gonad

9. Karen and Brad are thrilled to report to their neighbors that, 5 weeks after conception, a sonogram of their child-to-be revealed female sex organs. The neighbors are skeptical because:
   a. sonograms are never administered before the third trimester.
   b. sonograms only reveal the presence or absence of male sex organs.
   c. the fetus does not begin to develop female sex organs until about the ninth week.
   d. it is impossible to determine that a woman is pregnant until at least six weeks after conception.

10. Concern about a fetus's health would be greatest if the mother contracted rubella during the _____ week of her pregnancy.
    a. fourth   c. sixteenth
    b. ninth   d. thirty-second

11. Five-year-old Benjamin can't sit quietly and concentrate on a task for more than a minute. Dr. Simmons, who is a teratologist, suspects that Benjamin may have been exposed to _____ during prenatal development.
    a. human immunodeficiency virus
    b. a behavioral teratogen
    c. rubella
    d. lead

12. Sylvia and Stan, who are of British descent, are hoping to have a child. Doctor Caruthers asks for a complete nutritional history and is particularly concerned when she discovers that Sylvia may

have a deficiency of folic acid in her diet. Doctor Caruthers is probably worried about the risk of _____ in the couple's offspring.

a. FAS
b. brain damage
c. neural tube defects
d. ectopic pregnancy

13. Three-year-old Kenny was born underweight, premature, and temperamentally irritable. Today, he is small for his age and has learning disabilities in reading and spelling. His doctor suspects that:

a. Kenny is a victim of fetal alcohol syndrome.
b. Kenny suffers from fetal alcohol effects.
c. Kenny's mother smoked heavily during her pregnancy.
d. Kenny's mother used cocaine during her pregnancy.

14. Which of these fetuses is most likely to experience serious prenatal damage?

a. a male whose 15-year-old mother has an unusually stressful home life
b. a female whose mother did not begin to receive prenatal care until the second month of her pregnancy
c. a female whose 30-year-old mother is on welfare
d. a male whose mother was somewhat undernourished during the first month of her pregnancy

15. Fetal alcohol syndrome is much more common in newborns whose mothers were heavy drinkers during pregnancy than in those whose mothers were moderate drinkers. This finding shows that to assess and understand risk we must know:

a. the kind of alcoholic beverage (for example, beer, wine, or whiskey).
b. the level of exposure to the teratogen.
c. whether the substance really is teratogenic.
d. the timing of exposure to the teratogen.

Key Terms

Using your own words, write a brief definition or explanation of each of the following terms on a separate piece of paper .

1. germinal period
2. period of the embryo
3. period of the fetus
4. differentiation
5. implantation

6. infertility
7. endometriosis
8. artificial insemination
9. in vitro fertilization (IVF)
10. surrogate motherhood
11. embryonic disk
12. ectoderm
13. mesoderm
14. endoderm
15. neural tube
16. cephalo-caudal development
17. proximo-distal development
18. placenta
19. trimester
20. age of viability
21. teratology
22. teratogens
23. risk analysis
24. critical period
25. behavioral teratogens
26. rubella
27. human immunodeficiency virus (HIV)
28. acquired immune deficiency syndrome (AIDS)
29. toxoplasmosis
30. thalidomide
31. fetal alcohol syndrome (FAS)
32. folic acid
33. social support

ANSWERS
CHAPTER REVIEW

1. three; two; germinal; three; eight; embryo; fetus
2. fourth; differentiation; one; placenta; embryo
3. implantation; is not

Implantation triggers hormonal changes that halt the usual menstrual cycle, elevate body temperature, and increase the supply of blood to the breasts.

4. relationship; economic status; age
5. unintended; welcomed
6. 15; infertility; one year
7. 20; 7
8. neither sex
9. sperm production; sperm

Sperm production is affected by age and by other factors that can impair normal body functioning, such as an illness with high fever, medical therapy involving radiation, a high dosage of prescription drugs, drug abuse, or exposure to environmental toxins.

10. ovulation; blocked Fallopian tubes; endometriosis; uterine; 25; 35; one-third

11. artificial insemination; in vitro fertilization; gametes; zygotes

12. surrogate motherhood

Who really are the child's parents? Should children be informed of their parentage if it involved a third-party donor? Should children be legally permitted a chance to learn who their biological parents are upon request?

13. inner; embryonic disk; ectoderm; skin and nervous system; mesoderm; muscles, bones, and the circulatory, excretory, and reproductive systems; endoderm; key elements of the digestive and respiratory systems

14. neural tube; central nervous system

15. cephalo-caudal development; proximo-distal development; cardiovascular

16. placenta

Following the proximo-distal sequence, the upper arms, then the forearms, hands, and fingers appear. Legs, feet, and toes follow. At eight weeks, the embryo's head is more rounded, and the facial features are fully formed. The tail is no longer visible.

17. 1/30 of an ounce (1 gram); 1 inch (2.5 centimeters); fetus

18. stomach; heart; lungs; kidneys; third

19. sixth; indifferent gonad

20. Y; male; female; ninth; twelfth

21. third; 3 ounces (87 grams); 3 inches (7.5 centimeters)

22. trimester

23. ten; six

The heartbeat is stronger and can be heard. The digestive and excretory systems develop more fully. Occasional bursts of electrical activity reveal that the brain is becoming functional.

24. age of viability; twenty; twenty-six

25. breathing; circulatory; sleeping; waking

26. fat

27. thirty-eight

28. nine; fourteenth; breathe

29. sensory; hearing; recognize

30. teratology; teratogens; viruses and bacteria, drugs, chemicals, and types of radiation and environmental pollutants

31. risk analysis

32. timing; amount; genetic vulnerability

33. critical period; behavioral; brain; nervous system

34. cumulative; threshold; interaction

35. Y; male; spontaneous abortions; stillbirths

36. sperm

37. rubella; mumps, chicken pox, polio, and measles

38. human immunodeficiency virus (HIV); acquired immune deficiency syndrome (AIDS); adolescence; ten

39. syphilis; toxoplasmosis

40. thalidomide; tetracycline, anticoagulants, bromides, phenobarbital, retinoic acid, most psychoactive drugs, and most hormones

41. alcohol, tobacco, marijuana, cocaine, and heroine; behavioral; learning difficulties; self-control; irritability; oxygen; brain; more

42. fetal alcohol syndrome; five

Smoking increases risk of ectopic pregnancy, stillbirth, premature separation from the uterus, and premature birth. Babies born to regular smokers weigh less; are shorter; and tend to have behavioral problems, including learning disabilities and temperamental irritability.

43. central nervous; tremors, sleeplessness, voracious sucking, hyperactive reflexes, low birthweight, jaundice, breathing difficulties, mental retardation, poor motor development, and a variety of behavioral problems

In early pregnancy, use of cocaine increases the risk of structural damage, especially to the sex organs. In addition, cocaine use causes overall growth retardation and may cause certain kinds of brain damage. In later pregnancy, cocaine use can cause fetal convulsions.

44. maternal feelings

45. carbon monoxide, lead, mercury, PCBs, and radiation

46. physically or psychologically stressful

Spontaneous abortions when severe fetal damage is likely tend to promote normal development. The lengthy growth process, especially of the brain, means that harm to the fetus at one point can generally be overcome if the rest of the pregnancy is healthy.

47. nutrition; prenatal care; social support

48. 25; 35

49. vitamin

50. folic acid; neural tube
51. counseling; screening
52. barefoot doctors
53. are not

Supportive social networks can ease the financial and material stresses of life during pregnancy and facilitate the expectant mother's efforts to maintain good health habits and regular prenatal care.

PROGRESS TEST 1

Multiple-Choice Questions

1. **a.** is the answer. (p. 110)

   b. This term, which refers to the germinal period, is not used in the text.

   c. The period of the fetus is from the ninth week until birth.

   d. The germinal period covers the first two weeks.

2. **b.** is the answer. (p. 128)

3. **c.** is the answer. (p. 114)

4. **a.** is the answer. (p. 114)

   b. This term refers to all development that occurs from the ninth week after conception until birth.

   c. This describes development from the center outward.

   d. There is no such thing as "teratogenic development"; teratogens are substances that can lead to prenatal abnormalities.

5. **c.** is the answer. The sex organs do not begin to take shape until the period of the fetus. (p. 115)

6. **b.** is the answer. (p. 118)

7. **c.** is the answer. (pp. 116–117)

8. **c.** is the answer. (p. 117)

   a. During the final trimester the fetus actually gains about 5 1/2 pounds in weight.

   b. This occurs during the second trimester.

   d. This occurs during the first trimester.

9. **d.** is the answer. (p. 135)

   c. This is one of the biochemical bases of the genetic code.

10. **a.** is the answer. (p. 116)

11. **d.** is the answer. (p. 119)

    a. In general, teratogens can cross the placenta at any time.

    b. Teratogens are agents in the environment, not

heritable genes (although *susceptibility* to individual teratogens has a genetic component).

   c. Although nutrition is an important factor in healthy prenatal development, the text does not suggest that nutrition alone can usually counteract the harmful effects of teratogens.

12. **d.** is the answer. (pp. 120–121)

    a., b., & c. There are no such periods; development proceeds proximo-distally *throughout* prenatal development.

13. **b.** is the answer. (p. 128)

14. **a.** is the answer. (pp. 126–127)

15. **b.** is the answer. (p. 133)

Matching Items

1. h (p. 120)
2. e (p. 119)
3. b (p. 117)
4. i (p. 114)
5. f (p. 123)
6. j (pp. 126–127)
7. g (p. 124)
8. c (p. 114)
9. k (p. 111)
10. a (p. 114)
11. d (p. 116)

PROGRESS TEST 2

Multiple-Choice Questions

1. **d.** is the answer. (pp. 129, 132)

2. **c.** is the answer. (p. 110)

3. **b.** is the answer. (pp. 119–122)

   a. These were not mentioned in the text.

   c. Nutrition and social support are two of the protective factors that moderate the risk of teratogenic exposure.

4. **c.** is the answer. (p. 114)

5. **c.** is the answer. (p. 110)

6. **c.** is the answer. (p. 114)

7. **d.** is the answer. (p. 118)

8. **a.** is the answer. (p. 125)

9. **a.** is the answer. (p. 126)

10. **d.** is the answer. (p. 129)

11. **b.** is the answer. (p. 112)

    a. & c. These are disorders caused by teratogens.

    d. There is no such thing.

12. **a.** is the answer. (p. 123)

13. **b.** is the answer. (p. 114)

    a. This is the organ in which the zygote implants itself.

    c. This is the precursor of the central nervous system.

d. Fertilization normally takes place in these tubes, which link the mother's ovaries with her uterus.

14. **c.** is the answer. (p. 133)

15. **c.** is the answer. (pp. 136–137)

True or False Items

1. F   This occurs during the third trimester. (p. 118)

2. T (p. 118)

3. F   Normal-weight women should gain between 25 and 35 pounds. (p. 134)

4. F   It is estimated that 58 percent of all conceptions never achieve implantation. (p. 111)

5. T (p. 115)

6. T (p. 114)

7. T (p. 134)

8. F   Behavioral teratogens can affect the fetus at any time during the prenatal period. (p. 121)

9. F   There is no controversy about the damaging effects of smoking during pregnancy. (p. 128)

10. F   Until middle age, both sexes contribute about equally to fertility problems. (p. 112)

THINKING CRITICALLY ABOUT CHAPTER 4

1. **d.** is the answer. (p. 137)

2. **c.** is the answer. These behaviors are the result of instability of the central nervous system, caused by cocaine in the newborn's bloodstream. (p. 129)

3. **b.** is the answer. (p. 126)

4. **d.** is the answer. (p. 134)

5. **a.** is the answer. (pp. 126–127)

   b. HIV is a teratogenic virus.

   c. Although it has other harmful effects, alcohol is not linked to preterm births.

   d. Anoxia is a temporary lack of oxygen, usually experienced by low-birthweight infants.

6. **b.** is the answer. (p. 123)

7. **d.** is the answer. (p. 131)

8. **b.** is the answer. (p. 115)

   a. The zygote is the fertilized ovum.

   c. The developing organism is designated a fetus starting at the ninth week.

   d. The indifferent gonad is the mass of cells that will eventually develop into female or male sex organs.

9. **c.** is the answer. (p. 116)

10. **a.** is the answer. The third through the eighth weeks of pregnancy (period of the embryo) are a critical period in prenatal development; exposure to teratogens at this time is particularly hazardous. (pp. 120, 123)

11. **b.** is the answer. (p. 121)

    a. This is the virus that causes AIDS.

    c. Rubella may cause blindness, deafness, and brain damage.

    d. The text does not discuss the effects of exposure to lead.

12. **c.** is the answer. (p. 135)

    a. FAS is caused in genetically vulnerable infants by the mother-to-be drinking five or more drinks daily during pregnancy.

    b. Brain damage is caused by the use of social drugs during pregnancy.

    d. Risk of ectopic (tubal) pregnancy is increased when the mother smokes, but it is not linked to folic acid deficiency.

13. **c.** is the answer. (p. 128)

14. **a.** is the answer. (pp. 122, 133)

15. **b.** is the answer. (p. 122)

KEY TERMS

1. The first two weeks of development are called the **germinal period.** (p. 110)

   Memory aid: A *germ cell* is one from which a new organism can develop. The *germinal period* is the first stage in the development of the new organism.

2. The **period of the embryo** is the third through the eighth week of prenatal development. (p. 110)

3. From the ninth week until birth is the **period of the fetus.** (p. 110)

4. **Differentiation** is the process by which the cells of the developing organism begin to take on distinct traits and move toward particular locations in the body. (p. 110)

5. **Implantation** is the process by which the outer cells of the organism burrow into the uterine lining and rupture its blood vessels to obtain nourishment and trigger the bodily changes that signify the beginning of pregnancy. (p. 111)

6. Approximately 15 percent of all married couples experience **infertility,** usually defined as being unable to conceive a child after a year or more of trying. (p. 112)

7. A fairly common cause of female infertility is **endometriosis,** a condition in which fragments of

the uterine lining become implanted and grow on the surface of the ovaries or the Fallopian tubes. (p. 112)

8. Some fertility problems are remedied through **artificial insemination**, in which sperm are injected directly into the woman's cervix, increasing the likelihood that they will reach the ovum. (p. 112)

9. With **in vitro fertilization (IVF)**, ova are surgically removed from the ovaries and fertilized by sperm in the laboratory. The resulting embryos are then inserted into the uterus. (p. 112)

10. In **surrogate motherhood**, a woman volunteers to become impregnated by the father-to-be (usually through artificial insemination) and carries the baby to term. (p. 112)

11. During the period of the embryo, the cell cluster called the **embryonic disk** forms and differentiates into three layers that will develop into specialized parts and systems of the body. (p. 114)

12. The **ectoderm** is the outer layer of the embryonic disk. It will develop into the skin and nervous system. (p. 114)

13. The **mesoderm**, which is the middle layer of the embryonic disk, develops into the muscles, bones, and the circulatory, excretory, and reproductive systems. (p. 114)

14. The **endoderm**, which is the inner layer of the embryonic disk, develops into key elements of the digestive and respiratory systems. (p. 114)

15. The **neural tube** forms from a fold that develops in the ectoderm during the period of the embryo; it is the precursor of the central nervous system. (p. 114)

Memory aid: Neural means "of the nervous system." The **neural tube** is the precursor of the central nervous system.

16. **Cephalo-caudal development** refers to growth that proceeds from the head downward. (p. 114)

Memory aid: Cephalo-caudal literally means "of the head-of the tail." Think of *cephalic*, an adjective which also means "of the head."

17. **Proximo-distal development** refers to growth that proceeds from "near to far." According to this process, the most vital organs and body parts form first, before the extremities. (p. 114)

Memory aid: Something that is *proximal* is situated very near. *Proximo-distal development* begins with the very near organs at the center of the body.

18. The **placenta** is the life-giving organ that makes it possible for the developing person to have its

own bloodstream, and, at the same time, to receive oxygen and nourishment from the mother's bloodstream and to rid itself of body wastes. (p. 114)

19. Pregnancy is often divided into three-month-long segments called **trimesters**. (p. 116)

Memory aid: A semester is one of two terms during an academic year; a **trimester** is one of three, three-month-long periods during pregnancy.

20. Sometime between the twentieth and twenty-sixth week after conception the fetus attains the **age of viability**, at which point it has at least some slight chance of survival outside the uterus. (p. 117)

21. **Teratology** is the scientific study of the factors that can contribute to, or protect against, birth defects. (p. 119)

22. **Teratogens** are harmful agents, such as viruses, bacteria, drugs, chemicals, and radiation, that can cause damage to the developing organism. (p. 119)

23. The science of teratology is a science of **risk analysis**, meaning that it attempts to evaluate what factors make prenatal harm more, or less, likely to occur. (p. 119)

24. The first eight weeks of prenatal development is often called the **critical period** because teratogenic exposure during this time can produce malformations of basic body organs and structure. (pp. 120–121)

25. **Behavioral teratogens** tend to damage the brain and nervous system, impairing the future child's intellectual and emotional functioning. (p. 121)

26. **Rubella** (German measles) is a teratogenic disease that, if contracted by the expectant mother early in pregnancy, is likely to cause birth handicaps, including blindness, deafness, heart abnormalities, and brain damage. (p. 123)

27. **Human immunodeficiency virus (HIV)** is the most devastating viral teratogen. HIV gradually overwhelms the body's immune system, making the individual vulnerable to the host of diseases and infections that constitute AIDS. (p. 124)

28. The **acquired immune deficiency syndrome (AIDS)** is the conglomerate of diseases and infections caused by the HIV virus. (p. 124)

29. **Toxoplasmosis** is a teratogenic disease caused by a parasite in raw meat, cat feces, and yard dirt. Toxoplasmosis can severely damage the fetal brain, causing death, retardation, and blindness. (p. 125)

30 **Thalidomide** is a nausea-reducing tranquilizer that was administered to thousands of pregnant women, causing severe birth defects in their offspring. (p. 125)

31. Prenatal alcohol exposure may cause **fetal alcohol syndrome (FAS)**, which includes abnormal facial characteristics, slowed growth, behavior problems, and mental retardation. Likely victims are those who are genetically vulnerable and whose mothers drink five or more drinks daily during pregnancy. (pp. 126–127)

32. **Folic acid** is an important nutrient that is found in dark-green leafy vegetables, as well as certain fruits, grains, and organ meats. Folic acid can sometimes prevent neural tube defects. (p. 135)

33. **Social support** refers to the emotional and material assistance provided by others to an expectant mother. (p. 137)

CHAPTER 5

Birth

Chapter Overview

For the developing person, birth marks the most radical transition of the entire life span. No longer sheltered from the outside world, the fetus becomes a separate human being who begins life almost completely dependent upon its caregivers. Chapter 5 examines the process of birth, its possible variations and problems, and its significance for child, mother, father, and siblings.

The normal birth process, the subject of the first section, begins with uterine contractions and ends when the placenta is expelled. Those attending the birth, however, have much to do after the birth to ensure the well-being of the newborn. This section concludes with a description of the normal newborn.

The next section discusses the causes and consequences of the most common and potentially serious birth complications, including low birthweight, preterm birth, and respiratory distress syndrome. The text reviews the various medical procedures that can aid, or hinder, the birth process and takes a "Closer Look" at the medicalization of birth.

The birth experience has long-lasting effects on all members of the family—the baby, the parents, and the baby's siblings. The third section examines how the movement toward "prepared" or more natural childbirth has changed the typical birth experience in North America and Europe over the past forty years.

The chapter concludes with a discussion of the significance of the parent-newborn bond, including factors that affect its development.

NOTE: Answer guidelines for all Chapter 5 questions begin on page 76.

Guided Study

The text chapter should be studied one section at a time. Before you read, preview each section by skimming it, noting headings and boldface items. Then read the appropriate section objectives from the following outline. Keep these objectives in mind and, as you read the chapter section, search for the information that will enable you to meet each objective. Once you have finished a section, write out answers for its objectives.

The Normal Birth (pp. 142–144)

1. Describe the process of birth, specifying the events of each stage.

2. Describe the neonate and the test used to assess its condition at birth.

Variations, Problems, and Solutions (pp. 144–160)

3. Distinguish between preterm and small-for-gestational-age infants; identify the most critical problem for low birthweight, preterm infants.

4. List three causes of low birthweight. Specifically, discuss the relationship of poverty to low birthweight.

5. (text and Research Report) Note several possible problems in the development of low-birthweight infants, and discuss the effects of early hospital experiences on these infants and the steps that have been taken to prevent problems.

6. Identify the major problems for infants who undergo stressful birth. Explain how obstetricians know when the fetus is experiencing stress, and describe the most likely medical interventions.

7. (A Closer Look) Explain what is meant by the "medicalization" of birth and discuss the issues that surround common medical interventions.

Birth as a Family Event (pp. 160–167)

8. Define prepared childbirth and discuss its advantages for both the baby and the new parents; characterize the experience of siblings in the birth event.

The Beginning of Bonding (pp. 167–169)

9. Explain the concept of parent-newborn bonding and the current view of most developmentalists regarding bonding in humans.

Chapter Review

When you have finished reading the chapter, work through the material that follows to review it. Complete the sentences and answer the questions. As you proceed, evaluate your performance for each section by consulting the answers on page 76. Do not continue with the next section until you understand each answer. If you need to, review or reread the appropriate section in the textbook before continuing.

The Normal Birth (pp. 142–144)

1. In number, there are _____ stages of labor.

2. The birth process begins when contractions of the _____ become strong and regular. Contractions push the fetus downward until the _____ dilates to about _____ in diameter.

3. When the cervix is almost fully dilated, the process called _____ begins, as the fetus descends from the uterus into the birth canal, or vagina. After this point, the baby's

_____ appears at the opening of the vagina. The second stage of labor may last as long as _____ for first pregnancies.

4. Minutes after the baby is born, the third stage of labor occurs when the _____ is expelled.

5. The newborn _____ , or _____ , is usually rated on the _____ , which assigns a score of 0, 1, or 2 to each of the following five characteristics: _____ _____ .

A score below _____ indicates that the newborn is in critical condition and requires immediate attention; if the score is _____ or better, all is well. This rating is made twice, at _____ minute(s) after birth and again at _____ minutes.

6. At birth, the bones of the skull overlap; they eventually fuse together when the _____ (soft spots) on the head close, several months after birth.

Variations, Problems, and Solutions (pp. 144–160)

7. Most newborns weigh about _____ and are born full-term about _____ days after conception.

8. One newborn in every seven weighs less than _____ and is classified as a _____-_____ infant. Infants are called _____ if they are born _____ or more weeks early. Infants who weigh substantially less than they should, given how much time has passed since conception, are called _____ _____ _____ .

Describe the most common immediate difficulties facing low-birthweight infants.

9. The leading cause of preterm death is _____ _____ .

10. Within developed countries, medical intervention _____ (before/after) birth now allows most low-birthweight infants to survive, including very-low-birthweights, defined as those weighing under _____ .

11. Since 1970, infant mortality in the United States has _____ (increased/ decreased/not changed); seventeen other countries have even lower infant death rates, primarily because of better _____ (prenatal/postnatal) care.

12. In general, the survival of low-birthweight preterm infants depends more on maturation of the _____ and _____ than on body weight alone.

13. The most common causes of low birthweight are _____ _____ .

14. Other factors in birthweight are the mother's _____ and the _____ between pregnancies.

15. Compared to a single fetus, twins tend to weigh _____ (more/less) and to be born _____ (earlier/later).

16. Poverty is related to low birthweight, perhaps because poverty is linked to _____ _____ .

Give some statistical evidence that low birthweight is more common among infants from impoverished areas than among others.

17. Many low-birthweight infants experience _____ damage as the result of episodes of _____ , a temporary lack of oxygen, or of _____ .

18. Because they are often confined to an isolette or hooked up to medical machinery, low-birthweight infants may be deprived of normal kinds of _____ , such as

_____ .

Parents of preterm low-birthweight babies also tend to be more _____ of them than are parents of full-term babies.

19. Preterm babies tend to be _____ (more/less) active than full-term babies. Preterm infants may also experience difficulties in _____ and _____ development. For example, as time goes by they are more _____ , slower to _____ , and at risk for later difficulties in _____ competence.

20. Preterm infants who receive extra soothing stimulation while in the hospital _____ (do/do not) show physical and intellectual gains over infants who do not receive extra stimulation.

21. Low-birthweight infants born into families of lower socioeconomic status _____ (are/are not) more likely to continue to have learning problems than are children raised in middle-class families.

22. The deficits related to low birthweight usually _____ (can/cannot) be overcome.

23. In terms of stressful birth, the second stage of labor becomes longer and more difficult when the fetus presents itself buttocks-first in the _____ position.

State several other potential causes of a stressful birth.

24. The use of a _____ _____ can alert doctors to potential problems in the delivery room. However, recent research has indicated that the _____ method of monitoring labor may actually contribute to better outcomes.

25. Mothers in labor are generally more comfortable when they have constant _____ , such as that provided in Guatemala by an experienced woman, called a _____ .

26. For many mothers, _____ _____ ease the experience of labor and delivery. However, this may cause grogginess or irritation in the baby, which _____ (does/does not) disappear in time.

27. During the _____ stage of labor, other techniques that may be used to hasten delivery include _____ or a _____ _____ .

28. Once the fetal head begins to emerge, a small incision called an _____ is often performed to speed birth.

29. When a normal vaginal delivery is likely to be hazardous, a doctor may recommend a surgical procedure called a _____ _____ . This procedure now accounts for nearly one birth in _____ (how many?) in the United States.

(A Closer Look) Briefly state the position of those who believe that medical procedures tend to be overused in the birth process.

Birth as a Family Event (pp. 160–167)

30. When a more detailed assessment of the newborn is needed, the twenty-six item _____ _____ _____ _____ is often used.

31. A delivery technique that stresses active control in the birth process through breathing, concentration, and the father's assistance as a labor "coach" is the _____ method.

32. Before 1970, fathers usually _____ (were/were not) permitted in the delivery room.

33. The _____ _____ and _____ of the birth attendant are powerful determinants in how smooth and satisfying the birth process is for all concerned.

Describe how parents can prepare a child for the presence of a new baby in the family.

The Beginning of Bonding (pp. 167–169)

34. The term used to describe the close parent-child relationship that begins within the first hours after birth is _____ .

35. Insofar as it exists in humans, this process is _____ (less/more) biologically determined than in other animal species. In certain cases, such as when mothers are

_____ , _____ ,

or under _____ _____ ,

immediate contact with the infant seems to be especially important.

Progress Test 1

Multiple-Choice Questions

Circle your answers to the following questions and check them with the answers on page 76. If your answer is incorrect, read the explanation for why it is incorrect and then consult the appropriate pages of the text (in parentheses following the correct answer).

1. The birth process begins:
   a. when the fetus moves into the right position.
   b. when the uterus begins to contract at regular intervals to push the fetus out.
   c. about eight hours (in the case of first-borns) after the uterus begins to contract at regular intervals.
   d. when the baby's head appears at the opening of the vagina.

2. Transition occurs when:
   a. uterine contractions begin.
   b. the placenta is expelled.
   c. the fetus's head moves into the birth canal.
   d. the fetus's head emerges fully.

3. The third stage of labor occurs when:
   a. uterine contractions begin.
   b. the placenta is expelled.
   c. the fetus's head moves into the birth canal.
   d. the fetus's head emerges fully.

4. The Apgar is administered:
   a. only if the newborn is in obvious distress.
   b. once, just after birth.
   c. twice, 1 minute and 5 minutes after birth.
   d. repeatedly during the newborn's first hours.

5. Most newborns weigh about:
   a. 5 pounds.
   b. 6 pounds.
   c. 7 1/2 pounds.
   d. 8 1/2 pounds.

6. Low-birthweight babies born near the due date but weighing substantially less than they should:
   a. are classified as preterm.
   b. are called small for gestational age.
   c. usually have no sex organs.
   d. show many signs of immaturity.

7. The most common cause of low birthweight is:
   a. maternal malnutrition.
   b. the mother's poor overall health.
   c. a genetic handicap.
   d. maternal drug abuse.

8. Low birthweight infants are:
   a. more distractible.
   b. slower to talk.
   c. at risk for later problems in social competence.
   d. characterized by all of the above.

9. One reason for a long and stressful labor is:
   a. the fetus's head is large relative to the mother's pelvis.
   b. uterine contractions are too strong.
   c. fetal monitoring is inaccurate.
   d. transition does not occur in the proper sequence.

10. Forceps or a vacuum extractor may be used to:
   a. hasten a vaginal birth.
   b. perform an emergency Cesarean section.
   c. make an episiotomy.
   d. monitor the fetus's progress.

11. Which Apgar score indicates that a newborn is in normal health?
   a. 4
   b. 5
   c. 6
   d. 7

12. Minimal medical assistance, psychological encouragement, and adequate preparation are factors in:
    a. "natural" or Lamaze childbirth.
    b. the Apgar method.
    c. Cesarean delivery.
    d. birth trauma.

13. The idea of a parent-newborn bond in humans arose from:
    a. observations in the delivery room.
    b. data on adopted infants.
    c. animal studies.
    d. studies of disturbed mother-newborn pairs.

14. Studies of fathers present during delivery found that:
    a. 50 percent were emotionally disoriented.
    b. most were glad they had been there.
    c. the fathers introduced infection into the delivery room.
    d. most would not repeat the experience.

15. Birth anesthetics that are intended to reduce the mother's discomfort during labor:
    a. are prevented from entering the bloodstream of the fetus by the placenta.
    b. often have a significant effect on the fetus before it is born, resulting in diminished alertness.
    c. typically strengthen labor contractions.
    d. often lengthen labor.

Matching Items

Match each definition or description with its corresponding term.

Definitions or Descriptions

_____ 1. a baby born three or more weeks early
_____ 2. the leading cause of preterm death
_____ 3. a temporary lack of oxygen
_____ 4. a device that automatically charts the fetus's heart rate
_____ 5. a suction cup used to pull the fetus through the birth canal
_____ 6. an infant weighing less than 5 1/2 pounds at birth
_____ 7. a fetus presents itself buttocks-first
_____ 8. low-birthweight infants who are born close to the due date but who weigh less than they should
_____ 9. another word for newborn
_____ 10. a small surgical incision in the skin surrounding the vagina, made to facilitate birth

Terms

a. neonate
b. preterm
c. anoxia
d. vacuum extractor
e. breech position
f. small for gestational age
g. low birthweight
h. respiratory distress syndrome
i. fetal monitor
j. episiotomy

Progress Test 2

Progress Test 2 should be completed during a final chapter review. Answer the following questions after you thoroughly understand the correct answers for the Chapter Review and Progress Test 1.

Multiple-Choice Questions

1. The longest stage of labor is:
   a. the first stage.   c. the third stage.
   b. the second stage.   d. transition.

2. The second stage of labor begins when:
   a. uterine contractions begin.
   b. the placenta is expelled.
   c. the fetus's head moves into the birth canal.
   d. the fetus's head moves to the vaginal opening.

3. Among the characteristics rated on the Apgar are:
   a. shape of the newborn's head and nose.
   b. presence of body hair.
   c. interactive behaviors.
   d. muscle tone and color.

4. Among the characteristics rated on the Brazelton Neonatal Behavioral Assessment Scale are:
   a. shape of the newborn's head and nose.
   b. presence of body hair.
   c. interactive behaviors.
   d. muscle tone and color.

5. A newborn is classified as low birthweight if he or she weighs less than:
   a. 7 pounds.
   b. 6 pounds.
   c. 5 1/2 pounds.
   d. 4 pounds.

6. The most critical problem for preterm babies is:
   a. the immaturity of the sex organs—for example, undescended testicles.
   b. spitting up or hiccupping.
   c. infection from intravenous feeding.
   d. breathing difficulties.

7. Which of the following was *not* cited as evidence that social-contextual factors are an underlying cause of low birthweight?
   a. In many developed countries, the rate of low birthweight is higher in inner cities than in suburbs.
   b. Developing countries in the same general region, with similar ethnic populations, typically have similar rates of low birthweight.
   c. The rate of low-birthweight infants is much higher in developing, than developed, countries.
   d. Ethnic-group variations in low-birthweight rates within nations tend to follow socioeconomic, rather than genetic, patterns.

8. Many low-birthweight infants experience brain damage as the result of:
   a. anoxia.
   b. cerebral hemorrhaging.
   c. anoxia or cerebral hemorrhaging.
   d. genetic defects.

9. A fetal monitor attached to the mother's abdomen measures and records the:
   a. fetal heart rate.
   b. dilation of the cervix.
   c. position of the fetus.
   d. degree of fetal brain damage.

10. A Cesarean section may be performed when fetal monitoring shows a weak or erratic fetal heartbeat and when:
    a. labor is progressing too rapidly.
    b. the fetus is overmedicated.
    c. the fetus has rotated spontaneously at transition.
    d. the mother shows signs of physical stress and exhaustion.

11. Postnatal depression refers to the:
    a. insensitivity of birth attendants.
    b. aftereffects of local anesthesia.
    c. role of the midwife.
    d. "baby blues" of the new mother.

12. Extra early mother-newborn contact seems to be *most* beneficial to mothers of preterms and to:
    a. low-income, first-time mothers.
    b. mothers who have attended childbirth-preparation classes.
    c. mothers of female infants.
    d. mothers who have had only routine contact with infants.

13. Many of the factors that contribute to low birthweight are related to poverty; for example, women of lower socioeconomic status tend to:
    a. be less well nourished.
    b. have less education.
    c. be subjected to stressful living conditions.
    d. be all of the above.

14. (Public Policy) In the case of very-very-low-birthweight infants, the medical interventions that save their lives may cause blindness as a result of:
    a. the administration of high concentrations of oxygen to enhance breathing.
    b. the brain damage that occurred during the emergency birth.
    c. hemorrhaging during surgery.
    d. all of the above.

15. Respiratory distress syndrome results in:
    a. an inability to breathe normally.
    b. preterm birth.
    c. low birthweight.
    d. all of the above.

True or False Items

Write *true* or *false* on the line in front of each statement.

_____ 1. Physical appearance is the best indication of the newborn's health.

_____ 2. The Apgar is used to measure vital signs such as heart rate and breathing.

_____ 3. Newborns usually cry on their own, moments after birth.

_____ 4. A misshapen or pointed head in the neonate is often a permanent disfigurement.

_____ 5. Cesarean sections are less common in the United States today than they were 20 years ago.

_____ 6. For siblings, the birth of a new baby typically results in a loss of parental attention, leading to intellectual or learning difficulties that persist into adulthood.

_____ 7. Research shows that immediate mother-newborn contact at birth is necessary for the normal emotional development of the child.

_____ 8. Low-birthweight babies are more likely than other children to experience developmental difficulties in early childhood.

_____ 9. Parent-newborn bonding in humans is probably less biologically determined than it is in other mammals.

_____ 10. Women who attend childbirth classes generally use less anesthesia and feel less pain in the birth process.

Thinking Critically About Chapter 5

Answer these questions the day before an exam as a final check on your understanding of the chapter's terms and concepts.

1. A mother gives birth in a crowded, understaffed hospital and it is several hours before her newborn is brought to her. The most likely result of this separation is that:
   a. the mother will initially reject the infant.
   b. the mother will have difficulty bonding with the infant, especially if it is a female.
   c. the infant will experience difficulties in interacting with the mother during the first year or so.
   d. the mother will develop a normal attachment to her infant, and vice versa.

2. Your sister and brother-in-law, who are about to adopt a 1-year-old, are worried that the child will never bond with them. What advice should you offer?
   a. Tell them that, unfortunately, this is true; they would be better off waiting for a younger child who has not yet bonded.
   b. Tell them that, although the first year is a biologically determined critical period for attachment, there is a fifty-fifty chance that the child will bond with them.

   c. Tell them that bonding is a long-term process between parent and child that is determined by the nature of interaction throughout infancy, childhood, and beyond.
   d. Tell them that if the child is female, there is a good chance that she will bond with them, even at this late stage.

3. Antonia and Fernando wanted very much to have natural childbirth, so they attended Lamaze classes. Because she received no medication during childbirth, Antonia probably:
   a. felt mostly negative about the whole event and the baby.
   b. had a short labor and a positive reaction to birth and the baby.
   c. felt positive about the baby, but negative about the birth process itself.
   d. felt generally positive or neutral about birth and the baby.

4. Which of the following newborns would be most likely to have problems in body structure and functioning?
   a. Anton, whose Apgar score is 6
   b. Debora, whose Apgar score is 7
   c. Sheila, whose Apgar score is 3
   d. Simon, whose Apgar score is 5

5. In concluding your presentation on infant mortality, you note that the main reason infant mortality in the United States decreased substantially between 1970 and 1992 is:
   a. the increased survival of very-low-birthweight infants.
   b. better education of expectant mothers regarding nutrition.
   c. the decreased use of general anesthesia during delivery.
   d. the increased survival rate of preterm infants.

6. At birth, Clarence was classified as small for gestational age. It is likely that Clarence:
   a. was born in a rural hospital.
   b. suffered several months of prenatal malnutrition.
   c. was born in a large city hospital.
   d. comes from a family with a history of such births.

7. Of the following, who is *most* likely to give birth to a low-birthweight child?
   a. twenty-one-year-old Janice, who lives in the North
   b. twenty-five-year-old May Ling, who lives in China

c. sixteen-year-old Donna, who lives in a remote, rural part of the United States

d. thirty-year-old Maria, who lives in southern California

8. Among Hispanic-American groups, the rate of low-birthweight for infants of Puerto Rican heritage is higher than that for Cuban-Americans. This demonstrates that:

a. low birthweight is an inherited disorder.

b. low birthweight is unpredictable.

c. ethnic-group variations within nations tend to follow socioeconomic, rather than genetic, patterns.

d. None of the above is necessarily true.

9. A preterm infant is usually placed in an isolette. The purpose of this action is to:

a. protect the newborn from disease and infection.

b. isolate the newborn from its parents.

c. limit the infant's activity, in order to minimize weight loss after birth.

d. accomplish all of the above.

10. A 1980 study showed that first-time mothers who had learned about birth from other women and popular culture were most likely to experience:

a. pain and discomfort.

b. positive attitudes about birth.

c. negative feelings about birth.

d. normal labor and quick recuperation.

11. An infant born 266 days after conception, weighing 4 pounds, would be designated a _____ infant.

a. preterm

b. low-birthweight

c. small-for-gestational-age

d. b. & c.

12. An infant who was born at thirty-five weeks, weighing 6 pounds, would be called a _____ infant.

a. preterm

b. low-birthweight

c. small-for-gestational-age

d. premature

13. Although birth is a physically stressful experience for the newborn, its impact is buffered somewhat by:

a. the release of stress hormones into the bloodstream.

b. the fact that infants do not remember the experience.

c. the oxygen-rich environment of the birth canal.

d. all of the above.

14. The Lamaze technique is based on principles of _____ that relieve pain.

a. operant conditioning

b. classical conditioning

c. hypnosis

d. counterconditioning

15. The five characteristics evaluated by the Apgar are:

a. heart rate, length, weight, muscle tone, and color.

b. orientation, muscle tone, reflexes, interaction, and responses to stress.

c. reflex irritability, breathing, muscle tone, heart rate, and color.

d. pupillary response, heart rate, reflex irritability, alertness, and breathing.

Key Terms

Using your own words, write a brief definition or explanation of each of the following terms on a separate piece of paper.

1. first stage of labor

2. transition

3. second stage of labor

4. third stage of labor

5. neonate

6. Apgar

7. low-birthweight infants

8. preterm

9. small for gestational age (SGA)

10. very-low-birthweight (VLBW) infants

11. anoxia

12. breech position

13. fetal monitor

14. forceps

15. vacuum extractor

16. episiotomy

17. Cesarean section

18. Brazelton Neonatal Behavioral Assessment Scale (NBAS)

19. Lamaze method

20. dethronement

21. parent-newborn bond

ANSWERS

CHAPTER REVIEW

1. three

2. uterus; cervix; 10 centimeters (4 inches)

3. transition; head; one to two hours

4. placenta

5. neonate; Apgar; heart rate, breathing, muscle tone, color, and reflexes; 4; 7; 1; 5

6. fontanelles

7. 3,400 grams (7 1/2 pounds); 266

8. 2,500 grams (5 1/2 pounds); low-birthweight; preterm; three; small for gestational age

Low-birthweight infants may have difficulty maintaining body heat, digesting food, resisting infection, and getting sufficient oxygen.

9. respiratory distress syndrome

10. after; 1,500 grams (3 1/2 pounds)

11. decreased; prenatal

12. brain; lungs

13. maternal malnutrition; poor maternal health or health habits, including drug abuse; prenatal infections; genetic handicaps; and malfunctioning of the placenta or umbilical cord

14. age; interval

15. less; earlier

16. maternal malnutrition, less education, more stressful living conditions, poorer health, pregnancies at younger ages, and greater exposure to teratogens

The vast majority of low-birthweight infants born each year are from developing countries. In the United States, the rate of low birthweight in inner cities is more than double that in the suburbs; in poorer states, it is also almost twice that of some richer states. Ethnic-group variations in low-birthweight births tend to follow socioeconomic, rather than genetic, patterns.

17. brain; anoxia; cerebral hemorrhaging

18. stimulation; rocking (or regular handling); protective

19. less; cognitive; language; distractible; talk; social

20. do

21. are

22. can

23. breech

Other causes include a large fetal head relative to the mother's pelvis; contractions that are not strong enough; and a mother who is overtired, overanxious, or overmedicated.

24. fetal monitor; stethoscope

25. companionship; *doula*

26. anesthetic medications; does

27. second; forceps; vacuum extractor

28. episiotomy

29. Cesarean section; four

While medical procedures have been credited with saving lives, they have also been criticized for sometimes interfering needlessly with the natural process of birth. Many doctors believe that medical procedures are overused, resulting in a more expensive, riskier, and less humane birth process.

30. Brazelton Neonatal Behavioral Assessment Scale (NBAS)

31. Lamaze

32. were not

33. personal traits; attitude

Parents can help an older child prepare for the arrival of a new child by telling him or her what to expect in the days surrounding the birth and reassuring the child that becoming a big brother or sister will have its benefits. Parents can also relieve the anxiety the child feels when the mother goes to the hospital by showing him or her photographs of his or her early days at the hospital, and making plans for a special outing with the father while the mother is away.

34. bonding

35. less; young; poor; special stress

PROGRESS TEST 1

Multiple-Choice Questions

1. **b.** is the answer. (p. 142)

2. **c.** is the answer. (p. 142)

    a. This describes the first stage of labor.

    b. This describes the third stage of labor.

    d. This describes the second stage of labor.

3. **b.** is the answer. (p. 143)

4. **c.** is the answer. (p. 143)

5. **c.** is the answer. (p. 144)

6. **b.** is the answer. (p. 145)

7. **a.** is the answer. (p. 146)

8. **d.** is the answer. (p. 149)

9. **a.** is the answer. (p. 154)

 b. Labor is prolonged when uterine contractions are too *weak*.

 c. Fetal monitoring does not directly influence the course of labor.

 d. Transition occurs when the fetus's head moves into the birth canal; it cannot occur "out of sequence."

10. **a.** is the answer. (p. 156)

 b. Forceps are used to pull the baby through the birth canal; in a Cesarean section the baby is delivered through the mother's abdomen.

 c. An episiotomy is a surgical incision in the skin surrounding the vagina, made to facilitate birth.

 d. A fetal monitor is used for this purpose.

11. **d.** is the answer. (p. 143)

12. **a.** is the answer. (p. 162)

 b. The Apgar is a scale that rates a newborn's condition; there is no such thing as an "Apgar method" of delivery.

 c. A Cesarean delivery is a surgical procedure in which the baby is delivered through the mother's abdomen.

 d. The notion of birth as traumatic has not been supported by scientific evidence.

13. **c.** is the answer. (p. 167)

14. **b.** is the answer. (p. 166)

15. **b.** is the answer. (p. 156)

 a. Most drugs administered to the mother *do* pass through the placenta.

 c. & d. Although drugs are sometimes used to strengthen labor contractions (c) and *shorten* labor (d), anesthetics generally do not have these effects.

Matching Items

1. b (p. 145)
2. h (p. 146)
3. c (p. 148)
4. i (p. 154)
5. d (p. 156)
6. g (p. 144)
7. e (p. 154)
8. f (p. 145)
9. a (p. 143)
10. j (p. 156)

PROGRESS TEST 2

Multiple-Choice Questions

1. **a.** is the answer. (p. 142)

2. **d.** is the answer. (p. 142)

3. **d.** is the answer. (p. 143)

4. **c.** is the answer. (p. 160)

5. **c.** is the answer. (p. 144)

6. **d.** is the answer. (p. 146)

7. **b.** is the answer. Developing countries in the same general region, with similar ethnic populations, often have *different* rates of low birthweight. (p. 147)

8. **c.** is the answer. (p. 148)

9. **a.** is the answer. (p. 154)

10. **d.** is the answer. (p. 156)

11. **d.** is the answer. Postnatal depression is experienced by about 10 percent of all mothers in the days and weeks after birth. (p. 165)

12. **a.** is the answer. (p. 168)

13. **d.** is the answer. (p. 147)

14. **a.** is the answer. (p. 153)

 b. Brain damage may cause cerebral palsy.

 c. Hemorrhaging during surgery may cause cognitive deficits.

15. **a.** is the answer. (p. 146)

 b. & c. Respiratory distress syndrome is a *consequence*, rather than a cause, of preterm birth and low birthweight.

True or False Items

1. F   Many normal newborns look abnormal to someone who has never seen one before. (p. 144)

2. T (p. 143)

3. T (p. 143)

4. F   Newborns' heads often are elongated; however, this usually causes no lasting damage. (p. 144)

5. F   Nearly one in four births in the United States are now Cesarean. (p. 156)

6. F   Although the birth of a younger sibling is often stressful, the text does not suggest that it leads to persistent intellectual or learning difficulties. (pp. 166–167)

7. F   Though highly desirable, mother-newborn contact at birth is not necessary for the child's normal development, or for a good parent-child relationship. Many opportunities for bonding occur throughout childhood. (pp. 168–169)

8. T (p. 149)

9. T (p. 168)

10. T (p. 162)

THINKING CRITICALLY ABOUT CHAPTER 5

1. **d.** is the answer. (p. 169)

   a., b., & c. Most developmentalists now believe that the importance of early contact between mother and child has been overly popularized and that the strength of their bond is determined by the nature of their interaction throughout infancy, childhood, and beyond.

2. **c.** is the answer. (p. 169)

   a. & b. Bonding in humans is not a biologically determined event limited to a critical period, as it is in many other animal species.

   d. There is no evidence of any gender differences in the formation of the parent-newborn bond.

3. **b.** is the answer. (p. 162)

4. **c.** is the answer. If a neonate's Apgar score is below 4, the infant is in critical condition and needs immediate medical attention. (p. 143)

5. **a.** is the answer. (p. 146)

   b., c., & d. Although each of these is true, the main reason for the decreased infant mortality rate in the United States is the increased survival of very-low-birthweight infants.

6. **b.** is the answer. (pp. 146–147)

   a., c., & d. Prenatal malnutrition is the most common cause of a small-for-dates neonate.

7. **c.** is the answer. (p. 147)

   a., b., & d. The incidence of low birthweight is higher among mothers under 15 or over 40.

8. **d.** is the answer. Hispanic-Americans of Puerto Rican descent and those of Cuban descent come from the same basic ethnic group. Cuban-Americans, however, are more affluent as a group than are Americans of Puerto Rican heritage. (p. 148)

9. **a.** is the answer. (p. 148)

10. **c.** is the answer. (p. 161)

11. **d.** is the answer. (pp. 144–145)

   a. & c. At 266 days, this infant is full-term.

12. **a.** is the answer. (p. 145)

   b. Low birthweight is defined as weighing less than 5 1/2 pounds.

   c. Although an infant can be both preterm and small for gestational age, this baby's weight is within the normal range of healthy babies.

   d. This term is no longer used to describe early births.

13. **a.** is the answer. (p. 160)

   b. Although babies do not have permanent memories of the experience, birth is nevertheless stressful.

   c. The presence of oxygen does not make passage through the birth canal less stressful, especially since at this point, babies have not taken their first breath!

14. **b.** is the answer. (p. 162)

15. **c.** is the answer. (p. 143)

KEY TERMS

1. From the first tentative contractions of the uterus until full dilation of the cervix, the **first stage of labor** lasts eight to twelve hours in first births and four to seven hours in subsequent births. (p. 142)

2. During the **transition** period of labor, the fetus's head descends from the uterus through the birth canal to the vaginal opening. (p. 142)

3. The **second stage of labor**, which may last as long as one to two hours for first pregnancies, but perhaps only a few minutes for subsequent ones, begins when the fetus's head appears at the opening of the vagina. (p. 142)

4. Minutes after the baby is born, the **third stage of labor** occurs when contractions expel the placenta. (p. 143)

5. **Neonate** is another word for newborn. (p. 143)

6. Newborns are rated at one and then at five minutes after birth according to the **Apgar**. This scale assigns a score of 0, 1, or 2 to each of five characteristics: heart rate, breathing, muscle tone, color, and reflex irritability. A score of 7 or better indicates that all is well. (p. 143)

7. Newborns who weigh less than 2,500 grams (5 1/2 pounds) are called **low-birthweight infants**. Such infants are at risk for many immediate and long-term problems. (p. 144)

8. Infants who are born three or more weeks before the due date are called **preterm**. (p. 145)

9. Infants who weigh substantially less than they should, given how much time has passed since conception, are called **small for gestational age (SGA)**, or small-for-dates. (p. 145)

10. Infants weighing under 1,500 grams (less than 3 1/2 pounds) are referred to as **very-low-birthweight (VLBW) infants**. (p. 146)

11. **Anoxia** is a temporary lack of fetal oxygen during the birth process that can cause brain damage or even death. (p. 148)

12. When the fetus presents itself for birth with buttocks first, it is said to be in the **breech position**. (p. 154)

13. The electronic **fetal monitor** automatically charts fetal heart rate, the frequency of contractions, and other information, such as anoxia, to help reduce the possibility of a long and stressful labor. (p. 154)

14. During the second stage of labor, **forceps**—an instrument that fits around the fetal head—can be used to pull the fetus through the birth canal. (p. 156)

15. A **vacuum extractor** is a special suction cup that fits over the top of the fetal head and can be used to pull the fetus through the birth canal. (p. 156)

16. A small surgical incision in the skin surrounding the vagina, made to facilitate birth, is called an **episiotomy**. (p. 156)

17. When birth is not progressing as it should, a **Cesarean section** can be performed to remove the baby quickly through an incision in the mother's abdomen and uterus. (p. 156)

18. The **Brazelton Neonatal Behavioral Assessment Scale (NBAS)** is a twenty-six item test that assesses the infant's skill and style in responding to the environment. (p. 160)

19. The **Lamaze method** of childbirth emphasizes breathing and concentration techniques and the presence of a labor coach. This method often results in a less painful and more rapid delivery requiring less anesthesia. (p. 162)

20. The only-child's adjustment to the arrival of a new sibling is referred to as **dethronement** by some psychologists: The former little autocrat suddenly has to relinquish his or her power. (p. 167)

21. The term **parent-newborn bond** describes the tangible and metaphorical fastening of parent to child in the early moments of their relationship together. Insofar as bonding exists in humans, it is much less biologically determined than in other animal species. (p. 167)

CHAPTER 6

The First Two Years: Biosocial Development

Chapter Overview

Chapter 6 is the first of a three-chapter unit that describes the developing person from birth to age 2 in terms of biosocial, cognitive, and psychosocial development. Physical development is the first to be examined.

The chapter begins with observations on the overall growth and health of infants, including their size and shape and the importance of immunizations during the first two years. Following is a discussion of brain growth and maturation and the role of the brain in regulating the infant's physiological states. The chapter then turns to a discussion of motor abilities, and the ages at which the average infant acquires them. Vision and hearing and the development of these and other sensory abilities are discussed next, along with recent research on infant perception and the role of sensory experience in normal development. The final section discusses the importance of nutrition during the first two years, and the consequences of severe malnutrition and undernutrition.

NOTE: Answer guidelines for all Chapter 6 questions begin on page 91.

Guided Study

The text chapter should be studied one section at a time. Before you read, preview each section by skimming it, noting headings and boldface items. Then read the appropriate section objectives from the following outline. Keep these objectives in mind and, as you read the chapter section, search for the information that will enable you to meet each objective. Once you have finished a section, write out answers for its objectives.

Physical Growth and Health (pp. 176–183)

1. Describe the size and proportions of an infant's body, including how they change during the first two years and how they compare with those of an adult.

2. List several reasons for the twentieth-century improvement in the survival of young children.

3. Identify risk factors and possible explanations for sudden infant death syndrome.

Brain Growth and Maturation (pp. 183–186)

4. Describe the ways in which the brain changes or matures during infancy.

5. Discuss the role of the brain in regulating the infant's physiological states and name four normal physiological states of the infant.

Motor Skills (pp. 186–194)

6. Describe the basic reflexes of the newborn and distinguish between gross motor skills and fine motor skills.

7. Describe the basic pattern of motor-skill development and discuss variations in the timing of motor-skill acquisition.

Sensory and Perceptual Capacities (pp. 194–200)

8. Distinguish between sensation and perception and describe how and why habituation is used in research on infant perception.

9. Describe the extent and development of an infant's perceptual abilities in terms of the senses of vision, hearing, taste, smell, and touch.

10. Discuss the role of sensory experience in brain development.

Nutrition (pp. 200–207)

11. Describe the nutritional needs of infants and discuss the causes and results of malnutrition and undernutrition in the first years.

Chapter Review

When you have finished reading the chapter, work through the material that follows to review it. Complete the sentences and answer the questions. As you proceed, evaluate your performance for each section by consulting the answers on page 91. Do not continue with the next section until you understand each answer. If you need to, review or reread the appropriate section in the textbook before continuing.

Physical Growth and Health (pp. 176–183)

1. With the exception of _____ development, infancy is the period of the fastest and most notable increases in _____ and changes in _____.

2. The average North American newborn measures _____ and weighs _____.

3. In the first days of life, most newborns _____ (gain/lose) between 5 and 10 percent of their body weight.

4. By age 1, the typical baby weighs about _____ and measures almost _____.

5. Newborns often seem top-heavy because their heads are equivalent to about _____ (what proportion?) of their total length, compared to about _____ at one year and _____ in adulthood.

6. Newborns' legs represent about _____ (what proportion?) of their total length, whereas an adult's legs represent about _____ of it.

7. Proportionally, the smallest part of a newborn's body is the _____ .

8. The chance of infants dying within the first year in North America and most developed nations is less than _____ in 100. The single most important cause of the improvement in child survival is _____ .

State several other reasons for the increased survival of young children.

9. For most of the illnesses of infancy, _____ is much easier, cheaper, and less painful than _____ ;

sometimes, it is _____ (easy/difficult) to put into practice.

10. Most infant deaths occur in the first _____ of life, and are related to problems such as _____ _____ .

11. One common cause of infant death that is not related to any obvious problem is _____ _____ _____ _____ , which ranks as the _____ leading cause of infant death in the United States.

Identify several SIDS risk factors.

12. There is less of a risk for SIDS when healthy infants sleep on their _____ .

13. In terms of ethnicity, babies of _____ descent are more likely, and babies of _____ descent less likely, to succumb to SIDS than are babies of _____ descent. Two risk factors that may explain the SIDS-ethnicity correlation are _____ _____ and _____ _____ in high risk groups. An alternative explanation focuses on _____-_____ routines that vary from group to group.

Brain Growth and Maturation (pp. 183–186)

14. At birth the brain has attained about _____ percent of its adult weight; by age 2 the brain is about _____ percent of its adult weight. In comparison, body weight at age 2 is about _____ percent of what it will be in adulthood.

15. The nervous system is made up of long, thin nerve cells called _____ . Most

of these cells _____ (are/are not) present at birth.

16. During the first months of life, brain development is most noticeable in its outer layer, which is called the _____ . This area of the brain controls _____ and _____ .

17. From birth until age 2, the communication networks of the cortex, which are called _____ , show an estimated five-fold increase in density. These networks also become coated with the insulating substance called _____ , which makes neural transmission more efficient. This coating process continues through _____ .

18. The _____ area of the cortex, which assists in _____ and _____ , becomes more mature during infancy, giving infants greater regulation of their _____ states, and _____ -_____ patterns and increasing control over their early _____ .

19. The various conditions of sleep and waking in an infant are referred to as physiological _____ .

List and briefly describe the most distinctive of these conditions in the infant.

20. Patterns of electrical activity in the brain can be measured and recorded by the device called an _____ .

21. While the infant's total daily sleep _____ (does/does not) change much between birth and age 1, the length and _____ of sleep episodes more closely match the family pattern. Approximately _____ (what proportion?) of all

3-month-olds and _____ percent of all 1-year-olds sleep through the night. In comparison, preterm infants sleep _____ (more/less) with _____ (greater/lesser) regularity than full-term infants.

22. (Research Report) By _____ months of age the infant's physiological states become more predictable. The predictability of these states, however, varies with specific _____ -_____ practices, which in turn reflect the particular values of a family's _____ .

23. (Research Report) Industrialized countries tend to place _____ (more/less) emphasis on schedules than do less developed countries.

Motor Skills (pp. 186–194)

24. An involuntary physical response to a stimulus is called a _____ .

25. The involuntary response of breathing, which causes the newborn to take the first breath even before the umbilical cord is cut, is called the _____ . Because breathing is irregular during the first few days, other reflexive behaviors, such as _____ , _____ , and _____ , are common.

26. Shivering, crying, and tucking the legs close to the body are examples of reflexes that help to maintain _____ .

27. A third set of reflexes fosters _____ . One of these is the tendency of the newborn to suck anything that touches the lips; this is the _____ reflex. Another is the tendency of newborns to turn their heads and start to suck when something brushes against their cheek; this is the _____ reflex.

28. The tendency of a baby's toes to fan upward when the feet are stroked is called the _____ reflex.

29. The tendency of babies to move their feet as if to walk when the feet touch a flat surface is called the _____ reflex.

30. The tendency of a baby's arms and legs to stretch out when he or she is held horizontally on the stomach is called the _____ reflex.

31. The tendency of a baby's hands to close tightly when something touches the palm is called the _____ _____ reflex.

32. The tendency of newborns to fling their arms outward and then bring them together on the chest when someone bangs the table on which they are lying is called the _____ reflex.

33. Large movements such as running and climbing are called _____ _____ skills; abilities that require more precise, small movements, such as picking up a coin, are called _____ _____ skills.

34. Most infants are able to crawl on all fours (sometimes called creeping) between _____ and _____ months of age.

List the major landmarks in children's mastery of walking.

35. Babies who have just begun to walk are given the name _____ for the characteristic way they move their bodies from side to side.

36. By _____ of age, most babies can reach for, grab, and hold onto almost any object of the right size.

Briefly describe the development of the ability to pick up and manipulate small objects.

37. Although the _____ in which motor skills are mastered is the same in all healthy infants, the _____ of acquisition of skills varies greatly.

38. The average ages at which most infants master major motor skills are known as _____ . These averages are based on a large sample of infants drawn from _____ (a single/many) ethnic group(s).

39. Motor skill norms vary from one _____ group to another.

List several factors that account for the variation in the acquisition of motor skills.

40. Motor skill acquisition in identical twins _____ (is/is not) more similar than in fraternal twins, suggesting that genes _____ (do/do not) play an important role.

41. Most developmentalists would say that the age at which a particular baby first displays a particular skill depends on the interaction between _____ and _____ factors.

Sensory and Perceptual Capacities (pp. 194–200)

42. The process by which the visual, auditory, and other sensory systems detect stimuli is called _____ ; _____ occurs when the brain tries to make sense out of a stimulus so that the individual becomes aware of it. At birth, both of these processes _____ (are/are not) apparent.

Briefly describe the sensory abilities of the newborn.

43. An infant presented with an unfamiliar stimulus will respond with intensified sucking on a pacifier, or concentrated gazing. When the stimulus becomes so familiar that these responses no longer occur, _____ is said to have occurred. If the infant reacts to a new stimulus, researchers conclude that the infant can _____ between the stimuli.

44. Newborns' visual focusing is best for objects between _____ and _____ inches away, giving them distance vision of about 20/_____ . Distance vision improves rapidly, reaching 20/20 by _____ of age. This improvement is due mostly to changes that have taken place in the newborn's _____ .

45. Increasing maturation of the visual cortex accounts for improvements in other visual abilities, such as _____ . The ability to use both eyes together to focus on one object, which is called _____ , develops at about _____ of age. As a result of these changes, _____ and _____ perception improves dramatically.

46. Color vision _____ (is/is not) present at birth.

Describe infant visual preferences.

47. Generally speaking, newborns' hearing is _____ (more/less) sensitive than their vision. By _____ of age, infants can perceive differences between very similar speech sounds. Infants' hearing for low-frequency sounds is _____ (more/less) acute than their hearing for high-frequency sounds. Infants are less capable of _____ sounds than are older children.

48. Newborns' sense of taste is _____ (more/less) developed than their other senses. Newborns only 2 hours old display sensitivity to all the basic taste qualities except _____ .

49. Newborns' sense of smell is _____ (more/less) acute than their sense of taste.

50. By late infancy, the senses of _____ and _____ are more sensitive than at any other time in the entire life span.

51. In terms of their sense of touch, by 6 months, infants distinguish objects on the basis of their _____ , _____ , _____ , _____ , and _____ .

52. Sensory experience is an important factor in the development of _____ _____ , as well as in the development of the _____ and other brain structures that make seeing, hearing, and other sensory abilities possible.

Briefly describe the results of animal studies of sensory restriction.

53. Over the course of the first year, infants _____ (lose/gain) the ability to distinguish different _____ sounds that are not heard in their culture.

Nutrition (pp. 200–207)

54. More important than an infant's feeding schedule in fostering development is the overall _____ and _____ of the infant's nutritional intake.

State several advantages of breast milk over cow's milk for the developing infant.

55. Severe protein-calorie deficiency in early infancy causes a disease called _____ .
In toddlers, protein-calorie deficiency is more likely to cause a disease called
_____ , which involves swelling or bloating of the face, legs, and abdomen.

56. The primary cause of malnutrition in developing countries is _____
_____ .

Briefly explain why, in developing countries, bottle-fed babies have a higher risk of death and disease than do breast-fed babies.

57. In both developing and developed countries _____ is more prevalent than severe malnutrition. Worldwide, approximately _____ percent of all children in the least developed countries are undernourished.

Identify several possible causes of infant undernutrition.

58. Children who were undernourished as infants show impaired learning, especially in _____ and in _____ skills. Recovery from undernourishment is influenced by several factors, including _____
_____ .

Progress Test 1

Multiple-Choice Questions

Circle your answers to the following questions and check them with the answers on page 92. If your answer is incorrect, read the explanation for why it is incorrect and then consult the appropriate pages of the text (in parentheses following the correct answer).

1. The average North American newborn:
   a. weighs approximately 6 pounds.
   b. weighs approximately 7 pounds.
   c. is "overweight" because of the diet of the mother.
   d. weighs 10 percent less than is desirable.

2. Compared to the first year, growth during the second year:
   a. proceeds at a slower rate.
   b. continues at about the same rate.
   c. includes more insulating fat.
   d. includes more bone and muscle.

3. The major motor skill most likely to be mastered by an infant before the age of 6 months is:
   a. rolling over.
   b. sitting without support.
   c. turning the head in search of a nipple.
   d. grabbing an object with thumb and forefinger.

4. Norms suggest that the earliest walkers in the world are infants from:
   a. Western Europe.   c. Central Africa.
   b. the United States.   d. Denver.

5. The interaction between inherited and environmental factors is responsible for:
   a. variation in the age at which infants master specific motor skills.
   b. physical growth, but not the development of motor skills.
   c. the fact that babies in the United States walk earlier than do Ugandan babies.
   d. the fact that infants master motor skills more slowly today than they did fifty years ago.

6. The development of binocular vision at about 14 months results in:
   a. a dramatic improvement in depth and motion perception.
   b. the rapid development of distance vision.
   c. the refinement of the ability to discriminate colors.
   d. both a. and b.

7. Proportionally, the head of the infant is about
_____ of total body length; the head of an
adult is about _____ of total body length.
   a. one-fourth; one-third
   b. one-eighth; one-fourth
   c. one-fourth; one-eighth
   d. one-third; one-fourth

8. Research has shown that young animals prevented from moving or using their senses in a normal
way experience:
   a. no significant impairment.
   b. harmful overstimulation.
   c. deficits in behavior only.
   d. permanent impairment.

9. Compared with formula-fed infants, breast-fed
infants tend to have:
   a. greater weight gain.
   b. fewer allergies and digestive upsets.
   c. less frequent feedings during the first few
months.
   d. more social approval.

10. Marasmus and kwashiorkor are caused by:
   a. bloating.
   b. protein-calorie deficiency.
   c. living in a developing country.
   d. poor family food habits.

11. The infant's first motor skills are:
   a. fine motor skills.   c. reflexes.
   b. gross motor skills.   d. unpredictable.

12. Which of the following is not one of the basic
physiological states of infancy?
   a. quiet sleep
   b. active sleep
   c. alert wakefulness
   d. relaxed wakefulness

13. Babies are referred to as toddlers when:
   a. their newborn reflexes have disappeared.
   b. they can walk well unassisted.
   c. they begin to creep or crawl.
   d. they speak their first word.

14. Which of the following is true of motor skill
development in healthy infants?
   a. It follows the same basic sequence the world
over.
   b. It occurs at different rates from individual to
individual.
   c. It follows norms that vary from one ethnic
group to another.
   d. All of the above are true.

15. Most of the nerve cells a human brain will ever
possess are present:
   a. at conception.
   b. about 1 month following conception.
   c. at birth.
   d. at age 5 or 6.

Matching Items

Match each definition or description with its corresponding term.

Definitions or Descriptions
_____ 1. nerve cells
_____ 2. protein deficiency during the first year
_____ 3. picking up an object
_____ 4. newborn takes his or her first breath
even before the umbilical cord is cut
_____ 5. protein deficiency during toddlerhood
_____ 6. newborns suck anything that touches
their lips
_____ 7. communication networks among nerve
cells
_____ 8. declining physiological response to a
familiar stimulus
_____ 9. running or climbing
_____ 10. insulating substance for nerve cells
_____ 11. an involuntary response

Terms
a. neurons
b. dendrites
c. myelin
d. kwashiorkor
e. marasmus
f. habituation
g. gross motor skill
h. fine motor skill
i. reflex
j. sucking reflex
k. breathing reflex

Progress Test 2

Progress Test 2 should be completed during a final chapter review. Answer the following questions after you thoroughly understand the correct answers for the Chapter Review and Progress Test 1.

Multiple-Choice Questions

1. As a percentage of total body length, the head at birth comprises about _____ percent.
   a. 6
   b. 25
   c. 40
   d. 50

2. A reflex is best defined as a(n):
   a. fine motor skill.
   b. motor ability mastered at a specific age.
   c. involuntary physical response to a given stimulus.
   d. gross motor skill.

3. Habituation describes the:
   a. increased physiological arousal of the newborn to unfamiliar or interesting stimuli.
   b. decreased physiological arousal of the newborn to stimuli that are familiar or no longer interesting.
   c. preterm infant's immature brain-wave patterns.
   d. universal sequence of motor skill development in children.

4. Most babies can reach for, grasp, and hold onto an object by about the _____ month.
   a. second
   b. sixth
   c. ninth
   d. fourteenth

5. Activity level, rate of physical maturation, and body type affect the age at which an infant walks and acquires other motor skills. They are examples of:
   a. norms.
   b. environmental factors.
   c. inherited factors.
   d. the interaction of environment and heredity.

6. During the first weeks of life, babies seem to focus reasonably well on:
   a. little in their environment.
   b. objects at a distance of 4 to 30 inches.
   c. objects at a distance of 1 to 3 inches.
   d. objects several feet away.

7. At 12 months, the infant's senses of taste and smell are:
   a. relatively undeveloped.
   b. beginning a period of rapid development.
   c. more limited than those of an older child or adult.
   d. more sensitive than at any other age.

8. An EEG is best described as:
   a. a device that picks up and records electrical impulses from the nerve cells.
   b. a device that measures the physical growth of the skull and brain.
   c. a means of treating brain immaturity in preterm infants.
   d. a brain-wave pattern that is known as electrical silence.

9. An advantage of breast milk over formula is that:
   a. it is always sterile and at body temperature.
   b. it contains traces of medications ingested by the mother.
   c. it can be given without involving the father.
   d. it contains more protein and vitamin D than does formula.

10. The primary cause of malnutrition in developing countries is:
    a. formula feeding.
    b. inadequate food supply.
    c. disease.
    d. early cessation of breast-feeding.

11. The cause of sudden infant death syndrome (SIDS) is:
    a. an inborn heart defect.
    b. a neurological disorder.
    c. inadequate infant care.
    d. unknown.

12. Climbing is to using a crayon as _____ is to _____.
    a. fine motor skill; gross motor skill
    b. gross motor skill; fine motor skill
    c. reflex; fine motor skill
    d. reflex; gross motor skill

13. Some infant reflexes:
    a. are essential to life.
    b. disappear in the months after birth.
    c. provide the foundation for later motor skills.
    d. do all of the above.

14. When they are startled by a noise, newborns will fling their arms outward and then bring them together as if to hold on to something. This is an example of:
    a. a fine motor skill.
    b. a gross motor skill.
    c. the Babinski reflex.
    d. the Moro reflex.

15. A common cause of undernutrition in young children is:
   a. ignorance of the infant's nutritional needs.
   b. the absence of socioeconomic policies that reflect the importance of infant nutrition.
   c. problems in the family, such as maternal depression.
   d. all of the above.

True or False Items

Write *true* or *false* on the line in front of each statement.

_____ **1.** By age 2, boys are slightly taller than girls, but girls are slightly heavier.

_____ **2.** SIDS is the second leading cause of infant death in the United States.

_____ **3.** Reflexive hiccups, sneezes, and spit-ups are signs that the infant's reflexes are not functioning properly.

_____ **4.** Infants of all ethnic backgrounds develop the same motor skills at approximately the same age.

_____ **5.** Studies have shown that in the first few days of life, infants are unable to taste anything but sweet solutions.

_____ **6.** Vision is better developed than hearing in most newborns.

_____ **7.** Myelination and other processes of brain maturation are completed within the first few years of childhood.

_____ **8.** Certain basic sensory experiences seem necessary to ensure full brain development in the human infant.

_____ **9.** Breast-feeding is by far the most common method of infant feeding in the United States.

_____ **10.** Severe malnutrition is rare among young children in the United States.

Thinking Critically About Chapter 6

Answer these questions the day before an exam as a final check on your understanding of the chapter's terms and concepts.

1. Newborns cry, shiver, and tuck their legs close to their bodies. This set of reflexes helps them:
   a. ensure proper muscle tone.
   b. learn how to signal distress.
   c. maintain constant body temperature.
   d. communicate serious hunger pangs.

2. If a baby sucks harder on a nipple, evidences a change in heart rate, or stares longer at one image than at another when presented with a change of stimulus, the indication is that the baby:
   a. is annoyed by the change.
   b. is both hungry and angry.
   c. has become habituated to the new stimulus.
   d. perceives some differences between stimuli.

3. A classic experiment on hearing in infants (Eimas et al., 1971) showed that even 1-month-olds can detect:
   a. the father's voice more quickly than the mother's.
   b. sounds they won't be able to hear at age 2.
   c. differences between very similar sounds.
   d. the correct location of auditory stimuli about 80 percent of the time.

4. Mrs. Bartholomew opens the door to her infant's room to be sure everything is alright. She notices that her son's facial muscles are moving and his breathing is irregular and rapid. The infant is in which physiological state?
   a. quiet sleep
   b. active sleep
   c. alert wakefulness
   d. one somewhere between b. and c.

5. The brain development that permits seeing and hearing in human infants appears to be:
   a. totally dependent upon genetic programming, present at birth.
   b. totally dependent upon visual and auditory experiences in the first few months.
   c. "fine-tuned" by visual and auditory experiences in the first few months.
   d. independent of both genetic and environmental influences.

6. Disputing a classmate's contention that the high rate of SIDS among African-Americans implicates genetic causes in the syndrome, Renaldo notes that:
   a. the most recent statistics show that ethnic differences in SIDS rates among the major ethnic groups in the United States are decreasing.
   b. a higher proportion of low-birthweight infants and teenage mothers may explain this higher rate.
   c. African-American infants are almost always put to sleep on their stomachs.
   d. all of the above are true.

7. Michael has 20/400 vision and is able to discriminate subtle sound differences, as well as sweet, sour, and bitter tastes. Michael most likely:

a. is a preterm infant.
b. has brain damage in the visual processing areas of the cortex.
c. is a newborn.
d. is slow-to-mature.

8. A baby turns her head and starts to suck when her receiving blanket is brushed against her cheek. The baby is displaying the:
a. sucking reflex.
b. rooting reflex.
c. Babinski reflex.
d. Moro reflex.

9. Toddlers whose parents give them a bottle of milk before every nap and with every meal:
a. may be at increased risk of undernutrition, because the milk reduces the child's appetite for other foods.
b. are ensured of receiving a sufficient amount of iron in their diets.
c. are more likely to develop lactose intolerance.
d. are likely to be overweight throughout life.

10. Sensation is to perception as _____ is to _____.
a. hearing; seeing
b. detecting a stimulus; making sense of a stimulus
c. making sense of a stimulus; detecting a stimulus
d. tasting; smelling

11. Adults often speak to infants in a high-pitched voice. This is because they discover from experience that:
a. low-pitched sounds are more frightening to infants.
b. infants are more sensitive to high-pitched sounds.
c. high-pitched sounds are more soothing to infants.
d. all of the above are true.

12. Kittens who are blindfolded for the first several weeks of life:
a. do not develop the visual pathways in their brains to allow normal vision.
b. recover fully if visual stimulation is normal thereafter.
c. develop only binocular vision.
d. can see clearly, but lack sensitivity to color.

13. (text and A Closer Look) Your friend Isadore is a stockbroker in Chicago. She is also the mother of a 3-month-old. Isadora is concerned that her busy schedule prevents her from breast-feeding her infant. What should you tell Isadora?
a. "Spend as much time as possible cuddling your daughter to simulate the closeness you would have had with breast-feeding."
b. "Obtain a formula that simulates breast milk, because it's vital to your child's development."
c. "Don't worry. Children in developed countries who have not been breast-fed develop as well as those who have."
d. "It's never too late to breast-feed, and you should do so, because it's important to your child's development."

14. Three-week-old Nathan should have the *least* difficulty focusing on the sight of:
a. stuffed animals on a bookshelf across the room from his crib.
b. his mother's face as she holds him in her arms.
c. the checkerboard pattern in the wallpaper covering the ceiling of his room.
d. the family dog as it dashes into the nursery.

15. Geneva has been undernourished throughout childhood. It is likely that she will be:
a. smaller and shorter than her genetic potential would dictate.
b. slow in intellectual development.
c. less resistant to disease.
d. all of the above.

Key Terms

Using your own words, write a brief definition or explanation of each of the following terms on a separate piece of paper.

1. sudden infant death syndrome (SIDS)
2. neurons
3. dendrites
4. myelin
5. physiological states
6. electroencephalogram (EEG)
7. reflexes
8. breathing reflex
9. sucking reflex
10. rooting reflex
11. gross motor skills
12. toddler
13. fine motor skills

14. norms
15. sensation
16. perception
17. habituation
18. binocular vision
19. marasmus
20. kwashiorkor

ANSWERS
CHAPTER REVIEW

1. prenatal; size; body proportion
2. 20 inches (51 centimeters); 7 pounds (3.2 kilograms)
3. lose
4. 22 pounds (10 kilograms); 30 inches (75 centimeters)
5. one-fourth; one-fifth; one-eighth
6. one-fourth; one-half
7. feet
8. 1; immunization

Other reasons for the increased survival of young children include improved sanitation procedures that reduce the spread of disease; technological breakthroughs for high-risk infants; and improved health education for parents in developing nations.

9. prevention; remedy; difficult
10. month; heart defects or other inborn abnormalities, and very low birthweight
11. sudden infant death syndrome; second

SIDS risk factors include a young, poverty-level mother who smokes; a male child, 2-4 months of age, born in winter, who sleeps on his stomach.

12. backs
13. African; Asian; European; low birthweight; teenage mothers; infant-care
14. 25; 75; 20
15. neurons; are
16. cortex; perception; thinking
17. dendrites; myelin; adolescence
18. frontal; self-control; self-regulation; physiological; sleep-wake; reflexes
19. states

Quiet sleep: breathing is regular and slow and muscles are relaxed.

Active sleep: facial muscles move and breathing is less regular and more rapid.

Alert wakefulness: eyes are bright and breathing is relatively regular and rapid.

Active crying: the characteristics are obvious.

20. electroencephalogram (EEG)
21. does not; timing; one-third; 80; more; lesser
22. 3; child-rearing; culture
23. more
24. reflex
25. breathing reflex; hiccups, sneezes, spit-ups
26. body temperature
27. feeding; sucking; rooting
28. Babinski
29. stepping
30. swimming
31. Palmar grasping
32. Moro
33. gross motor; fine motor
34. 8; 10

On average, a child can walk while holding a hand at 9 months, can stand alone momentarily at 10 months, and can walk well unassisted at 12 months.

35. toddler
36. 6 months

At first, infants use their whole hand, especially the palm and the fourth and fifth fingers to grasp. Then they use the middle fingers and the center of the palm, or the index finger and the side of the palm. Finally, they use thumb and forefinger together.

37. sequence; age
38. norms; many
39. ethnic

Of primary importance in variations in the acquisition of motor skills are inherited factors, such as activity level, rate of physical maturation, and body type. Particular patterns of infant care may also be influential.

40. is; do
41. inherited; environmental
42. sensation; perception; are

Although their sensory abilities are selective, newborns see, hear, smell, taste, and respond to pressure, motion, temperature, and pain.

43. habituation; discriminate

44. 4; 30; 400; 1 year; brain

45. scanning; binocular vision; 14 weeks; depth; motion

46. is

Infants prefer to look at novel images, complex patterns, stimuli with contrast and contour density, and visual events that represent incongruity or discrepancy from the usual.

47. more; 1 month; less; locating

48. less; salty

49. more

50. taste; smell

51. temperature; size; hardness; texture; weight

52. perceptual abilities; dendrites

Animals that were prevented from using their senses or moving their bodies in infancy became permanently handicapped. For example, kittens blindfolded for the first several weeks did not develop brain pathways to allow normal vision.

53. lose; speech

54. quality; quantity

Breast milk is always sterile and at body temperature; it is more digestible and contains more iron, vitamin C, and vitamin A; it contains antibodies that provide the infant some protection against disease; and it contains hormones that help regulate growth, encourage attachment, reduce pain, and regulate the brain, liver, intestines, and pancreas.

55. marasmus; kwashiorkor

56. early cessation of breast-feeding

For many people in the developing world, the hygienic conditions for the proper use of infant formula do not exist. The water and bottles are unclean and the formula is often diluted to make it last longer.

57. undernutrition; 56

Undernutrition is caused by the interaction of many factors, with insufficient food as the immediate cause, and problems in the family and/or society as underlying causes. For example, depressed mothers tend to feed their infants erratically, and emotional stresses in a child's life are sometimes reflected in less healthy eating habits.

58. concentration; language; the duration of the undernutrition and the quality of intellectual stimulation experienced after infancy

PROGRESS TEST 1

Multiple-Choice Questions

1. **b.** is the answer. (p. 176)

2. **a.** is the answer. (p. 176)

3. **a.** is the answer. (p. 192)

   b. The age norm for this skill is 7.8 months.

   c. This is a reflex, rather than an acquired motor skill.

   d. This skill is acquired between 9 and 14 months.

4. **c.** is the answer. (p. 193)

5. **a.** is the answer. (p. 193)

   b. Inherited and environmental factors are important for both physical growth *and* the development of motor skills.

   c. On average, Ugandan babies walk earlier than do babies in the United States.

   d. In fact, just the opposite is true.

6. **a.** is the answer. (p. 196)

7. **c.** is the answer. (p. 176)

8. **d.** is the answer. (p. 199)

   a. & c. Research has shown that deprivation of normal sensory experiences prevents the development of normal neural pathways that transmit sensory information.

   b. On the contrary, these studies demonstrate harmful sensory *restriction*.

9. **b.** is the answer. This is because breast milk is more digestible than cow's milk or formula. (p. 201)

   a., c., & d. Breast- and bottle-fed babies do not differ in these attributes.

10. **b.** is the answer. (p. 204)

11. **c.** is the answer. (p. 188)

    a. & b. These motor skills do not emerge until somewhat later; reflexes are present at birth.

    d. On the contrary, reflexes are quite predictable; this is the basis for the Brazelton Neonatal Behavioral Assessment Scale.

12. **d.** is the answer. (p. 185)

13. **b.** is the answer. (p. 191)

14. **d.** is the answer. (pp. 192–193)

15. **c.** is the answer. (p. 184)

Matching Items

1. a (p. 184)
2. e (p. 204)
3. h (p. 191)
4. k (p. 188)
5. d (p. 204)
6. j (p. 188)
7. b (p. 184)
8. f (pp. 194–195)
9. g (p. 189)
10. c (p. 184)
11. i (p. 188)

PROGRESS TEST 2

Multiple-Choice Questions

1. **b.** is the answer. (p. 176)

2. **c.** is the answer. (p. 188)

   a., b., & d. Each of these refers to voluntary responses that are acquired only after a certain amount of practice; reflexes are involuntary responses that are present at birth and require no practice.

3. **b.** is the answer. (p. 195)

4. **b.** is the answer. (p. 191)

5. **c.** is the answer. (p. 193)

   a. Norms are average ages at which certain motor skills are acquired.

6. **b.** is the answer. (p. 195)

   a. Although focusing ability seems to be limited to a certain range, babies do focus on many objects in this range.

   c. This is not within the range at which babies *can* focus.

   d. Babies have very poor distance vision.

7. **d.** is the answer. (p. 198)

8. **a.** is the answer. (p. 185)

9. **a.** is the answer. (p. 200)

   b. If anything, this is a potential *disadvantage* of breast milk over formula.

   c. So can formula.

   d. Breast milk contains more iron, vitamin C, and vitamin A than cow's milk; it does not contain more protein and vitamin D, however.

10. **d.** is the answer. (p. 204)

11. **d.** is the answer. (p. 181)

12. **b.** is the answer. (pp. 189, 191)

    c. & d. Reflexes are involuntary responses; climbing and using a crayon are both voluntary responses.

13. **d.** is the answer. (pp. 188–189)

14. **d.** is the answer. (p. 189)

    a. & b. Fine and gross motor skills are voluntary responses; the response described here is clearly reflexive.

    c. The Babinski reflex is the response that infants make when their feet are stroked.

15. **d.** is the answer. (pp. 205–206)

True or False Items

1. F   Boys are both slightly heavier and taller than girls at 2 years. (p. 176)

2. T   (p. 181)

3. F   Hiccups, sneezes, and spit-ups are common during the first few days, and they are entirely normal reflexes. (p. 188)

4. F   Although all healthy infants develop the same motor skills in the same sequence, the age at which these skills are acquired can vary greatly from infant to infant, group to group, and from place to place. (pp. 192–193)

5. F   Researchers have compiled evidence that even 2-hour-old infants react to sweet, sour, and bitter solutions. (p. 198)

6. F   Vision is relatively poorly developed at birth, whereas hearing is well developed. (pp. 195–197)

7. F   Myelination is not complete until adolescence. (p. 184)

8. T (p. 199)

9. F   Although there is a trend toward increased breast-feeding, bottle- or formula-feeding is more common in this country. (p. 201)

10. T (p. 204)

THINKING CRITICALLY ABOUT CHAPTER 6

1. **c.** is the answer. (p. 188)

2. **d.** is the answer. (p. 195)

   a. & b. These changes in behavior indicate that the newborn has perceived an unfamiliar stimulus, not that he or she is hungry, annoyed, or angry.

   c. Habituation refers to a *decrease* in physiological responsiveness to a familiar stimulus.

3. **c.** is the answer. (p. 197)

   a. & b. There is no evidence that infants can detect one parent's voice more easily than the other's, or that sounds perceived at 1 month can not be discriminated later.

   d. This experiment was not concerned with sound localization.

4. **b.** is the answer. (p. 185)

   a. This state is characterized by slow and regular breathing and relaxed muscles.

   c. This state is characterized by bright eyes and regular and rapid breathing.

5. **c.** is the answer. The evidence for this comes from studies in which animals were prevented from using their senses in infancy; such animals became permanently handicapped. (pp. 199–200)

   a. If this were true, research would show that restriction had no effect on sensory abilities.

   b. If this were true, sensory restriction would cause much more serious impairment than it does.

d. Sensory restriction research demonstrates that both genetic and environmental factors are important in the development of sensory abilities.

6. **b.** is the answer. (pp. 181–183)

7. **c.** is the answer. (pp. 195, 197, 198)

8. **b.** is the answer. (p. 188)

a. This is the reflexive sucking of newborns in response to anything that touches their *lips.*

c. This is the response that infants make when their feet are stroked.

d. In this response to startling noises, newborns fling their arms outward and then bring them together on their chests as if to hold on to something.

9. **a.** is the answer. (p. 206)

10. **b.** is the answer. (p. 194)

a. & d. Sensation and perception operate in all of these sensory modalities.

11. **b.** is the answer. (p. 198)

a. & c. The text does not suggest that whether a sound is soothing or frightening is determined by its pitch.

12. **a.** is the answer. (p. 199)

13. **c.** is the answer. (pp. 201–203)

14. **b.** is the answer. This is true because, at birth, focusing is best for objects between 4 and 30 inches away. (p. 195)

a., c., & d. Newborns have very poor distance vision; each of these situations involves a distance greater than the optimal focus range.

15. **d.** is the answer. (pp. 206–207)

KEY TERMS

1. The second leading cause of infant death in the United States, **sudden infant death syndrome (SIDS)**, is diagnosed when autopsy suggests that the infant simply stopped breathing, with other possible causes ruled out. (pp. 180–181)

2. **Neurons**, or nerve cells, are the basic building blocks of the nervous system. (p. 184)

3. **Dendrites** are the thin, branchlike extensions of neurons that comprise the communication networks among the billions of neurons in the nervous system. (p. 184)

4. **Myelin** is the fatty, insulating substance coating neurons that helps transmit neural impulses faster and more efficiently. (p. 184)

5. The **physiological states** of the infant include quiet sleep, active sleep, alert wakefulness, and active crying. (p. 185)

6. The **electroencephalogram (EEG)** is a device that picks up the electrical impulses or brain waves from neurons. (p. 185)

7. **Reflexes** are involuntary responses to specific stimuli. (p. 188)

8. The **breathing reflex** is an involuntary response that ensures that the infant has an adequate supply of oxygen. (p. 188)

9. The **sucking reflex** is the involuntary tendency of newborns to suck anything that touches their lips. This reflex fosters feeding. (p. 188)

10. The **rooting reflex**, which helps babies find a nipple, causes them to turn their heads and start to suck when something brushes against their cheek. (p. 188)

11. **Gross motor skills** are abilities that demand large body movements, such as climbing, jumping, or running. (p. 189)

12. When babies can walk well without assistance (usually at about 12 months), they are given the name **toddler** because of the characteristic way they move their bodies from side to side. (p. 191)

13. **Fine motor skills** are abilities that require precise, small movements, such as picking up a coin. (p. 191)

14. **Norms** are age averages for the acquisition of a particular behavior (p. 192)

15. **Sensation** is the process by which a sensory system detects a particular stimulus. (p. 194)

16. **Perception** is the process by which the brain tries to make sense of a stimulus such that the individual becomes aware of it. (p. 194)

17. **Habituation** refers to the decline in physiological responsiveness that occurs when a stimulus becomes familiar. Habituation to stimuli is used by researchers to assess infants' ability to perceive by testing their ability to discriminate between very similar stimuli. (pp. 194–195)

18. **Binocular vision** is the ability to use both eyes together to focus on one object. (p. 196)

Memory aid: Bi- indicates "two"; *ocular* means something pertaining to the eye. **Binocular vision** refers to vision using two eyes.

19. **Marasmus** is a disease caused by severe protein-calorie deficiency during the first year of life. Growth stops, body tissues waste away, and the infant dies. (p. 204)

20. **Kwashiorkor** is a disease caused by protein-calorie deficiency during toddlerhood. The child's face, legs, and abdomen swell with water, sometimes making the child appear well fed. Other body parts are degraded, including the hair, which becomes thin, brittle, and colorless. (p. 204)

The First Two Years: Cognitive Development

Chapter Overview

Chapter 7 explores the ways in which the infant comes to learn about, think about, and adapt to his or her surroundings. It focuses on the various ways in which infant intelligence is revealed: through perception, cognition, memory, sensorimotor intelligence, and language development. The chapter begins with a description of infant perception and the influential theory of Eleanor and James Gibson. Central to this theory is the idea that infants gain cognitive understanding of their world through the affordances of objects, that is, the activities they can do with them.

The second section discusses infant cognition, memory, and intelligence, as revealed by research using the habituation procedure. Researchers have found that the speed with which infants recognize familiarity and seek something novel is related to later cognitive skill.

The third section describes Jean Piaget's theory of sensorimotor intelligence, which maintains that infants think exclusively with their senses and motor skills. Piaget's six stages of sensorimotor intelligence are examined.

Finally, the chapter turns to the most remarkable cognitive achievement of the first two years, the acquisition of language. Beginning with a description of the infant's first attempts at language, the chapter follows the sequence of events that lead to the child's ability to utter two-word sentences. The chapter concludes with an examination of language learning as teamwork involving babies and adults, who, in a sense, teach each other the unique human process of verbal communication.

NOTE: Answer guidelines for all Chapter 7 questions begin on page 105.

Guided Study

The text chapter should be studied one section at a time. Before you read, preview each section by skim-ming it, noting headings and boldface items. Then read the appropriate section objectives from the following outline. Keep these objectives in mind and, as you read the chapter section, search for the information that will enable you to meet each objective. Once you have finished a section, write out answers for its objectives.

Perception (pp. 212–219)

1. Explain the Gibsons' contextual view of perception and discuss the idea of affordances, giving examples of affordances perceived by infants.

2. Explain how the infant's understanding of perceptual constancy, along with the infant's focus on movement and change, enhance sensory and perceptual skills.

3. Discuss the infant's ability to integrate perceptual information from different sensory systems, giving examples of intermodal and cross-modal perception.

Cognition, Memory, and Intelligence (pp. 219–231)

4. Explain what habituation research has revealed about the infant's ability to categorize and his or her understanding of number.

5. Explain what object permanence is, how it is tested in infancy, and what these tests reveal.

6. (text and A Closer Look) Discuss recent research findings on infant long-term memory and infants' understanding of causal relationships.

Piaget's Theory of Sensorimotor Intelligence (pp. 231–237)

7. Identify and describe the first three of Piaget's stages of sensorimotor intelligence.

8. Identify and describe stages 4 through 6 of Piaget's theory of sensorimotor intelligence.

Language Development (pp. 237–246)

9. Describe language development during infancy and identify its major landmarks.

10. Contrast the theories of Skinner and Chomsky regarding early language development and explain current views on language learning.

11. Explain the importance of baby talk and identify its main features.

Chapter Review

When you have finished reading the chapter, work through the material that follows to review it. Complete the sentences and answer the questions. As you proceed, evaluate your performance for each section by consulting the answers on page 105. Do not continue with the next section until you understand each answer. If you need to, review or reread the appropriate section in the textbook before continuing.

Perception (pp. 212–219)

1. The first major theorist to realize that infants are active learners was _____ .

2. Much of the current research in perception and cognition has been inspired by the work of the Gibsons, who stress that perception is a(n) _____ (active/passive/automatic) cognitive phenomenon.

3. According to the Gibsons, any object in the envi-

ronment offers diverse opportunities for interaction; this property of objects is called

_____ .

4. Which of these an individual perceives in an object depends on the individual's

_____ _____

and _____ _____

on his or her _____

_____ , and on his or her

_____ _____

of what the object might afford.

5. Infants perceive the affordance of

_____ long before their manual dexterity has matured.

List other affordances perceived by infants from a very early age.

6. Central to the infant's ability to perceive affordances is gaining an understanding of the

_____ of objects. This begins to occur by the age of _____ ,

when infants are able to distinguish the

_____ of separate objects, especially objects that are _____

_____ .

7. Infants also begin to develop an understanding of

_____ _____ ,

which is the awareness that the

_____ and _____

of objects remain the same despite changes in their appearance.

8. Perception that is primed to focus on movement and change is called _____

_____ .

Give several examples of how infants use movement cues in perceiving objects.

9. The ability to perceive where objects exist relative to each other in a three-dimensional world defines _____ _____ .

10. Once babies have mastered _____ ,
it becomes clear that they not only perceive vertical depth but also its _____ .

11. The ability to associate information from one sensory modality with information from another is called _____

_____ . This ability

_____ (is/is not) demonstrated by newborns.

12. The ability to use information from one sensory modality to imagine something in another is called _____-_____

_____ . Infants as young as

_____ have demonstrated this ability, at least in rudimentary form.

Cognition, Memory, and Intelligence (pp. 219–231)

13. From an early age infants coordinate and organize their perceptions into _____ .
Researchers use the phenomenon of infant

_____ to study these abilities.

14. Young infants also seem to form categories on the basis of the _____ between objects.

15. Infants younger than 8 months can categorize objects according to their _____ ,

_____ , and _____ .
By the end of the first year, they can categorize

_____ , _____ ,

and _____ . By age

_____ , infants begin to apply

_____ cues to distinguish male and female.

16. Preliminary research suggests that infants as young as _____ months possess basic number awareness and also some capacity to _____ .

17. A major cognitive accomplishment of infancy is the ability to understand that objects exist independently of _____

_____ . This awareness is called _____ _____ .

18. Using the habituation procedure, Renée Baillargeon has demonstrated that infants as young as _____ months have an awareness of object permanence that is concealed by the traditional Piagetian hidden-object tests.

19. Generally speaking, infants' long-term memory is quite _____ (good/poor).

20. When memory tasks are motivating and made more suitable to their abilities, infants as young as _____ months "remembered" events from two weeks earlier, if they were reminded prior to retesting.

21. Another important cognitive accomplishment of infancy is the ability to recognize and associate _____ relations. Research using the _____ _____ procedure reveals that infants as young as _____ months have a rudimentary understanding of such relations.

22. Traditional tests of infant intelligence _____ (are/are not) very accurate in predicting adult IQ. Recent research suggests that _____ speed may be a more valid measure of infant intelligence.

23. Infants who are _____ (faster/ slower) in habituating to familiar stimuli and who show a preference for _____ _____ tend to score higher on tests of childhood IQ.

Piaget's Theory of Sensorimotor Intelligence (pp. 231–237)

24. When infants begin to explore the environment through sensory and motor skills, they are displaying what Piaget called _____ intelligence. In number, Piaget described _____ stages of development of this type of intelligence.

25. According to Piaget, a _____ is a general way of thinking about, and interacting with, the environment. One of the most powerful inborn abilities of this type is the _____ reflex.

26. The first stage of sensorimotor intelligence lasts from birth to _____ of age.

Describe a typical stage-one behavior.

27. The second stage of sensorimotor intelligence, which occurs between _____ and _____ months of age, begins when infants _____ their reflexes to the environment. Piaget called these actions _____ _____ .

28. Situations in which a baby's action triggers a reaction that causes the baby to repeat the action are called _____ _____ . When the baby's own body is the source of the reaction, it is called a _____ _____ _____ .

Describe a typical stage-two behavior.

29. Piaget referred to stage three, which occurs between _____ and _____ months of age, as _____ . During this stage, infants repeat a specific action that has just elicited a pleasing response. Piaget called this a _____ _____ .

Describe a typical stage-three behavior.

30. In stage four, which lasts from _____ to _____ months of age, infants can better _____ events. At this stage babies also engage in purposeful actions, or _____ - _____ behavior.

31. Piaget referred to stage five, which lasts from _____ to _____ months, as the stage of _____ _____ . Typical of this stage are _____

    _____ _____ , in which babies experiment with variations of a particular action.

Explain what Piaget meant when he described the stage-five infant as a "little scientist."

32. Stage six, which lasts from _____ to _____ months, is the stage of achieving new means through _____

    _____ .

33. One sign that children have reached stage six is their ability to enjoy a broader range of _____ activities.

34. Piaget's analysis of infant cognition underscores the fact that infants are _____ (active/passive) learners.

Language Development (pp. 237–246)

35. Newborns show a preference for hearing _____ over other sounds. They also quickly learn to recognize that certain speech sounds go with specific _____

    _____ .

36. Children the world over follow the same _____ of accomplishments in language development, although their _____ may vary considerably.

37. By 5 months of age, most babies' verbal repertoire consists of _____

    _____ .

38. At _____ months of age, babies begin to repeat certain syllables, a phenomenon referred to as _____ . At the same time, _____ become part of the baby's efforts to communicate.

39. Deaf babies tend to show superiority over hearing babies in communicating with _____ and _____

    _____ .

40. Deaf babies begin oral babbling _____ (earlier/later) than hearing babies do. Deaf babies may also babble _____ , with this behavior emerging _____ (earlier than/at the same time as/later than) hearing infants begin oral babbling. The similar timing of babbling among hearing and deaf babies suggests that _____ maturation, more than maturation of the _____

    _____ , underlies language development.

41. At every stage of development, children understand _____ (more/less) than they express.

42. The average baby speaks one or two words at about _____ of age. At this time vocabulary increases at a rate of _____ words a month. When vocabulary reaches approximately fifty words, it suddenly begins to build rapidly, at a rate of _____ or more words a month.

43. One characteristic of infant speech is _____ , or overgeneralization, in which the infant applies a known word to a variety of objects and contexts. Initially, however, infants tend toward _____ of word meanings. Another characteristic is the use of the _____ , in which a single word expresses a complete thought.

44. Vocabulary size _____ (is/is not) the best measure of early language learning. The crux of early language is _____

    _____ .

45. Children begin to produce their first two-word sentences at about _____ months.

46. Reinforcement and other conditioning processes account for language development, according to the learning theory of _____ .

47. The theorist who stressed the infant's innate language abilities is _____ , who maintained that all children are born with a LAD, or _____ _____ _____ .

Summarize the conclusions of recent research regarding the theories of Skinner and Chomsky.

48. Adults talk to infants using a special form of language called _____ _____ , which is nicknamed _____ .

Briefly describe the type of speech adults use with infants.

49. The conversational aspect of parent-child communication tends to become stronger between _____ and _____ months of age.

Progress Test 1

Multiple-Choice Questions

Circle your answers to the following questions and check them with the answers on page 105. If your answer is incorrect, read the explanation for why it is incorrect and then consult the appropriate pages of the text (in parentheses following the correct answer).

1. In general terms, the Gibsons' concept of affordances emphasizes the idea that the individual perceives an object in terms of its:
   a. economic importance.
   b. physical qualities.
   c. function or use to the individual.
   d. role in the larger culture or environment.

2. According to Piaget, when a baby repeats an action that has just triggered a pleasing response from his or her caregiver, a _____ has occurred.
   a. primary circular reaction
   b. secondary circular reaction
   c. tertiary circular reaction
   d. launching event

3. Sensorimotor intelligence begins with a baby's first:
   a. attempt to crawl.
   b. reflex actions.
   c. auditory perception.
   d. adaptation of a reflex.

4. Between 1 and 4 months (sensorimotor stage two), babies begin to:
   a. grasp object permanence.
   b. look for toys that fall out of the crib.
   c. engage in goal-directed behavior.
   d. adapt their reflexes to the environment.

5. In Piaget's terms, a scheme is:
   a. an opportunity for interaction with the environment.
   b. a general way of thinking about, and interacting with, the environment.
   c. a mental combination.
   d. goal-directed behavior.

6. By the end of the first year, infants usually learn how to:
   a. accomplish simple goals.
   b. manipulate various symbols.
   c. solve complex problems.
   d. pretend.

7. When an infant begins to understand that objects exist even when they are out of sight, she or he has begun to understand the concept of object:
   a. displacement.   c. permanence.
   b. importance.   d. location.

8. Today, most cognitive psychologists view language acquisition as:
   a. primarily the result of imitation of adult speech.
   b. determined primarily by biological maturation.
   c. a behavior that is entirely determined by learning.
   d. determined by both biological maturation and learning.

9. Despite cultural differences, children all over the world attain very similar language skills:
   a. according to ethnically specific timetables.

b. at about the same age in the same sequence.

c. according to culturally specific timetables.

d. according to timetables that vary from child to child.

10. The average baby speaks one or two words at about:

   a. 6 months.   c. 12 months.
   b. 9 months.   d. 24 months.

11. A single word used by toddlers to express a complete thought is:

   a. a holophrase.   c. an overextension.
   b. baby talk.   d. an underextension.

12. Compared to children's *rate* of speech development, their *comprehension* of language develops:

   a. more slowly.
   b. at about the same pace.

c. more rapidly.

d. more rapidly in certain cultures than it does in other cultures.

13. A distinctive form of language, with a particular pitch, structure, etc., that adults use in talking to infants is called:

   a. a holophrase.   c. baby talk.
   b. the LAD.   d. conversation.

14. At 8 months, infants can categorize objects on the basis of

   a. angularity.   c. density.
   b. shape.   d. all of the above.

15. Recent studies suggest that infants possess a basic number awareness by:

   a. 5 months.   c. 10 months.
   b. 8 months.   d. 12 months.

Matching Items

Match each definition or description with its corresponding term.

Definitions or Descriptions

_____ 1. overgeneralization of a word to inappropriate objects, etc.

_____ 2. repetitive utterance of certain syllables

_____ 3. perception that focuses on movement and change

_____ 4. thinking through the senses and motor skills

_____ 5. the realization that something that is out of sight continues to exist

_____ 6. trying out actions mentally

_____ 7. opportunities for interaction that an object offers

_____ 8. associating information from one sensory modality with information from another

_____ 9. a single word used to express a complete thought

_____ 10. using information from one sensory modality to imagine something in another

Terms

a. mental combinations
b. affordances
c. object permanence
d. intermodal perception
e. cross-modal perception
f. dynamic perception
g. sensorimotor intelligence
h. babbling
i. holophrase
j. overextension

Progress Test 2

Progress Test 2 should be completed during a final chapter review. Answer the following questions after you thoroughly understand the correct answers for the Chapter Review and Progress Test 1.

Multiple-Choice Questions

1. Stage five (12 to 18 months) of sensorimotor intelligence is best described as:

a. first acquired adaptations.

b. new means through active experimentation.

c. procedures for making interesting sights last.

d. new means through symbolization.

2. Which of the following is *not* evidence of dynamic perception during infancy?

   a. Babies prefer to look at things in motion.

b. Babies form simple expectations of the path that a moving object will follow.

c. Babies use movement cues to discern the boundaries of objects.

d. Babies quickly grasp that even though objects look different when seen from different viewpoints, they are the same objects.

3. Recent research suggests that the concept of object permanence:
   a. fades after a few months.
   b. is a skill some children never acquire.
   c. may occur earlier and more gradually than Piaget recognized.
   d. involves pretending as well as mental combinations.

4. According to the Gibsons, graspability is:
   a. an opportunity perceived by a baby.
   b. a quality that resides in toys and other objects.
   c. an ability that emerges at about 6 months.
   d. evidence of manual dexterity in the infant.

5. Both intermodal and cross-modal perception necessarily involve:
   a. matching of sight and sound.
   b. hand-eye coordination.
   c. mental representation of a hidden object.
   d. the ability to integrate perceptual information.

6. The best and most accurate measure of early language learning is the:
   a. size of a child's vocabulary.
   b. number of grammatical errors made by a child.
   c. nature of the grammatical errors made by the child.
   d. child's ability and willingness to communicate.

7. For Noam Chomsky, the "language acquisition device" refers to:
   a. the human predisposition to acquire language.
   b. the portion of the human brain that processes speech.
   c. the vocabulary of the language the child is exposed to.
   d. all of the above.

8. The first stage of sensorimotor intelligence lasts until:
   a. infants can anticipate events that will fulfill their needs.
   b. infants begin to adapt their reflexes to the environment.

c. object permanence has been achieved.

d. infants are capable of thinking about past and future events.

9. Experiments demonstrate that intermodal and cross-modal perceptual abilities begin to develop in infants:
   a. less than 6 months old.
   b. between 6 and 12 months old.
   c. between 12 and 18 months old.
   d. more than 18 months old.

10. Whether or not an infant perceives certain characteristics of objects, such as "suckability" or "graspability," seems to depend on:
    a. his or her prior experiences.
    b. his or her needs.
    c. his or her cognitive awareness.
    d. all of the above.

11. Infants faster in habituating to familiar stimuli:
    a. score higher on tests of childhood IQ.
    b. generally make fewer grammatical errors as they acquire language.
    c. are more prone to develop childhood learning disabilities.
    d. also have a larger long-term memory capacity.

12. The purposeful actions that begin to develop in sensorimotor stage four ("new adaptation and anticipation") are called:
    a. reflexes.
    b. affordances.
    c. goal-directed behaviors.
    d. mental combinations.

13. What is the correct sequence of stages of language development?
    a. crying, babbling, cooing, first word
    b. crying, cooing, babbling, first word
    c. crying, babbling, first word, cooing
    d. crying, cooing, first word, babbling

14. Compared to hearing babies, deaf babies:
    a. are less likely to babble.
    b. are more likely to babble.
    c. begin to babble vocally at about the same age.
    d. begin to babble manually at about the same age as hearing babies begin to babble vocally.

15. According to Skinner, children acquire language:
    a. as a result of an inborn ability to use the basic structure of language.
    b. through reinforcement and conditioning.
    c. mostly because of biological maturation.
    d. in a fixed sequence of predictable stages.

Matching Items

Match each definition or description with its corresponding term.

Definitions or Descriptions

_____ 1. the awareness that the size and shape of an object remains the same despite changes in its appearance

_____ 2. perceptual ability facilitated by self-locomotion

_____ 3. research procedure for investigating cause-effect relations

_____ 4. situation in which a baby's actions trigger a self-reaction

_____ 5. situation in which a baby repeats an action that has elicited a pleasing response from some person or thing

_____ 6. situation in which a baby repeats an action, varying its exact form each time

_____ 7. a word is used more narrowly than its true meaning allows

_____ 8. a hypothetical device that facilitates language development

_____ 9. also called "Motherese"

_____ 10. a general way of thinking about, and interacting with, the environment

Terms

a. scheme
b. perceptual constancy
c. secondary circular reactions
d. baby talk
e. LAD
f. tertiary circular reactions
g. launching event
h. underextension
i. primary circular reaction
j. depth perception

Thinking Critically About Chapter 7

Answer these questions the day before an exam as a final check on your understanding of the chapter's terms and concepts.

1. A 9-month-old repeatedly reaches for his sister's doll, even though he has been told "no" many times. This is an example of:
   a. a tertiary circular reaction.
   b. an overextension.
   c. delayed imitation.
   d. goal-directed behavior.

2. An infant who comes to expect the sound of music to emanate from a revolving turntable is exhibiting:
   a. cross-modal perception.
   b. goal-directed behavior.
   c. intermodal perception.
   d. object permanence.

3. Experiments reveal that infants can "recognize" by sight an object that they have previously touched but not seen. This is an example of:
   a. delayed imitation.
   b. two related affordances.
   c. categorization.
   d. cross-modal perception.

4. According to Skinner's theory, an infant who learns to delight his father by saying "da-da" is probably benefiting from:
   a. social reinforcers, such as smiles and hugs.
   b. modeling.
   c. learning by imitation.
   d. an innate ability to use language.

5. The child's tendency to call every animal "doggie" is an example of:
   a. using a holophrase.
   b. babbling.
   c. Motherese.
   d. overextension.

6. About six months after speaking his or her first words, the typical child will:
   a. have a vocabulary of between 250 and 350 words.
   b. begin to speak in holophrases.
   c. put words together to form rudimentary sentences.
   d. do all of the above.

7. A 20-month-old girl who is able to try out various actions mentally without having to actually perform them is learning to solve simple problems by using:
   a. dynamic perception.
   b. schemes.
   c. intermodal perception.
   d. mental combinations.

8. A baby who repeats an action he or she has seen trigger a reaction in someone else is demonstrating an ability that Piaget called:
   a. cross-modal perception.
   b. circular reaction.
   c. intermodal perception.
   d. mental combinations.

9. (Research Report) In one experiment (reported by Bower, 1989), infants were found to look more intently at films that showed someone of their own sex, no matter how that person was dressed, or what kind of toy he or she played with. Boys who watched the films seemed to be puzzled by the sight of:
   a. girls who played with guns and drums.
   b. boys who played with dolls.
   c. boys who were dressed in frilly, feminine clothes.
   d. girls who were dressed in boyish pants.

10. (Research Report) Studies show that 6-month-old infants look longer at a photo of a male face when they are listening to a tape of a male voice, and longer at a female face when listening to a female voice. This is an example of:
    a. delayed imitation.
    b. a gender expectancy.
    c. cross-modal perception.
    d. intermodal perception.

11. A baby who realizes that a rubber duck that has fallen out of the tub must be somewhere on the floor has achieved:
    a. object permanence.
    b. intermodal perception.
    c. mental combinations.
    d. cross-modal perception.

12. As soon as her babysitter arrives, 21-month-old Christine holds on to her mother's legs and, in a questioning manner, says "bye-bye." Because Christine clearly is "asking" her mother not to leave, her utterance can be classified as:
    a. babbling.   c. a holophrase.
    b. an overextension. d. telegraphic speech.

13. The 6-month-old infant's continual repetition of sound combinations such as "ba-ba-ba" is called:
    a. cooing.   c. a holophrase.
    b. babbling.   d. an overextension.

14. Which of the following is an example of a linguistic overextension that a 2-year-old might make?
    a. saying "bye-bye" to indicate that he or she wants to go out
    b. pointing to a cat and saying "doggie"
    c. repeating certain syllables, such as "ma-ma"
    d. reversing word order, such as "want it, paper"

15. Many researchers believe that the infant's ability to detect the similarities and differences between shapes and colors marks the beginning of:
    a. cross-modal perception.
    b. intermodal perception.
    c. category or concept formation.
    d. full object permanence.

Key Terms

Using your own words, write a brief definition or explanation of each of the following terms on a separate piece of paper.

1. affordances
2. perceptual constancy
3. dynamic perception
4. depth perception
5. intermodal perception
6. cross-modal perception
7. object permanence
8. launching event
9. sensorimotor intelligence
10. circular reactions
11. primary circular reactions
12. secondary circular reactions
13. goal-directed behavior
14. tertiary circular reactions
15. mental combinations
16. babbling
17. underextension
18. overextension
19. holophrase
20. language acquisition device (LAD)
21. baby talk

ANSWERS
CHAPTER REVIEW

1. Piaget
2. active
3. affordances
4. developmental level; past experiences; present needs; cognitive awareness
5. graspability

From a very early age, infants understand which objects afford suckability, which afford noise-making, which afford movability, and so forth.

6. constancy; 3 months; boundaries; in motion
7. perceptual constancy; size; shape
8. dynamic perception

Infants use movement cues to discern not only the boundaries of objects but also their rigidity, wholeness, shape, and size. They even form expectations of the path that a moving object will follow.

9. depth perception
10. crawling; danger
11. intermodal perception; is
12. cross-modal perception; 1 month
13. categories; habituation
14. relationships
15. angularity; shape; density; faces; animals; birds; 1; cultural
16. 5; count
17. one's perception of them; object permanence
18. 4 1/2
19. poor
20. 3 months
21. causal; launching event; 6
22. are not; habituation
23. faster; new events
24. sensorimotor; 6
25. scheme; sucking
26. 1 month

Stage-one infants suck everything that touches their lips, grasp at everything that touches the center of their palms, stare at everything that comes within focus, and so forth.

27. 1; 4; adapt; acquired adaptations
28. circular reactions; primary circular reaction

During this stage, infants adapt their sucking to specific objects. For example, they learn that efficient breast-sucking requires a squeezing sucking, whereas efficient pacifier-sucking does not.

29. 4; 8; procedures for making interesting sights last; secondary circular reaction

A stage-three infant may squeeze a duck, hear a quack, and squeeze the duck again.

30. 8; 12; anticipate; goal-directed
31. 12; 18; new means through active experimentation; tertiary circular reactions

Having discovered some action or set of actions that is possible with a given object, stage-five "little scientists" seem to ask, "What else can I do with this?"

32. 18; 24; mental combinations
33. pretend
34. active
35. speech; mouth positions
36. sequence; timing
37. squeals, growls, grunts, croons, and yells
38. 6 or 7; babbling; gestures
39. gestures; facial expressions
40. later; manually; at the same time as; brain; vocal apparatus
41. more
42. 1 year; a few; one hundred
43. overextension; underextension; holophrase
44. is not; communication
45. 21
46. B. F. Skinner
47. Noam Chomsky; language acquisition device

Recent research has suggested that both Skinner's and Chomsky's theories have some validity, but both miss the mark. Developmentalists today believe that language acquisition is an interactional process between the infant's genetic predisposition and the communication that occurs in the caregiver-child relationship.

48. baby talk; Motherese

Baby talk is higher in pitch; has a characteristically low-to-high intonation pattern; uses simpler and more concrete vocabulary and shorter sentence length; and employs more questions, commands, and repetitions, and fewer past tenses, pronouns, and complex sentences.

49. 5; 7

PROGRESS TEST 1

Multiple-Choice Questions

1. **c.** is the answer. (p. 213)
2. **b.** is the answer. (p. 234)

a. In primary circular reactions, a baby's action triggers a *self*-reaction.

c. A tertiary circular reaction is Piaget's term for actions that infants repeat with slight variations.

d. This is a research technique used for studying infants' awareness of causal relationships.

3. **b.** is the answer. This was Piaget's most basic contribution to the study of infant cognition—that intelligence is revealed in behavior at every age. (p. 232)

4. **d.** is the answer. (p. 233)

a., b., & c. These behaviors are typical of stage-four infants.

5. **b.** is the answer. (p. 233)

6. **a.** is the answer. (p. 235)

b. & c. These abilities are not acquired until children are much older.

d. Pretending is associated with stage six (18 to 24 months).

7. **c.** is the answer. (p. 223)

8. **d.** is the answer. (p. 243)

9. **b.** is the answer. (p. 239)

a., c., & d. Children the world over, and in every Piagetian stage, follow the same sequence and approximately the same timetable for early language development.

10. **c.** is the answer. (p. 241)

11. **a.** is the answer. (p. 241)

b. Baby talk is the speech adults use with infants.

c. An overextension is a grammatical error in which a word is generalized to an inappropriate context.

d. An underextension is the use of a word to refer to a narrower category of objects or events than the term signifies.

12. **c.** is the answer. At every age, children understand more speech than they can produce. (pp. 240–241)

13. **c.** is the answer. (p. 243)

a. A holophrase is a single word uttered by a toddler to express a complete thought.

b. According to Noam Chomsky, the LAD, or language acquisition device, is an innate ability in humans to acquire language.

d. These characteristic differences in pitch and structure are precisely what distinguish baby talk from regular conversation.

14. **d.** is the answer. (p. 221)

15. **a.** is the answer. (p. 223)

Matching Items

1. j (p. 241)
2. h (p. 239)
3. f (p. 216)
4. g (p. 232)
5. c (p. 223)
6. a (p. 236)
7. b (p. 213)
8. d (p. 217)
9. i (p. 241)
10. e (p. 218)

PROGRESS TEST 2

Multiple-Choice Questions

1. **b.** is the answer. (p. 235)

a. This is stage two.

c. This is stage three.

d. This is not a stage of sensorimotor intelligence.

2. **d.** is the answer. This is an example of perceptual constancy. (p. 216)

3. **c.** is the answer. (p. 225)

4. **a.** is the answer. (p. 213)

b. Affordances are perceptual phenomena.

c. & d. Infants perceive graspability at an earlier age, and long before their manual dexterity enables them to actually grasp successfully.

5. **d.** is the answer. (pp. 217–218)

a. Intermodal and cross-modal perception are not limited to vision and hearing.

b. Intermodal and cross-modal perception are *perceptual* abilities and do not involve motor responses, as hand-eye coordination does.

c. This ability is called object permanence.

6. **d.** is the answer. (p. 242)

7. **a.** is the answer. Chomsky believed this device is innate. (pp. 242–243)

8. **b.** is the answer. (p. 233)

a. & c. Both of these occur later than stage one.

d. This is a hallmark of stage six.

9. **a.** is the answer. (pp. 217–218)

10. **d.** is the answer. (p. 213)

11. **a.** is the answer. (p. 231)

12. **c.** is the answer. (p. 235)

a. Reflexes are involuntary (and therefore unintentional) responses.

b. Affordances are perceived opportunities for interaction with objects.

d. Mental combinations are actions that are carried out mentally, rather than behaviorally. Moreover, mental combinations do not develop until a later age, during sensorimotor stage six.

13. **b.** is the answer. (pp. 238–240)

14. **d.** is the answer. (p. 240)

    a. & b. Hearing and deaf babies do not differ in the overall likelihood that they will babble.

    c. Deaf babies begin to babble vocally several months later than hearing babies do.

15. **b.** is the answer. (p. 242)

    a., c., & d. These views on language acquisition describe the theory offered by Noam Chomsky.

Matching Items

1. b (p. 216)	**5.** c (p. 234)	**8.** e (p. 243)
2. j (p. 217)	**6.** f (p. 235)	**9.** d (p. 243)
3. g (p. 229)	**7.** h (p. 241)	**10.** a (p. 233)
4. i (p. 233)		

THINKING CRITICALLY ABOUT CHAPTER 7

1. **d.** is the answer. The baby is clearly behaving purposefully, the hallmark of goal-directed behavior. (p. 235)

    a. Tertiary circular reaction is Piaget's term for actions that infants repeat with slight variations.

    b. An overextension occurs when the infant overgeneralizes the use of a word to an inappropriate object or context.

    c. Delayed imitation is the ability to imitate actions seen in the past.

2. **c.** is the answer. Intermodal perception is the ability to associate information from one sensory modality with information from another. In the example, the infant is associating visual information (the sight of the revolving turntable) with auditory information (the sound of a record album). (p. 217)

    a. Cross-modal perception is the ability to use information from one sensory modality to imagine something in another.

    b. Goal-directed behavior is purposeful action.

    d. Object permanence is the awareness that objects do not cease to exist when they are out of sight.

3. **d.** is the answer. (p. 218)

    a. Delayed imitation is the ability to imitate actions seen in the past.

    b. Affordances are perceived opportunities for interacting with objects.

    c. Categorization refers to cognitively classifying objects according to certain features.

4. **a.** is the answer. The father's expression of delight is clearly a reinforcer in that it has increased the likelihood of the infant's vocalization. (p. 242)

    b. & c. Modeling, or learning by imitation, would be implicated if the father attempted to increase the infant's vocalizations by repeatedly saying "da-da" himself, in the infant's presence.

    d. This is Chomsky's viewpoint; Skinner maintained that language is acquired through learning.

5. **d.** is the answer. The child is clearly overgeneralizing the word "dog" by applying it to other animals. (p. 241)

    a. The holophrase is a single word that is used to express a complete thought.

    b. Babbling is the repetitious uttering of certain syllables, such as "ma-ma," or "da-da."

    c. Motherese, or baby talk, is the characteristic manner in which adults change the structure and pitch of their speech when conversing with infants.

6. **c.** is the answer. (p. 242)

    a. At 18 months of age, most children have much smaller vocabularies.

    b. Speaking in holophrases is typical of younger infants.

7. **d.** is the answer. (p. 236)

    a. Dynamic perception is perception primed to focus on movement and change.

    b. Schemes are general ways of thinking about, and interacting with, the environment. In this example, the child is *mentally* exercising a particular scheme, not interacting with the environment.

    c. Intermodal perception is the ability to associate information from one sensory modality with information from another.

8. **b.** is the answer. (p. 227)

    a. Cross-modal perception is the ability to use information from one sensory modality to imagine something in another.

    c. Intermodal perception is the ability to associate information from one sensory modality with information from another.

    d. Mental combinations refers to the ability to play out a course of action before exercising it.

9. **c.** is the answer. (p. 222)

10. **d.** is the answer. In this experiment the infants are associating the visual information from the photograph with the auditory information from the tape recording. (p. 222)

11. **a.** is the answer. Before object permanence is

attained, an object that disappears from sight ceases to exist for the infant. (pp. 223–224)

b. Intermodal perception is the ability to associate information from one sensory modality with information from another.

c. Mental combinations are actions that are carried out mentally.

d. Cross-modal perception is the ability to use information from one sensory modality to imagine something in another.

12. c. is the answer. (p. 241)

a. Because Christine is expressing a complete thought, her speech is much more than babbling.

b. An overextension is the application of a word the child knows to an inappropriate context, such as "doggie" to all animals the child sees.

d. Telegraphic speech emerges later, when children begin forming 2- and 3-word sentences.

13. b. is the answer. (p. 239)

a. Cooing is the pleasant-sounding utterances of the infant at about 2 months.

c. The holophrase occurs later, and refers to the toddler's use of a single word to express a complete thought.

d. An overextension, or overgeneralization, is the application of a word to an inappropriate context, such as "doed" for the past tense of "do."

14. b. is the answer. In this example, the 2-year-old has overgeneralized the concept "doggie" to all four-legged animals. (p. 241)

15. c. is the answer. (p. 220)

a. & b. These perceptual abilities are based on the integration of perceptual information from different sensory systems.

d. Object permanence, or the awareness that objects do not cease to exist simply because they are not in view, is not based on perceiving similarities among objects.

KEY TERMS

1. **Affordances** are perceived opportunities for interacting with objects in the environment. Infants perceive sucking, grasping, noise-making, and many other affordances of objects at an early age. (p. 213)

2. **Perceptual constancy** is the awareness that the size and shape of an object remain the same despite changes in the object's appearance. (p. 216)

3. **Dynamic perception** is perception that is primed to focus on movement and change. (p. 216)

4. **Depth perception** is the ability to perceive where objects exist relative to each other in a three-dimensional world. (p. 217)

5. **Intermodal perception** is the ability to associate information from one sensory modality with information from another. (p. 217)

6. **Cross-modal perception** is the ability to use information from one sensory modality to imagine something in another. (p. 218)

7. **Object permanence** is Piaget's term for the understanding that objects continue to exist even when they are out of sight. (p. 223)

8. The **launching event** is a commonly used habituation technique for studying infants' awareness of causal relationships. (p. 229)

9. Piaget's stages of **sensorimotor intelligence** are based on his theory that infants think exclusively with their senses and motor skills. (p. 232)

10. **Circular reactions** is Piaget's term for situations in which a baby's action triggers a reaction (in the baby or in someone or something else) that, in turn, makes the baby repeat the action. (p. 233)

11. In **primary circular reactions**, a baby's action triggers a self-reaction. (p. 233)

12. In **secondary circular reactions**, a baby repeats an action that has just triggered a pleasing response from some person or thing. (p. 234)

13. **Goal-directed behavior** refers to purposeful actions initiated by infants in anticipation of events that will fulfill their needs and wishes. (p. 235)

14. Unlike primary and secondary circular reactions, in which babies repeat the same action again and again, **tertiary circular reactions** are distinguished by variations of a given behavior. (p. 235)

15. In Piaget's theory, **mental combinations** are actions that are carried out mentally. Mental combinations enable stage-six toddlers to begin to anticipate and solve problems without resorting to trial-and-error experiments. (p. 236)

16. The **babbling** stage of language development, which begins at 6 or 7 months, is characterized by the extended repetition of certain syllables (such as "ma-ma"). (p. 239)

17. An **underextension** of word meaning occurs when a baby applies a word more narrowly than its full meaning allows. (p. 241)

18. **Overextension** is a characteristic of infant speech in which the infant overgeneralizes a known word by applying it to a large variety of objects or contexts. (p. 241)

    Memory aid: In this behavior the infant *extends* a word or grammatical rule beyond, or *over* and above, its normal boundaries.

19. Another characteristic of infant speech is the use of the **holophrase**, in which a single word is used to convey a complete thought. (p. 241)

20. According to Chomsky, children possess an innate **language acquisition device (LAD)** that facilitates language development. (p. 243)

21. **Baby talk**, or Motherese, is a form of speech used by adults when talking to infants. Its hallmark is exaggerated expressiveness; it employs more questions, commands, and repetitions and fewer past tenses, pronouns, and complex sentences; it uses simpler vocabulary and grammar; it has a higher pitch and more low-to-high fluctuations. (pp. 243–244)

CHAPTER 8

The First Two Years: Psychosocial Development

Chapter Overview

Chapter 8 describes the emotional and social life of the developing person during the first two years. It begins with a discussion of the new ethological perspective, which argues that the significance of many behaviors—including infant emotions—is revealed in light of human evolution. A second section describes the infant's emerging emotions and how they reflect increasing cognitive abilities. The next section presents the theories of Freud, Erikson, and Mahler that help us understand how the infant's emotional and behavioral responses begin to take on the various patterns that form personality. Important research on the nature and origins of temperament, which informs virtually every characteristic of the individual's developing personality, is also considered.

In the fourth section, emotions and relationships are examined from a different perspective—that of parent-infant interaction. Videotaped studies of parents and infants, combined with laboratory studies of attachment, have greatly expanded our understanding of psychosocial development. The chapter concludes with a discussion of factors in the home environment that have been shown to correlate with child development. Peer interactions also contribute to children's social understanding and skills.

NOTE: Answer guidelines for all Chapter 8 questions begin on page 122.

Guided Study

The text chapter should be studied one section at a time. Before you read, preview each section by skimming it, noting headings and boldface items. Then read the appropriate section objectives from the following outline. Keep these objectives in mind and, as you read the chapter section, search for the information that will enable you to meet each objective. Once you have finished a section, write out answers for its objectives.

The Ethological Perspective (pp. 250–252)

1. State the contributions of the ethological perspective to our understanding of early development.

Emotional Development (pp. 252–261)

2. Describe the basic emotions that are expressed by infants during the first days and months.

3. Describe the main developments in the emotional life of the child between 6 months and about 1 year.

110

4. Discuss the effects of cognitive advances on emotional development during the second year, including the effects of the infant's emerging self-awareness.

5. Describe how social and cultural influences affect emotional development.

The Origins of Personality (pp. 261–269)

6. Describe the evolution of behaviorist views on personality development.

7. Describe Freud's psychosexual stages of infant development.

8. Describe Erikson's psychosocial stages of infant development and Mahler's separation-individuation period of infant development.

9. Identify the components of sensitivity, a feature shared by all psychological views.

10. Discuss the origins and development of temperament as an interaction of nature and nurture, and explain the significance of research on temperament for parents and caregivers.

Parent-Infant Interaction (pp. 269–284)

11. Describe the synchrony of parent-infant interaction during the first year and discuss its significance for the developing person.

12. (A Closer Look) Discuss contemporary views on the role of the father in infant psychosocial development.

13. Define attachment, explain how it is measured and how it is influenced by context, and discuss the long-term consequences of secure and insecure attachment.

Exploring the Environment and New Relationships (pp. 284–288)

14. Describe the environmental conditions that foster development during the second year, including the roles of parents and peers.

Chapter Review

When you have finished reading the chapter, work through the material that follows to review it. Complete the sentences and answer the questions. As you proceed, evaluate your performance for each section by consulting the answers on page 122. Do not continue with the next section until you understand each answer. If you need to, review or reread the appropriate section in the textbook before continuing.

1. Early developmentalists believed that infants come into the world with no _____ tendencies at all. Current views still emphasize the importance of _____ in promoting psychosocial growth, but they add the view that infants are born with a _____ to enjoy social contact.

The Ethological Perspective (pp. 250–252)

2. The study of patterns of animal behavior, includ-

ing their evolutionary origins, is called _____ .

3. When they hear an infant cry, adults become _____ aroused. Infant crying is a(n) _____ (learned/innate) behavior that signals caregivers about a baby's needs and contributes to the _____ of the human species.

Emotional Development (pp. 252–261)

4. Even very young infants express many emotions, including _____ _____ .

5. Infants' capacity for specific emotions emerges according to a developmental schedule, which is related to _____ maturation.

6. The first emotion that can be reliably discerned in infants is _____ .

7. The infant's smile in response to a moving face or a human voice, which is called a _____ _____ , begins to appear at about _____ of age. The development of smiling _____ (is/is not) universal in infants.

8. Stranger _____ is first noticeable at about _____ of age. All infants _____ (do/do not) experience this fear. How a baby responds to a stranger depends on aspects of the infant, such as _____ , as well as on the situation and the stranger.

9. An infant's fear of being left by the mother or other caregiver, called _____ _____ , peaks at about _____ of age and then gradually subsides. Whether separation distresses an infant depends on such factors as _____ .

10. As infants become older, emotions such as anger _____ (intensify/weaken) and smiling and laughing become _____ (more/less) selective. Another change that occurs in the infant's emotional life might be character-

ized as greater emotional _____ .
These emotional changes may be the result of
_____ maturation, such as
infants' growing awareness of
_____ .

11. Emotional growth is also influenced by the
infant's developing capacity to understand the
_____ _____
of others. For example, infants look to trusted
adults for emotional cues in uncertain situations;
this is called _____
_____ . The fact that this occurs as
the infant becomes more mobile indicates, from
an _____ viewpoint, that it is an
_____ protection strategy.

12. The emerging sense of "me and mine" is part of
what psychologists call _____ .
This makes possible many new self-conscious
emotions, including _____ ,
_____ , _____ ,
and _____ .

13. In the first few months infants _____
(do/do not) have a sense of self and/or an awareness of their bodies as their own.

Briefly describe the nature and findings of the classic
rouge-and-mirror experiment on self-awareness in
infants.

14. The development of self-awareness seems
_____ (universal/to vary from
culture to culture); its onset changes the
_____ and _____
of the toddler's reactions to others, including
affection and _____ .

15. Developing self-awareness also enhances the toddler's _____ reactions and emo-
tional responses such as _____ .

16. Social interaction plays a role in shaping

emotional development, as when mothers
_____ the baby's positive emotional expressions and _____
sadness or distress, or briefly _____
the baby's sadness and then switch to a positive
emotion.

17. Infants' expressive styles _____
(do/do not) begin to resemble their mothers' over
time.

18. The kinds of experiences parents provide their
offspring _____ (vary/do not
vary) from culture to culture.

The Origins of Personality (pp. 261–269)

19. An early prevailing view among psychologists
was that the individual's personality was permanently molded by the actions of his or her
_____ . Two versions of this
theory were the _____ and
_____ .

20. According to early behaviorist theory, personality
is molded through the processes of
_____ and _____
of the child's various behaviors. A strong proponent of this position was _____ .
Later theorists incorporated the role of
_____ learning, that is, infants'
tendency to _____ the personal-
ity traits of their parents. More recently, learning
theory recognizes the constraints of the innate
biological and _____ limits and
the wider _____ .

21. According to Freud, the experiences of the first
_____ years of life and the
child's relationship with his or her
_____ were decisive in personality formation.

22. In Freud's theory, development begins with the
_____ stage, so named because
the _____ is the infant's prime
source of gratification and pleasure.

23. According to Freud, in the _____

year the prime focus of gratification comes from stimulation and control of the bowels. Freud referred to this period as the _____ stage. This stage represents a shift in the way the infant interacts with others, from the more _____ mode of orality to the more _____ mode of anality.

Describe Freud's ideas on the importance of early oral experiences to later personality development.

24. Research has shown that the parents' overall pattern of _____ is more important to the child's emotional development than the particulars of feeding and weaning or toilet training.

25. The theorist who believed that development occurs through a series of crises is _____ . According to his theory, the crisis of infancy is one of _____ , while the crisis of toddlerhood is one of _____ . He maintained that experiences later in life _____ (can alter/have little impact on) the effects of early experiences on personality development.

26. The need for a proper balance between protection and freedom is also central to the theory proposed by _____ . According to this view, the period from 5 months to 3 years, during which the infant gains a sense of self apart from the mother, is the period of _____ - _____ .

27. The traditional views of personality emphasize the importance of early _____ ,

particularly that provided by a child's _____ . They also emphasize parental _____ as a crucial component of healthy nurturance.

28. A person's inherent, relatively consistent, basic dispositions define his or her _____ . This overall make up, which _____ (is/is not) evident at birth, begins in the _____ codes that guide the development of the brain, and is affected by many prenatal experiences, including _____ .

29. Mary Rothbart believes that temperament pertains primarily to differences in _____ and _____ . She measures such dimensions as _____ .

30. Arnold Buss proposes three dimensions of temperament: _____ , _____ , and _____ .

31. List the nine temperamental characteristics measured in the NYLS study:
_____
_____

32. Most young infants can be described as one of three types: _____ , _____ - _____ - _____ - _____ , or _____ .

33. Two aspects of temperament that are quite variable are _____ and _____ .

Describe two ways in which the environment can influence a child's temperamental characteristics.

34. (Research Report) Every ethnic and racial group _____ (has/does not have) a

portion of individuals who are very outgoing and another portion who are unusually shy. Among white American children, about _____ percent are consistently sociable and about _____ percent are consistently shy.

35. (Research Report) The personality trait of extroversion/shyness is readily observable by age _____ . A recent study found that infants who were high or low in both

_____ _____

and _____ at 4 months were, respectively, high or low in fear at 9 and 14 months. Results such as these suggest that extroversion/shyness is a(n) _____ (inherited/learned) trait. They further suggest that shyness is one manifestation of a more general physiological pattern of _____ to new stimuli and a trait that may be inherited in an additive fashion or _____ .

Parent-Infant Interaction (pp. 269–284)

36. Although infants are social from birth, they are not necessarily socially _____ .

37. By 2 to 3 months of age, growth in _____ and _____ perception enables babies to respond especially to their primary caregivers. At this time caregivers begin to initiate focused episodes of

_____ - _____ -

_____ play.

Describe the social play behaviors of adults with infants.

38. Episodes of face-to-face play _____ (are/are not) a universal feature of early interaction with infants.

39. Cultural variations in the _____ and _____ of social play are common.

40. The intricate dialogue, or coordinated interaction of response, between infant and caregiver is called _____ . Partly through this interaction, infants learn to _____ and _____ emotions.

41. During synchrony, caregivers _____ _____ and infants

_____ ;

the signs of dyssynchrony include _____

_____ .

42. The ease of synchrony is affected not only by the caregiver's personality, but also by the infant's _____ and _____ .

43. (A Closer Look) Traditional views of infant development focused _____ (exclusively on mothers/on both mothers and fathers). Overall, researchers _____ (have/have not) found evidence that women are biologically predisposed to be better parents than men are.

44. (A Closer Look) In contemporary marriages, with both parents working outside the home, most child caregiving is _____ (shared equally by mothers and fathers/done by the mother).

45. (A Closer Look) Even so, fathers spend more time _____ with their children.

Describe several differences in how mothers and fathers typically play with their children.

46. (A Closer Look) In one study, the _____ (mother's/father's) presence made toddlers more likely to smile and play with a stranger than did the presence of the other parent.

47. The emotional bond that develops between parents and infants is called _____ . An infant who derives comfort and confidence from the secure base provided by the caregiver is displaying _____

_____ . By contrast,

_____ _____
is characterized by an infant's fear, anger, or
seeming indifference to the caregiver.

48. The procedure developed by Ainsworth to measure attachment is called the _____
_____ . Approximately
_____ (what proportion?) of
American infants tested with this procedure
demonstrate secure attachment.

Briefly describe three types of insecure attachment.

49. Among the features of caregiving that affect the
quality of attachment are the following:

   a. _____

   b. _____

   c. _____

50. Cross-cultural comparisons of the Strange
Situation reveal that children from
_____ and _____
show a higher rate of resistance and anxiety than
do American infants, while infants from some
Western European countries show higher rates of
_____ . Overall, such studies
demonstrate that the majority of infants in the
Strange Situation exhibit _____
attachment.

51. Most infants _____ (do/
do not) show signs of attachment to other caregivers, such as fathers, siblings, and day-care
workers.

52. List several characteristics of 3- and 4-year-olds
who, at age 1, were rated as follows:

securely attached _____

insecurely attached _____

53. (Public Policy) According to Jay Belsky, extended
infant day care _____ (is/is
not) likely to result in negative developmental
outcomes. Belsky admits, however—and other
research has convincingly demonstrated—that
when preschoolers experience early and extended
amounts of high quality day care, they show
more _____ (positive/negative)
outcomes than children without such experience.

54. By itself, a secure or insecure attachment in
infancy _____ (determines/ does
not determine) a child's later social relationships.

55. Mary Main has found that adults can be classified
into one of four categories of attachment:
_____ adults who value attach-
ment relationships, but can discuss them objectively; _____ adults who deval-
ue attachment; _____ adults
who dwell on past relationships; and
_____ adults who have not yet
reconciled their past experiences with the present.

56. Autonomous mothers tend to have infants who
are _____ attached, dismissing
mothers tend to have _____
babies, and preoccupied mothers tend to have
_____ infants.

State several possible reasons for the link between
adult and infant attachment.

Exploring the Environment and New Relationships
(pp. 284–288)

57. Guidelines for toddler care have been suggested
by the project called _____ ,
which rates the environment of young children

in terms of _____ (how many?) subscales.

List the subscales of HOME.

58. Unlike children in previous generations, many infants today have their first encounters with other infants at a(n) _____ (younger/older) age.

59. With the growth of social skills, _____-awareness, and _____ vitality during the second year, peer relationships flourish.

Progress Test 1

Multiple-Choice Questions

Circle your answers to the following questions and check them with the answers on page 123. If your answer is incorrect, read the explanation for why it is incorrect and then consult the appropriate pages of the text (in parentheses following the correct answer).

1. One of the first emotions that can be discerned in infancy is:
   a. shame.
   b. distress.
   c. guilt.
   d. pride.

2. The social smile begins to appear:
   a. at about 6 weeks.
   b. at about 8 months.
   c. after stranger wariness has been overcome.
   d. after the infant has achieved a sense of self.

3. An infant's fear of being left by the mother or other caregiver, called _____, peaks at about _____ .
   a. separation anxiety; 14 months
   b. stranger wariness; 8 months
   c. separation anxiety; 8 months
   d. stranger wariness; 14 months

4. Social referencing refers to:
   a. parenting skills that change over time.
   b. changes in community values regarding, for example, the acceptability of using physical punishment with small children.
   c. the support network for new parents provided by extended family members.
   d. the infant response of looking to trusted adults for emotional cues in uncertain situations.

5. According to Margaret Mahler, separation-individuation is the period during which:
   a. dependence on the mother is strongest.
   b. infants feel as though they are part of their mother.
   c. the mother focuses exclusively on toilet training.
   d. the infant gradually develops a sense of self.

6. Psychologists who favored the _____ perspective believed that the personality of the child was virtually "created" through reinforcement and punishment.
   a. psychoanalytic
   b. behaviorist
   c. psychosocial
   d. separation-individuation

7. Freud's oral stage corresponds to Erikson's crisis of:
   a. orality versus anality.
   b. trust versus mistrust.
   c. autonomy versus shame and doubt.
   d. secure versus insecure attachment.

8. Erikson feels that the development of a sense of trust in early infancy depends on the quality of the:
   a. infant's food.
   b. child's genetic inheritance.
   c. maternal relationship.
   d. introduction of toilet training.

9. Like Freud and Erikson, Mahler believes that:
   a. the social environment of the infant overshadows the effects of heredity on development.
   b. the personality of the child is created through reinforcement and punishment.
   c. each stage of development is important for later psychological health.
   d. development occurs through a series of basic crises.

10. "Easy," "slow-to-warm-up," and "difficult" are descriptions of different:
    a. forms of attachment.
    b. types of temperament.
    c. types of parenting.
    d. toddler responses to the Strange Situation.

11. (Research Report) Most developmentalists believe that social shyness:
    a. is an inherited trait.
    b. is one manifestation of a more general, physiological pattern of inhibition to new stimuli.
    c. can be modified by the reaction of parents, caregivers, and others in the environment.
    d. is characterized by all of the above.

12. Synchrony is a term that describes:
    a. the carefully coordinated interaction between parent and infant.
    b. a mismatch of the temperaments of parent and infant.
    c. a research technique involving videotapes.
    d. separation-individuation.

13. The emotional tie that develops between an infant and his or her primary caregiver is called:
    a. self-awareness.   c. affiliation.
    b. synchrony.   d. attachment.

14. An important effect of secure attachment is the promotion of:
    a. self-awareness.
    b. curiosity and self-directed behavior.
    c. dependency.
    d. all of the above.

15. Ethology is the study of:
    a. emotional development.
    b. patterns of animal behavior.
    c. social interactions.
    d. parent-infant attachment.

True or False Items

Write *true* or *false* on the line in front of each statement.

_____ 1. Emotions in infancy emerge according to a developmental schedule.
_____ 2. Joy and sadness are emotions present by about age 1; fear and anger, however, do not appear for another 6 months, at about age 1 1/2.
_____ 3. A baby at 11 months is likely to display both stranger wariness and separation anxiety.
_____ 4. Emotional development affects cognitive development, and vice versa.
_____ 5. A securely attached toddler is most likely to stay close to his or her mother even in a familiar environment.
_____ 6. (Public Policy) Current research shows that the majority of infants in day care are insecurely attached.
_____ 7. Adults become physiologically aroused when hearing a baby cry.
_____ 8. (Research Report) Infants' facial expressions are foolproof indicators of emotion.
_____ 9. Infants' expressive reactions come to resemble their mothers' over time.
_____ 10. Adult attachment classifications parallel those of infancy.

Progress Test 2

Progress Test 2 should be completed during a final chapter review. Answer the following questions after you thoroughly understand the correct answers for the Chapter Review and Progress Test 1.

Multiple-Choice Questions

1. Infants give their first real smiles, called _____ , when they are about _____ of age.
   a. play smiles; 3 months
   b. play smiles; 6 weeks
   c. social smiles; 3 months
   d. social smiles; 6 weeks

2. Freud's anal stage corresponds to Erikson's crisis of:
   a. autonomy versus shame and doubt.
   b. trust versus mistrust.
   c. orality versus anality.
   d. identity versus role confusion.

3. Not until the sense of self begins to emerge do babies realize that they are seeing their own faces in the mirror. This realization usually occurs:
   a. shortly before 3 months.
   b. at about 6 months.
   c. between 15 and 24 months.
   d. after 24 months.

4. According to the ethological perspective, adults become physiologically aroused at the sound of a baby's cry because:
   a. they have developed an emotional attachment to the infant.
   b. this tendency promotes the nurturance and protection of infants by adults.
   c. their own caregivers nurtured them as infants.
   d. of all of the above reasons.

5. Emotions such as shame, guilt, embarrassment, and pride emerge at the same time that:
   a. the social smile appears.
   b. aspects of the infant's temperament can first be discerned.

c. self-awareness begins to emerge.

d. parents initiate toilet training.

6. According to the research, the NYLS temperamental characteristics that are not particularly stable are quality of mood and:

 a. rhythmicity.

 b. activity level.

 c. self-awareness.

 d. sociability (or shyness).

7. In the second six months, stranger wariness is a:

 a. result of insecure attachment.

 b. result of social isolation.

 c. normal emotional response.

 d. setback in emotional development.

8. The caregiving environment can affect a child's temperament through:

 a. the child's temperamental pattern and the demands of the home environment.

 b. parenting style.

 c. both a. and b.

 d. neither a. nor b.

9. Compared to children who are insecurely attached, those who are securely attached are:

 a. more independent.

 b. more cooperative.

 c. more sociable.

 d. characterized by all of the above.

10. The later consequences of secure attachment and insecure attachment for children are:

 a. balanced by the child's current rearing circumstances.

 b. irreversible, regardless of the child's current rearing circumstances.

 c. more significant in girls than in boys.

 d. more significant in boys than in girls.

11. Beginning at _____ of age, infants begin to associate emotional meaning with different facial expressions of emotion.

 a. 2 months   c. 4 months

 b. 3 months   d. 6 months

12. (Research Report) Compared to mothers, fathers are more likely to:

 a. engage in noisier, more boisterous play.

 b. encourage intellectual development in their children.

 c. encourage social development in their children.

 d. read to their toddlers.

13. The text suggests that infants smile and laugh more as they get older because:

 a. their mothers selectively reinforce and model positive emotions.

 b. cognitive growth gives rise to a more fully developed sense of humor.

 c. brain maturation enables these emotions to occur more readily.

 d. of all the above reasons.

14. Which of the following most accurately summarizes the relationship between early attachment and later social relationships?

 a. Attachment in infancy determines whether a child will grow to be sociable.

 b. Attachment relationships are sometimes, though rarely, altered as children grow older.

 c. There is, at best, only a weak correlation between early attachment and later social relationships.

 d. Early attachment biases, but does not inevitably determine, later social relationships.

15. In her research, Mary Main has discovered that:

 a. adult attachment classifications parallel those of infancy.

 b. autonomous mothers tend to have insecurely attached babies.

 c. preoccupied mothers tend to have avoidant babies.

 d. all of the above are true.

Matching Items

Match each theorist, term, or concept with its corresponding description or definition.

Theorists, Terms, or Concepts

_____ **1.** temperament
_____ **2.** Erikson
_____ **3.** the Strange Situation
_____ **4.** synchrony
_____ **5.** trust versus mistrust
_____ **6.** Freud
_____ **7.** sensitivity
_____ **8.** autonomy versus shame and doubt
_____ **9.** Mahler
_____ **10.** Ainsworth

Descriptions or Definitions

a. responsiveness to a child's needs, desires, and abilities
b. the crisis of infancy
c. the crisis of toddlerhood
d. theorist who described psychosexual stages of development
e. researcher who devised a laboratory procedure for studying attachment
f. laboratory procedure for studying attachment
g. the relatively consistent, basic dispositions inherent in a person
h. coordinated interaction between parent and infant
i. theorist who described psychosocial stages of development
j. theorist who described the period of separation-individuation

Thinking Critically About Chapter 8

Answer these questions the day before an exam as a final check on your understanding of the chapter's terms and concepts.

1. In laboratory tests of attachment, when the mother returns to the playroom after a short absence, a securely attached infant is most likely to:
   a. cry and protest the mother's return.
   b. climb into the mother's lap, then leave to resume play.
   c. climb into the mother's lap and stay there.
   d. continue playing without acknowledging the mother.

2. Dr. Jacobs believes that infants' wariness of strangers derives from an evolved predisposition to fear potentially dangerous circumstances. Dr. Jacobs is evidently working from a(n):
   a. behavioral perspective.
   b. ethological perspective.
   c. psychoanalytic perspective.
   d. cognitive perspective.

3. Which of the following is a clear sign of an infant's attachment to a particular person?
   a. The infant turns to that person when distressed.
   b. The infant protests when that person leaves a room.
   c. The infant may cry when strangers appear.
   d. All of the above are signs of infant attachment.

4. At about 8 months of age, babies are more likely to laugh in anticipation of happy experiences—in part, because they have developed expectations about what will happen. This infant behavior shows the:
   a. effect of cognitive development on infant emotions.
   b. infant's discovery of his or her own body parts.
   c. validity of Freud's and Erikson's theories.
   d. importance of attachment.

5. Kenny becomes very emotional when talking about his relationship with his parents; consequently, he is unable to discuss his early attachment experiences objectively. Kenny's attachment classification is probably:
   a. autonomous.   **c.** preoccupied.
   b. dismissing.   **d.** unresolved.

6. Which of the following mothers is most likely to have an avoidant son or daughter?
   a. Claudia, who is still coping with the loss of her parents
   b. Kaleen, who idealizes her parents, yet devalues the importance of her own relationships

c. Pearl, who is able to discuss her own early attachment experiences quite objectively, despite their painful nature

d. Carmen, who spends a lot of time thinking about her own relationship with her parents

7. One way in which infant psychosocial development has changed is that today:

a. many infants have their first encounters with other infants at a younger age.

b. parental influence is less important than in the past.

c. social norms are nearly the same for the sexes.

d. infants tend to have fewer social encounters than in the past.

8. (Research Report) Jack, who is about to become a father and primary caregiver, is worried that he will never have the natural caregiving skills that the child's mother has. Studies on father-infant relationships show that:

a. infants nurtured by single fathers are more likely to be insecurely attached.

b. fathers can provide the emotional and cognitive nurturing necessary for healthy infant development.

c. women are biologically predisposed to be better parents than men are.

d. social development is usually slightly delayed in children whose fathers are the primary caregiver.

9. Kalil's mother left him alone in the room for a few minutes. When she returned, Kalil seemed indifferent to her presence. According to Mary Ainsworth's research with children in the Strange Situation, Kalil is probably:

a. a normal, independent infant.

b. an abused child.

c. insecurely attached.

d. securely attached.

10. Connie and Lev, who are first-time parents, are concerned because their 1-month-old baby is difficult to care for and hard to soothe. They are worried that they are doing something wrong. You inform them that their child is probably that way because:

a. they are reinforcing the child's tantrum behaviors.

b. they are not meeting some biological need of the child's.

c. of his or her inherited temperament.

d. at 1 month of age all children are difficult to care for and hard to soothe.

11. Two-year-old Anita and her mother visit a day-care center. Seeing an interesting toy, Anita runs a few steps toward it, then stops and looks back to see if her mother is coming. Margaret Mahler would probably say that Anita is experiencing:

a. the crisis of autonomy versus shame and doubt.

b. synchrony.

c. dyssynchrony.

d. the need for greater psychological separation from her mother.

12. Felix has a biting, sarcastic manner. Freud would probably say that Felix is:

a. anally expulsive.

b. anally retentive.

c. fixated in the oral stage.

d. experiencing the crisis of trust versus mistrust.

13. A researcher at the child development center places a dot on an infant's nose and watches to see if the infant reacts to her image in a mirror by touching her nose. Evidently, the researcher is testing the child's:

a. attachment.

b. temperament.

c. self-awareness.

d. separation-individuation.

14. Four-month-old Carl and his 13-month-old sister Carla are left in the care of a baby-sitter. As their parents are leaving, it is to be expected that:

a. Carl will become extremely upset, while Carla will calmly accept her parents' departure.

b. Carla will become more upset over her parents' departure than will Carl.

c. Carl and Carla will both become quite upset as their parents leave.

d. Neither Carl nor Carla will become very upset as their parents leave.

15. You have been asked to give a presentation on "Mother-Infant Attachment" to a group of expectant mothers. Basing your presentation on the research of Mary Ainsworth, you conclude your talk by stating that mother-infant attachment depends mostly on:

a. an infant's innate temperament.

b. the amount of time mothers spend with their infants.

c. sensitive and responsive caregiving in the early months.

d. whether the mother herself was securely attached as an infant.

Key Terms

Using your own words, write a brief definition or explanation of each of the following terms on a separate piece of paper.

1. ethology
2. social smile
3. stranger wariness
4. separation anxiety
5. social referencing
6. self-awareness
7. oral stage
8. anal stage
9. trust versus mistrust
10. autonomy versus shame and doubt
11. separation-individuation
12. sensitivity
13. temperament
14. goodness of fit
15. synchrony
16. attachment
17. secure attachment
18. insecure attachment
19. Strange Situation
20. HOME

ANSWERS

CHAPTER REVIEW

1. social; nurturance; predisposition
2. ethology
3. physiologically; innate; survival
4. joy, surprise, anger, fear, disgust, interest, and sadness
5. brain
6. distress
7. social smile; 6 weeks; is
8. wariness; 6 months; do not; temperament and the security of the mother-infant relationship
9. separation anxiety; 14 months; the baby's prior experiences with separation and the manner in which the parent departs
10. intensify; more; vitality; cognitive; causality
11. emotional expressions; social referencing; ethological; innate

12. self-awareness; pride; guilt; shame; embarrassment
13. do not

In the classic self-awareness experiment, babies look in a mirror after a dot of rouge is put on their nose. If the babies react to the mirror image by touching their nose, it is clear they know they are seeing their own face. Most babies demonstrate this self-awareness between 15 and 24 months of age.

14. universal; intensity; conditions; jealousy
15. self-critical; guilt
16. mimic; ignore; imitate
17. do
18. vary
19. parents; behaviorist; psychoanalytic
20. reinforcement; punishment; John Watson; social; imitate; maturational; social context
21. four; mother
22. oral; mouth
23. second; anal; passive; active

Freud believed that the oral and anal stages are fraught with potential conflict that can have long-term consequences for the infant. If nursing is a hurried or tense event, for example, the child may become fixated at the oral stage, excessively eating, drinking, smoking, or talking in quest of oral satisfaction.

24. warmth and sensitivity or strict domination
25. Erikson; trust versus mistrust; autonomy versus shame and doubt; can alter
26. Mahler; separation-individuation
27. nurture; mother; sensitivity
28. temperament; is; genetic; the nutrition and health of the mother
29. reactivity; self-regulation; smiling and laughing, fear, soothability, distress when thwarted, persistence at one task, and activity level
30. activity; emotionality; sociability
31. activity level; rhythmicity; approach-withdrawal; adaptability; intensity of reaction; threshold of responsiveness; quality of mood; distractibility; attention span
32. easy; slow-to-warm-up; difficult
33. rhythmicity; quality of mood

One way is through the "goodness of fit" between the child's temperamental patterns and the demands of the home environment. Parenting style also can influence temperament.

34. has; 25; 10

35. 1 year; motor activity; crying; inherited; inhibition; discretely

36. competent

37. visual; intermodal; face-to-face

Adults tend to open their eyes and mouths wide in exaggerated expressions, make rapid clicking noises or repeated one-syllable sounds, raise and lower the pitch of their voice, change the pace of their movements, and imitate the infant's actions.

38. are

39. frequency; duration

40. synchrony; express; read

41. modify the timing or pace of their initiatives to accord with the baby's readiness; modify their social and emotional expressiveness to match or complement the caregiver's; averted eyes, stiffening or abrupt shifting of the body, and/or an unhappy noise

42. personality; predispositions

43. exclusively on mothers; have not

44. done by the mother

45. playing

Fathers' play is noisier, more boisterous, and idiosyncratic. Mothers are more likely to read to their toddlers, help them play with toys, or play conventional games.

46. father's

47. attachment; secure attachment; insecure attachment

48. Strange Situation; two-thirds

Some infants are anxious and *resistant*: they cling nervously to their mother, are unwilling to explore, cry loudly when she leaves, and refuse to be comforted when she returns. Others are *avoidant*: they engage in little interaction with their mother before and after her departure. Others are *disoriented*: they show an inconsistent mixture of behavior toward the mother.

49. a. general sensitivity to the infant's needs

    b. responsiveness to the infant's specific signals

    c. talking and playing with the infant in ways that actively encourage growth and development

50. Israel; Japan; avoidance; secure

51. do

52. *securely attached*: more competent in certain social and cognitive skills; more curious, outgoing, and self-directed

    insecurely attached: overly dependent on teachers, demanding their attention unnecessarily instead of playing or exploring; boys tend to be aggressive

53. is; positive

54. does not determine

55. autonomous; dismissing; preoccupied; unresolved

56. securely; avoidant; resistant

Parents who value attachment may be more sensitive to their offspring, and inspire secure attachment as a result; or innate temperament may predispose a certain attachment pattern across most relationships; or the nature of parents' attachment with their children may influence their memories of, and attitudes about, other attachments.

57. HOME; six

    a. emotional and verbal responsiveness of mother

    b. avoidance of restriction and punishment

    c. organization of the physical environment

    d. provision of appropriate play materials

    e. maternal involvement with child

    f. opportunities for variety in daily stimulation

58. younger

59. self; emotional

PROGRESS TEST 1

Multiple-Choice Questions

1. **b.** is the answer. (p. 252)

    a., c., & d. These emotions emerge later in infancy at about the same time as self-awareness emerges.

2. **a.** is the answer. (p. 253)

3. **a.** is the answer. (p. 256)

    b. & d. This fear, which is also called fear of strangers, peaks by 10 to 14 months.

4. **d.** is the answer. (p. 258)

5. **d.** is the answer. (p. 264)

    a. & b. According to Mahler, these describe the symbiotic mother-child relationship at an earlier age—during the first months of life.

6. **b.** is the answer. (p. 261)

    a. Reinforcement and punishment have no place in the psychoanalytic perspective.

    c. This is Erikson's theory, which sees development as occurring through a series of basic crises.

    d. This is a concept in Mahler's theory, which describes the development of the infant's sense of self, apart from the mother.

7. **b.** is the answer. (p. 263)

   a. Orality and anality refer to personality traits that result from fixation in the oral and anal stages, respectively.

   c. According to Erikson, this is the crisis of toddlerhood, which corresponds to Freud's anal stage.

   d. These are not developmental crises in Erikson's theory.

8. **c.** is the answer. (pp. 263–264)

9. **c.** is the answer. (p. 264)

   a. This is not true of any theory.

   b. This is the behaviorist approach.

   d. This is Erikson's idea.

10. **b.** is the answer. (p. 267)

    a. "Secure" and "insecure" are different forms of attachment.

    c. The chapter does not describe different types of parenting.

    d. The Strange Situation is a test of attachment, rather than temperament.

11. **d.** is the answer. (pp. 270–271)

12. **a.** is the answer. (p. 273)

13. **d.** is the answer. (p. 277)

    a. Self-awareness refers to the infant's developing sense of "me and mine."

    b. Synchrony describes the coordinated interaction between infant and caregiver.

    c. Affiliation describes the tendency of people at any age to seek the companionship of others.

14. **b.** is the answer. (p. 280)

    a. The text does not link self-awareness to secure attachment.

    c. On the contrary, secure attachment promotes *independence* in infants and children.

15. **b.** is the answer. (p. 250)

True or False Items

1. T (p. 252)
2. F Fear, sadness, joy, and anger are all present by age 1. (p. 252)
3. T (p. 256)
4. T (pp. 257–258)
5. F A securely attached toddler is most likely to explore the environment, the mother's presence being enough to give him or her the courage to do so. (p. 277)

6. F The effects of early and extended day care continue to be studied and debated. However, Jay Belsky believes that high-quality day care is not likely to harm the child. (p. 281)
7. T (p. 250)
8. F Infant facial expressions sometimes appear in incongruous situations. (p. 254)
9. T (pp. 257–258)
10. T (p. 283)

PROGRESS TEST 2

Multiple-Choice Questions

1. **d.** is the answer. (p. 253)
2. **a.** is the answer. (pp. 263, 264)

   b. This crisis corresponds to Freud's oral stage.

   c. These describe fixation in Freud's oral and anal stages, respectively.

   d. This is a crisis which, according to Erikson, occurs much later in development.

3. **c.** is the answer. (p. 259)
4. **b.** is the answer. (p. 250)
5. **c.** is the answer. (p. 259)

   a. & b. The social smile, as well as temperamental characteristics, emerge well before the first signs of self-awareness.

   d. Contemporary developmentalists link these emotions to self-consciousness, rather than any specific environmental event such as toilet training.

6. **a.** is the answer. (p. 267)

   b. & d. Activity level and sociability are much less variable than rhythmicity and quality of mood.

   c. Self-awareness is not a temperamental characteristic.

7. **c.** is the answer. (p. 256)
8. **c.** is the answer. (pp. 268–269)
9. **d.** is the answer. (p. 280)
10. **a.** is the answer. (pp. 281–282)

    c. & d. The text does not suggest that the consequences of secure and insecure attachment differ in boys and girls.

11. **c.** is the answer. (p. 258)
12. **a.** is the answer. (p. 274)
13. **a.** is the answer. (p. 260)
14. **d.** is the answer. (pp. 281–282)

15. a. is the answer. (p. 283)

b. Autonomous mothers tend to have securely attached infants.

c. Preoccupied mothers tend to have resistant infants.

Matching Items

1. g (p. 265) 5. b (p. 263) 8. c (p. 264)
2. i (p. 263) 6. d (p. 263) 9. j (p. 264)
3. f (p. 278) 7. a (p. 265) 10. e (p. 278)
4. h (p. 273)

THINKING CRITICALLY ABOUT CHAPTER 8

1. b. is the answer. (p. 278)

a., c., & d. These responses are more typical of insecurely attached infants.

2. b. is the answer. (pp. 250–251)

3. d. is the answer. (p. 278)

4. a. is the answer. (p. 257)

5. c. is the answer. (p. 283)

a. Autonomous adults are able to talk objectively about their own early attachments.

b. Dismissing adults devalue the importance of attachment relationships.

d. Unresolved adults have not yet reconciled their own early attachments.

6. b. is the answer. (p. 283)

a. Claudia would be classified as "unresolved."

c. Autonomous adults, such as Pearl, tend to have securely attached infants.

d. Preoccupied adults, such as Carmen, tend to have resistant offspring.

7. a. is the answer. (p. 284)

8. b. is the answer. (p. 274)

9. c. is the answer. (p. 278)

a. & d. When their mothers return following an absence, securely attached infants usually reestablish social contact (with a smile or by climbing into their laps) and then resume playing.

b. There is no evidence in this example that Kalil is an abused child.

10. c. is the answer. (p. 267)

a. & b. There is no evidence in the question that the parents are reinforcing tantrum behavior, or

failing to meet some biological need of the child's.

d. On the contrary, about 40 percent of infants are "easy" in temperamental style.

11. d. is the answer. (p. 264)

a. According to Erikson, this is the crisis of toddlerhood.

b. This describes a moment of coordinated and mutually responsive interaction between a parent and an infant.

c. Dyssynchrony occurs when the coordinated pace and timing of a synchronous interaction are temporarily lost.

12. c. is the answer. (p. 263)

a. & b. In Freud's theory, a person who is fixated in the anal stage exhibits messiness and disorganization, or compulsive neatness.

d. Erikson, rather than Freud, proposed crises of development.

13. c. is the answer. (p. 259)

14. b. is the answer. The fear of being left by a caregiver (separation anxiety) emerges at about 8 or 9 months, and peaks at about 14 months. For this reason, 4-month-old Carl can be expected to become less upset than his older sister. (p. 256)

15. c. is the answer. (pp. 278–279)

KEY TERMS

1. **Ethology** is the study of patterns of animal behavior, particularly as that behavior is related to evolutionary origins and species survival. (p. 250)

2. The **social smile**—a smile that is a response to a moving face or a human voice—appears at about 6 weeks. (p. 253)

3. A common early fear, **stranger wariness** (also called fear of strangers) is first noticeable at about 6 months. (p. 256)

4. **Separation anxiety**, which is the infant fear of being left by the mother or other caregiver, emerges at about 8 or 9 months, peaks at about 14 months, and then gradually subsides. (p. 256)

5. When infants engage in **social referencing**, they are looking to trusted adults for emotional cues in uncertain situations. (p. 258)

6. **Self-awareness** refers to the infant's emerging sense of "me and mine" that makes possible many new self-conscious emotions, including shame, guilt, embarrassment, and pride. (p. 259)

7. In Freud's first stage of psychosexual development, the **oral stage**, the mouth is the most important source of gratification for the infant. (p. 263)

8. According to Freud, during the second year infants are in the **anal stage** of psychosexual development and derive sensual pleasure from the stimulation of the bowels and psychological pleasure from their control. (p. 263)

9. In Erikson's theory, the crisis of infancy is one of **trust versus mistrust**, in which the infant learns whether the world is a secure place in which basic needs will be met. (p. 263)

10. In Erikson's theory, the crisis of toddlerhood is one of **autonomy versus shame and doubt**, in which toddlers strive to rule their own actions and bodies. (p. 264)

11. In Mahler's theory, between the ages of 5 months and 3 years the infant is in a period of **separation-individuation** as he or she gradually develops a sense of self that is separate and apart from the mother. (p. 264)

12. **Sensitivity** refers to a caregiver's awareness of, and responsiveness to, a child's needs, desires, and abilities. (p. 265)

13. **Temperament** refers to the "relatively consistent, basic dispositions inherent in the person that underlie and modulate the expression of activity, reactivity, emotionality, and sociability." (p. 265)

14. **Goodness of fit** is the match between the child's temperamental pattern and the demands of the environment. (p. 268)

15. **Synchrony** refers to the coordinated interaction between caregiver and infant that helps infants learn to express and read emotions. (p. 273)

16. **Attachment** is the enduring emotional tie that a person or animal forms with another. (p. 277)

17. A **secure attachment** is one in which the infant derives comfort and confidence from the "secure base" provided by a caregiver. (p. 277)

18. **Insecure attachment** is characterized by the infant's fear, anger, or seeming indifference toward the caregiver. (p. 277)

19. The **Strange Situation** is a laboratory procedure developed by Ainsworth for assessing attachment. Infants are observed in a playroom, in several successive episodes, with their mother and/or a stranger, and by themselves. (p. 278)

20. **HOME** (an acronym for Home Observation for the Measurement of the Environment) is a list of family and household characteristics that have been shown to correlate with children's development. (p. 285)

CHAPTER 9

The Play Years: Biosocial Development

Chapter Overview

Chapter 9 introduces the developing person between the ages of 2 and 6. This period is called the play years, emphasizing the central importance of play to the biosocial, cognitive, and psychosocial development of preschoolers.

The chapter begins by outlining the changes in size and shape that occur from age 2 through 6. This is followed by a look at the most important physiological development during early childhood—brain maturation. The discussion focuses on hemispheric specialization and its role in the development of physical and cognitive abilities, including activity level.

A description of the acquisition of gross and fine motor skills precedes a Public Policy box on accidents, the leading cause of death in young children. The chapter concludes with an in-depth exploration of child maltreatment, including its prevalence, contributing factors, consequences for future development, treatment, and prevention.

NOTE: Answer guidelines for all Chapter 9 questions begin on page 138.

Guided Study

The text chapter should be studied one section at a time. Before you read, preview each section by skimming it, noting headings and boldface items. Then read the appropriate section objectives from the following outline. Keep these objectives in mind and, as you read the chapter section, search for the information that will enable you to meet each objective. Once you have finished a section, write out answers for its objectives.

Size and Shape (pp. 295–298)

1. Describe normal physical growth during the play years and account for variations in height and weight.

2. Describe changes in eating habits during the preschool years.

Brain Maturation (pp. 298–301)

3. Discuss brain maturation and its effect on development during the play years.

4. Identify the specialized functions of the two halves of the brain and discuss flexibility in brain specialization.

5. Discuss trends in the activity level of children during the play years and identify factors that contribute to variation.

Mastering Motor Skills (pp. 301–306)

6. Distinguish between gross and fine motor skills and discuss the development of each during the play years.

7. (Public Policy) Explain what is meant by "injury control" and identify several factors that contribute to variation in the risk of injury among children; describe some measures that have significantly reduced accidental death rates for children.

Child Maltreatment (pp. 307–325)

8. (text and A Closer Look) Identify the various categories of child maltreatment and discuss several factors that contribute to the relatively high incidence of maltreatment in the United States.

9. (text and Public Policy) Discuss the consequences of child maltreatment, and identify several approaches to its treatment or prevention in terms of the four categories of maltreating families.

Chapter Review

When you have finished reading the chapter, work through the material that follows to review it. Complete the sentences and answer the questions. As you proceed, evaluate your performance for each section by consulting the answers on page 138. Do not continue with the next section until you understand each answer. If you need to, review or reread the appropriate section in the textbook before continuing.

Size and Shape (pp. 295–298)

1. During the preschool years, from age
_____ to _____ ,
children add almost _____ in
height and gain about _____ in
weight per year. By age 6, the average child in a developed nation weighs about
_____ and measures
_____ in height.

2. The range of normal physical development is quite _____ (narrow/broad).

3. Of the many factors that influence height and weight, the most influential are the child's
_____ _____ ,

_____ _____ ,
and _____ .

4. The dramatic differences between physical development in developed and developing countries are largely due to differences in the average child's _____ .

Compare the size and shape of boys and girls during childhood.

5. In North America, children who are in the heaviest 10th percentile are more likely to be _____ (girls/boys). This is because they have a higher proportion of

_____ _____

when they have access to ample food.

6. During the preschool years, annual height and weight gain is much _____ (greater/less) than during infancy. This means that children need _____ (fewer/more) calories per pound during this period.

7. The most prevalent nutritional problem in developed countries during the preschool years is

_____ _____

_____ , the chief symptom of which is _____

_____ . This problem stems from a diet deficient in _____

_____ .

This problem is _____ (more/less) common among poor families than among nonpoor ones.

8. An additional problem for American children is that they, like most American adults, consume too much _____ .

Brain Maturation (pp. 298–301)

9. The most important physiological development during early childhood is the continued maturation of the _____

_____ .

By age 5, the brain has attained about _____ percent of its adult weight; in contrast, total body weight is about _____ percent of that of the average adult.

10. Part of the brain's increase in size during childhood is due to the continued proliferation of _____ networks, and to the ongoing process of _____ . This latter process is important to many of the child's developing abilities, including _____-

_____ _____ ,

as well as _____ and _____ , which enhance the ability to process more _____

_____ .

11. The band of nerve fibers that connects the two halves of the brain, called the _____

_____ , is not fully myelinated until about age _____ .

12. Each half of the brain controls the functioning of the _____ (same/opposite) side of the body. In 95 percent of right-handed adults and about 70 percent of left-handed adults, the _____ brain contains key areas associated with logical analysis and _____ development. The opposite half is the location of areas associated with various visual and _____ skills, including _____

_____ .

13. Because advanced motor skills and higher-order cognition require both halves of the brain and body to work together effectively, the myelination and maturation of the _____

_____ is an important factor for the development of these skills.

14. During infancy and early childhood _____ (fewer/more) areas of the brain are dedicated to specific functions than in adulthood. Consequently, when damage occurs to one area, the functions of that area usually _____ (can/cannot) be

taken over by some other area. During adulthood, this type of recovery of function is _____ (more/less) likely to occur.

15. The flexibility of brain functioning and specialization during infancy and childhood is evident in _____ . Even by age _____ , most children can learn to use their nonpreferred hand for certain skills. By the end of childhood, such learning is _____ (more/less) difficult to accomplish.

16. At birth, the two halves of the brain _____ (have not yet/have already) begun to specialize.

17. Some children are poor readers because they have difficulty connecting visual symbols with their sounds and meanings. This is because they _____ .

18. How much and how often a person moves his or her body defines _____ _____ . Brain maturation _____ (is/is not) linked to this characteristic.

19. In the first two or three years of life, activity level _____ (increases/decreases), and then _____ (increases/decreases) throughout childhood. This developmental trend _____ (is universal/varies from culture to culture).

20. The factors that contribute to individual variation in activity level are _____ and _____ factors.

State the relevance of the developmental trend in activity level during childhood.

Mastering Motor Skills (pp. 301–306)

21. Large body movements such as running, climbing, jumping, and throwing are called _____ _____

_____ . These skills, which improve dramatically during the preschool years, require _____ , as well as a certain level of _____ _____ . Most children learn these skills _____ (by themselves/from parents).

22. Skills that involve small body movements, such as pouring liquids and cutting food, are called _____ _____ _____ . Preschoolers have greater difficulty with these skills primarily because they have not developed the _____ control, patience, or _____ needed, in part because the _____ of the central nervous system is not complete.

23. Many developmentalists believe that _____ is a form of play that enhances the child's sense of accomplishment. This form of play also provides a testing ground for another important skill, _____ . Mastery of this skill is related to overall _____ growth.

24. (Public Policy) In all but the most disease-ridden or war-torn countries of the world, the leading cause of childhood death is _____ .

25. (Public Policy) The accident risk for a particular child depends on several factors, including _____ _____ _____ _____ .

26. (Public Policy) Injuries and accidental deaths are _____ (more/less) frequent among boys than girls.

27. (Public Policy) Among American ethnic groups, _____ have the lowest accident rate, while _____ and _____ have the highest.

28. (Public Policy) The clearest risk factor in accident rates is _____ _____ , with _____

(high/low)-status children more likely than other children to die an accidental death.

29. (Public Policy) Instead of "accident prevention," many experts speak of _____ _____ , an approach based on the belief that most accidents _____ (are/are not) preventable.

30. (Public Policy) The best approaches to safety education are those that _____ _____ .

31. (Public Policy) New and expectant parents are _____ (more/less) likely than experienced parents to heed safety suggestions, such as using an infant car seat.

32. (Public Policy) Safety laws that include penalties for noncompliance seem to be even _____ (less/more) effective than educational measures in reducing injury rates.

33. (Public Policy) The accidental death rate for American children between the ages of 1 and 5 has _____ (increased/ decreased) over the past twenty years.

Child Maltreatment (pp. 307–325)

34. The most common form of child maltreatment is a persistent pattern of psychological abuse and neglect that, over the years, affects the child's _____ .

35. Forty years ago, the concept of child maltreatment was mostly limited to gross _____ abuse, which was thought to be the outburst of a mentally disturbed person. Today, it is known that most perpetrators of maltreatment _____ (are/are not) mentally ill.

36. Intentional harm to, or avoidable endangerment of, someone under age 18 defines child _____ . Actions that are deliberately harmful to a child's well-being are classified as _____ . A failure to act appropriately to meet a child's basic needs is classified as _____ .

37. Child abuse and neglect can be divided into 5 subcategories:

   a. _____ _____
   b. _____ _____
   c. _____ _____
   d. _____ _____
   e. _____ _____

38. (A Closer Look) An important factor in understanding child maltreatment in context is _____ _____ .

39. (A Closer Look) The acceptability of physical punishment for children _____ (varies/does not vary) from culture to culture.

40. (A Closer Look) The seriousness of an act of maltreatment depends partly on a particular child's _____ , _____ , and _____ .

List four cultural values that protect children from abuse.

41. (Research Report) It is estimated that about one out of every _____ American children under age 18 has experienced some form of severe maltreatment within the past year.

42. (Research Report) Four methods are commonly used to estimate the prevalence of child maltreatment:

   a. _____
   b. _____
   c. _____
   d. _____

The method that leads to the highest reported abuse rate is _____ .

Give four reasons for the prevalence of child maltreatment in the United States.

List several characteristics of children who are more likely to be maltreated.

43. The daily routines of maltreating families typically are either very rigid in their
_____ and _____
_____ such that no one can
measure up, or they are so _____
and _____ that no one can be certain of what is expected.

44. Maltreatment is more likely if the family is
_____ and distrusting of others.
Also, maltreatment may result when there are
_____ _____
among other family members. In families where
there are more than _____
young children, maltreatment is more common.
Low-income single mothers are
_____ (no more/more) abusive
than their married counterparts.

45. It is estimated that only about _____
percent or fewer of maltreating parents are pathological.

List several personality traits of maltreating parents.

46. Maltreating parents are more likely to misread
their children's _____ , viewing
their cries of distress as displays of anger.

47. Drug dependency _____
(increases/does not increase) the likelihood of
child maltreatment.

48. The difficult nature of some abused and neglected children is often a _____
(result/cause) of their maltreatment.

Describe some of the deficits of children who have been maltreated.

49. The phenomenon of maltreated children growing
up to become abusive or neglectful parents themselves is called _____
_____ . A widely held misconception is that this phenomenon
_____ (is/is not) avoidable.

50. Approximately _____ percent
of abused children actually become abusive parents. This rate is about _____
times that of the general population.

51. Maltreating families who are experiencing
unusual problems, such as divorce or the loss of a
job, are classified as _____
_____ _____ .
It is relatively _____ (easy/difficult) to help these families overcome their dysfunctional ways.

52. Maltreating families that have many problems,
caused by their immediate situation, past history,
and temperament, that seriously impair their parenting abilities, are classified as
_____ . Treatment of these families is _____ (more/less) difficult.

53. Maltreating families who will probably never be
able to function adequately and independently of

the help of social workers, therapists, and others until the children are grown are classified as

_____ .

54. Maltreating families that are so impaired by deep emotional problems or serious cognitive deficiencies that they may never be able to meet the needs of their children are classified as

_____ . For children born into these families, long-term _____

_____ is the best solution.

55. A reason that foster care has been stereotyped as inadequate care is that, compared with children overall, foster children tend to do less well in

_____ and have fewer

_____ , and are more likely to

become _____ .

56. Those children who fare worst with foster care tend to be those whose earlier maltreatment left them with such low _____ , impaired

_____ _____ , and

_____ that they would encounter difficulty anywhere.

57. Many programs for preventing child maltreatment are targeted at families that are considered particularly vulnerable, such as those with

_____ parents, _____-

_____ families, or those with a child who needs special care.

58. (Public Policy) One promising strategy for preventing child maltreatment focuses on mothers, especially _____

_____ .

This strategy is known as _____

_____ .

59. (Public Policy) Another prevention strategy is called _____ _____

_____ , in which a caseworker meets with the family frequently and intensively.

Progress Test 1

Multiple-Choice Questions

Circle your answers to the following questions and check them with the answers on page 139. If your answer is incorrect, read the explanation for why it is incorrect and then consult the appropriate pages of the text (in parentheses following the correct answer).

1. During the preschool years, the most common nutritional problem in developed countries is:
   a. serious malnutrition.
   b. excessive intake of sweets.
   c. iron deficiency anemia.
   d. excessive caloric intake.

2. The brain center for speech is usually located in the:
   a. right brain.
   b. left brain.
   c. corpus callosum.
   d. space just below the right ear.

3. An indication of brain specialization in early childhood is:
   a. the clear emergence of hand preference.
   b. rapid acquisition of gross motor skills.
   c. increased bladder and bowel control.
   d. the incidence of growth problems.

4. After age 6, the child's overall activity level:
   a. increases until adolescence.
   b. continues to decline.
   c. begins to decline rapidly.
   d. remains the same until about age 10.

5. Like most Americans, children tend to have too much _____ in their diet.
   a. iron   c. sugar
   b. fat   d. b. and c.

6. Skills that involve large body movements, such as running and jumping, are called:
   a. activity-level skills.
   b. fine motor skills.
   c. gross motor skills.
   d. left-brain skills.

7. Differences in activity level among children have been linked to:
   a. age differences.
   b. genetic differences.
   c. cultural differences regarding "acceptable" levels of activity.
   d. all of the above.

8. (Public Policy) The leading cause of death in childhood is:
   a. accidents.   c. malnutrition.
   b. untreated diabetes. d. iron deficiency anemia.

9. (Public Policy) Among American ethnic groups, _____ have the lowest accident rate, while _____ have the highest.
   a. Asian-Americans; African-Americans and Native Americans
   b. Native Americans; African-Americans
   c. European-Americans; Native Americans
   d. Asian-Americans; European-Americans

10. Which of the following factors is *most* responsible for differences in height and weight between children in developed and developing countries?
    a. the child's genetic background
    b. health care
    c. nutrition
    d. age of weaning

11. In which of the following age periods is serious malnutrition *least* likely to occur?
    a. infancy
    b. early childhood
    c. adolescence
    d. Serious malnutrition is equally likely in each of these age groups.

12. (Public Policy) The relationship between accident rate and SES can be described as:
    a. a positive correlation.
    b. a negative correlation.
    c. curvilinear.
    d. no correlation.

13. Which of the following is true of the corpus callosum?
    a. It enables short-term memory.
    b. It connects the two halves of the brain.
    c. It must be fully myelinated before gross motor skills can be acquired.
    d. All of the above are correct.

14. Hand-eye coordination improves during the play years, in part because:
    a. the brain areas associated with this ability becomes more fully myelinated.
    b. the corpus callosum begins to function.
    c. fine motor skills have matured by age 2.
    d. gross motor skills have matured by age 2.

15. A factor that may contribute to a higher incidence of child maltreatment in the United States is the common acceptance of:
    a. violence.
    b. mental illness.
    c. the economic value of children.
    d. dual-career families.

True or False Items

Write *true* or *false* on the line in front of each statement.

_____ 1. Growth between ages 2 and 6 is more rapid than at any other period in the life span.

_____ 2. During childhood, the legs develop faster than any other part of the body.

_____ 3. For most right-handed people, the brain center for speech is located in the left brain.

_____ 4. The ability to sit quietly would be expected to improve between the ages of 4 and 7.

_____ 5. The high activity level of the American 2-year-old is directly related to the cultural values of a fast-paced society.

_____ 6. Fine motor skills are usually easier for preschoolers to master than are gross motor skills.

_____ 7. (Public Policy) Most serious childhood injuries truly are "accidents."

_____ 8. (Public Policy) Accidents cease to be a major cause of death after age 3.

_____ 9. Concern for and protection of the well-being of children varies markedly from culture to culture.

_____ 10. Most child maltreatment does not involve serious physical abuse.

Progress Test 2

Progress Test 2 should be completed during a final chapter review. Answer the following questions after you thoroughly understand the correct answers for the Chapter Review and Progress Test 1.

Multiple-Choice Questions

1. Each year from ages 2 to 6, the average child gains and grows, respectively:
   a. 2 pounds and 1 inch.
   b. 3 pounds and 2 inches.
   c. 4 1/2 pounds and 3 inches.
   d. 6 pounds and 6 inches.

2. In which area of the brain is the center for perceiving various types of spatial relations usually located?
   a. the right brain
   b. the left brain
   c. either the right or the left brain
   d. the corpus callosum

3. After brain specialization is complete, the brain is:
   a. less able to compensate for loss of function if a particular area is damaged.
   b. better able to compensate for loss of function if a particular area is damaged.
   c. more likely to be injured.
   d. less able to learn new intellectual tasks.

4. The text emphasizes that art provides an important opportunity for the child to develop the skill of:
   a. realistic representation of objects.
   b. reading.
   c. perspective.
   d. self-correction.

5. Which of the following best describes parents who abuse their children?
   a. They are older and unintelligent.
   b. They are older and reclusive.
   c. They are less adaptable and more immature.
   d. There are no predictable traits of abusive parents.

6. A form of maltreatment in which parents or caregivers do not provide adequate food, shelter, attention, or supervision is referred to as:
   a. physical abuse.
   b. physical neglect.
   c. endangering.
   d. psychological abuse.

7. Which of the following is *not* typical of nonabusive cultures?
   a. Children are valued, as a psychological joy and an economic asset.
   b. Child care is considered the responsibility of the community.
   c. Children are expected to be responsible for their actions.
   d. Violence in any context is disapproved of.

8. Most families involved in maltreatment of children are classified as _____ , which means that while they have the potential to provide adequate care, they have many problems that seriously impair their parenting abilities.
   a. vulnerable to crisis.
   b. restorable.
   c. supportable.
   d. inadequate.

9. Which of the following is an example of a fine motor skill?
   a. kicking a ball
   b. running
   c. drawing with a pencil
   d. jumping

10. In infancy and early childhood:
    a. myelination of the central nervous system is completed.
    b. fewer areas of the brain are dedicated to specific functions than in adulthood.
    c. the legs develop faster than any other part of the body.
    d. hand preference has not yet emerged in most children.

11. The child with the highest activity level is most likely a:
    a. 1-year-old.
    b. 2-year-old.
    c. 5-year-old who has an extremely active identical twin.
    d. 5-year-old who has mastered such fine motor skills as using a spoon.

12. Most gross motor skills can be learned by healthy children by about age:
    a. 2.   c. 5.
    b. 3.   d. 7.

13. Two of the most important factors that affect height during the play years are:
    a. socioeconomic status and health care.
    b. gender and health care.
    c. heredity and nutrition.
    d. heredity and activity level.

14. (Public Policy) Over the past two decades, the accidental death rate for American children between the ages of 1 and 5 has:
    a. decreased, largely as a result of new city, state, and federal safety laws.
    b. decreased, largely because parents are more knowledgeable about safety practices.
    c. increased.
    d. remained unchanged.

15. During the play years, because growth is slow, children's appetites seem _____ they were in the first two years of life.
    a. larger than
    b. smaller than
    c. about the same as
    d. erratic, sometimes smaller and sometimes larger than

Matching Items

Match each term or concept with its corresponding
description or definition.

Terms or Concepts

_____ 1. activity level
_____ 2. gross motor skills
_____ 3. fine motor skills
_____ 4. restorable
_____ 5. vulnerable to crisis
_____ 6. injury control
_____ 7. supportable
_____ 8. inadequate
_____ 9. abuse
_____ 10. neglect

Descriptions or Definitions

a. maltreating family for which foster care of children is the best solution
b. maltreating family that needs temporary help to
   resolve unusual problems
c. maltreating family that requires a variety of helping services until the children are grown
d. maltreating family that seems to have the potential to provide adequate care, but has serious
   problems that impair its parenting abilities
e. running and jumping
f. actions that are deliberately harmful to a child's
   well-being
g. painting a picture or tying shoelaces
h. failure to appropriately meet a child's basic needs
i. an approach emphasizing "accident" prevention
j. how much and how often a person moves his or
   her body

Thinking Critically About Chapter 9

Answer these questions the day before an exam as a
final check on your understanding of the chapter's
terms and concepts.

1. Two-year-old Bonnie fidgets more and has a
   higher activity level than her 1-year-old brother.
   Her parents:
   a. should not worry since preschoolers typically
      have a higher activity level than infants.
   b. were probably very active preschoolers them-
      selves.
   c. should be concerned since boys typically are
      more active than girls.
   d. are probably feeding Bonnie too many sugary
      foods.

2. Four-year-old Deon is tired all the time. On questioning Deon's mother, the pediatrician learns
   that Deon's diet is deficient in quality meats,
   whole grains, and dark-green vegetables. The
   doctor believes that Deon may be suffering from:
   a. malnutrition.
   b. protein anemia.
   c. iron deficiency anemia.
   d. an inherited fatigue disorder.

3. Following an automobile accident, Amira developed severe problems with her speech. Her doc-

tor believes that the accident injured the
_____ of her brain.
   a. left half   c. dendrite network
   b. right half   d. corpus callosum

4. Two-year-old Ali is quite clumsy, falls down frequently, and often bumps into stationary objects.
   Ali most likely:
   a. has a neuromuscular disorder.
   b. has an underdeveloped right brain.
   c. is suffering from iron deficiency anemia.
   d. is a normal 2-year-old whose gross motor
      skills will improve dramatically during the
      preschool years.

5. Climbing a fence is an example of a:
   a. fine motor skill.   c. circular reaction.
   b. gross motor skill.   d. launching event.

6. (Public Policy) To prevent accidental death in
   childhood, some experts urge forethought and
   planning for safety, and measures to limit the
   damage of such accidents as do occur. This
   approach is called:
   a. protective analysis.   c. injury control.
   b. safety education.   d. childproofing.

7. Recent research reveals that some children are
   poor readers because they have trouble connect-

ing visual symbols, phonetic sounds, and verbal meanings. This occurs because:

a. their sugary diets make concentration more difficult.

b. the brain areas involved in reading have not become localized in the left brain.

c. they use one side of the brain considerably more than the other.

d. their underdeveloped corpus callosums limit communication between the two brain halves.

8. Which of the following activities would probably be the most difficult for a 5-year-old child?

a. climbing a ladder

b. catching a ball

c. throwing a ball

d. pouring juice from a pitcher without spilling

9. When brain damage affects the language areas of the brain, children are likely to experience an impairment in overall cognition, whereas adults are likely to lose a specific set of verbal abilities. This demonstrates that:

a. compared to adults, children's cognitive abilities are more dependent on their mastery of language.

b. the incomplete myelination of the childhood brain makes it more vulnerable to global damage.

c. adults have more extensive dendrite networks that resist global brain damage.

d. the greater flexibility in functioning of children's brains enables the functions of a damaged area of the brain to be taken over by some other area.

10. Adults find it much harder to learn to perform a skill with their nonpreferred hand than young children do, because:

a. their fine motor skills are more developed.

b. they are more disciplined in practicing new skills.

c. patterns in the brain for such skills become localized and habitual.

d. of all the above reasons.

11. Claude, who is an abusive parent, is more likely than a nonabusive parent to:

a. view any crying as a sign the baby is frightened.

b. misinterpret a baby's cries as displays of anger.

c. leave a baby who continues to fuss after his or her needs have been met.

d. do all of the above.

12. A factor that would figure very little in the development of fine motor skills, such as drawing and writing, is:

a. strength.   c. judgment.

b. muscular control.   d. short, fat fingers.

13. Parents who were abused as children:

a. almost always abuse their children.

b. are more likely to neglect, but not necessarily abuse, their children.

c. are no more likely than anyone else to mistreat their children.

d. do none of the above.

14. Which aspect of brain development during the play years contributes most to enhancing communication among the brain's various specialized areas?

a. increasing brain weight

b. proliferation of dendrite networks

c. myelination

d. increasing specialization of brain areas

15. Three-year-old Kalil's parents are concerned because Kalil, who generally seems healthy, doesn't seem to have the hefty appetite or rate of growth he had as an infant. Should they be worried?

a. Yes, since both appetite and growth rate normally increase throughout the preschool years.

b. Yes, since appetite (but not necessarily growth rate) normally increases during the preschool years.

c. No, since growth rate (and hence caloric need) is less during the preschool years than during infancy.

d. There is not enough information to determine whether Kalil is developing normally.

Key Terms

Using your own words, write a brief definition or explanation of each of the following terms on a separate piece of paper.

1. corpus callosum

2. activity level

3. injury control

4. child maltreatment

5. abuse

6. neglect

7. intergenerational transmission

8. foster care

ANSWERS

CHAPTER REVIEW

1. 2; 6; 3 inches (7 centimeters); 4 $1/2$ pounds (2 kilograms); 46 pounds (21 kilograms); 46 inches (117 centimeters)

2. broad

3. genetic background; health care; nutrition

4. nutrition

Generally, boys are more muscular, have less body fat, and are slightly taller and heavier than girls throughout childhood.

5. girls; body fat

6. less; fewer

7. iron deficiency anemia; chronic fatigue; quality meats, whole grains, and dark-green vegetables; more

8. fat

9. central nervous system; 90; 30

10. dendrite; myelination; hand-eye coordination; language; reasoning; abstract thought

11. corpus callosum; 8

12. opposite; left; language; artistic; recognizing faces, responding to music, and perceiving various types of spatial relations

13. corpus callosum

14. fewer; can; less

15. handedness; 5; more

16. have already

17. use one half of the brain considerably more than the other

18. activity level; is

19. increases; decreases; is universal

20. heredity; environmental

It suggests that it is a mistake to expect young children to sit quietly for very long. It is also a mistake to think that all children have the same activity level.

21. gross motor skills; practice; brain maturation; by themselves

22. fine motor skills; muscular; judgment; myelination

23. drawing; self-correction; intellectual

24. accidents

25. the child's own judgment, motor skills, and activity level; caregivers' knowledge of, and attentiveness to, potential hazards, along with the quality of their supervision; and community standards and cultural norms that either foster or impede safety practices

26. more

27. Asian-Americans; African-Americans, Native Americans

28. socioeconomic status (SES); low

29. injury control; are

30. reach both parents and children in situations where motivation is high

31. more

32. more

33. decreased

34. self-concept, social interactions, and intellectual growth

35. physical; are not

36. maltreatment; abuse; neglect

37. physical abuse; psychological abuse; sexual abuse; physical neglect; psychological neglect

38. community standards

39. varies

40. age; temperament; abilities

   a. Children are highly valued.
   b. Child care is considered the responsibility of the community.
   c. Young children are not expected to be responsible for their actions.
   d. Violence is disapproved of.

41. 30

42. counting the number of complaints; interviewing trained professionals; interviewing caregivers; asking adults if they were abused or neglected; the latter

   a. Children are often considered to be a financial and personal burden.
   b. Social support for parents and young children is scarce.
   c. The emphasis on the child's ability to learn may cause parents to forget that children are immature and dependent on others.
   d. Violence is prevalent.

43. schedules; role demands; chaotic; disorganized

44. isolated; dysfunctional relationships; three; more

45. 10

Maltreating parents are less trusting, less self-assured, less adaptable, less mature, and tend to view the world as a hostile and difficult place.

46. communications

47. increases

Babies who are unwanted, who are born too early, who are the product of an unhappy love affair or a difficult pregnancy, who are the "wrong" sex, or who have physical problems can all become victims of maltreatment.

48. result

Compared to well-cared-for children, chronically abused and neglected children are slower to talk, underweight, less able to concentrate, and behind in school. They also tend to regard others as hostile and exploitative, and are less friendly, more aggressive, and more isolated than other children. As adolescents and adults, they often engage in self-destructive and/or other destructive behaviors.

49. intergenerational transmission; is not

50. 30; 6

51. vulnerable to crisis; easy

52. restorable; more

53. supportable

54. inadequate; foster care

55. school; friends; delinquents

56. self-esteem; social skills; anger

57. teenage; low-income

58. first-time mothers who are young and alone and whose child is newborn; home visitation

59. intensive family preservation

PROGRESS TEST 1

Multiple-Choice Questions

1. **c.** is the answer. (p. 297)

    a. Serious malnutrition is much more likely to occur in infancy or in adolescence than in early childhood.

    b. Although an important health problem, eating too much candy or other sweets is not as serious as iron deficiency anemia.

    d. Since growth is slower during the preschool years, children need fewer calories per pound during this period.

2. **b.** is the answer. (p. 299)

    a. & d. The right brain is the location of areas associated with various visual and artistic skills.

    c. The corpus callosum helps integrate the functioning of the two halves of the brain; it does not contain areas specialized for particular skills.

3. **a.** is the answer. (p. 300)

4. **b.** is the answer. (p. 301)

    a., c., & d. In the first two or three years of life, activity level increases in all children, and then decreases throughout childhood.

5. **d.** is the answer. (p. 298)

6. **c.** is the answer. (p. 302)

7. **d.** is the answer. (p. 301)

8. **a.** is the answer. (p. 304)

9. **a.** is the answer. (p. 304)

10. **c.** is the answer. (p. 296)

11. **b.** is the answer. (p. 297)

12. **b.** is the answer. Children with *lower* SES have *higher* accident rates. (p. 304)

13. **b.** is the answer. (p. 299)

    a. The corpus callosum is not directly involved in memory.

    c. Myelination of the central nervous system is important to the mastery of *fine* motor skills.

14. **a.** is the answer. (p. 299)

    b. The corpus callosum begins to function long before the play years.

    c. & d. Neither fine nor gross motor skills have fully matured by age 2.

15. **a.** is the answer. (p. 314)

True or False Items

1. F Growth actually slows down during the play years. (p. 297)

2. F During childhood, the brain develops faster than any other part of the body. (p. 298)

3. T (p. 299)

4. T (p. 301)

5. F In all cultures, activity level is highest in the first three years. (p. 301)

6. F Fine motor skills are more difficult for preschoolers to master than are gross motor skills. (p. 303)

7. F Most serious accidents involve someone's lack of forethought. (p. 304)

8. F Accidents continue to be the leading cause of death until age 15. (p. 304)

9. T (p. 310)

10. T (p. 307)

PROGRESS TEST 2

Multiple-Choice Questions

1. **c.** is the answer. (p. 296)

2. **a.** is the answer. (p. 299)

    b. The left half of the brain contains areas associated with logical analysis and language development.

c. In most people, including those who are left-handed, the right half of the brain processes spatial relations.

d. The corpus callosum does not contain areas for specific behaviors.

3. **a.** is the answer. (p. 299)

b. *Before* brain specialization is complete, the brain is better able to compensate for loss of function following an injury.

c. & d. The likelihood of injury and the ease of learning new tasks are no different once brain specialization is complete.

4. **d.** is the answer. (p. 303)

5. **c.** is the answer. (p. 316)

6. **b.** is the answer. (p. 309)

a. Physical abuse is deliberate, harsh injury to the body.

c. Endangerment was not discussed.

d. Psychological abuse is deliberate destruction of self-esteem.

7. **c.** is the answer. In nonabusive cultures, children are *not* expected to be responsible for their actions. (p. 311)

8. **b.** is the answer. (p. 320)

a. Families that are vulnerable to crisis are experiencing unusual problems, such as divorce or loss of a job, and need temporary help to resolve these problems.

c. Supportable families will probably never be able to function adequately and independently until the children are grown.

d. Inadequate families are so impaired by problems that long-term foster care of the children is usually the best solution.

9. **c.** is the answer. (p. 303)

a., b., & d. These are gross motor skills.

10. **b.** is the answer. (p. 299)

a. Myelination of some areas of the brain is not complete until adolescence.

c. During childhood, the brain develops faster than any other part of the body.

d. By age 5, more than 90 percent of all children are clearly right- or left-handed.

11. **b.** is the answer. (p. 301)

12. **c.** is the answer. (p. 302)

13. **c.** is the answer. (p. 296)

14. **a.** is the answer. (p. 306)

b. Although safety education is important, the decrease in accident rate is largely the result of new safety laws.

15. **b.** is the answer. (p. 297)

Matching Items

1. j (p. 301)   5. b (p. 319)   8. a (p. 321)
2. e (p. 302)   6. i (p. 304)   9. f (p. 308)
3. g (p. 303)   7. c (p. 321)   10. h (p. 308)
4. d (p. 320)

THINKING CRITICALLY ABOUT CHAPTER 9

1. **a.** is the answer. (p. 301)

2. **c.** is the answer. Chronic fatigue is the major symptom of iron deficiency anemia, which is caused by a diet deficient in quality meats, whole grains, and dark-green vegetables and is the most prevalent nutritional deficiency in developed countries. (p. 297)

3. **a.** is the answer. In most people, the left brain contains centers for language and speech. (p. 299)

4. **d.** is the answer. (p. 302)

5. **b.** is the answer. (p. 302)

a. Fine motor skills involve small body movements, such as the hand movements used in painting.

c. & d. These events were not discussed in this chapter.

6. **c.** is the answer. (p. 304)

7. **c.** is the answer. Analysis of the brain's electrical activity reveals that areas in both halves of the brain are involved in reading. (p. 300)

8. **d.** is the answer. (p. 303)

a., b., & c. Preschoolers find these gross motor skills easier to perform than fine motor skills such as that described in d.

9. **d.** is the answer. (p. 299)

10. **c.** is the answer. (p. 300)

11. **b.** is the answer. (p. 316)

12. **a.** is the answer. Strength is a more important factor in the development of gross motor skills. (p. 303)

13. **d.** is the answer. Approximately 30 percent of adults who were abused as children themselves become abusive parents. (p. 319)

14. **b.** is the answer. (p. 298)

15. **c.** is the answer. (p. 297)

KEY TERMS

1. The **corpus callosum** is the band of nerve fibers that connects the two halves of the brain. (p. 299)

2. **Activity level** refers to how much and how often a person moves his or her body. (p. 301)

3. **Injury control** is an approach to accident prevention that focuses on broad-based safety education, stricter enforcement of safety regulations, "childproofing" homes, and related measures. (pp. 304–305)

4. **Child maltreatment** is intentional harm to, or avoidable endangerment of, anyone under age 18. (p. 308)

5. **Abuse** refers to actions that are deliberately harmful to a child's well-being. (p. 308)

6. **Neglect** refers to failure to appropriately meet a child's basic needs. (p. 308)

7. **Intergenerational transmission** is the phenomenon in which some maltreated children grow up to become abusive or neglectful parents themselves. (p. 318)

8. **Foster care** is a legally sanctioned, publicly supported arrangement in which children are removed from their original parents and given to another adult to nurture. (p. 321)

CHAPTER

10

The Play Years: Cognitive Development

Chapter Overview

In countless everyday instances, as well as in the findings of numerous research studies, preschoolers reveal themselves to be remarkably thoughtful, insightful, and perceptive thinkers whose grasp of the causes of everyday events, memory of the past, and mastery of language is sometimes astonishing. Chapter 10 begins by describing how preschoolers think, including their competence in understanding number concepts, solving problems, storing and retrieving memories, and theorizing about the world.

The chapter focuses next on Piaget's theory of preschool cognition. According to this view, the most significant cognitive gain in early childhood is the emergence of symbolic thought, which opens up a whole new world of pretend play. Despite this development, preschoolers' thought is still preoperational: children between the ages of 2 and 7 are unable to perform many logical operations and are limited by irreversible, centered, and static thinking.

Much of the recent research on preschool thinking is inspired by the writings of Lev Vygotsky, a contemporary of Piaget's who saw learning as a social activity more than as a matter of individual discovery. Vygotsky's views regarding the "zone of proximal development" and the relationship between language and thought are the focus of the following section, which leads into a description of language development during the play years. Although preschoolers demonstrate rapid improvement in vocabulary, grammar, and pragmatics, they have difficulty with abstractions, metaphorical speech, and certain rules of grammar.

The chapter concludes with a discussion of preschool education, including a description of "quality" preschool programs and an evaluation of their lifelong impact on children.

NOTE: Answer guidelines for all Chapter 10 questions begin on page 154.

Guided Study

The text chapter should be studied one section at a time. Before you read, preview each section by skimming it, noting headings and boldface items. Then read the appropriate section objectives from the following outline. Keep these objectives in mind and, as you read the chapter section, search for the information that will enable you to meet each objective. Once you have finished a section, write out answers for its objectives.

How Preschoolers Think (pp. 331–347)

1. Discuss preschoolers' understanding of number concepts.

2. Describe problem-solving ability during the play years.

3. Discuss young children's memory abilities and limitations, noting the role of meaning in their ability to recall events.

4. (Public Policy) Discuss the reliability of children's eyewitness testimony.

5. Explain the typical preschool child's theory of mind.

Piaget's Theory of Preoperational Thought
(pp. 347–351)

6. Explain how the cognitive potential of young children is expanded by symbolic thought.

7. Describe and discuss the major characteristics of preoperational thought, according to Piaget.

8. Discuss recent research on conservation and explain why findings have led to qualification or revision of Piaget's description of cognition during the play years.

Vygotsky's Theory of Children as Apprentices
(pp. 351–354)

9. Contrast Vygotsky's views on cognitive development with those of Piaget.

10. Explain the significance of scaffolding and the zone of proximal development in promoting cognitive growth.

Language Development (pp. 354–363)

11. Outline the sequence by which vocabulary and grammar develop during the play years and discuss limitations in the preschool child's language abilities.

12. Describe pragmatic developments and difficulties associated with language acquisition during the play years.

13. Discuss possible explanations for differences in the language development of children during the play years.

14. Discuss the relationship between language and thought in the child's cognitive development during the play years.

Preschool Education (pp. 363–367)

15. Identify the characteristics of a high-quality preschool program and discuss the long-term benefits of preschool education for the child and family.

Chapter Review

When you have finished reading the chapter, work through the material that follows to review it. Complete the sentences and answer the questions. As you proceed, evaluate your performance for each section by consulting the answers on page 154. Do not continue with the next section until you understand each answer. If you need to, review or reread the appropriate section in the textbook before continuing.

1. For many years, researchers maintained that young children's thinking abilities were sorely limited by _____ .

How Preschoolers Think (pp. 331–347)

2. Although preschoolers generally cannot count well, they often possess sophisticated number concepts, such as the _____-_____-_____ principle, the _____-_____ principle, and the _____ principle.

3. At about age _____ , children begin to use numbers symbolically.

4. The preschoolers' developing understanding of number is influenced by _____ development and the emerging ability to use _____ to conceptualize number, as well as the flowering of the child's innate _____ . The overall importance the child's _____ places on number competence also plays an important role.

5. The structure of the _____ in a particular culture may promote preschool number competence. One hypothesis for the superiority of _____ _____ children over _____ and _____ children in math is that languages such as _____ , _____ , and _____ are more logical in their labeling of numbers.

6. A final factor in promoting number competence is the _____ and _____ provided by parents, other adults, and older children. By providing _____ _____ in shared number activities, parents help to stimulate the growth of numerical understanding.

7. Although they have limited formal problem-solving ability, preschoolers are quite skilled in solving _____ problems.

8. Efficient problem solving requires many skills, including the ability to use systematic _____-_____-_____ to plan a sequence of _____ toward the problem's solution, and to notice, evaluate, and correct one's _____ .

9. Preschoolers are notorious for having a poor _____ . This shortcoming is due to the fact that they have not yet acquired

skills for deliberate _____ and efficient _____ of information.

10. One way in which preschoolers are quite capable of storing in mind a representation of past events is by retaining _____ of familiar, recurrent past experiences. These devices reflect an awareness of the correct _____ and causal _____ of remembered events.

11. Another reason young children sometimes appear deficient in their memory ability is that they often do not _____ _____ .

12. Parents vary in how they guide young children's recall of past events. Parents described as _____ tend to ask specific questions, and then repeat the child's answer. Parents described as _____ also supplement the child's recall with additional information about an experience. One study found that 2-year-olds whose mothers used an _____ style remembered more and could better answer questions about a prior experience.

13. A recent study compared preschoolers' memory of Disneyworld in response to a series of focused questions (a procedure called _____ _____) with that in response to a series of open-ended questions (a procedure called _____ _____). The results showed that age _____ (did/did not) significantly affect the amount of information the children remembered. Older children recalled more information under the _____ _____ condition than did the younger children, and their recollections tended to contain more _____ . In general, all the children provided much more information during the _____ _____ procedure.

14. The "Disneyworld" study strongly suggests that

even very young preschoolers can recall a great deal of information when they are given appropriate _____ .

15. (Public Policy) Until recently, young children in most countries _____ (were/ were not) prohibited from providing courtroom testimony.

16. (Public Policy) Recent research has found that, particularly for young children, the _____ context in which children considered to be eyewitnesses are questioned is an important factor in the accuracy of their memory. Specifically, the _____ of the child to the questioner, the _____ of the questioner, and the _____ of the interview have a substantial influence on his or her testimony.

17. (Public Policy) Research demonstrates that the great majority of children when questioned as eyewitnesses _____ (resist/fail to resist) suggestive questioning.

18. By the early preschool years, children elaborate their categorical system to include not only the physical attributes of objects and people but also their distinctive _____ , _____ , and _____ . In essence, the _____ understanding of the infant becomes the _____ understanding of the preschooler.

19. Many developmentalists believe that preschoolers act like _____ _____ as they conceptualize the world; that is, they gradually construct coherent, internally consistent _____ about "how things work."

20. As a result of their experiences with others, young children acquire a _____ _____ _____ that reflects their developing concepts about human mental processes.

21. Developmentalists have discovered that, in contrast with the traditional view of preschoolers as

_____ , young children are quite aware of _____ psychological perspectives.

Describe the young child's theory of mind at age 4.

22. An important advance in preschoolers' theory of mind occurs when they realize that mental states may not accurately reflect _____ .

23. The growth of children's theory of mind has broader implications for _____ understanding. For example, children become far more capable of _____ and _____ the thoughts, emotions, and intentions of others.

Piaget's Theory of Preoperational Thought
(pp. 347–351)

24. Piaget _____ (overestimated/ underestimated) certain aspects of children's cognitive abilities, and underestimated the power of the _____ _____ in influencing cognitive development.

25. To Piaget, the most important feature of cognitive development during the preschool years is that children become able to think _____ ; that is, they can think by forming

_____ _____

of things and events that they are not immediately experiencing.

26. Each new level of the child's symbolic play is accompanied by more elaborate use of _____ , itself an indication of symbolic thought.

27. According to Piaget, between the ages of 2 and 7, thinking is characterized by _____ thought. One example of this operational inability is the preschooler's failure to grasp the logical idea of _____—that reversing a process will restore the original conditions from which the process began.

28. The preschooler's tendency to think about one aspect of a situation at a time is called

_____ .

29. Preschoolers' understanding of the world tends to be _____ (static/ dynamic), which means that they tend to think in terms of _____ (absolutes/a range of possibilities). As a result, they have trouble understanding transitions and

_____ .

30. The idea that amount is unaffected by changes in shape or placement is called _____ . In the case of _____

_____ _____ ,

preschoolers who are shown pairs of checkers in two even rows and who then observe one row being spaced out will say that the spaced-out row has more checkers.

31. Piaget believed that it is _____ (possible/impossible) for preoperational children to grasp the ides of conservation and other logical reasoning processes.

32. It is now clear that with special training and more playful test conditions, children as young as age _____ can succeed at some tests of conservation.

Vygotsky's Theory of Children as Apprentices
(pp. 351–354)

33. The idea that children are "apprentices in thinking" emphasizes that children's intellectual growth is stimulated by their _____ in _____ experiences of their environment.

34. Much of this new research and perspective on the young child's emerging cognition is inspired by the Russian psychologist _____ .

35. Unlike Piaget, this psychologist believed that cognitive growth is a _____ _____ more than a matter of individual discovery.

36. Vygotsky suggested that each individual is surrounded by a _____ _____ _____ , which represents the cognitive distance between the child's actual level of development and his or her developmental potential.

37. How and when new skills are developed depends, in part, on the willingness of tutors to _____ the child's participation in learning encounters.

Identify several steps that contribute to effective scaffolding.

38. Vygotsky believed that language is essential to the advancement of thinking in two crucial ways. The first is through the internal dialogue in which a person talks to himself or herself, called _____ _____ . In preschoolers, this dialogue is likely to be _____ (expressed silently/ uttered aloud).

39. According to Vygotsky, another way language advances thinking is as the _____ of social interaction.

Language Development (pp. 354–363)

40. During the preschool years a dramatic increase in language occurs, with _____ , _____ , and _____ of language showing rapid improvement.

41. Through the process called _____ _____ preschoolers often learn words after only one hearing.

42. The learning of new words _____ (does/does not) follow a predictable sequence according to parts of speech.

43. In building vocabulary, preschoolers generally learn _____ more readily than _____ , which are learned more readily than _____ .

44. Generally, children are able to map new words more quickly when words, categories, and concepts are _____ (explained in a formal lesson/used in the course of normal speech).

45. Abstract nouns, metaphors, and analogies are _____ (more/no more) difficult for preschoolers to understand.

46. Because preschool children tend to think in absolute terms, they have difficulty with words that express _____ , as well as words expressing relativities of _____ and _____ .

47. The structures, techniques, and rules that a language uses to communicate meaning define its _____ . By age _____ , children typically demonstrate extensive understanding of this aspect of language.

48. Following the ideas of _____ , some developmentalists believe that humans possess an innate _____ _____ _____ that facilitates their mastery of grammar. In support of this view, researchers point out that certain areas of the _____ are specifically responsible for language. The part known as _____ _____ is associated with language production, while _____ _____ is associated with language comprehension.

49. Chomsky's theory is also supported by evidence

that children worldwide proceed through similar
_____ and _____
in language acquisition.

50. This view also suggests that during the period
from _____ _____
through _____ _____
humans are primed to acquire language. This
helps explain why learning a _____
_____ is easier for children
than for adults.

51. One way in which preschoolers acquire grammar
is by "_____
_____," in which, over time,
they use their knowledge of words to deduce sentence structure.

52. Preschoolers' tendency to apply rules of grammar
when they should not is called
_____ .

Give several examples of overregularization.

53. During the preschool years children are able to
comprehend _____ (more/less)
complex grammar and vocabulary than they can
produce.

54. The practical communication between one person
and another in terms of the overall context in
which language is used is called
_____ . The major emphasis of
the study of this phenomenon concerns how children learn to adjust vocabulary and grammar to
the _____ _____ .

Give an example of the pragmatic development in
language use that occurs during the play years.

55. By the time children enter kindergarten, differences among them in language skills are
_____ (small/great).

56. In terms of the relationship between language
proficiency and gender, socioeconomic class,
birth order, and multiple births,
_____ (boys/girls),
_____ (middle-income/lower-
income) children, _____ (first-
borns/later-borns), and _____
(single-borns/twins/triplets) tend to be more
proficient.

Discuss how researchers explain these differences in
language development.

57. As Piaget noted, language ability builds on the
_____ and _____
accomplishments of infancy and toddlerhood.
This explains why the first words that children
learn refer to _____ .

58. As Vygotsky and other sociocultural theorists
note, language also provides a basis for the
_____ _____
that contribute to cognitive growth. Vygotsky
believed that initially language and thought
_____ (may develop indepen-
dently/are mutually influential), but that after
age _____ , they
_____ (develop independent-
ly/are mutually influential).

Preschool Education (pp. 363–367)

59. In most industrialized nations and many of the
developing ones, most children
_____ (do/do not) enter some

form of school during the "preschool" years. Two related reasons for this historical change are a shift in _____ and _____ _____ .

List several characteristics of a high-quality preschool program.

60. In the 1960s, _____ _____ was inaugurated to give low-income children some form of compensatory education during the preschool years. Longitudinal research found that, as they made their way through elementary school, graduates of this program scored _____ (higher/no higher) on achievement tests and had more positive school report cards than their non-Headstart counterparts.

61. Most developmentalists believe that disadvantaged children will benefit from early education beginning at age _____ or even sooner.

Progress Test 1

Multiple-Choice Questions

Circle your answers to the following questions and check them with the answers on page 155. If your answer is incorrect, read the explanation for why it is incorrect and then consult the appropriate pages of the text (in parentheses following the correct answer).

1. Piaget believed that children are in the preoperational stage from ages:
   a. 6 months to 1 year.   c. 2 to 7 years.
   b. 1 to 3 years.   d. 5 to 11 years.

2. According to Piaget, the most significant cognitive gain of preschoolers is the emergence of:
   a. egocentrism.   c. logical thought.
   b. symbolic thought.   d. pragmatic language.

3. (Public Policy) When questioned as eyewitnesses to an event, most young children:
   a. are unable to resist suggestive questioning.
   b. are able to resist suggestive questioning.

c. provide very inaccurate answers.
d. have reliable short-term memories, but very unreliable long-term memories.

4. The results of recent experiments on preschoolers' understanding of number concepts demonstrate that:
   a. supportive guidance provided by adults can stimulate the growth of number understanding in preschoolers.
   b. preschoolers have little or no number understanding.
   c. early developmentalists overestimated preschoolers' understanding of number.
   d. preschoolers are able to master the cardinal principle but not the one-to-one principle.

5. Preschoolers' poor performance on memory tests is primarily due to:
   a. their tendency to rely too extensively on scripts.
   b. their lack of efficient storage and retrieval skills.
   c. the incomplete myelination of cortical neurons.
   d. their short attention span.

6. The vocabulary of preschool children consists primarily of:
   a. metaphors.
   b. self-created words.
   c. abstract nouns.
   d. verbs and concrete nouns.

7. Preschoolers sometimes apply the rules of grammar even when they shouldn't. This tendency is called:
   a. overregularization.   c. pragmatics.
   b. literal language.   d. single-mindedness.

8. The Russian psychologist Vygotsky emphasized that:
   a. language helps children form ideas.
   b. children form concepts first, then find words to express them.
   c. language and other cognitive developments are unrelated at this stage.
   d. preschoolers learn language only for egocentric purposes.

9. Private speech can be described as:
   a. a way of formulating ideas to oneself.
   b. fantasy.
   c. an early learning difficulty.
   d. the beginnings of deception.

10. The child who has not yet grasped the principle of conservation is likely to:
   a. insist that a tall, narrow glass contains more liquid than a short, wide glass, even though both glasses actually contain the same amount.
   b. be incapable of egocentric thought.
   c. be unable to think animistically.
   d. do all of the above.

11. In later life, Headstart graduates showed:
   a. better report cards, but more behavioral problems.
   b. significantly higher IQ scores.
   c. higher scores on achievement tests and higher aspirations.
   d. alienation from their original neighborhoods and families.

12. The best preschool programs are generally those that provide the greatest amount of:
   a. behavioral control.
   b. adult-child conversation.
   c. instruction in conservation and other logical principles.
   d. demonstration of toys by professionals.

13. Compared to their rate of speech development, children's understanding of language develops:
   a. more slowly.
   b. at about the same pace.
   c. more rapidly.
   d. more rapidly in certain cultures than others.

14. Recent experiments have demonstrated that preschoolers *can* succeed at tests of conservation when:
   a. they are allowed to work cooperatively with other children.
   b. the test is presented as a competition.
   c. the children are informed that they are being observed by their parents.
   d. the test is presented in a simple, gamelike way.

15. Through the process called fast mapping, children:
   a. immediately assimilate new words by connecting them through their assumed meaning to categories of words they have already mastered.
   b. acquire the concept of conservation at an earlier age than Piaget believed.
   c. are able to move beyond egocentric thinking.
   d. become skilled in the pragmatics of language.

True or False Items

Write *true* or *false* on the line in front of each statement.

_____ 1. Piaget's description of cognitive development in early childhood has been universally rejected by contemporary developmentalists.

_____ 2. In conservation problems, many preschoolers are unable to understand the transformation because they focus exclusively on appearances.

_____ 3. Young children's thinking abilities are sorely limited by their egocentrism.

_____ 4. Whether or not a preschooler demonstrates conservation in an experiment depends in part on the conditions of the experiment.

_____ 5. One reason Japanese children are superior to American children in math may be that the Japanese language is more logical in its labeling of numbers.

_____ 6. Piaget believed that preschoolers' acquisition of language makes possible their cognitive development.

_____ 7. With the beginning of symbolic thought, most preschoolers can understand abstract words.

_____ 8. A preschooler who says "You comed up and hurted me" is demonstrating a lack of understanding of English grammar.

_____ 9. Successful preschool programs generally have a low teacher-to-child ratio and are expensive.

_____ 10. Children who have many older siblings are usually the most advanced in language use.

Progress Test 2

Progress Test 2 should be completed during a final chapter review. Answer the following questions after you thoroughly understand the correct answers for the Chapter Review and Progress Test 1.

Multiple-Choice Questions

1. (Public Policy) When children are required to give eyewitness testimony:
   a. they should be interviewed by a neutral professional.
   b. they should be interviewed by a family member.

c. the atmosphere of the interview should be fairly intense, to impress upon them the importance of their answers.
d. both b. and c. should be done.

2. In one study, 3- and 4-year-old children were interviewed after visiting Disneyworld. The results demonstrated that:
a. age did not significantly affect the amount of information children remembered.
b. the children provided much more information in response to open-ended questions than they did to directive questions.
c. older children recalled less information spontaneously than did younger children.
d. all of the above were true.

3. A preschooler who focuses his or her attention on only one feature of a situation is demonstrating a characteristic of preoperational thought called:
a. centration.
b. pragmatic thinking.
c. reversibility.
d. egocentrism.

4. One characteristic of preoperational thought is:
a. the ability to categorize objects.
b. the ability to count in multiples of 5.
c. the inability to perform logical operations.
d. difficulty adjusting to changes in routine.

5. The zone of proximal development represents the:
a. cognitive distance between a child's actual level of development and his or her potential development.
b. influence of a child's peers on cognitive development.
c. explosive period of language development during the play years.
d. normal variations in children's language proficiency.

6. According to Vygotsky, language advances thinking through private speech, and by:
a. helping children to privately review what they know.
b. helping children explain events to themselves.
c. serving as a mediator of the social interaction that is a vital part of learning.
d. facilitating the process of fast mapping.

7. Reversibility refers to the:
a. awareness that other people view the world from a different perspective than one's own.
b. ability to think about more than one idea at a time.
c. understanding that changing the arrangement of a group of objects doesn't change their number.
d. understanding that undoing a process will restore the original conditions.

8. According to Piaget:
a. it is impossible for preoperational children to grasp the concept of conservation, no matter how carefully it is explained.
b. preschoolers fail to solve conservation problems because they center their attention on the transformation that has occurred and ignore the changed appearances of the objects.
c. with special training, even preoperational children are able to grasp some aspects of conservation.
d. preschoolers fail to solve conservation problems because they have no theory of mind.

9. Pretend play with dolls and other toys is an indication of the preschooler's:
a. egocentric thinking.
b. centration.
c. symbolic thinking.
d. understanding of reversibility.

10. Which theorist would be most likely to agree with the statement, "Learning is a social activity more than it is a matter of individual discovery"?
a. Piaget   c. both a. and b.
b. Vygotsky   d. neither a. nor b.

11. Children first demonstrate some understanding of grammar:
a. as soon as the first words are produced.
b. once they begin to use language for pragmatic purposes.
c. through the process called fast mapping.
d. in their earliest two-word sentences.

12. Pragmatics refers to the:
a. structures, techniques, and rules that a language uses to communicate meaning.
b. practical communication between one person and another in terms of the overall context in which language is used.
c. way children sometimes use language to deceive other people.
d. cognitive limitations of preschool children.

13. During the preschool years, the learning of new words tends to follow this sequence:
a. verbs, followed by nouns, then adjectives, adverbs, and interrogatives.

b. nouns, followed by verbs, then adjectives, adverbs, and interrogatives.

c. adjectives, followed by verbs, then nouns, adverbs, and interrogatives.

d. interrogatives, followed by nouns, then verbs, adjectives, and adverbs.

14. In general, which of the following is a good predictor of a child's language competence?

a. the strength of parental attachment

b. the amount of time the child spends with his or her parents

c. the extent to which parents provide specific comments in response to their child's utterances

d. All of the above are good predictors.

15. Regarding the value of preschool education, most developmentalists believe that:

a. most disadvantaged children will not benefit from an early preschool education.

b. most disadvantaged children will benefit from an early preschool education.

c. because of sleeper effects, the early benefits of preschool education are likely to disappear by grade 3.

d. the relatively small benefits of antipoverty measures such as Headstart do not justify their huge costs.

Matching Items

Match each term or concept with its corresponding description or definition.

Terms or Concepts

_____ 1. script
_____ 2. scaffold
_____ 3. theory of mind
_____ 4. zone of proximal development
_____ 5. overregularization
_____ 6. fast mapping
_____ 7. reversibility
_____ 8. centration
_____ 9. conservation
_____ 10. pragmatics
_____ 11. guided participation

Descriptions or Definitions

a. the idea that amount is unaffected by changes in shape or placement

b. memory-facilitating outline of past experiences

c. the cognitive distance between a child's actual and potential levels of development

d. the tendency to think about one aspect of a situation at a time

e. the process whereby the child learns through social interaction with a "tutor"

f. our understanding of mental processes in ourselves and others

g. the process by which words are learned after only one hearing

h. an inappropriate application of rules of grammar

i. the study of the practical use of language

j. a logical operation through which original conditions are restored by the undoing of some process

k. sensitively structure a child's participation in learning encounters

Thinking Critically About Chapter 10

Answer these questions the day before an exam as a final check on your understanding of the chapter's terms and concepts.

1. An experimenter first shows a child two rows of checkers that each have the same number of checkers. Then, with the child watching, the experimenter elongates one row and asks the child if each of the two rows still has an equal number of checkers. This experiment tests the child's understanding of:

a. reversibility.

b. conservation of matter.

c. conservation of number.

d. centration.

2. A preschooler believes that a "party" is the one and only attribute of a birthday. She says that

Daddy doesn't have a birthday because he never has a party. This thinking demonstrates the tendency Piaget called:

a. egocentrism.
b. centration.
c. conservation of events.
d. mental representation.

3. A child who understands that 3 + 4 = 7 means that 7 − 4 = 3 has had to master the concept of:

a. reversibility.
b. number.
c. conservation.
d. egocentrism.

4. A 4-year-old tells the teacher that a clown should not be allowed to visit the class because "Pat is 'fraid of clowns." The 4-year-old thus shows that he can anticipate how another will feel. This is evidence of the beginnings of:

a. egocentrism.
b. deception.
c. a theory of mind.
d. conservation.

5. Evidence that 6-year-old Hilary has mastered the pragmatics of language can best be seen in the fact that:

a. her conversation consists largely of concrete nouns.
b. she engages in overregularization.
c. she speaks "baby talk" to toys and pets but not to adults.
d. she believes people understand communications when they do not.

6. A nursery school teacher is given the job of selecting holiday entertainment for a group of preschool children. If the teacher agrees with the ideas of Vygotsky, she is most likely to select:

a. a simple TV show that every child can understand.
b. a hands-on experience that requires little adult supervision.
c. brief, action-oriented play activities that the children and teachers will perform together.
d. holiday puzzles for children to work on individually.

7. Based on averages, the child who is most likely to score highest on a test that measures language production is a:

a. middle-class girl who has no siblings.
b. later-born middle-class boy.
c. boy from a large, economically disadvantaged family.
d. boy who is one of twins.

8. That a child produces sentences that follow such rules of word order as "the initiator of an action precedes the verb, the receiver of an action follows it" demonstrates a knowledge of:

a. grammar.
b. semantics.
c. pragmatics.
d. phrase structure.

9. The 2-year-old child who says, "We goed to the store," is making a grammatical:

a. centration.
b. overregularization.
c. extension.
d. pragmatic.

10. An experimenter who makes two balls of clay of equal amount, then rolls one into a long skinny rope and asks the child if the amounts are still the same, is testing the child's understanding of:

a. conservation.
b. reversibility.
c. perspective-taking.
d. centration.

11. Dr. Jones, who believes that children's language growth greatly contributes to their cognitive growth, evidently is a proponent of the ideas of:

a. Piaget.
b. Chomsky.
c. Flavell.
d. Vygotsky.

12. Broca's area is to language _____ as Wernicke's area is to language _____.

a. comprehension; production
b. production; comprehension
c. grammar; vocabulary
d. vocabulary; grammar

13. In describing the limited logical reasoning of preschoolers, a *contemporary* developmentalist is *least* likely to emphasize:

a. irreversibility.
b. centration.
c. egocentrism.
d. its static nature.

14. A preschooler fails to put together a difficult puzzle on her own, so her mother encourages her to try again, this time guiding her by asking questions such as, "For this space do we need a big piece or a little piece?" With Mom's help, the child successfully completes the puzzle. Lev Vygotsky would attribute the child's success to:

a. additional practice with the puzzle pieces.
b. imitation of her mother's behavior.
c. the social interaction with her mother that restructured the task to make its solution more attainable.
d. modeling and reinforcement.

15. Mark is answering an essay question that asks him to "discuss the positions of major developmental theorists regarding the relationship between language and cognitive development." To help organize his answer, Mark jots down a reminder that _____ believed that language is essential to the advancement of thinking,

while _____ believed that cognitive development precedes language.

a. Piaget; Vygotsky   c. Piaget; Skinner
b. Vygotsky; Piaget   d. Vygotsky; Skinner

Key Terms

Using your own words, write a brief definition or explanation of each of the following terms on a separate piece of paper.

1. scripts
2. theory of mind
3. symbolic thinking
4. preoperational thought
5. guided participation
6. zone of proximal development
7. scaffold
8. private speech
9. fast mapping
10. overregularization
11. pragmatics
12. Project Headstart

ANSWERS

CHAPTER REVIEW

1. egocentrism
2. one-to-one; stable-order; cardinal
3. 2
4. brain; language; culture
5. language; East Asian; European; American; Japanese; Korean; Chinese
6. structure; support; guided participation
7. practical
8. trial-and-error; steps; errors
9. memory; storage; retrieval
10. scripts; sequence; flow
11. attend to the features of an event that an older person would consider pertinent
12. repetitors; elaborators; elaborative
13. directed recall; spontaneous recall; did not; spontaneous recall; elaboration; directive recall
14. cues (or prompts)
15. were
16. social; relationship; age; atmosphere
17. resist
18. characteristics; actions; origins; categorical; conceptual
19. scientific theorists; theories
20. theory of mind
21. egocentric; divergent (or different)

By age 3 or 4, young children distinguish between mental phenomena and the physical events to which they refer; they appreciate how mental states arise from experiences in the world; they understand that mental phenomena are subjective; they recognize that people have differing opinions and preferences; and they realize that beliefs and desires can form the basis for human action.

22. reality
23. social; anticipating; affecting
24. underestimated; social context
25. symbolically; mental representations
26. language
27. preoperational; reversibility
28. centration
29. static; absolutes; transformations
30. conservation; conservation of number
31. impossible
32. 4
33. guided participation; social
34. Lev Vygotsky
35. social activity
36. zone of proximal development
37. scaffold

Parents who scaffold effectively recruit and maintain the child's interest, simplify tasks, anticipate and indicate errors in performance, control frustration, and model correct solutions.

38. private speech; uttered aloud
39. mediator
40. vocabulary; grammar; practical use
41. fast mapping
42. does
43. nouns; verbs; adjectives, adverbs, conjunctions, or interrogatives
44. used in the course of normal speech
45. more
46. comparisons; time; place

47. grammar; 3

48. Noam Chomsky; language acquisition device; brain; Broca's area; Wernicke's area

49. stages; sequences

50. late infancy; late childhood; second language

51. semantic bootstrapping

52. overregularization

Many preschoolers overapply the rule of adding "s" to form the plural, as well as the rule of adding "ed" to form the past tense. Thus, preschoolers are likely to say "foots" and "snows," and that someone "broked" a toy.

53. more

54. pragmatics; social situation

Preschoolers may use high-pitched "baby talk" when talking with dolls, and deeper, more formal "adult" speech when giving commands to dogs and cats.

55. great

56. girls; middle-income; first-borns; single-borns

Researchers generally explain these differences as being due to familial and cultural variations in the language children hear. In general, mothers talk more to daughters than to sons; middle-class parents provide their children with more elaborate explanations, more responsive comments, and fewer commands than lower-income parents do; and parents talk more to first-borns and single-borns than to later-borns or twins.

57. sensorimotor; conceptual; objects they can manipulate

58. shared experiences; develop independently; 2; are mutually influential

59. do; maternal work patterns; research on child development showing that young children can learn at least as well outside the home as within it

High-quality preschools are characterized by (a) a low teacher-child ratio, (b) a staff with training and credentials in early childhood education, (c) a curriculum geared toward cognitive development rather than behavioral control, and (d) an organization of space that facilitates creative and constructive play.

60. Project Headstart; higher

61. 3

PROGRESS TEST 1

Multiple-Choice Questions

1. **c.** is the answer. (p. 348)

2. **b.** is the answer. (p. 347)

    a. Egocentrism, or thinking that is self-centered, is generally not viewed as a cognitive gain.

    c. Because thinking is "preoperational," logical thought is not characteristic of children at this time.

    d. An emerging understanding of pragmatics does appear during the preschool years; however, this gain is not as significant as symbolic thought. Also, Piaget did not deal with language.

3. **b.** is the answer. (pp. 342–343)

    c. & d. Research demonstrates that even young children often have very accurate *long*-term recall.

4. **a.** is the answer. (p. 333)

    b. & c. Recent experiments demonstrate that preschoolers have *greater* number awareness than was once believed.

    d. Preschoolers are able to recognize *both* of these principles.

5. **b.** is the answer. (pp. 335–336)

    a. Scripts tend to *improve* preschoolers' memory.

    c. & d. Although true, neither of these is the *primary* reason for preschoolers' poor memory.

6. **d.** is the answer. (pp. 355, 357)

    a. & c. Preschoolers generally have great difficulty understanding, and therefore using, metaphors and abstract nouns.

    b. Other than the grammatical errors of overregularization, the text does not indicate that preschoolers use a significant number of self-created words.

7. **a.** is the answer. (p. 360)

    b. & d. These are not terms identified in the text.

    c. Pragmatics is the practical communication between one person and another in terms of the overall context in which language is used.

8. **a.** is the answer. (p. 354)

    b. This expresses the views of Piaget.

    c. Because he believed that language facilitates thinking, Vygotsky obviously felt that language and other cognitive developments are intimately related.

    d. Vygotsky did not hold this view.

9. **a.** is the answer. (p. 354)

10. **a.** is the answer. (p. 349)

    b., c., & d. Failure to conserve is the result of thinking that is centered on appearances. Egocentrism and animism are also examples of centered thinking.

11. **c.** is the answer. (p. 366)

    b. Although there was a slight early IQ advantage

in Headstart graduates, the difference disappeared by grade 3.

a. & d. There was no indication of greater behavioral problems or alienation in Headstart graduates.

12. b. is the answer. (p. 363)

13. c. is the answer. (p. 360)

14. d. is the answer. (p. 351)

15. a. is the answer. (p. 355)

True or False Items

1. F   More recent research has found that children may understand conservation earlier than Piaget thought, given a more gamelike presentation. His theory has not been rejected overall, however. (pp. 350–351)

2. T (p. 349)

3. F   Recent studies demonstrate that preschoolers are not nearly as egocentric as was once believed. (p. 330)

4. T (pp. 350–351)

5. T (p. 333)

6. F   Piaget believed that language ability builds on the sensorimotor and conceptual accomplishments of infancy and toddlerhood. (p. 362)

7. F   Preschoolers have difficulty understanding abstract words; their vocabulary consists mainly of concrete nouns and verbs. (p. 357)

8. F   In adding "ed" to form a past tense, the child has indicated an understanding of the grammatical rule for making past tenses in English, even though the construction in these two cases is incorrect. (p. 360)

9. T (p. 363)

10. F   Presumably because of opportunities for contact with adults, first-born children tend to be more advanced in language learning than are children who have many older siblings. (p. 362)

PROGRESS TEST 2

Multiple-Choice Questions

1. a. is the answer. (p. 343)

2. a. is the answer. (p. 339)

b. The children provided more information in response to *directive* questions.

c. Older children recalled *more* information spontaneously than did younger children.

3. a. is the answer. (p. 349)

b. Pragmatics is the practical use of language; a child who demonstrated pragmatic thinking would vary his or her language to fit the social situation.

c. Reversibility is the concept that reversing an operation, such as addition, will restore the original conditions.

d. This term is used to refer to the preschool child's belief that people think as he or she does.

4. c. is the answer. This is why the stage is called pre*operational*. (p. 348)

5. a. is the answer. (p. 353)

6. c. is the answer. (p. 354)

a. & b. These are both advantages of private speech.

d. Fast mapping is the process by which new words are acquired, often after only one hearing.

7. d. is the answer. (p. 348)

a. This describes perspective-taking.

b. This is the opposite of centration.

c. This defines conservation of number.

8. a. is the answer. (pp. 349–350)

b. According to Piaget, preschoolers fail to solve conservation problems because they focus on the *appearance* of objects and ignore the transformation that has occurred.

d. Piaget did not relate conservation to a theory of mind.

9. c. is the answer. (p. 347)

a. Egocentric thinking is self-centered thinking.

b. Centration refers to focusing awareness on only one aspect of a situation.

d. Reversibility is the understanding that reversing an operation will restore the original conditions.

10. b. is the answer. (p. 352)

a. Piaget believed that learning is a matter of individual discovery.

11. d. is the answer. Preschoolers almost always put subject before verb in their two-word sentences. (pp. 357–358)

12. b. is the answer. (p. 361)

a. This defines grammar.

13. b. is the answer. (p. 355)

14. c. is the answer. (p. 362)

a. & b. The strength and amount of attachment are *not* good predictors of language development.

15. b. is the answer. (p. 366)

Matching Items

1. b (p. 336)   5. h (p. 360)   9. a (p. 349)
2. k (p. 353)   6. g (p. 355)   10. i (p. 361)
3. f (p. 344)   7. j (p. 348)   11. e (p. 352)
4. c (p. 353)   8. d (p. 349)

THINKING CRITICALLY ABOUT CHAPTER 10

1. **c.** is the answer. (p. 349)

    a. A test of reversibility would ask a child to perform an operation, such as adding 4 to 3, and then reverse the process (subtract 3 from 7) to determine whether the child understood that the original condition (the number 4) was restored.

    b. A test of conservation of matter would transform the appearance of an object, such as a ball of clay, to determine whether the child understood that the object remained the same.

    d. A test of centration would involve the child's ability to see various aspects of a situation.

2. **b.** is the answer. (p. 349)

    a. Egocentrism is thinking that is self-centered.

    c. This is not a concept in Piaget's theory.

    d. Mental representation is an example of symbolic thought.

3. **a.** is the answer. (p. 348)

4. **c.** is the answer. (pp. 344–345)

    a. Egocentrism is self-centered thinking.

    b. Although deception provides evidence of a theory of mind, the child in this example is not deceiving anyone.

    d. Conservation is the understanding that the amount of a substance is unchanged by changes in its shape or placement.

5. **c.** is the answer. (p. 361)

6. **c.** is the answer. In Vygotsky's view, learning is a social activity more than a matter of individual discovery. Thus, social interaction that provides motivation and focuses attention facilitates learning. (p. 352)

    a., b., & d. These situations either provide no opportunity for social interaction (b. & d.), or do not challenge the children (a.).

7. **a.** is the answer. (p. 362)

    b., c., & d. On measures of language production, girls are more proficient than boys; middle-class children, more proficient than lower-income children; first-borns, more proficient than later-borns; and single-born children more proficient than twins.

8. **a.** is the answer. (p. 357)

    b. & d. The text does not discuss these aspects of language.

    c. Pragmatics refers to the practical use of language in varying social contexts.

9. **b.** is the answer. (p. 360)

10. **a.** is the answer. (p. 349)

11. **d.** is the answer. (p. 354)

    a. Piaget believed that cognitive growth precedes language development.

    b. & c. These theorists' views regarding the relationship between language and thought were not discussed.

12. **b.** is the answer. (p. 358)

13. **c.** is the answer. (pp. 344–345)

14. **c.** is the answer. (p. 353)

15. **b.** is the answer. (pp. 362–363)

    c. & d. The text does not present Skinner's views on the relationship of language to thinking.

KEY TERMS

1. **Scripts** are mental outlines of familiar, recurrent past experiences used to facilitate the storage and retrieval of memories. (p. 336)

2. All adults have what psychologists call a **theory of mind**, an understanding of mental processes, that is, of one's own or another's emotions, perceptions, and thoughts. (p. 344)

3. **Symbolic thinking** is the ability to use words, objects, and actions as symbols in one's thinking and communication. (p. 347)

4. According to Piaget, thinking between ages 2 and 7 is characterized by **preoperational thought**, meaning that children cannot yet perform logical operations; that is, they cannot use ideas and symbols. (p. 348)

    Memory aid: Operations are mental transformations involving the manipulation of ideas and symbols. *Pre*operational children, who lack the ability to perform transformations, are "before" this developmental milestone.

5. According to Vygotsky, intellectual growth in young children is stimulated and directed by their **guided participation** in learning experiences. As guides, parents, teachers, and older children provide challenges for learning, offer assistance, and support the child's interest and motivation. (p. 352)

6. According to Vygotsky, for each individual there is a **zone of proximal development**, which represents the cognitive distance between the child's actual level of development and his or her potential development. (p. 353)

7. Tutors who **scaffold** sensitively structure children's learning experiences by simplifying tasks, maintaining children's interest, and modeling correct performance, among other things. (p. 353)

8. **Private speech** is the internal dialogue in which a person talks to himself or herself. Preschoolers' private speech, which often is uttered aloud, helps them think, review what they know, and decide what to do. (p. 354)

9. **Fast mapping** is the process by which children rapidly learn new words by quickly connecting them to words and categories that are already understood. (p. 355)

10. **Overregularization** occurs when children apply rules of grammar when they should not. It is seen in English, for example, when children add "s" to form the plural even in irregular cases that form the plural in a different way. (p. 360)

11. **Pragmatics** refers to the practical features of communication between one person and another in terms of the overall context in which language is used. (p. 361)

12. **Project Headstart** is a preschool program that was initiated in the 1960s in response to a perceived need to improve the educational future for low-income children. (p. 365)

11

The Play Years: Psychosocial Development

Chapter Overview

Chapter 11 explores the ways in which preschoolers begin to relate to others in an ever-widening social environment. The chapter begins where social understanding begins, with the emergence of the sense of self. With their increasing self-awareness, preschoolers become more concerned with how others evaluate them. They also experience a wider range of emotions and become increasingly adept at coping with them.

The next section describes the increasing complexity of children's interactions with others, paying special attention to the parent-child relationship in terms of different styles of parenting and how factors such as a child's personality and behavior, the quality of the marital relationship, and the cultural, ethnic, and community context influence the effectiveness of parenting. The section concludes with a description of sibling and peer relationships, noting the role of play in the preschoolers' social development.

A final section explores the development of gender roles and stereotypes and the alternative viewpoint of androgyny.

NOTE: Answer guidelines for all Chapter 11 questions begin on page 170.

Guided Study

The text chapter should be studied one section at a time. Before you read, preview each section by skimming it, noting headings and boldface items. Then read the appropriate section objectives from the following outline. Keep these objectives in mind and, as you read the chapter section, search for the information that will enable you to meet each objective. Once you have finished a section, write out answers for its objectives.

The Self and the Social World (pp. 372–376)

1. Discuss the relationship between the child's developing sense of self and social awareness, as well as the importance of positive self-evaluation during this period.

2. Explain how preschoolers' emotions, and understanding of emotions, change during the play years.

Relationships and Psychosocial Growth (pp. 376–396)

3. Compare and contrast six patterns of parenting and their effect on children.

4. Discuss the impact of the child, the quality of the marital relationship, and the cultural, ethnic, and community contexts on the effectiveness of the various styles of parenting.

5. (Research Report) Identify and discuss three concerns of critics of preschool TV viewing.

6. Describe sibling relationships during the play years and discuss the impact of being an only-child, noting the developmental significance of each situation.

7. Describe the nature of peer relationships during the play years.

8. Discuss the nature and significance of four varieties of play during the play years.

Gender Roles and Stereotypes (pp. 396–405)

9. (text and A Closer Look) Describe the preschooler's developing understanding of gender roles and identify and discuss the nature and possible explanation of gender distinctions in play patterns.

10. Summarize the three theories of gender-role development during the play years, noting important contributions of each.

11. Discuss the concept of androgyny, emphasizing what research has shown regarding the impact of traditional and androgynous gender roles on children and their parents.

Chapter Review

When you have finished reading the chapter, work through the material that follows to review it. Complete the sentences and answer the questions. As you proceed, evaluate your performance for each section by consulting the answers on page 170. Do not continue with the next section until you understand each answer. If you need to, review or reread the appropriate section in the textbook before continuing.

The Self and the Social World (pp. 372–376)

1. The play years are filled with examples of the child's emerging _____. During these years, children begin to perceive themselves not just in terms of their _____

attributes or abilities, but also in terms of their _____ and _____ .

2. The growth of preschoolers' self-awareness is especially apparent in their _____ with others.

Give several examples of the limited nature of preschoolers' understanding of themselves and others.

3. Psychologists emphasize the importance of children developing a positive _____ . Preschoolers typically form impressions of themselves that are quite _____ . One manifestation of this tendency is that preschoolers regularly _____ (overestimate/underestimate) their own abilities. Most preschoolers think of themselves as competent _____ (in all/only in certain) areas.

4. As they grow, preschoolers become _____ (more/less) concerned with how others evaluate their behavior. As Erikson theorized, between toddlerhood and age 3, children are in the stage of _____ _____ , when their feelings about themselves depend largely on the _____ .

5. Later in the play years, the basis for a child's self-evaluation becomes the _____ adult reaction to the child's success or failure. At this point, according to Erikson, children are in the stage of _____ .

6. During the play years, children's emotions become aroused by a _____ (narrower/broader) range of circumstances. Preschoolers also become _____ (more/less) empathic and increasingly adept at _____ with their own emotions.

7. Preschoolers' increasing ability to deal with their emotions comes about partly as a result of their greater understanding of the _____ and _____ of emotion in other people. By age _____ chil-

dren begin to perceive emotion as arising from internal as well as situational causes.

8. One study found that preschoolers who had had more frequent family _____ about emotions were better at making judgments about the emotions of others.

Relationships and Psychosocial Growth
(pp. 376–396)

9. Although the preschooler's social world is considerably broader than that of the infant, psychosocial growth remains fundamentally guided by close relationships shared with

_____ , _____ , and, secondarily, with _____ .

10. The _____ perspective focuses on the awareness that preschoolers' psychosocial growth emerges mainly from experience in close _____ , which are

_____ .

11. The most significant influence on early psychosocial growth is the style of _____ that characterizes a child's family life.

12. There _____ (is/is not) a single best style of parenting that will guarantee a child's successful upbringing. The seminal research on parenting styles, which was conducted by _____ , found that parents varied in their _____ toward offspring, in their efforts to _____ , in how well they _____ , and in their

_____ _____ .

13. Parents who adopt the _____ style demand unquestioning obedience from their children. In this style of parenting, nurturance tends to be _____ (low/high), maturity demands are _____ (low/high), and parent-child communication tends to be _____ (low/high).

14. Parents who adopt the _____ style make few demands on their children and are lax in discipline. Such parents _____ (are/are not very) nurturant, communicate _____ (well/poorly), and make _____ (few/extensive) maturity demands.

15. Parents who adopt the _____
    style democratically set limits and enforce rules.
    Such parents make _____
    (high/low) maturity demands, communicate
    _____ (well/poorly), and
    _____ (are/are not) nurturant.

16. Follow-up studies indicate that children raised by
    _____ parents are likely to be
    obedient but unhappy; those raised by
    _____ parents are likely to lack
    self-control; and those raised by
    _____ parents are more likely
    to be successful, happy with themselves, and gen-
    erous with others.

17. Permissive parents who are warm and responsive
    are called _____-
    _____ . Permissive parents who
    are cold and unengaged are called
    _____-_____ .
    Parents who take somewhat old-fashioned male
    and female roles are labeled _____
    parents.

18. Longitudinal research suggests that traditional
    and democratic-indulgent parenting is less suc-
    cessful than _____ parenting
    but more successful than _____
    or _____-_____
    parenting.

Identify several influences that contribute to shaping
parenting style.

19. Over time, the most effective type of discipline is
    that associated with the _____
    parenting style. This is so not because of the
    absence of _____ , but rather
    because of these parents' use of
    _____

for enlisting the child's cooperation. These parents also provide a positive _____
for expected behavior.

20. An important factor in the effect of parenting
    style on children is the particular child's
    _____ . The impact of parenting
    styles also varies according to the child's
    _____ .

21. (Research Report) Today, most parents believe
    that spanking _____ (is/is not)
    acceptable at times.

22. (Research Report) A recent study investigated the
    relationship between spanking and aggressive
    behavior in the child. Observers scored kinder-
    garteners for three types of aggression:
    _____ , used to obtain or retain
    a toy or other object; _____ ,
    used in angry retaliation against an intentional or
    accidental act committed by a peer; and
    _____ , used in an unprovoked
    attack on a peer. Compared to children who were
    not spanked, those children who were spanked
    were more likely to engage in _____
    aggression.

23. When a marriage is satisfying and mutually sup-
    portive, both parents tend to be _____
    or _____ . When a marriage is
    unhappy, parents tend to be
    _____ . When a marriage is
    falling apart, parents are particularly likely to be
    _____-_____ .
    Marital _____ can also indirect-
    ly affect parenting practices.

24. The efficacy of various parenting styles is also
    influenced by the _____ ,
    _____ , and _____
    context, especially its stability and safety.

25. The relationship perspective highlights the fact
    that the family consists of _____
    _____ that influence each other
    and are, in turn, affected by the beliefs, supports,
    and demands of the broader _____
    _____ in which the family lives.

26. For many children, the first lesson in social inter-
    action comes from their _____ .

For a younger child, an older sibling provides an important _____ and source of learning; for an older child, a younger sibling is an important benchmark of _____ _____ .

27. Siblings _____ (are/are not) more likely to quarrel with each other than they are with nonrelated children. Siblings are _____ (more/less) likely to have positive interactions with each other, and tend to show more _____ and _____ than with unrelated children. According to the text, _____ may be the best description of the typical sibling relationship.

28. The home experiences of each child in a given family are _____ (quite different from/much the same as) those of the other children. Earlier researchers incorrectly assumed that differences in personality and intelligence among children in a given family must be _____ .

Briefly discuss environmental factors that account for the experiential differences between siblings.

29. In most ways, only-children fare _____ (as well as or better/worse) than children with siblings. Only-children are particularly likely to benefit _____ , becoming more _____ and more _____ . A potential problem for only-children is in their development of _____ skills.

30. Today, most young children spend a large portion of their time in a _____ program or _____- _____ .

Such programs generally _____ (do/do not) benefit children's psychosocial development. One consideration is that children in group day care may become more _____ than children without extensive day-care experience.

31. In their peer encounters, preschoolers learn to distinguish among other children in terms of their _____ , _____ , and _____ . This may explain why friendships are remarkably _____ during the play years.

32. An important factor in children's "likability" is the nature of the _____-_____ relationship. Popular children tend to have the most _____ of these relationships.

33. Most developmentalists believe that _____ is the work of early childhood.

34. Play is important not only as a means of social interaction but also because of the opportunities it provides for _____ , _____ , and _____ .

35. Play that captures the pleasures of using the senses and motor abilities is called _____ play.

36. In _____ play, children practice new physical and intellectual skills.

37. The type of physical play that mimics aggression is called _____-_____-_____ play. A distinctive feature of this form of play, which _____ (occurs only in some cultures/is universal), is the positive facial expression that characterizes the _____ _____ .

38. Gender and cultural differences _____ (are/are not) evident in rough-and-tumble play.

39. In _____ play, children act out various roles and themes in stories of their own creation.

Gender Roles and Stereotypes (pp. 396–405)

40. By age _____ , children prefer to play with gender-typed toys. By age _____ , children can consistently apply gender labels and have a rudimentary understanding of the permanence of their own gender. By age _____ , most children express stereotypic ideas of each sex. Such stereotyping _____ (does/does not) occur in children whose parents provide nontraditional gender role models.

41. A number of developmentalists believe that gender differences are primarily displayed in the context of children's _____ .

42. All-boy groups tend to be _____ , and more often oriented toward _____ and _____ . Girls' groups are _____ , with members using _____ and _____ to consolidate friendship.

43. (A Closer Look) A basic question for psychologists is whether differences between males and females are _____ differences— arising from the differences between male and female chromosomes and hormones—or _____ differences—arising from the special customs, values, and expectations that a particular culture attaches to one sex or the other.

(A Closer Look) Describe several gender distinctions in play patterns.

44. (A Closer Look) Because the physical differences between the sexes during the preschool years are _____ (slight/many), gender differences in play patterns may largely be due to _____ pressure for children to conform. Indeed, cross-cultural research finds that, in all societies, children are encouraged to engage in activities that teach them their culture's traditional _____ _____ .

45. Freud called the period from age 3 to 7 the _____ _____ . According to this view, boys in this stage develop sexual feelings about their _____ and become jealous of their _____ . Freud called this phenomenon the _____ _____ .

46. In Freud's theory, preschool boys resolve their guilty feelings defensively through _____ with their father.

47. According to Freud, during the phallic stage little girls may experience the _____ _____ , in which they want to get rid of their mother and become intimate with their father. Alternatively, they may become jealous of boys because they have a penis; this emotion Freud called _____ _____ .

48. According to learning theory, preschool children develop gender-role ideas by being _____ for behaviors deemed appropriate for their sex, and _____ for behaviors deemed inappropriate. This type of learning may be strongest within peer groups that _____ (are/are not) segregated by sex.

49. Social-learning theorists maintain that children learn gender-appropriate behavior by _____ . Most adults are _____ (more/less) gender-stereotyped in their behaviors and _____ when their children are young than they are earlier or later in life.

50. In explaining gender identity and gender-role development, cognitive theorists focus on children's understanding of _____ , as well as _____-_____ differences.

51. According to _____-_____ theory, preschoolers' understanding of gender is limited by their belief that gender differences depend on differences in appearance or behavior rather than on biology. It is not until after age _____ that children realize that they are permanently male or female; this realization is called _____ _____ . Research has shown that children _____ (do/do not) behave in gender-typed ways before they have acquired this realization.

52. According to _____-_____ theory, children organize their ideas about people in terms of gender-based categories and evaluations that are acquired very early in life.

53. As developmentalists use the term, _____ refers to a person's having a balance of what are commonly regarded as "male" and "female" psychological characteristics.

54. Androgynous people are generally _____ (more/less) flexible in their gender roles. Early studies showed that androgynous individuals are generally more _____ and have higher _____ than people who follow traditional gender-role behavior.

55. Recent research indicates that traditional gender-role values may _____ (foster/diminish) self-esteem at certain other stages of life.

Progress Test 1

Multiple-Choice Questions

Circle your answers to the following questions and check them with the answers on page 171. If your answer is incorrect, read the explanation for why it is incorrect and then consult the appropriate pages of the text (in parentheses following the correct answer).

1. Preschool children have a clear (but not necessarily accurate) concept of self. Typically, the preschooler believes that she or he:
   a. owns all objects in sight.
   b. is great at almost everything.
   c. is much less competent than peers and older children.
   d. is more powerful than her or his parents.

2. According to Freud, the third stage of psychosexual development, during which the penis is the focus of psychological concern and pleasure, is the:
   a. oral stage.   c. phallic stage.
   b. anal stage.   d. latency period.

3. Because it helps children rehearse social roles, work out fears and fantasies, and learn cooperation, an important form of social play is:
   a. sociodramatic play.
   b. mastery play.
   c. rough-and-tumble play.
   d. sensorimotor play.

4. The three *basic* patterns of parenting described by Diana Baumrind are:
   a. hostile, loving, and harsh.
   b. authoritarian, permissive, and authoritative.
   c. positive, negative, and punishing.
   d. democratic-indulgent, rejecting-neglecting, and traditional.

5. Authoritative parents are receptive and loving, but they also normally:
   a. set limits and enforce rules.
   b. have difficulty communicating.
   c. withhold praise and affection.
   d. encourage aggressive behavior.

6. Preschoolers who tend to be hostile and aggressive are frequently found to have parents who:
   a. are rejecting.
   b. are authoritative.
   c. are neglectful.
   d. overuse physical punishment.

7. The most significant influence on a child's early psychosocial growth is:
   a. family size.
   b. parenting style.

c. whether the child is placed in a day-care program.

d. sibling relationships.

8. During the play years, a child's self-concept is defined largely by his or her:
   a. expanding range of skills and competencies.
   b. physical appearance.
   c. gender.
   d. relationship with family members.

9. Learning theorists emphasize the importance of _____ in the development of the preschool child.
   a. identification
   b. praise and blame
   c. initiative
   d. a theory of mind

10. Children apply gender labels, and have definite ideas about how boys and girls behave, as early as age:
    a. 3.
    b. 4.
    c. 5.
    d. 7.

11. A concept that counters the idea that masculinity and femininity are exact opposites is called:
    a. modeling.
    b. Freudianism.
    c. gender stereotyping.
    d. androgyny.

12. According to some psychologists, children very early label themselves as male and female, try to conform to these schemas, and use them in interpreting others' behavior. This is the _____ theory.
    a. cognitive-developmental
    b. gender-constancy
    c. gender-schema
    d. social-learning

13. Compared to children with siblings, only-children are likely to:
    a. be less verbal.
    b. fare as well or better in most ways.
    c. have greater competence in social skills.
    d. be less creative.

14. Which of the following was *not* identified as a factor that influences the effectiveness of various parenting styles?
    a. the child's behavior
    b. the marital relationship
    c. the stability and safety of the larger society
    d. the parents' ages

15. Research on parenting styles reveals that traditional parents:
    a. tend to be less child-centered than authoritarian parents.
    b. often do a better job of child-rearing than authoritarian parents.
    c. often raise children with lower self-esteem than authoritarian parents.
    d. often raise children with more behavior problems than authoritarian parents.

True or False Items

Write *true* or *false* on the line in front of each statement.

_____ 1. According to Baumrind, only authoritarian parents make maturity demands on their children.

_____ 2. Children of authoritative parents tend to be successful, happy with themselves, and generous with others.

_____ 3. Because of sibling rivalry, a typical child is more likely to help a friend than to come to the aid of a brother or sister.

_____ 4. Day-care programs generally benefit a child's psychosocial development.

_____ 5. The most popular children tend to have the most permissive parents.

_____ 6. Children from feminist or nontraditional homes seldom have stereotypic ideas about feminine and masculine roles.

_____ 7. The concept of androgyny suggests that people can be flexible in their gender roles, incorporating the best qualities of men and women.

_____ 8. By age 3, most children have definite ideas about what constitutes typical masculine and feminine behavior.

_____ 9. Identification was defined by Freud as a defense mechanism in which people identify with others who may be stronger and more powerful than they.

_____ 10. Sociodramatic play is free-wheeling, creative, and fluid.

Progress Test 2

Progress Test 2 should be completed during a final chapter review. Answer the following questions after you thoroughly understand the correct answers for the Chapter Review and Progress Test 1.

Multiple-Choice Questions

1. Children of permissive parents are *most* likely to lack:

a. social skills.
b. self-control.
c. initiative and guilt.
d. care and concern.

2. Children learn reciprocity, nurturance, and cooperation most readily from their interaction with:
   a. their mothers.
   b. their fathers.
   c. friends.
   d. others of the same sex.

3. (Research Report) Critics of television-viewing for preschoolers are concerned about the effect of commercials, the violent content of many programs, and:
   a. television censorship by parents.
   b. the time that TV robs from valuable social and creative activities.
   c. the deprivation of deaf children.
   d. the realistic nature of cartoons.

4. Which of the following is *not* a factor affecting parenting style?
   a. the child's behavior
   b. the number of children
   c. the parents' relationship
   d. the influence of the cultural, ethnic, and community context

5. Research has shown that whether androgynous values enhance self-esteem depends on the:
   a. consistency of parenting.
   b. stage of life.
   c. influence of peers on the individual.
   d. socioeconomic status of the parents.

6. According to Freud, a young boy's jealousy of his father's relationship with his mother, and the guilt feelings produced by this jealousy, are part of the:
   a. Electra complex.
   b. Oedipus complex.
   c. phallic complex.
   d. penis envy complex.

7. The style of parenting in which the parents make few demands on children, the discipline is lax, and the parents are warm and responsive is:
   a. authoritarian.
   b. authoritative.
   c. democratic-indulgent.
   d. rejecting-neglecting.

8. Compared to their interactions with friends, siblings tend to:
   a. have more positive interactions.
   b. quarrel more often.

c. be more cooperative.
d. do all of the above.

9. In a satisfying and mutually supportive marriage, both parents tend to adopt the _____ style of parenting; when they are unhappy with each other, they are more likely to be _____ .
   a. permissive; authoritative
   b. permissive; authoritarian
   c. authoritarian; authoritative
   d. authoritative; authoritarian

10. At an early age, children begin to organize their knowledge about people into the categories of "male" and "female"; that is, they acquire:
    a. gender constancy.
    b. gender identity.
    c. gender schemas.
    d. androgyny.

11. Compared to children with siblings, only-children are more likely to be:
    a. overly dependent upon their parents.
    b. very spoiled.
    c. both a. and b.
    d. neither a. nor b.

12. The preschooler's readiness to learn new tasks and play activities reflects his or her:
    a. emerging competency and self-awareness.
    b. theory of mind.
    c. relationship with parents.
    d. growing identification with others.

13. The awareness that psychosocial growth emerges mainly from a child's interactions with parents, siblings, and peers has led to the emergence of:
    a. the sociocultural perspective.
    b. the relationship perspective.
    c. psychosociology.
    d. social-learning theory.

14. In which style of parenting is the parents' word law and misbehavior strictly punished?
    a. permissive
    b. authoritative
    c. authoritarian
    d. rejecting-neglecting

15. Erikson notes that preschoolers eagerly begin many new activities but are vulnerable to criticism and feelings of failure; they experience the crisis of:
    a. identity versus role confusion.
    b. initiative versus guilt.
    c. basic trust versus mistrust.
    d. efficacy versus helplessness.

Matching Items

Match each term or concept with its corresponding description or definition.

Terms or Concepts

_____ 1. mastery play
_____ 2. sensorimotor play
_____ 3. sociodramatic play
_____ 4. rejecting-neglecting
_____ 5. democratic-indulgent
_____ 6. Electra complex
_____ 7. Oedipus complex
_____ 8. authoritative
_____ 9. authoritarian
_____ 10. identification

Descriptions or Definitions

a. uninvolved parents are permissive and ignorant of their child's activities
b. Freudian theory that every daughter secretly wishes to replace her mother
c. parenting style associated with high maturity demands and low parent-child communication
d. a child delights in feeling the textures of various foods
e. Freudian theory that every son secretly wishes to replace his father
f. parenting style associated with high maturity demands and high parent-child communication
g. a child develops her hand skills by dressing her dolls
h. parents are warm and responsive, yet quite permissive
i. two children act out roles in a story of their own creation
j. a defense mechanism through which children cope with their feelings of guilt during the phallic stage

Thinking Critically About Chapter 11

Answer these questions the day before an exam as a final check on your understanding of the chapter's terms and concepts.

1. The 4-year-old's realization that she is permanently female, will never grow a penis, and will not grow up to be a "Daddy" is called:
   a. identification.
   b. gender constancy.
   c. penis envy.
   d. the Electra complex.

2. A little girl who says she wants her mother to go on vacation so that she can marry her father is voicing a fantasy consistent with the _____ described by Freud.
   a. Oedipus complex
   b. Electra complex
   c. theory of mind
   d. crisis of initiative versus guilt

3. According to Erikson, before the preschool years children are incapable of feeling guilt because:
   a. guilt depends on a sense of self, which is not sufficiently established in preschoolers.

b. they do not yet understand that gender is constant.
   c. this emotion is unlikely to have been reinforced at such an early age.
   d. guilt is associated with the resolution of the Oedipus complex, which occurs later in life.

4. Parents who are strict and aloof are *most* likely to make their children:
   a. cooperative and trusting.
   b. obedient but unhappy.
   c. violent.
   d. withdrawn and anxious.

5. The belief that children's love, jealousy, and fear of their parents are primary determinants in the learning of gender roles would find its strongest adherents among _____ theorists.
   a. psychoanalytic   c. humanist
   b. cognitive   d. learning

6. The belief that almost all sexual patterns are learned rather than inborn would find its strongest adherents among:
   a. cognitive theorists.

b. learning theorists.

c. psychoanalytic theorists.

d. ethological theorists.

7. (A Closer Look) The fact that physical differences between boys and girls during the preschool years are slight suggests that many distinctions in their play patterns are actually:

a. sex differences.

b. gender differences.

c. nonexistent.

d. biological in their origin.

8. Five-year-old Rodney has a better-developed sense of self and is more confident than Darnell. According to the text, it is likely that Rodney will also be more skilled at:

a. tasks involving verbal reasoning.

b. social interaction.

c. deception.

d. all of the above.

9. Your sister and brother-in-law are thinking of having a second child, because they are worried that only-children miss out on the benefits of social play. You tell them that:

a. parents can compensate for this by making sure the child has regular contact with other children.

b. only-children are likely to possess *superior* social skills because of the greater attention they receive from their parents.

c. the style of parenting, rather than the presence of siblings, is the most important factor in social and intellectual development.

d. unfortunately, this is true and nothing can replace the opportunities for acquiring social skills that siblings provide.

10. Concerning children's concept of gender, which of the following statements is true?

a. Before the age of 3 or so, children think that boys and girls can change gender as they get older.

b. Children as young as 18 months have a clear understanding of the physical differences between girls and boys and can consistently apply gender labels.

c. Not until age 5 or 6 do children show a clear preference for gender-typed toys.

d. All of the above are true.

11. Which of the following is *not* one of the features of parenting used by Baumrind to differentiate authoritarian, permissive, and authoritative parents?

a. maturity demands for the child's conduct

b. efforts to control the child's actions

c. nurturance

d. adherence to stereotypic gender roles

12. Jan recalls her mother as being nurturant and permissive, while her father was much more authoritarian. It is likely that Jan's parents would be classified as _____ by Diana Baumrind.

a. democratic-indulgent   c. androgynous

b. traditional   d. authoritative

13. (Research Report) Concerning the effect that observing violence on television has on children, which of the following is *not* true?

a. Children who watch a lot of television are likely to be more aggressive than children who do not.

b. Children who are aggressive are likely to watch a lot of TV violence.

c. Children who see a lot of violence on television are more likely to regard violence as a "normal" part of everyday life.

d. The impact of TV violence on preschoolers remains a controversial issue among social scientists.

14. Dr. Rubenstein believes that young preschoolers' understanding of gender is limited by their belief that sex differences depend on differences in appearance or behavior rather than on biology. Evidently, Dr. Rubenstein is an advocate of _____ theory.

a. psychoanalytic

b. learning

c. cognitive-developmental

d. gender-schema

15. Of the following individuals, who is likely to have the highest self-esteem?

a. 16-year-old Emilio, who takes pride in his masculine qualities

b. 16-year-old Martin, whose parents have always encouraged his androgynous behavior

c. 43-year-old Diana, who has always tried to be as "feminine" as possible

d. 23-year-old Tricia, who is attempting to raise her infant in an "androgynous" environment

Key Terms

Using your own words, write a brief definition or explanation of each of the following terms on a separate piece of paper.

1. initiative versus guilt

2. relationship perspective
3. authoritarian parenting
4. permissive parenting
5. authoritative parenting
6. democratic-indulgent parenting
7. rejecting-neglecting parenting
8. traditional parenting
9. sensorimotor play
10. mastery play
11. rough-and-tumble play
12. sociodramatic play
13. sex differences
14. gender differences
15. Oedipus complex
16. identification
17. Electra complex
18. gender constancy
19. gender schemas
20. androgyny

ANSWERS
CHAPTER REVIEW

1. self-concept; physical; dispositions; traits
2. negotiations

Preschoolers do not grasp the variability of a person's competencies. They also are unable to clearly distinguish the different psychological causes of their actions or skills.

3. self-concept; positive; overestimate; in all
4. more; autonomy versus shame and doubt; reactions of adults
5. anticipated; initiative versus guilt
6. broader; more; coping
7. causes; consequences; 4 or 5
8. conversations
9. parents; siblings; peers
10. relationship; relationships; mutually influencing
11. parenting
12. is not; Baumrind; nurturance; control; communicate; maturity demands
13. authoritarian; low; high; low
14. permissive; are; well; few
15. authoritative; high; well; are

16. authoritarian; permissive; authoritative
17. democratic-indulgent; rejecting-neglecting; traditional
18. authoritative; authoritarian; rejecting-neglecting

Parenting style derives, in part, from the parents' child-rearing goals, and from beliefs about the nature of children, the proper role of parents, and the best way to raise children. The parents' personality, economic well-being, and memory of their own upbringing are also important influences.

19. authoritative; punishment; positive strategies; model
20. temperament (or personality); age
21. is
22. instrumental; reaction; bullying; reaction
23. authoritative; traditional; authoritarian; rejecting-neglecting; stress
24. cultural; ethnic; community
25. multiple relationships; social context
26. siblings; model; social comparison
27. are; more; nurturance; cooperation; ambivalence
28. quite different from; genetic

One of the most important factors is parents' differential treatment of children, which fuels feelings of jealousy, anger, dominance, or inferiority. Sibling relationships are also a factor, since siblings guide, challenge, and encourage a child's social interactions.

29. as well as or better; intellectually; verbal; creative; social
30. preschool; day-care center; do; assertive and aggressive
31. cooperativeness; friendliness; "likability"; consistent
32. parent-child; supportive
33. play
34. motor development; intellectual growth; self-discovery
35. sensorimotor
36. mastery
37. rough-and-tumble; is universal; play face
38. are
39. sociodramatic
40. 2; 3; 6; does
41. relationships
42. larger; competition; dominance; smaller; cooperation; support
43. sex; gender

There are several gender distinctions in play patterns:

(a) boys typically spend more playtime outside, engaging in gross motor activities, such as running, climbing, and playing ball; (b) boys engage in more playful aggression and competition; (c) girls spend more time indoors, typically engaging in fine motor activities and cooperative games; (d) beginning in infancy both boys and girls prefer same-sex activities.

44. slight; social; adult roles
45. phallic stage; mother; father; Oedipus complex
46. identification
47. Electra complex; penis envy
48. reinforced; punished; are
49. observing other people; more; self-concept
50. gender; male-female
51. cognitive-developmental; 4 or 5; gender constancy; do
52. gender-schema
53. androgyny
54. more; competent; self-esteem
55. foster

PROGRESS TEST 1

Multiple-Choice Questions

1. **b.** is the answer. (pp. 373–374)
2. **c.** is the answer. (p. 400)

   a. & b. In Freud's theory, the oral and anal stages are associated with infant and early childhood development, respectively.

   d. In Freud's theory, the latency period is associated with development during the school years.
3. **a.** is the answer. (p. 395)

   b. Mastery play is play that helps children develop new physical and intellectual skills.

   c. Rough-and-tumble play is physical play that mimics aggression.

   d. Sensorimotor play captures the pleasures of using the senses and motor skills.
4. **b.** is the answer. (p. 378)

   d. These are variations of the basic styles uncovered by later research.
5. **a.** is the answer. (p. 378)

   b. & c. Authoritative parents communicate very well and are quite affectionate.

   d. This is not typical of authoritative parents.
6. **d.** is the answer. (p. 380)
7. **b.** is the answer. (p. 377)
8. **a.** is the answer. (p. 372)
9. **b.** is the answer. (p. 402)

a. This is the focus of Freud's phallic stage.

c. This is the focus of Erikson's psychoanalytic theory.

d. This is the focus of cognitive theorists.

10. **a.** is the answer. (p. 397)
11. **d.** is the answer. (p. 404)

    a. Through modeling children learn by observing others.

    b. & c. Freud's theory and gender stereotyping tend to perpetuate, rather than counter, this idea.
12. **c.** is the answer. (p. 403)

    a. According to this theory, preschoolers' understanding of gender is limited by their belief that differences between the sexes depend on differences in appearance or behavior.

    b. This is an aspect of the cognitive-developmental theory of gender-role development.

    d. According to this theory, children learn much of their gender behavior by observing other people.
13. **b.** is the answer. (p. 391)

    a. & d. Only-children often benefit intellectually, becoming more verbal and more creative.

    c. Because only-children may miss out on the benefits of social play, they may be weaker in their social skills.
14. **d.** is the answer. (pp. 382–383, 386–387)
15. **b.** is the answer. (pp. 379–380)

    a. Traditional parents tend to be *more* child-centered than authoritarian parents.

    c. & d. In fact, just the opposite is true.

True or False Items

1. F All parents make some maturity demands on their children; maturity demands are high in both the authoritarian and authoritative parenting styles. (p. 378)
2. T (p. 379)
3. F Siblings are more likely to help each other than to help an unrelated child; of course, siblings are also more likely to fight with each other than with other children. (p. 389)
4. T (p. 391)
5. F The most popular children tend to have the most *supportive* parents. (p. 392)
6. F Children from feminist or nontraditional homes often surprise their parents by expressing stereotypic ideas about feminine and masculine roles. (p. 397)

7. T (pp. 404–405)

8. T (p. 397)

9. T (p. 400)

10. F Although sociodramatic play appears creative and fluid, it actually involves complex rules and structures. (p. 396)

PROGRESS TEST 2

Multiple-Choice Questions

1. **b.** is the answer. (p. 379)

2. **c.** is the answer. (p. 392)

   a. & b. Siblings often provide better instruction than adults, since they are likely to guide, challenge, and encourage a child's social interactions more frequently and intimately.

   d. The text does not indicate that same-sex friends are more important in learning these than friends of the other sex.

3. **b.** is the answer. (p. 385)

4. **b.** is the answer. (pp. 382–383, 386–387)

5. **b.** is the answer. Although androgynous college students have higher self-esteem, this is not the case at certain other stages of life, such as during the early years. (p. 405)

6. **b.** is the answer. (p. 400)

   a. & d. These are Freud's versions of phallic-stage development in little girls.

   c. There is no such thing as the "phallic complex."

7. **c.** is the answer. (p. 379)

   a. & b. Both authoritarian and authoritative parents make high demands on their children.

   d. Rejecting-neglecting parents are quite cold and unengaged.

8. **d.** is the answer. (pp. 388–390)

9. **d.** is the answer. (p. 383)

10. **c.** is the answer. (p. 403)

    a. Gender constancy is the realization that one is permanently male or female.

    b. Gender identity is one's personal sense of being male or female.

    d. Androgyny refers to a person's having a balance of what are commonly regarded as "male" and "female" psychological characteristics.

11. **d.** is the answer. (p. 391)

12. **a.** is the answer. (p. 372)

    b. This viewpoint is associated only with cognitive theory.

c. Although parent-child relationships are important to social development, they do not determine readiness.

d. Identification is a Freudian defense mechanism.

13. **b.** is the answer. (p. 377)

14. **c.** is the answer. (p. 378)

15. **b.** is the answer. (p. 374)

    a. & c. According to Erikson, these are the crises of adolescence and infancy, respectively.

    d. This is not a crisis described by Erikson.

Matching Items

1. g (p. 393)   5. h (p. 379)   8. f (p. 378)
2. d (p. 393)   6. b (p. 400)   9. c (p. 378)
3. i (p. 395)   7. e (p. 400)   10. j (p. 400)
4. a (p. 379)

THINKING CRITICALLY ABOUT CHAPTER 11

1. **b.** is the answer. (p. 403)

   a. Identification is the defense mechanism through which children were believed by Freud to resolve the guilt of their phallic-stage urges.

   c. & d. These are Freudian descriptions of phallic-stage development in girls.

2. **b.** is the answer. (p. 400)

   a. According to Freud, the Oedipus complex refers to the male's sexual feelings toward his mother and resentment toward his father.

   c. & d. These are concepts introduced by cognitive theorists and Erik Erikson, respectively.

3. **a.** is the answer. (p. 374)

   b. Erikson did not equate gender constancy with the emergence of guilt.

   c. & d. These reflect the viewpoints of learning theory and Freud, respectively.

4. **b.** is the answer. (p. 379)

5. **a.** is the answer. (p. 400)

   b. Cognitive theorists focus on children's understanding of gender and male-female differences, and on how their changing perceptions of gender motivate their efforts to behave consistently with their gender role.

   c. The text does not discuss a humanist theory of gender-role development.

   d. Learning theorists believe that role patterns are learned through reinforcement, punishment, and, in the case of social-learning theorists, modeling.

6. **b.** is the answer. (p. 402)

7. **b.** is the answer. Since physical differences between the sexes are slight, play differences (which *are* reliable, making c. incorrect) are likely to be the result of social pressure rather than biology (a. and d.). (pp. 398–399)

8. **b.** is the answer. (pp. 372–373)

   a. & c. The chapter does not link self-understanding with verbal reasoning or deception.

9. **a.** is the answer. (p. 391)

10. **a.** is the answer. (p. 397)

    b. Not until about age 3 can children consistently apply gender labels.

    c. By age 2, children prefer gender-typed toys.

11. **d.** is the answer. (p. 378)

12. **b.** is the answer. (p. 379)

    a. Democratic-indulgent parents are warm and responsive, yet make fewer demands on their children than do authoritarian parents.

    c. Androgynous parents, although not specifically mentioned in the text, would be more flexible in their gender roles than Jan's parents evidently were.

    d. Authoritative parents are more democratic than Jan's father evidently was.

13. **d.** is the answer. The negative impact of TV violence is now accepted as a fact by social scientists. (p. 384)

14. **c.** is the answer. (p. 403)

    a. According to psychoanalytic theory, children copy the behaviors and moral standards of their same-sex parents as they resolve the guilt associated with the sexual urges of the phallic stage.

    b. Learning theorists believe that role patterns are acquired through reinforcement, punishment, and, in the case of social-learning theorists, modeling.

    d. According to gender-schema theory, young children's motivation to behave in gender-appropriate ways derives from the ways they organize their knowledge about people in terms of gender-based categories.

15. **a.** is the answer. (p. 405)

    b. & d. During adolescence, and when raising young children, those who consider themselves relatively traditional for their gender tend to have high self-esteem.

    c. Some of the first studies on androgyny showed that androgynous individuals generally have a higher sense of self-esteem than do people who follow traditional gender-role behavior (like Diana in this example).

KEY TERMS

1. According to Erikson, the crisis of the preschool years is **initiative versus guilt**. In this crisis, preschoolers eagerly take on new tasks and play activities and feel guilty when their efforts result in failure or criticism. (p. 374)

2. According to the **relationship perspective**, psychosocial growth emerges mainly from the child's experience in close relationships with parents, siblings, and friends. (p. 377)

3. **Authoritarian parents** show little affection or nurturance for their children; maturity demands are high and parent-child communication is low. (p. 378)

   Memory aid: Someone who is an *authoritarian* demands unquestioning obedience and acts in a dictatorial way.

4. **Permissive parents** make few demands on their children, yet are nurturant and accepting, and communicate well with their children. (p. 378)

5. **Authoritative parents** set limits and enforce rules, but do so more democratically than do authoritarian parents. (p. 378)

   Memory aid: **Authoritative** parents act as *authorities* do on a subject—by discussing and explaining why certain family rules are in place.

6. **Democratic-indulgent parents** adopt the undemanding, uncoercive style of permissive parents, yet are warm and responsive toward their children. (p. 379)

7. **Rejecting-neglecting parents** adopt the undemanding, uncoercive style of permissive parents, yet are cold, unengaged, and even ignorant about what their children actually do. (p. 379)

8. **Traditional parents** take somewhat old-fashioned male and female roles, the mother being quite nurturant and permissive, while the father is more authoritarian. (p. 379)

9. **Sensorimotor play** is play that captures the pleasures of using the senses and motor abilities. (p. 393)

10. **Mastery play** is play that helps children to develop new physical, intellectual, and language skills. (p. 393)

11. **Rough-and-tumble play** is physical play that often mimics aggression, but involves no intent to harm. (p. 394)

12. In **sociodramatic play**, children act out roles and themes in stories of their own creation, allowing them to examine personal concerns in a non-threatening manner. (p. 395)

13. **Sex differences** are physical and behavioral differences between males and females that arise from hormonal and chromosomal differences. (p. 398)

14. **Gender differences** are male-female differences that arise from cultural customs, values, and expectations. (p. 398)

15. According to Freud, boys in the phallic stage develop a collection of feelings, known as the **Oedipus complex**, that center on sexual attraction to the mother and resentment of the father. (p. 400)

16. In Freud's theory, **identification** is the defense mechanism through which people imagine themselves to be like a person more powerful than themselves. (p. 400)

17. According to Freud, girls in the phallic stage may develop a collection of feelings, known as the **Electra complex**, that center on sexual attraction to the father and resentment of the mother. (p. 400)

18. **Gender constancy** is the realization that emerges after age 4 or 5 that one is permanently male or female. (p. 403)

19. **Gender schemas** refer to the ways children organize their knowledge about people in terms of gender-based categories and evaluations. (p. 403)

20. **Androgyny** refers to a person's having a balance of what are commonly regarded as "male" and "female" psychological characteristics. (p. 404)

CHAPTER

12

The School Years: Biosocial Development

Chapter Overview

This chapter introduces middle childhood, the years from 7 to 11. Changes in physical size and shape are described, and the problem of obesity is addressed. The discussion then turns to the continuing development of motor skills during the school years. A final section examines the experiences of children with special needs, such as autistic children, children with learning disabilities, and those diagnosed as having attention-deficit hyperactivity disorder. The causes of and treatments for these problems are discussed, with emphasis placed on insights arising from the new developmental psychopathology perspective. This perspective makes it clear that the manifestations of any special childhood problem will change as the child grows older, and that treatment must often focus on all three domains of development.

NOTE: Answer guidelines for all Chapter 12 questions begin on page 185.

Guided Study

The text chapter should be studied one section at a time. Before you read, preview each section by skimming it, noting headings and boldface items. Then read the appropriate section objectives from the following outline. Keep these objectives in mind and, as you read the chapter section, search for the information that will enable you to meet each objective. Once you have finished a section, write out answers for its objectives.

Size and Shape (pp. 412–417)

1. Describe normal physical growth and development during middle childhood and account for the usual variations among children.

2. Discuss the problems—both physical and psychological—of obese children in middle childhood.

3. Identify the major causes of obesity and outline the best approaches to treating obesity.

175

Motor Skills (pp. 417–419)

4. Describe motor-skiill development during the school years and discuss the major reason for limited abilities during this period.

Children with Special Needs (pp. 419–434)

5. Explain the new developmental psychopathology perspective and discuss its value in treating children with special needs.

6. Identify the symptoms of autism, discuss its possible causes, and describe its most effective treatment.

7. Discuss the symptoms and possible causes of learning disabilities.

8. Describe the symptoms and possible causes of attention-deficit hyperactivity disorder and attention-deficit hyperactivity disorder with aggression.

9. Discuss the types of treatment available for children with attention-deficit hyperactivity disorder.

Chapter Review

When you have finished reading the chapter, work through the material that follows to review it. Complete the sentences and answer the questions. As you proceed, evaluate your performance for each section by consulting the answers on page 185. Do not continue with the next section until you understand each answer. If you need to, review or reread the appropriate section in the textbook before continuing.

1. Compared to that in other periods of the life span, biosocial development during middle childhood is _____ (relatively smooth/often fraught with problems). For example, disease and death during these years are _____ (more common/rarer) than during any other period. For another, sex differences in physical development and ability are _____ (very great/ minimal).

Size and Shape (pp. 412–417)

2. Children grow _____ (faster/more slowly) during middle childhood than they did earlier or than they will in adolescence. The typical child gains about _____ pounds and _____ inches per year.

Describe several other features of physical development during the school years.

3. In some undeveloped countries, most of the variation in children's height and weight is caused by _____ . In developed countries, most children grow as tall as their _____ allow. These factors affect not only size but rate of _____ as well.

4. Among Americans, those of African descent tend to mature more _____ (quickly/slowly) than those of European descent, who tend to mature more _____ (quickly/slowly) than those of Asian descent.

5. The precise point at which a child is considered obese depends on _____ _____ , on the proportion of _____ to _____ , and on _____ _____ . At least _____ percent of American children are 20 pounds or more above the average weight for their age.

6. Two physical problems associated with childhood obesity are _____ and _____ problems.

Identify several psychological problems commonly associated with childhood obesity.

Identify several inherited characteristics that might contribute to obesity.

7. Inactive people burn _____ (more/fewer) calories and are _____ (no more/more) likely to be obese than active people.

8. American children whose parents were immigrants from developing countries are _____ (more/less) likely to be overweight. This demonstrates the importance of another factor in obesity: _____ .

Give an example of how parents' attitudes toward food might contribute to obesity in their children.

9. Diets that emphasize _____ do not lead to excess weight gain, whereas diets that are high in _____ obviously do.

10. The diet of North American families who are below the poverty line tends to be high in _____ . The types of food eaten also vary with _____ food preferences.

11. Throughout life, the number of fat cells in a person's body _____ (remains relatively constant/increases). Overfeeding during _____ is likely to increase the number of fat cells in a person's body and _____ (speed up/slow down) the rate of cell multiplication. Underfeeding or malnutrition decreases the number of fat cells in a person's body and tends to _____ (speed up/slow down) the rate of cell multiplication.

12. Excessive television-watching by children _____ (is/is not) directly correlated with obesity. When children watch TV their metabolism _____ (slows down/speeds up).

Identify three factors that make television-watching fattening.

13. The onset of childhood obesity
_____ (is/is not) commonly associated with a traumatic experience.

14. Less than 1 percent of all cases of childhood obesity are caused by _____ problems.

15. Obesity is usually fostered by entrenched _____ that promote a fattening diet and sedentary lifestyle.

16. Fasting and/or repeated dieting _____ (lowers/raises) the rate of metabolism. For this reason, after a certain amount of weight loss, additional pounds become _____ (more/less) difficult to lose.

17. Strenuous dieting during childhood _____ (is/is not) potentially dangerous. A diet that is deficient in protein or calcium can hinder _____ and _____ growth.

18. The best way to get children to lose weight is to increase their _____ _____. Developmentalists agree that treating obesity early in life _____ (is/is not) very important in ensuring the child's overall health later in life.

Motor Skills (pp. 417–419)

19. Children become more skilled at controlling their bodies during the school years, in part because they _____.

20. Because boys have greater _____ strength during childhood than girls, they tend to have an advantage in sports like

_____, whereas girls have an advantage in sports like _____.

21. The length of time it takes a person to respond to a particular stimulus is called _____ _____; a key factor in this motor skill is _____ _____.

22. Most of the sports that adults value _____ (are/are not) well-suited for children.

Children with Special Needs (pp. 419–434)

23. Some psychological disorders originate from physiological impairment of the _____; others stem from the _____ and _____ consequences of certain physical disabilities; and still others originate in the child's _____.

24. The field of study that is concerned with childhood psychological disorders is _____ _____.

25. Traditionally, clinicians treated disturbed children through _____ therapy. Because of their _____ approach, developmental psychopathologists have broadened their treatment approach to include _____ members in _____ therapy.

26. One of the most severe disturbances of early childhood is _____, which, when all symptoms are taken into account, may affect as many as one child in _____. This disorder is more common in _____ (boys/girls).

27. In early childhood autism, severe deficiencies appear in three areas: _____, _____, _____, and _____ _____.

28. The first noticeable symptom of autism is usually the lack of _____ _____.

29. Some autistic children engage in a type of speech called _____ , in which they repeat, word for word, things they have heard.

30. The unusual play patterns of autistic children are characterized by repetitive _____ and an absence of spontaneous, _____ play.

31. The most devastating problem of autistic children often proves to be the lack of

    _____ _____ .

    Autistic children appear to lack a

    _____ _____

    _____ . This problem

    _____ (is usually temporary/remains lifelong).

32. Although the precise cause of autism is

    _____ , there is strong evidence that it has a _____ origin.

33. Monozygotic twins _____ (always/do not always) share the disorder with their autistic twin. This finding suggests that _____ vulnerability in combination with some form of _____ damage leads to autism. This is also suggested by the increased prevalence of abnormal

    _____ patterns, _____ ,

    _____ , previous exposure to

    _____ , and _____

    abnormalities among autistic children.

34. The most crucial period for intervention in the treatment of autism are the years between ages

    _____ and _____ .

    This is so because _____ skills develop most rapidly during these years.

35. The most successful treatment methods for autism combine _____

    _____ with _____

    techniques that shape particular

    _____ .

36. Some children have difficulty in school due to an overall slowness in development; that is, they suffer _____ .

    If that difficulty _____ (is/is

not) attributable to an overall intellectual slowness, a physical handicap, a severely stressful situation, or a lack of basic education, the child is said to have a _____

_____ . The key criterion for diagnosis is a significant discrepancy between measures of _____

_____ and measures of

_____ in a particular area.

Using this criterion, about _____ percent of all 6- to 11-year-olds are so designated.

37. A disability in reading is called

    _____ ; in math, it is called

    _____ . Other specific academic subjects that may show a learning disability are

    _____ and _____ .

38. Learning disabilities _____ (are/are not) caused by a lack of effort on the child's part. Many professionals believe that the origin of learning disabilities is _____ , perhaps caused by _____

    _____ that have a detrimental effect on brain functioning, particularly in the

    _____ area.

39. Learning disabilities _____ (do/do not) tend to run in families. Teratogens such as _____ may also be a precipitating factor. The rate of learning disabilities is particularly high among children who were _____-

    _____-_____ .

40. If a learning disability is of proven organic origin, it _____ (is/is not) impossible to correct.

41. Help for children with learning disabilities should focus on the specific problem, and on the child's _____ skills, which are often affected by the underlying problem.

42. A disability that manifests itself in a difficulty in concentrating for more than a few moments and a need to be active, often accompanied by excitability and impulsivity is called _____-

    _____ _____ . Children with this

disorder who are prone to _____ are at risk for developing _____ disorders. In some cases, when hyperactivity or aggression is missing, the child may be prone to _____ or _____ . The crucial problem in these conditions seems to be a neurological difficulty in _____ _____ .

43. For every girl diagnosed with ADHD, _____ boys are so diagnosed.

44. Twin studies indicate that hereditary differences _____ (do/do not) contribute to ADHD.

45. Brain activity tends to be _____ (higher/lower) in ADHD individuals than in control subjects, especially in areas of the brain associated with _____ _____ .

46. ADHD also may result from prenatal damage due to _____ . Poisoning due to exposure to _____ can also lead to impaired concentration and hyperactivity.

Identify several family and environmental influences on ADHD.

47. More than half of all children with ADHD _____ (do/do not) have continuing problems as adults.

48. The most frequent therapy for children with ADHD is _____ . Certain drugs that stimulate adults, such as _____ and _____ , have a reverse effect on hyperactive children.

49. The most effective types of psychological therapy for ADHD have generally been those developed

from _____ theory, such as teaching parents how to use _____-_____ techniques with their child.

50. Some classroom environments, called

_____ _____ ,

tend to increase ADHD problems. Others, called

_____ _____ ,

tend to reduce ADHD problems.

Describe these two types of classroom environments.

Progress Test 1

Multiple-Choice Questions

Circle your answers to the following questions and check them with the answers on page 186. If your answer is incorrect, read the explanation for why it is incorrect and then consult the appropriate pages of the text (in parentheses following the correct answer).

1. As children move into middle childhood:
   a. the rate of accidental death increases.
   b. sexual urges intensify.
   c. the rate of weight gain increases.
   d. biological growth slows and steadies.

2. During middle childhood:
   a. girls are usually stronger than boys.
   b. boys have greater physical flexibility than girls.
   c. boys have greater forearm strength than girls.
   d. the development of motor skills slows drastically.

3. To help obese children, nutritionists usually recommend:
   a. strenuous dieting to counteract early overfeeding.
   b. the use of amphetamines and other drugs.

c. more exercise, stabilization of weight, and time to "grow out" of the fat.

d. no specific actions.

4. A factor that is *not* primary in the development of motor skills during middle childhood is:

a. practice.
b. gender.
c. brain maturation.
d. age.

5. Dyslexia is a learning disability that affects the ability to:

a. do math.
b. read.
c. write.
d. speak.

6. In relation to weight in later life, childhood obesity:

a. is not an accurate predictor of adolescent or adult weight.
b. is predictive of adolescent but not adult weight.
c. is predictive of adult but not adolescent weight.
d. is predictive of both adolescent and adult weight.

7. The developmental psychopathology perspective is characterized by its:

a. contextual approach.
b. emphasis on individual therapy.
c. emphasis on the cognitive domain of development.
d. concern with all of the above.

8. The time—usually measured in fractions of a second—it takes for a person to respond to a particular stimulus is called:

a. the interstimulus interval.
b. reaction time.
c. the stimulus-response interval.
d. response latency.

9. Researchers have suggested that excessive television-watching is a possible cause of childhood obesity because:

a. TV bombards children with persuasive junk food commercials.
b. children often snack while watching TV.
c. body metabolism slows while watching TV.
d. of all the above reasons.

10. The underlying problem in attention-deficit hyperactivity disorder appears to be:

a. low overall intelligence.
b. a neurological difficulty in screening out distracting stimuli.

c. a learning disability in a specific academic skill.
d. the existence of a conduct disorder.

11. Classroom environments that seem to aggravate or increase problems in children with attention-deficit hyperactivity disorder are sometimes labeled:

a. provocation ecologies.
b. rarefaction ecologies.
c. open classrooms.
d. homogeneous groupings.

12. In developed countries, most of the variation in children's size and shape can be attributed to:

a. the amount of daily exercise.
b. nutrition.
c. genes.
d. the interaction of the above factors.

13. Autistic children generally have severe deficiencies in all but which of the following?

a. social skills
b. imaginative play
c. echolalia
d. communication ability

14. The most likely cause of autism is:

a. abnormal genes.
b. prenatal exposure to teratogens.
c. maternal stress.
d. genetic vulnerability in combination with prenatal or early postnatal damage.

15. Psychoactive drugs are most effective in treating attention-deficit hyperactivity disorder when they are administered:

a. before the diagnosis becomes certain.
b. for several years after the basic problem has abated.
c. as part of the labeling process.
d. with psychological support or therapy.

True or False Items

Write *true* or *false* on the line in front of each statement.

_____ 1. Physical variations in North American children are usually caused by diet rather than heredity.

_____ 2. Childhood obesity usually does not correlate with adult obesity.

_____ 3. Research shows a direct correlation between television-watching and obesity.

_____ 4. The quick reaction time that is crucial in

some sports can be readily achieved with practice.

_____ 5. Despite the efforts of teachers and parents, most children with learning disabilities can expect their disabilities to persist and even worsen as they enter adulthood.

_____ 6. The best way for children to lose weight is through strenuous dieting.

_____ 7. Parental coldness toward infants is a primary cause of autism.

_____ 8. Most learning disabilities are caused by a difficult birth or other early trauma to the child.

_____ 9. Most of the children who have attention-deficit hyperactivity disorder are girls.

_____ 10. The drugs sometimes given to children to reduce hyperactive behaviors have a reverse effect on adults.

Progress Test 2

Progress Test 2 should be completed during a final chapter review. Answer the following questions after you thoroughly understand the correct answers for the Chapter Review and Progress Test 1.

Multiple-Choice Questions

1. During the years from 7 to 11, the average child:
   a. becomes slimmer.
   b. gains about 12 pounds a year.
   c. has decreased lung capacity.
   d. is more likely to become obese than at any other period in the life span.

2. Among the factors that are known to contribute to obesity are activity level, quantity and types of food eaten, and:
   a. a traumatic event.
   b. television-watching.
   c. attitude toward food.
   d. all of the above.

3. A specific learning disability that becomes apparent when a child experiences unusual difficulty in learning to read is:
   a. dyslexia.   c. ADHD.
   b. dyscalcula.   d. ADHDA.

4. Problems in learning to write, read, and do math are collectively referred to as:
   a. learning disabilities.
   b. attention-deficit hyperactivity disorder.

   c. hyperactivity.
   d. dyscalcula.

5. A classroom environment that seems to decrease the problems of the child with attention-deficit hyperactivity disorder is called a(n):
   a. provocation ecology.
   b. rarefaction ecology.
   c. ecological niche.
   d. therapeutic classroom.

6. Diets that emphasize _____ are unlikely to promote obesity.
   a. fat
   b. protein
   c. fruits, vegetables, and grains
   d. simple carbohydrates

7. The *most frequent* therapy for children with attention-deficit hyperactivity disorder is:
   a. behavior modification.
   b. medication with drugs such as amphetamines.
   c. family counseling.
   d. medication with tranquilizers.

8. A key factor in reaction time is:
   a. whether the child is male or female.
   b. brain maturation.
   c. whether the stimulus to be reacted to is an auditory or visual one.
   d. all of the above.

9. The first noticeable symptom of autism is usually:
   a. the lack of spoken language.
   b. abnormal social responsiveness.
   c. self-focused, ritualized play.
   d. unpredictable.

10. Which of the following is true of children with a diagnosed learning disability?
    a. They are, in most cases, average in intelligence.
    b. They often have a specific physical handicap, such as hearing loss.
    c. They often lack basic educational experiences.
    d. All of the above are true.

11. During the school years:
    a. boys are, on average, at least a year ahead of girls in the development of physical abilities.
    b. girls are, on average, at least a year ahead of boys in the development of physical abilities.
    c. boys and girls are about equal in physical abilities.

d. motor-skill development proceeds at a slower pace, since children grow more rapidly at this age than at any other time.

12. Whether a particular child is considered obese depends on:
   a. the child's body type.
   b. the proportion of fat to muscle.
   c. cultural standards.
   d. all of the above.

13. Compared with other children, children with attention-deficit hyperactivity disorder come from families who:
   a. tend to stress academic performance.
   b. move infrequently.

c. have many children.
d. are especially concerned with controlling their children's behavior.

14. Most experts contend that at least _____ percent of American children need to lose weight.
   a. 10   c. 20
   b. 15   d. 25

15. The most effective treatment for autism is a combination of individual attention and:
   a. group therapy.
   b. cognitive therapy.
   c. psychoanalysis.
   d. behavior therapy.

Matching Items

Match each term or concept with its corresponding description or definition.

Terms or Concepts

_____ 1. dyslexia
_____ 2. dyscalcula
_____ 3. mental retardation
_____ 4. attention-deficit hyperactivity disorder
_____ 5. provocation ecologies
_____ 6. echolalia
_____ 7. autism
_____ 8. developmental psychopathology
_____ 9. rarefaction ecologies
_____ 10. learning disability

Descriptions or Definitions

a. an unexpected difficulty with one or more academic skills
b. speech that repeats, word for word, what has just been heard
c. flexible, yet structured classroom environment
d. a pervasive delay in cognitive development
e. applies insights from studies of normal development to the study of childhood disorders
f. disorder characterized by the absence of a theory of mind
g. difficulty in reading
h. unusually rigid or freewheeling classroom environment
i. behavior problem involving difficulty in concentrating, as well as excitability and impulsivity
j. difficulty in math

Thinking Critically About Chapter 12

Answer these questions the day before an exam as a final check on your understanding of the chapter's terms and concepts.

1. According to developmentalists, the best game for a typical group of 8-year-olds would be:
   a. football or baseball.
   b. basketball.
   c. one in which reaction time is not crucial.
   d. games involving one-on-one competition.

2. Dr. Rutter, who believes that "we can learn more about an organism's normal functioning by

studying its pathology and, likewise, more about its pathology by studying its normal condition," evidently is working from which of the following perspectives?
   a. clinical psychology
   b. developmental psychopathology
   c. behaviorism
   d. psychoanalysis

3. Nine-year-old Jack has difficulty concentrating on his classwork for more than a few moments, repeatedly asks his teacher irrelevant questions, and is constantly disrupting the class with loud noises. If his difficulties persist, Jack is likely to be diagnosed as suffering from:

    a. dyslexia.
    b. dyscalcula.
    c. autism.
    d. attention-deficit hyperactivity disorder.

4. Of the following 9-year-olds, who is likely to mature physically at the youngest age?
    a. Britta, who is of European descent
    b. Michael, who is of European descent
    c. Malcolm, who is of African descent
    d. Lee, who is of Asian descent

5. Ten-year-old Clarence is quick-tempered, easily frustrated, and is often disruptive in the classroom. Clarence may be suffering from:
    a. dyslexia.
    b. dyscalcula.
    c. attention-deficit disorder.
    d. attention-deficit hyperactivity disorder.

6. Because 11-year-old Wayne is obese, he runs a greater risk of developing:
    a. orthopedic problems.
    b. respiratory problems.
    c. psychological problems.
    d. all of the above.

7. Of the following individuals, who is likely to have the fastest reaction time?
    a. a 7-year-old   c. an 11-year-old
    b. a 9-year-old   d. an adult

8. Harold weighs about 20 pounds more than his friend Jay. During school recess, Jay can usually be found playing soccer with his classmates, while Harold sits on the sidelines by himself. Harold's rejection is likely due to his:
    a. being physically different.
    b. being dyslexic.
    c. intimidating his schoolmates.
    d. being hyperactive.

9. In determining whether an 8-year-old has a learning disability, a teacher looks primarily for:
    a. discrepant performance in a subject area.
    b. the exclusion of other explanations.
    c. a family history of the learning disability.
    d. both a. and b.

10. Which of the following American children is *most* likely to be overweight?
    a. Caledonia, whose diet is high in fiber
    b. Sperry, who comes from an affluent family
    c. David, whose parents are below the poverty line

    d. It is impossible to predict from the information given.

11. If you were to ask an autistic child with echolalia, "what's your name?" the child would probably respond by saying:
    a. nothing.
    b. "what's your name?"
    c. "your name what's?"
    d. something that was unintelligible.

12. Although 12-year-old Brenda is quite intelligent, she has low self-esteem, few friends, and is often teased. Knowing nothing else about Brenda, you conclude that she may be:
    a. unusually aggressive.   c. arrogant.
    b. obese.   d. socially inept.

13. Danny has been diagnosed as having attention-deficit hyperactivity disorder. A scan of his brain is likely to reveal:
    a. nothing out of the ordinary.
    b. an abnormally high overall rate of brain metabolism.
    c. abnormally low brain metabolism in the areas of the brain associated with the control of attention and motor activity.
    d. an unusually thin cortical layer in the frontal lobe.

14. In concluding her presentation entitled "Facts and falsehoods regarding childhood obesity," Cheryl states that contrary to popular belief _____ is *not* a common cause of childhood obesity.
    a. television-watching
    b. a traumatic event
    c. overeating of high-fat foods
    d. abnormal physiology

15. Debbie, who was overfed as a child and has dieted most of her life, wants to know the effect of overeating and dieting on the body. You tell her that the number of fat cells in a person's body:
    a. is fixed at the moment of conception.
    b. increases in response to overeating and decreases in response to dieting.
    c. increases in response to overeating but does not decrease in response to dieting.
    d. is fixed by age 1.

Key Terms

Using your own words, write a brief definition or explanation of each of the following terms on a separate piece of paper.

1. obesity
2. reaction time
3. developmental psychopathology
4. autism
5. mental retardation
6. learning disability
7. dyslexia
8. dyscalcula
9. attention-deficit hyperactivity disorder (ADHD)
10. provocation ecologies
11. rarefaction ecologies

ANSWERS
CHAPTER REVIEW

1. relatively smooth; rarer; minimal
2. more slowly; 5; 2 1/2

During the school years, children generally become slimmer, muscles become stronger, and lung capacity increases.

3. malnutrition; genes; maturation
4. quickly; quickly
5. body type; fat; muscle; cultural standards; 10
6. orthopedic; respiratory

Obese children are teased, picked on, and rejected, and so tend to have fewer friends than other children and are more likely to experience diminished self-esteem, depression, and behavior problems.

Body type, including the amount and distribution of fat, as well as height and bone structure; individual differences in metabolic rate; and activity level are all influenced by heredity and can contribute to obesity.

7. fewer; more
8. more; attitudes toward food

Parents who consider food a symbol of love and comfort may feed their babies whenever they cry, rather than first figuring out if the baby is lonely or uncomfortable rather than hungry.

9. fruits, vegetables, and grains; fat and sugar
10. fat; ethnic and subcultural
11. remains relatively constant; the prenatal period, the first two years of life, and early adolescence; speed up; slow down
12. is; slows down

While watching television, children (a) are bombarded with commercials for junk food, (b) consume many snacks, and (c) burn fewer calories than they would if they were actively playing.

13. is
14. physiological
15. family attitudes and habits
16. lowers; more
17. is; brain; bone
18. physical activity; is
19. grow more slowly
20. forearm; baseball; gymnastics
21. reaction time; brain maturation
22. are not
23. brain; social; emotional; environment
24. developmental psychopathology
25. individual; contextual; family; group
26. autism; 100; boys
27. communication ability; social skills; imaginative play
28. spoken language
29. echolalia
30. rituals; imaginative
31. social understanding; theory of mind; remains lifelong
32. unknown; genetic
33. do not always; genetic; environmental; neurological; seizures; anoxia; viruses; hearing
34. 1; 4; language
35. individual attention; behavior; skills
36. mental retardation; is not; learning disability; general aptitude; performance; 7
37. dyslexia; dyscalcula; spelling; handwriting
38. are not; organic; prenatal factors; auditory
39. do; prenatal exposure to drugs or to other toxins, such as mercury and PCBs, and postnatal exposure to lead; very-low-birthweight
40. is not
41. social
42. attention-deficit hyperactivity disorder; aggression; conduct; anxiety; depression; screening out irrelevant and distracting stimuli
43. four
44. do
45. lower; the control of attention and motor activity
46. maternal drug use during pregnancy or pregnancy complications; lead

Compared with other children, children with ADHD come from families who move often, are stressed, have fewer children, and are less concerned about the child's academic performance than about controlling the child's behavior. ADHD may also be exacerbated by being in an exciting but unstructured situation or in a situation with many behavioral demands. Similarly, children with no place to play or who watch too much television may be affected.

47. do

48. medication; amphetamines; methylphenidate (Ritalin)

49. learning; behavior-modification

50. provocation ecologies; rarefaction ecologies

In provocation ecologies, classroom structure is either unusually rigid or completely absent, and noise is either completely forbidden or tolerated to a distracting degree. In rarefaction ecologies, teachers tend to be more flexible in their reactions to minor disruptions, but also provide sufficient structure so that children know what they should be doing and when. Alternating short periods of concentrated schoolwork with opportunities for physical activity also tends to be helpful.

PROGRESS TEST 1

Multiple-Choice Questions

1. **d.** is the answer. (p. 412)

2. **c.** is the answer. (p. 418)

    a. Especially in forearm strength, boys are usually stronger than girls during middle childhood.

    b. During middle childhood, girls usually have greater overall flexibility than boys.

    d. Motor-skill development improves greatly during middle childhood.

3. **c.** is the answer. (p. 417)

    a. Strenuous dieting can be physically harmful and often makes children irritable, listless, and even sick—adding to the psychological problems of the obese child.

    b. The use of amphetamines to control weight is not recommended at any age.

4. **b.** Boys and girls are just about equal in physical abilities during the school years. (p. 418)

5. **b.** is the answer. (p. 426)

    a. This is dyscalcula.

    c. & d. The text does not give labels for learning disabilities in writing or speaking.

6. **d.** is the answer. (p. 417)

7. **a.** is the answer. (pp. 420–421)

    b. & c. Because of its contextual approach, developmental psychopathology emphasizes *group* therapy and *all* domains of development.

8. **b.** is the answer. (p. 418)

9. **d.** is the answer. (pp. 415–416)

10. **b.** is the answer. (p. 430)

11. **a.** is the answer. (p. 434)

    b. These classroom environments often reduce ADHD behaviors.

    c. Open classrooms were not discussed in the text.

    d. Homogeneous groupings are classrooms that segregate slow learners in one class, gifted in another, and learning disabled in still another.

12. **c.** is the answer. (p. 412)

    a. The amount of daily exercise a child receives is an important factor in his or her tendency toward obesity; exercise does not, however, explain most of the variation in childhood physique.

    b. In some parts of the world malnutrition accounts for most of the variation in physique; this is not true of developed countries, where most children get enough food to grow as tall as their genes allow.

13. **c.** is the answer. Echolalia *is* a type of communication difficulty. (p. 422)

14. **d.** is the answer. (p. 424)

15. **d.** is the answer. (p. 433)

True or False Items

1. F   Physical variations in children from developed countries are caused primarily by heredity. (p. 412)

2. F   If obesity is established in middle childhood, it tends to continue into adulthood. (p. 417)

3. T (p. 415)

4. F   Reaction time depends on brain maturation and is not readily affected by practice. (p. 418)

5. F   With the proper assistance, many learning-disabled children develop into adults who are virtually indistinguishable from other adults in their educational and occupational achievements. (p. 427)

6. F   Strenuous dieting during childhood can be dangerous. The best way to get children to lose weight is by increasing their activity level. (p. 416)

7. F   This was an early myth regarding the origins of autism. (p. 424)

8. F The causes of learning disabilities are difficult to pinpoint, and cannot be specified with certainty. (p. 426)

9. F Most children who suffer from attention-deficit hyperactivity disorder are boys. (p. 430)

10. T (pp. 431–432)

PROGRESS TEST 2

Multiple-Choice Questions

1. **a.** is the answer. (p. 412)

   b. & c. During this period children gain about 5 pounds per year and experience increased lung capacity.

   d. Although childhood obesity is a common problem, the text does not indicate that a person is more likely to become obese at this age than at any other.

2. **d.** is the answer. (pp. 414–416)

3. **a.** is the answer. (p. 426)

   b. This learning disability involves math, rather than reading.

   c. & d. These disorders do not manifest themselves in a particular academic skill but instead appear in psychological processes that affect learning in general.

4. **a.** is the answer. (p. 425)

   b. & c. ADHD is a general learning disability that usually does not manifest itself in specific subject areas. Hyperactivity is a facet of this disorder.

   d. Dyscalcula is a learning disability in math only.

5. **b.** is the answer. (p. 434)

   a. This classroom environment tends to increase the problems of children with ADHD.

   c. & d. These classroom environments are not discussed in the text.

6. **c.** is the answer. (p. 415)

   a. & d. Diets high in fat and sugar are likely to promote obesity.

   b. Diets that emphasize protein are more likely to promote obesity than are diets that emphasize fruits, vegetables, and grains.

7. **b.** is the answer. (p. 431)

8. **b.** is the answer. (p. 418)

9. **a.** is the answer. (p. 422)

10. **a.** is the answer. (p. 425)

11. **c.** is the answer. (p. 418)

12. **d.** is the answer. (p. 413)

13. **d.** is the answer. (p. 431)

   a., b., & c. The families of children with ADHD typically place less stress on academic performance than on controlling their children's behavior, move frequently, and have few children.

14. **a.** is the answer. (p. 413)

15. **d.** is the answer. (p. 424)

Matching Items

1. g (p. 426)
2. j (p. 426)
3. d (p. 425)
4. i (p. 429)
5. h (p. 434)
6. b (p. 422)
7. f (pp. 421–423)
8. e (p. 420)
9. c (p. 434)
10. a (p. 425)

THINKING CRITICALLY ABOUT CHAPTER 12

1. **c.** is the answer. (p. 418)

   a. & b. Each of these games involves skills that are hardest for schoolchildren to master.

   d. Because one-on-one sports are likely to accentuate individual differences in ability, they may be especially discouraging to some children.

2. **b.** is the answer. (p. 420)

3. **d.** is the answer. (p. 429)

   a. & b. Jack's difficulty is in concentrating, not in reading (dyslexia) or math (dyscalcula).

   c. Autism is characterized by a lack of communication skills.

4. **c.** is the answer. (p. 412)

   a., b., & d. Among Americans, those of African descent tend to mature more quickly than those of European descent, who, in turn, tend to be maturationally ahead of those of Asian descent.

5. **d.** is the answer. (p. 429)

6. **d.** is the answer. (pp. 413–414)

7. **d.** is the answer. (p. 418)

8. **a.** is the answer. (p. 414)

   b., c., & d. Obese children are no more likely to be dyslexic, physically intimidating, or hyperactive than other children.

9. **d.** is the answer. (p. 425)

10. **c.** is the answer. (p. 415)

   a. This type of diet is less likely to promote obesity than one that is high in fat.

   b. The diet of families who are *below* the poverty line tends to be high in fat, and therefore more likely to promote obesity.

11. **b.** is the answer. (p. 422)

12. b. is the answer. (p. 414)

13. c. is the answer. (p. 430)

14. d. is the answer. Physiological problems account for less than 1 percent of all cases of childhood obesity. (p. 416)

15. c. is the answer. (p. 415)

KEY TERMS

1. **Obesity** is the condition of being significantly and unhealthily overweight. (p. 413)

2. **Reaction time** is the length of time it takes a person to respond to a particular stimulus. (p. 418)

3. **Developmental psychopathology** is a new field that applies the insights from studies of normal development to the study and treatment of childhood disorders. (p. 420)

4. **Autism** is a severe disturbance of early childhood characterized by deficiencies in communication ability, social skills, and imaginative play. (pp. 421–422)

5. **Mental retardation** is a pervasive delay in cognitive development. (p. 425)

6. A **learning disability** is a difficulty in a particular cognitive skill that is not attributable to an overall intellectual slowness, a physical handicap, a severely stressful living condition, or a lack of basic education. (p. 425)

7. **Dyslexia** is a learning disability in reading. (p. 426)

8. **Dyscalcula** is a learning disability in math. (p. 426)

9. The **attention-deficit hyperactivity disorder (ADHD)** is a behavior problem in which the individual has great difficulty concentrating, is often excessively excitable and impulsive, and is sometimes aggressive. (pp. 429–430)

10. **Provocation ecologies** are unusually rigid or free-wheeling classroom environments that tend to increase ADHD behaviors. (p. 434)

11. **Rarefaction ecologies** are classroom environments that are more flexible than provocation ecologies, yet provide enough structure to reduce ADHD behaviors. (p. 434)

The School Years: Cognitive Development

Chapter Overview

Chapter 13 looks at the development of cognitive abilities in children from age 7 to 11. The first section focuses on changes in the child's selective attention, memory strategies, processing speed and capacity, knowledge base, and problem-solving strategies, as well as their relevance to education, the special province of the information-processing perspective. The second section discusses the Piagetian approach, which describes the growth of logical and reasoning abilities during middle childhood.

The following section looks at language learning in the school years. During this time, children develop a more analytic understanding of words and show a marked improvement in pragmatic skills, such as changing from one form of speech to another when the situation so demands. The educational and social challenges facing children who use nonstandard English, as well as those who are taught in a language other than their native tongue, are discussed. A Research Report examines educational and environmental conditions that are conducive to fluency in a second language.

The final section describes innovative new teaching methods, which emphasize active rather than passive learning and are derived from the developmental theories of Piaget, Vygotsky, and others. Studies that contrast these methods with more traditional methods have shown their effectiveness in reading and math education. A Research Report comparing education in the United States, Japan, and the Republic of China explores the reasons for the disparities. The chapter concludes by examining measures of cognitive growth and variations in cultural standards.

NOTE: Answer guidelines for all Chapter 13 questions begin on page 200.

Guided Study

The text chapter should be studied one section at a time. Before you read, preview each section by skimming it, noting headings and boldface items. Then read the appropriate section objectives from the following outline. Keep these objectives in mind and, as you read the chapter section, search for the information that will enable you to meet each objective. Once you have finished a section, write out answers for its objectives.

The Growth of Thinking, Memory, and Knowledge (pp. 438–445)

1. Discuss advances in selective attention, memory skills, and processing speed and capacity during middle childhood.

2. Discuss advances in knowledge and metacognition during the school years and describe the role these and related advances play in formal education.

Concrete Operational Thought (pp. 445–447)

3. Identify and discuss the logical operations of concrete operational thought and give examples of how these operations are demonstrated by schoolchildren.

4. Discuss recent modifications of Piaget's theory.

Language (pp. 447–456)

5. Describe language development during the school years, noting changing abilities in vocabulary, grammar, and pragmatics.

6. Explain code-switching and discuss the academic and social challenges facing children whose primary language is a nonstandard form.

7. (text and Research Report) Identify several conditions that foster the learning of a second language and describe the best approaches to bilingual education.

Thinking, Learning, and Schooling (pp. 456–468)

8. Discuss historical and cultural variations in the schooling of children and explain why such variations have recently become troubling.

9. Discuss the influences of Piaget, the information-processing perspective, and Vygotsky on classroom education.

10. (Research Report) Compare the academic performance of children in Japan, the Republic of China, and the United States and identify differences in school and home life that may account for differences in academic performance.

11. Explain how achievement and aptitude tests are used in evaluating individual differences in cognitive growth and discuss why use of such tests is controversial.

12. Describe how self-perceptions of cognitive competence change during middle childhood and explain how cultural needs and standards direct cognitive growth.

Chapter Review

When you have finished reading the chapter, work through the material that follows to review it. Complete the sentences and answer the questions. As you proceed, evaluate your performance for each section by consulting the answers on page 200. Do not continue with the next section until you understand each answer. If you need to, review or reread the appropriate section in the textbook before continuing.

The Growth of Thinking, Memory, and Knowledge (pp. 438–445)

1. During middle childhood, children not only know more but are more resourceful in _____ and using their cognitive resources when solving a problem. In the words of John Flavell, they have acquired "a sense of the _____ " of thinking.

2. Researchers who take the _____-_____ perspective believe that the advances in thinking that accompany middle childhood occur because of basic changes in how children _____ and _____ information.

3. The ability to use _____ _____—to screen out distractors and concentrate on relevant information—improves steadily during the school years.

4. During middle childhood, children's use of _____ _____ for retaining new information broadens significantly. For example, they begin to use _____ to repeat information to be remembered and _____ to improve the memorability of material through regrouping. Children's use of _____ _____ to access previously learned information also improves.

5. Taken together, storage strategies and retrieval strategies are called _____ .

6. Children in the school years are better learners and problem-solvers than younger children because they have faster _____ _____ , and they have a larger _____ _____ . This helps account for the stage differences that Piaget found in children's ability to _____ .

7. Some researchers believe that _____ maturation accounts for the cognitive advances of middle childhood, especially the _____ of nerve pathways and maturation of the

_____ _____ .

Others believe that processing becomes more efficient as children learn to use their

_____ _____

better.

8. Processing capacity also becomes more efficient through _____ , as familiar mental activities become routine.

9. Memory ability improves during middle childhood in part because of the child's expanded

_____ _____ .

10. Research suggests that adults _____ (are/are not) always more cognitively competent than children, and that many differences between schoolchildren's and adult's memory and reasoning may be due to children's limited _____ about topics.

11. The ability to evaluate a cognitive task to determine what to do—and to monitor one's performance—is called _____ .

List some indicators of this developmental change during the school years.

12. Children benefit from educational practices that not only impart knowledge but also foster

_____ _____ .

13. Children become much more educable when they can deliberately use _____

_____ , _____ ,

and _____ to assist their learning.

Concrete Operational Thought (pp. 445–447)

14. Another reason older children are more educable is that they are _____ thinkers

who seek explanations that are _____ ,

_____ _____ ,

and _____ .

15. According to Piaget, between ages 7 and 11 children are in the stage of _____

_____ .

16. The logical principle that an object remains the same despite changes in its appearance is _____ . The idea that a transformation process can be reversed to restore the original condition is _____ . The idea that a transformation in one dimension is compensated for by one in another is

_____ .

17. Many concrete operations underlie the basic ideas of elementary-school _____ and _____ .

18. Many recent studies have found that cognitive development is _____ (less/more) heterogeneous than Piaget's descriptions would suggest. Two of the factors that may account for this are _____ differences among individuals in their abilities and aptitudes, and _____ differences in cultural, educational, and experiential background.

Language (pp. 447–456)

19. During middle childhood language development is much more _____ (subtle/ obvious) than in the preschool years. Children become more _____ and _____ in their processing of vocabulary and are better able to define words by analyzing their _____ to other words.

20. Although most grammatical constructions of the child's native language are mastered before age _____ , knowledge of _____ continues to develop throughout elementary school.

21. Children younger than 6 often have trouble understanding the _____ voice

in grammar. In addition to improved understanding of this voice, school-age children begin to understand other grammatical constructions, such as the correct use of _____ , the _____ , and

_____ .

22. Children's use of pragmatics _____ (improves/does not improve) significantly during the school years. A clear demonstration is found in schoolchildren's _____-_____ , which is beyond the ability of most preschool children. Another example is found in their developing ability to learn various forms of _____

_____ .

23. Changing from one form of speech to another is called _____-_____ . The _____ _____ , which children use in situations such as the classroom, is characterized by extensive

_____ , complex _____ , and lengthy _____ . With their friends, children tend to use the _____

_____ , which has a more limited use of vocabulary and syntax and relies more on _____ and _____ to convey meaning.

24. Compared with the elaborated code, which is context- _____ (free/bound), the restricted code is context-_____ (free/bound). While adults often stress the importance of mastery of the elaborated code, the restricted code is also important in helping the child develop _____ skills.

25. Language differences are likely to form a distinct code in groups that are _____ ,

_____ _____ ,

and _____ distinct.

26. The best path for a child whose primary language is a nonstandard form is to _____ (learn standard English as a distinct code/suppress the use of nonstandard English).

Describe some of the academic and social difficulties facing a child whose primary language is a nonstandard form.

27. Most of the citizens of the world

_____ (are/are not) bilingual. Cognitively and linguistically, it is a(n)

_____ (advantage/disadvantage) for children to learn more than one language. Specifically, it may enhance children's grasp of _____

_____ and _____ .

28. (text and Research Report) The approach to bilingual education in which the child's instruction occurs entirely in the second language is called _____ . These programs seem to work best with _____ (younger/older) children. In another approach to bilingual education, children are taught the dominant language in much the same way native children might be taught a foreign language. This is called the _____-

_____ approach. In the

_____-_____

approach, children maintain their native language, learning various content areas in it, while studying the new language.

Thinking, Learning, and Schooling (pp. 456–468)

29. There _____ (is/is not) universal agreement on how best to educate schoolchildren.

30. Historically, _____ (boys/girls) and wealthier children have been most likely to be formally taught, and to have the greatest educational demands placed upon them.

31. Schools vary extensively in the _____

offered and the _____

_____ used.

32. Achievement scores show that American children are _____ (ahead of/behind) their counterparts in most other industrialized countries, especially in the subjects of _____ and _____ .

33. Passive learning _____ (is/is not) the most appropriate form of instruction for most schoolchildren.

34. The information-processing perspective has led to a reemphasis on _____ _____ and the realization that there _____ (is/is not) a standard curriculum that should be taught to everyone in a given grade.

35. Teaching that is based on Vygotsky's perspective emphasizes the importance of _____ _____ in learning. A recent study found that children taught according to this model had _____ (higher/lower) reading achievement scores than those taught by more traditional methods.

36. A new approach in math replaces rote learning with _____-_____ materials and active discussion, promoting a problem-solving approach to learning.

37. (Research Report) Achievement tests today demonstrate that children from three countries, _____ _____ , have the highest scores. Research attributes this superiority to _____ _____ .

(Research Report) Give several examples of how schooling in the United States differs from that in Japan and the Republic of China.

38. (Research Report) Compared to American parents, parents in Japan and China tend to be _____ (more/less) involved in their children's education.

39. (Research Report) Values in the macrosystem are highly influential as well. As compared to _____ (American/Japanese) teachers, _____ (American/Japanese) teachers are greatly esteemed and receive a proportionately _____ (higher/lower) salary.

40. Tests that are designed to measure what a child has learned are called _____ tests. Tests that are designed to measure learning potential are called _____ tests. In the original version of the most commonly used of the latter tests, a person's score was translated into a _____ _____ and that was divided by the person's

_____ _____

to determine his or her _____ . On current tests, two-thirds of all children score within a year or two of their age-mates, somewhere between _____ and _____ . Children who score above _____ are considered gifted, while those who score in the _____-_____ range are considered to be slow learners.

41. The most widely used IQ tests are the _____-_____ and the _____ tests; the latter test has special versions for _____ , _____ , and _____ .

42. Testing is controversial in part because a child's test performance can be affected by nonintellectual factors, such as _____ _____ .

43. Children's perceptions of their intellectual competence generally _____ (improve/decline) through the school years. One reason is that older children are more likely to use _____

_____ to evaluate their abilities and attributes.

44. Students who approach schoolwork with a _____ orientation believe that intellectual growth depends on persistence and hard work. By contrast, students with a _____ orientation tend to shy away from challenges in which they might fail.

45. The shift to more structured schooling during middle childhood reflects the traditional values of _____ culture, where _____ achievement, _____ , and _____ accuracy are highly regarded. In other cultures, more emphasis is placed on _____ learning, _____ mastery, and respect for _____ styles.

Progress Test 1

Multiple-Choice Questions

Circle your answers to the following questions and check them with the answers on page 201. If your answer is incorrect, read the explanation for why it is incorrect and then consult the appropriate pages of the text (in parentheses following the correct answer).

1. According to Piaget, the stage of cognitive development in which a person understands specific logical ideas and can apply them to concrete problems is called:
   a. preoperational thought.
   b. operational thought.
   c. concrete operational thought.
   d. formal operational thought.

2. Aptitude and achievement testing are controversial because:
   a. most tests are unreliable with respect to the individual scores they yield.
   b. test performance can be affected by many factors other than the child's intellectual potential or academic achievement.
   c. they often fail to identify serious learning problems.
   d. of all of the above reasons.

3. The idea that an object that has been transformed in some way can be restored to its original form by undoing the process is:

a. identity.
b. reversibility.
c. reciprocity.
d. automatization.

4. Information-processing theorists contend that major advances in cognitive development occur during the school years because:
   a. the child's mind becomes more like a computer as he or she matures.
   b. children become better able to process and analyze information.
   c. most mental activities become automatic by the time a child is about 13 years old.
   d. the major improvements in reasoning that occur during the school years involve increased long-term memory capacity.

5. The ability to filter out distractions and concentrate on relevant details is called:
   a. metacognition.
   b. information processing.
   c. selective attention.
   d. decentering.

6. The best example of a retrieval strategy is:
   a. reconstructing a lecture from notes.
   b. organizing terms to be learned in categories.
   c. studying in an environment that is free of distractions.
   d. repeating a multiplication table until it is automatic.

7. A term that refers to the ability to monitor one's cognitive performance—to think about thinking—is:
   a. pragmatics.
   b. information processing.
   c. selective attention.
   d. metacognition.

8. During middle childhood, children become more analytic and logical in their understanding of words. This means that they:
   a. learn more words per year than they did during the play years.
   b. can first learn a second language.
   c. are less bound by context, appearance, and personal experience.
   d. no longer engage in verbal play.

9. Tests that measure a child's potential to learn a new subject are called _____ tests.
   a. aptitude
   b. achievement
   c. vocational
   d. intelligence

10. A type of speech used in formal situations—for example, when speaking to teachers—that is characterized by extensive vocabulary and lengthy sentences is the:
    a. restricted code.
    b. elaborated code.
    c. pragmatic code.
    d. grammatical code.

11. To encourage competence in standard English in children whose primary language is a nonstandard form without damaging self-esteem, teachers should:
    a. accept nonstandard English as legitimate in all school contexts.
    b. reinforce the idea that all nonstandard English is incorrect.
    c. allow children to select their own form of expression.
    d. help children with the pragmatics of code-switching between standard and nonstandard English.

12. The educational emphasis on the importance of social interaction in the classroom is most directly derived from the developmental theory of:
    a. Vygotsky.
    b. Piaget.
    c. information processing.
    d. those who advocate immersion learning.

13. Critics of Piaget contend that:
    a. cognitive development is more homogeneous than Piaget predicted.
    b. children's progress through the cognitive stages is more uniform than Piaget thought.
    c. children demonstrate partial entrance into concrete operational thought earlier than Piaget predicted.
    d. individual differences in progress through the cognitive stages are minimal.

14. Historically, boys and wealthier children were more likely to be formally taught and to have greater educational demands placed upon them than girls or poor children. Today, this inequality:
    a. can be found only in developing countries.
    b. has largely disappeared.
    c. persists, even in developed countries.
    d. has been eliminated for girls, but not for poor children.

15. (Research Report) To what do cross-cultural researchers attribute the superior achievement test scores of Pacific-rim students?
    a. genetics
    b. the high quality of home and classroom educational experiences
    c. a shorter school day and year
    d. classroom environments that emphasize passive learning

True or False Items

Write *true* or *false* on the line in front of each statement.

_____ 1. One major objection to Piagetian theory is that it describes the schoolchild as an active learner, a term appropriate only for preschoolers.

_____ 2. Children master many grammatical constructions of their native language before age 6.

_____ 3. Children's perceptions of their intellectual competence generally improve through the school years.

_____ 4. Western classrooms today emphasize collaborative learning.

_____ 5. The process of telling a joke involves pragmatic language skills usually not mastered before age 7.

_____ 6. Code-switching, especially the occasional use of slang, is a behavior characteristic primarily of children in the lower social strata.

_____ 7. (Research Report) American parents are more likely than Japanese parents to be dissatisfied with their children's academic performance.

_____ 8. (Research Report) During the early school years, children learn a second language best if they have not already achieved proficiency in their native language.

_____ 9. (Research Report) Most developmentalists agree that there should be a standard educational system for all children.

_____ 10. New standards of math education in many nations emphasize problem-solving skills rather than simple memorization of formulas.

Progress Test 2

Progress Test 2 should be completed during a final chapter review. Answer the following questions after you thoroughly understand the correct answers for the Chapter Review and Progress Test 1.

Multiple-Choice Questions

1. According to Piaget, 8- and 9-year-olds can reason only about concrete things in their lives. "Concrete" means:

a. logical.
b. abstract.
c. tangible or specific.
d. mathematical or classifiable.

2. In the earliest aptitude tests, a person's score was translated into a(n) _____ age that was divided by the person's _____ age to find the _____ quotient.
   a. mental; chronological; intelligence
   b. chronological; mental; intelligence
   c. intelligence; chronological; mental
   d. intelligence; mental; chronological

3. Tests that measure what a child has already learned are called _____ tests.
   a. aptitude   c. achievement
   b. vocational   d. intelligence

4. When psychologists look at the ability of children to receive, store, and organize information, they are examining cognitive development from a view based on:
   a. the observations of Piaget.
   b. information processing.
   c. learning theory.
   d. the idea that the key to thinking is the sensory register.

5. The aptitude test that has special versions for preschoolers, schoolchildren, and adults is the:
   a. IQ test.   c. Wechsler test.
   b. Stanford-Binet.   d. WAIS-R.

6. The logical operations of concrete operational thought are particularly important to an understanding of the basic ideas of elementary-school:
   a. spelling.   c. math and science.
   b. reading.   d. social studies.

7. One mnemonic technique that develops toward the end of middle childhood is the regrouping of items to be remembered into categories. This technique is called:
   a. metacognition.   c. rehearsal.
   b. selective attention. d. organization.

8. Which of the following is *not* a Piagetian idea that is widely accepted by contemporary developmentalists?
   a. The thinking of school-age children is characterized by a more comprehensive logic than that of preschoolers.
   b. Children are active learners.
   c. How children think is as important as what they know.

d. Once a certain type of reasoning ability emerges in children, it is evenly apparent in all domains of thinking.

9. Processing capacity refers to:
   a. the ability to selectively attend to more than one thought.
   b. the amount of information that a person is able to hold in working memory.
   c. the size of the child's knowledge base.
   d. all of the above.

10. Procedures for retaining new information are called:
    a. retrieval strategies.
    b. storage strategies.
    c. mnemonics.
    d. metacognition.

11. A form of speech children use among themselves in informal situations that includes slang, shared understandings, and meaningful gestures is the:
    a. elaborated code.   c. restricted code.
    b. grammatical code.   d. open code.

12. (Research Report) When the dominant language is used for instruction in reading, writing, and math, second-language learning of students using another language is fostered by:
    a. instruction based on bilingual-bicultural education.
    b. instruction that completely immerses the student in the new language.
    c. instruction that focuses on rote memorization of grammatical rules.
    d. group instruction.

13. Research on metacognition shows that school-age children learn problem solving best when they are:
    a. shown the correct answer to the problem.
    b. shown the specific shortcomings in their strategies.
    c. criticized for an incorrect answer, then told to try again.
    d. left to work the problem on their own.

14. A new approach to math education focuses on:
    a. rote memorization of formulas before problems are introduced.
    b. "hands-on" materials and active discussion of concepts.
    c. one-on-one tutorials.
    d. pretesting children and grouping them by ability.

15. Regarding bilingual education, many contemporary developmentalists believe that:
    a. the attempted learning of two languages is confusing to children and delays proficiency in either one or both languages.
    b. bilingual education is linguistically, culturally, and cognitively advantageous to children.
    c. second-language education is most effective when the child has not yet mastered the native language.
    d. bilingual education programs are too expensive to justify the few developmental advantages they confer.

Matching Items

Match each term or concept with its corresponding description or definition.

Terms or Concepts

_____ 1. automatization
_____ 2. reversibility
_____ 3. reciprocity
_____ 4. identity
_____ 5. information processing
_____ 6. selective attention
_____ 7. retrieval strategies
_____ 8. mnemonics
_____ 9. metacognition
_____ 10. immersion

Descriptions or Definitions

a. the ability to screen out distractions and concentrate on relevant information
b. the idea that a transformation process can be undone to restore the original conditions
c. the idea that an object remains the same despite changes in its appearance
d. developmental perspective that conceives of cognitive development as the result of changes in the processing and analysis of information
e. the idea that a transformation in one dimension is compensated for by a transformation in another
f. educational technique in which instruction occurs entirely in the second language
g. procedures to access previously learned information
h. memory aids
i. familiar mental activities become routine
j. the ability to evaluate a cognitive task and to monitor one's performance on it

Thinking Critically About Chapter 13

Answer these questions the day before an exam as a final check on your understanding of the chapter's terms and concepts.

1. Angela was born in 1984. In 1992, she scored 125 on an intelligence test. Using the original formula, what was Angela's mental age when she took the test?
    a. 6   c. 10
    b. 8   d. 12

2. Damon chooses challenging tasks because he believes that he will learn from them even if he doesn't succeed. Damon clearly has a(n):
    a. mastery orientation.
    b. performance orientation.
    c. external locus of control.
    d. restricted code.

3. Compared to her 4-year-old sister, 9-year-old Andrea is more likely to seek explanations that are:
    a. intuitive.   c. subjective.
    b. generalizable.   d. all of the above.

4. Dr. Larsen believes that the cognitive advances of middle childhood occur because of basic changes in children's thinking speed, knowledge base, and memory retrieval skills. Dr. Larsen evidently is working from the _____ perspective.
    a. Piagetian
    b. Vygotskian
    c. information-processing
    d. psychoanalytic

5. Some researchers believe that cognitive processing speed and capacity increase during middle childhood because of:

a. the myelination of nerve pathways.
b. maturation of the frontal cortex.
c. better use of cognitive resources.
d. all of the above.

6. A child's ability to tell a joke that will amuse his or her audience always depends on:
a. the child's mastery of reciprocity and reversibility.
b. code-switching.
c. the child's ability to consider another's perspective.
d. an expansion of the child's processing capacity.

7. For a 10-year-old, some mental activities have become so familiar or routine as to require little mental work. This development is called:
a. selective attention.
b. mnemonics.
c. metacognition.
d. automatization.

8. A child who sings "i before e except after c" is using a memory-aiding device called:
a. rehearsal.
b. automatization.
c. a mnemonic.
d. class inclusion.

9. (Research Report) The existence or effectiveness of bilingual education may be limited because:
a. it is expensive.
b. trained teachers are scarce.
c. parents and the community do not always support it.
d. of all of the above reasons.

10. A 9-year-old will typically cling less stubbornly to grammatical mistakes than a 4-year-old because the 9-year-old:
a. has mastered the concept of conservation.
b. is less egocentric in learning and applying rules.
c. has more experience in humor and joke-telling.
d. understands the subjunctive.

11. Russian-speaking children do not master the subjunctive very much earlier than English-speaking children, even though the subjunctive is less complicated in the Russian language. The reason for this is that:
a. cultural patterns make the subjunctive more difficult for Russian children to grasp.
b. mastery of the subjunctive requires a particular level of cognitive development.
c. the use of the subjunctive in Russian is very rare.

d. Russian children score lower on language aptitude tests.

12. A second-grader says, "I don't know nothing about nothing." The teacher corrects the child because his double negative is:
a. unacceptable in a school with primarily middle-class students.
b. illogical and confused.
c. incorrect in standard English.
d. incorrect in nonstandard English.

13. Compared with her mother, who attended elementary school in the 1950s, Bettina, who is now in the third grade, is likely to be in a class that places greater emphasis on:
a. individualized learning.
b. active learning.
c. learning by discovery, discussion, and deduction.
d. all of the above.

14. Compared to his 5-year-old brother, 10-year-old Wyeth is less confident of his intellectual abilities. The most likely explanation for this is that:
a. older children are more likely to use social comparison to evaluate their competencies.
b. Wyeth has a performance orientation.
c. Wyeth's brother has a mastery orientation.
d. all of the above are true.

15. (Research Report) Concluding her class presentation on differences between the educational experiences of Japanese and American children, Nogumi states that:
a. Japanese children devote more time to nonacademic activities than American children.
b. American children spend less time in school than Japanese children.
c. Japanese children appear to be less happy and less responsive in the classroom than American children.
d. Japanese teachers are more likely to employ individual, as opposed to group, instruction.

Key Terms

Using your own words, write a brief definition or explanation of each of the following terms on a separate piece of paper.

1. selective attention
2. storage strategies
3. rehearsal

4. organization
5. retrieval strategies
6. mnemonics
7. automatization
8. metacognition
9. concrete operational thought
10. identity
11. reversibility
12. reciprocity
13. code-switching
14. elaborated code
15. restricted code
16. immersion
17. achievement tests
18. aptitude tests
19. IQ tests
20. social comparison
21. mastery orientation
22. performance orientation

ANSWERS

CHAPTER REVIEW

1. planning; game
2. information-processing; process; analyze
3. selective attention
4. storage strategies; rehearsal; organization; retrieval strategies
5. mnemonics
6. processing speed; processing capacity; conserve
7. neurological; myelination; frontal cortex; cognitive resources
8. automatization
9. knowledge base
10. are not; knowledge
11. metacognition

School-age children's better use of selective attention, mnemonics, and other cognitive strategies all derive from metacognitive growth. Furthermore, they know how to identify challenging tasks and devote greater effort to them; are more likely to spontaneously monitor and evaluate their progress than are preschoolers; and are more likely to use external aids to enhance memorization and problem solving.

12. cognitive strategies
13. selective attention; mnemonics; metacognition
14. logical; rational; internally consistent; generalizable
15. concrete operations
16. identity; reversibility; reciprocity
17. math; science
18. more; hereditary; environmental
19. subtle; analytic; logical; relationships
20. 6; syntax
21. passive; comparatives; subjunctive; metaphors
22. improves; joke-telling; polite speech
23. code-switching; elaborated code; vocabulary; syntax; sentences; restricted code; gestures; intonation
24. free; bound; pragmatic
25. cohesive; geographically isolated; culturally
26. learn standard English as a distinct code

Such children may be teased by classmates for their unusual speech and have greater difficulty learning to read and write standard English. If the teacher and school take the stance that nonstandard English is illegitimate, children may experience a loss of self-esteem and be troubled by this attack on their cultural identity.

27. are; advantage; linguistic rules; concepts
28. immersion; younger; second-language; bilingual-bicultural
29. is not
30. boys
31. curriculum; pedagogical techniques
32. behind; math; science
33. is not
34. explicit instruction; is not
35. social interaction; higher
36. hands-on
37. Japan, Korea, and the Republic of China; educational experiences in the school and home

Japanese and Chinese children are in school more hours weekly than American children are. They also are more likely to attend supplemental classes at special schools if they fall behind and to have more of their classroom time devoted to academic activities. Teachers in Japan and the Republic of China tend to emphasize group instruction, while American teachers emphasize individual or small-group instruction.

38. more
39. American; Japanese; higher

40. achievement; aptitude; mental age; chronological age; IQ; 85; 115; 130; 70–85

41. Stanford-Binet; Wechsler; preschoolers; school-children; adults

42. the capacity to pay attention and concentrate, emotional stress, health, language difficulties, and educational background

43. decline; social comparison

44. mastery; performance

45. Western; individual; competition; technical; collaborative; group; individual

PROGRESS TEST 1

Multiple-Choice Questions

1. c. is the answer. (p. 445)

   a. Preoperational thought is "pre-logical" thinking.

   b. There is no such stage in Piaget's theory.

   d. Formal operational thought extends logical reasoning to abstract problems.

2. b. is the answer. (p. 464)

3. b. is the answer. (p. 446)

   a. This is the concept that an object remains the same despite changes in its appearance.

   c. This is the concept that a change in one dimension of an object can be compensated for by a change in another dimension.

   d. This is the process by which familiar mental activities become routine and automatic.

4. b. is the answer. (p. 438)

   a. Information-processing theorists use the mind-computer metaphor at every age.

   c. Although increasing automatization is an important aspect of development, the information-processing perspective does not suggest that most mental activities become automatic by age 13.

   d. Most of the important changes in reasoning that occur during the school years are due to the improved processing capacity of the person's *working memory.*

5. c. is the answer. (p. 439)

   a. This is the ability to evaluate a cognitive task and to monitor one's performance on it.

   b. Information processing is a perspective on cognitive development that focuses on how the mind analyzes, stores, retrieves, and reasons about information.

   d. Decentering, which refers to the school-age child's ability to consider more than one aspect of a problem simultaneously, is not discussed in this chapter.

6. a. is the answer. (pp. 440–441)

   b. & d. These are examples of storage strategies.

   c. This is a good idea, but it is not a retrieval strategy.

7. d. is the answer. (p. 443)

   a. Pragmatics refers to the practical use of language to communicate with others.

   b. The information-processing perspective views the mind as being like a computer.

   c. This is the ability to screen out distractions in order to focus on important information.

8. c. is the answer. (p. 448)

   a. Vocabulary development is more subtle during the school years than the preschool years.

   b. The learning of a second language does *not* depend on this linguistic advance.

   d. Verbal play, such as joke-telling, most certainly does *not* decrease during the school years.

9. a. is the answer. (pp. 463–464)

   b. Achievement tests measure what has already been learned.

   c. Vocational tests are achievement tests.

   d. Intelligence tests measure *general* aptitude, rather than aptitude for a specific subject.

10. b. is the answer. (p. 451)

    a. This less formal type of speech is more often used with friends.

    c. & d. No such codes were discussed.

11. d. is the answer. (pp. 452–453)

    a. & c. These would be impractical; furthermore, children need to learn standard English in order to further their own academic development.

    b. This would be a blow to the child's cultural identity and self-esteem.

12. a. is the answer. (p. 459)

13. c. is the answer. (p. 447)

    a., b., & d. Just the opposite is true.

14. c. is the answer. (p. 456)

15. b. is the answer. (p. 460)

True or False Items

1. F Most educators agree that the school-age child, like the preschooler, is an active learner. (p. 458)

2. T (p. 448)

3. F Older children are more realistic than younger

children. They also are more likely to use social comparison to evaluate their emerging competencies. (p. 465)

4. F   Western classrooms tend to emphasize competition and individual achievement. (p. 466)

5. T (p. 450)

6. F   Code-switching (including occasional use of slang) is a behavior demonstrated by all children. (p. 451)

7. F   Although the academic performance of American children lags behind that of Japanese children, American parents are more likely than Japanese (or Chinese) parents to express satisfaction with their children's academic performance. (p. 460)

8. F   Studies of Finnish children immersed in Swedish indicate that children seem to learn a second language best when they have already achieved proficiency in their native language. (p. 455)

9. F   The complexity of the learning process, as described by information-processing researchers, indicates that there is no basic educational system that will work for everyone. (p. 461)

10. T (p. 459)

PROGRESS TEST 2

Multiple-Choice Questions

1. c. is the answer. (p. 445)

2. a. is the answer. (p. 463)

3. c. is the answer. (p. 462)

4. b. is the answer. (p. 438)

5. c. is the answer. (p. 463)

    a. "IQ test" is too vague an answer. Both the Wechsler and the Stanford-Binet are IQ tests.

    d. The WAIS-R is the *adult* revision of the Wechsler test.

6. c. is the answer. (pp. 445–446)

7. d. is the answer. (p. 440)

    a. This is the ability to evaluate a cognitive task and to monitor one's performance on it.

    b. This is the ability to screen out distractions and focus on important information.

    c. This is the repeating of information in order to remember it.

8. d. is the answer. (p. 447)

9. b. is the answer. (p. 441)

10. b. is the answer. (p. 440)

    a. These are strategies for *accessing* already learned information.

c. Mnemonics include both storage and retrieval strategies.

d. This is the ability to evaluate a task and to monitor one's performance on it.

11. c. is the answer. (p. 451)

    a. This is a type of speech used in the classroom and other more formal situations.

    b. & d. No such codes were discussed.

12. b. is the answer. (p. 454)

13. b. is the answer. (p. 443)

14. b. is the answer. (p. 459)

15. b. is the answer. (p. 453)

Matching Items

1. i (p. 442)   5. d (p. 438)   8. h (p. 441)
2. b (p. 446)   6. a (p. 439)   9. j (p. 443)
3. e (p. 446)   7. g (p. 440)   10. f (p. 456)
4. c (p. 445)

THINKING CRITICALLY ABOUT CHAPTER 13

1. c. is the answer. At the time she took the test, Angela's chronological age was 8. Knowing that her IQ was 125, solving the equation for mental age yields a value of 10. (p. 463)

2. a. is the answer. (pp. 465–466)

    b. Students with a performance orientation tend to shy away from challenges in which they might fail.

    c. The text did not discuss the relationship between locus of control and students' approach to schoolwork.

    d. A restricted code is an informal form of speech.

3. b. is the answer. (p. 445)

4. c. is the answer. (p. 438)

    a. This perspective emphasizes the logical, active nature of thinking during middle childhood.

    b. This perspective emphasizes the importance of social interaction in learning.

    d. This perspective does not address the development of cognitive skills.

5. d. is the answer. (p. 441)

6. c. is the answer. Joke-telling is one of the clearest demonstrations of schoolchildren's improved pragmatic skills, including the ability to know what someone else will think is funny. (p. 450)

7. d. is the answer. (p. 442)

    a. Selective attention is the ability to focus on important information and screen out distractions.

b. Mnemonics are memory aids.

c. Metacognition is the ability to evaluate a task and to monitor one's performance on it.

8. c. is the answer. (p. 441)

a. Rehearsal is the repetition of to-be-learned information.

b. Automatization refers to the tendency of well-rehearsed mental activities to become routine and automatic.

d. Class inclusion is the idea that a particular object may belong to more than one class.

9. d. is the answer. (pp. 454–455)

10. b. is the answer. (p. 449)

11. b. is the answer. (p. 449)

12. c. is the answer. (p. 452)

13. d. is the answer. (pp. 458–459)

14. a. is the answer. (p. 465)

b. & c. There is no basis for determining either brother's orientation.

15. b. is the answer. (p. 460)

a. & d. In fact, the opposites are true.

c. This is untrue.

KEY TERMS

1. **Selective attention** is the ability to screen out distractions and concentrate on relevant information. (p. 439)

2. **Storage strategies** are procedures for retaining new information. (p. 440)

3. **Rehearsal** is the repeating of information to be remembered. (p. 440)

4. **Organization** is the regrouping of information to make it easier to remember. (p. 440)

5. **Retrieval strategies** are procedures for accessing previously learned information. (p. 440)

6. **Mnemonics** are storage and retrieval strategies used to aid memory. (p. 441)

7. **Automatization** is the process by which familiar and well-rehearsed mental activities become routine and automatic. (p. 442)

8. **Metacognition** is the ability to evaluate a cognitive task to determine what to do, and to monitor one's performance on that task. (p. 443)

9. During Piaget's stage of **concrete operational thought**, lasting from ages 7 to 11, children can think logically about events and objects but are not able to reason abstractly. (p. 445)

10. **Identity** is the logical principle that an object remains the same despite changes in its appearance. (p. 445)

11. **Reversibility** is the logical principle that a transformation process can be reversed to restore the original conditions. (p. 446)

12. **Reciprocity** is the logical principle that a transformation in one dimension of an object is compensated for by a transformation in another. (p. 446)

Example: A child who understands **reciprocity** realizes that rolling a ball of clay into a thin rope makes it longer, but also skinnier, than its original shape.

13. **Code-switching** is changing from one form of speech to another. (p. 451)

14. The **elaborated code**, which is characterized by extensive vocabulary, complex syntax, and lengthy sentences, is the formal speech children use in situations such as the classroom. (p. 451)

15. The **restricted code**, which has a limited vocabulary and syntax, relies more on gestures and intonation, and is context-specific, is the informal speech children use with their friends. (p. 451)

16. **Immersion** is an approach to bilingual education in which the child's instruction occurs entirely in the new language. (p. 456)

17. **Achievement tests** are tests that measure what a child has already learned in a particular academic subject or subjects. (p. 462)

18. **Aptitude tests** are designed to measure how well and how quickly a person could learn a new subject if given the chance. (p. 463)

19. **IQ tests** are aptitude tests that measure an individual's intelligence. Originally, IQ scores were calculated as a quotient—the child's mental age divided by the child's chronological age times 100. (p. 463)

20. During middle childhood, children use **social comparison** to evaluate their competencies, comparing their abilities against those of their peers. (p. 465)

21. Students with a **mastery orientation** choose challenging tasks, believing that intellectual growth will occur through persistence and hard work. (pp. 465–466)

22. Students with a **performance orientation** tend to shy away from challenging tasks at which they might fail, regarding failures as a sign of inadequacy that is unlikely to change. (p. 466)

14

The School Years: Psychosocial Development

Chapter Overview

This chapter brings to a close the unit on the school years. We have seen that from ages 7 to 11, the child becomes stronger and more competent, mastering the biosocial and cognitive abilities that are important in his or her culture. Psychosocial accomplishments are equally impressive.

The first section of the chapter begins by exploring the growing social competence of children, as described by Freud, Erikson, and learning, cognitive, and sociocultural theorists. The section continues with a discussion of the growth of social cognition and self-understanding. Children's interaction with peers and others in their ever-widening social world is the subject of the next section.

Following this, the chapter examines moral development during middle childhood. Kohlberg's stage theory is outlined, as well as current reevaluations of his theory. The section raises a crucial and practical question: what is the relationship between moral thinking and moral behavior.

The following two sections explore the problems and challenges that are often experienced by school-age children in our society, including the experience of parental divorce and remarriage, living in single-parent and blended families, as well as that of poverty. The chapter closes with a discussion of the ways children cope with stressful situations.

NOTE: Answer guidelines for all Chapter 14 questions begin on page 216.

Guided Study

The text chapter should be studied one section at a time. Before you read, preview each section by skimming it, noting headings and boldface items. Then read the appropriate section objectives from the following outline. Keep these objectives in mind and, as you read the chapter section, search for the information that will enable you to meet each objective. Once you have finished a section, write out answers for its objectives.

An Expanding Social World (pp. 472–477)

1. Identify the common themes or emphases of three theoretical views of the psychosocial development of school-age children.

2. Define social cognition and explain how children's theory of mind evolves during middle childhood.

3. Describe the development of self-understanding during middle childhood and its implications for children's self-esteem and their vulnerability to learned helplessness.

The Peer Group (pp. 477–487)

4. Discuss the importance of peer groups, providing examples of how school-age children develop their own subculture and explaining the importance of this development.

5. Discuss the ways in which children's social problem-solving skills and friendship circles change during the school years.

6. (text and A Closer Look) Identify three groups of unpopular children who merit special concern; discuss the reasons for this unpopularity, noting whether anything can be done to help such children.

Moral Development (pp. 488–494)

7. Outline Kohlberg' stage theory of moral development.

8. Identify and evaluate several criticisms of Kohlberg's theory.

9. Discuss children's growing awareness of social conventions, as well as the relationship between moral reasoning and moral behavior.

Family Structure and Child Development (pp. 494–505)

10. Describe how American family structures have changed in recent decades, and discuss the benefits of children living with both biological parents.

11. Discuss the impact of divorce and single-parent households on the psychosocial development of the school-age child.

12. Discuss the impact of blended families and grandparent households on the psychosocial development of the school-age child.

Poverty in Middle Childhood (pp. 505–511)

13. Discuss the effect of socioeconomic status on the biosocial, cognitive, and psychosocial development of school-age children.

Coping with Life (pp. 511–514)

14. Identify the variables that influence the impact of stresses on schoolchildren and discuss those factors that seem especially important in helping children cope with stress.

Chapter Review

When you have finished reading the chapter, work through the material that follows to review it. Complete the sentences and answer the questions. As you proceed, evaluate your performance for each section by consulting the answers on page 216. Do not continue with the next section until you understand each answer. If you need to, review or reread the appropriate section in the textbook before continuing.

An Expanding Social World (pp. 472–477)

1. Freud describes middle childhood as the period of _____ , when emotional

drives are _____ , psychosexual needs are _____ , and unconscious conflicts are _____ .

2. According to Erikson, the crisis of middle childhood is _____

_____ _____ .

3. Developmentalists influenced by behaviorism or social learning theory, or by the cognitive or sociocultural perspectives, are more concerned with children's _____ of new cognitive abilities. Middle childhood is seen as a time when many distinct competencies _____ .

4. School-age children advance in their understanding of other people and groups; that is, they advance in _____

_____ . At this time, the preschooler's one-step theory of mind begins to evolve into a complex, _____ view of others.

5. In experiments on children's social cognition, older children are more likely to focus on _____ (observable behaviors/ underlying motives) when asked to predict another person's behavior in a situation.

6. Another example of children's advancing social cognition is that, as compared to younger children, older children are more likely to focus on _____ (physical characteristics/personality traits) when asked to describe other children.

7. During the school years children's emotional sensitivity to others _____ (increases/does not increase).

Give several examples of how the expansion of emotional understanding influences children's social interaction.

8. In the beginning of the school years children often explain their actions by referring to the events of the immediate _____ ; a few years later they more readily relate their actions to their _____ _____ and _____ .

9. Along with greater self-understanding during the school years comes greater self- _____ , as children learn to control their reactions for strategic purposes.

10. As their self-understanding sharpens, children gradually become _____ (more/less) self-critical, and their self-esteem _____ (rises/dips). As they mature, children are also _____ (more/less) likely to feel personally to blame for their shortcomings. This is especially true for _____ (girls/boys).

11. During the school years children's perceptions of their intellectual competencies _____ (decline steadily/remain optimistic).

12. Compared with younger children, older children are more vulnerable to _____ _____ ; that is, their past failures in a particular area have taught them to believe that they are unable to do anything to improve their performance. Many such children attribute their _____ (failures/ successes/failures and successes) to their ability rather than to things beyond their control.

The Peer Group (pp. 477–487)

13. A peer group is defined as _____ _____ .

14. Some social scientists call the peer group's subculture the _____ _____ _____ , highlighting the distinctions between children's groups and the general culture.

Identify several distinguishing features of this subculture.

15. A certain amount of _____ , _____ , and _____ is expected in children's peer interactions. Variation in the norms for such behaviors _____ (has/has not) been found to occur by age, by ethnic and economic group, by neighborhood, and by the specific _____ _____ .

16. As children's social awareness increases, assisting or sharing with others, referred to as _____ behavior, is increasingly seen as a sign and an obligation of friendship. However, children become _____ (more/less) exclusive in giving help to those they know, for example.

17. Peer conflict during the school years, as compared to the preschool years, is _____ (more/less) likely to result in retaliation, an appeal to an adult authority, or distress. This demonstrates that social problem-solving skills _____ (advance/do not advance) during the school years.

18. When asked what makes their best friends different from other acquaintances, older children are more likely than younger children to cite _____ _____ . Older children also increasingly regard friendship as a forum for _____ .

19. Friendship groups typically become _____ (larger/smaller) and _____ (more/less) rigid during the school years.

20. An estimated _____ percent of schoolchildren are unpopular most of the time. Researchers have identified several categories of such children, including _____ children who are actively disliked by others, _____ children who are ignored by peers because they are shy and withdrawn, and _____ children toward whom others are ambivalent.

21. Children who are rejected by their peers often are

immature in their _____ .
_____ .

Give a specific example of this immaturity.

22. According to the relationship perspective, unpopular children acquire social tendencies at
_____ that may lead to their lack of
acceptance. For example, _____ ,
and especially _____-
_____ , children report feeling
more family _____ and less
affection and support from their
_____ than do other children.

23. (A Closer Look) Several strategies have been
used, each with some success, to help children
who lack acceptance among peers. They are social
_____ _____ ,
_____ _____ ,
social-_____ training, and
_____ _____ .

Moral Development (pp. 488–494)

24. The development of moral actions, attitudes, and
arguments is _____ (mostly
complete by adolescence/lifelong).

Explain why the first significant growth in moral
development occurs during the school years.

25. The theorist who has extensively studied moral
development by presenting children, adolescents,
and adults with stories that pose ethical dilemmas is _____ . According to his
theory, the three levels of moral reasoning are
_____ , _____ ,
and _____ .

26. In preconventional reasoning, emphasis is on

_____ _____ .
"Might makes right" describes stage
_____ (1/2), while "look out for number one" describes stage _____ (1/2).

27. In conventional reasoning, emphasis is on
_____ _____ ,
such as being a dutiful citizen, in stage
_____ (3/4), or winning
approval from others, in stage _____
(3/4).

28. In postconventional reasoning, emphasis is on
_____ _____ ,
such as _____ _____
(stage 5) and _____ _____
_____ (stage 6).

29. In Kohlberg's theory, the moral conclusions people reach when reacting to ethical dilemmas are
_____ (more/less) important than
how they reason.

30. One criticism of Kohlberg's theory is that the
stages reflect values associated with
_____ , _____
cultures. A second is that moral thinking is less
_____ than Kohlberg implied.
A third is that the theory overemphasized
_____ thought and underesti-
mated _____
_____ . A fourth is that the theory was validated only on _____
(males/females).

31. The criticism that Kohlberg's theory is biased
against females has been most compellingly
expressed by _____ . Research
studies _____ (have/have not)
consistently supported this criticism. Some studies do find that, compared with males, females
tend to focus more on _____
_____ than on _____
_____ .

32. As their moral judgment develops, children also
become aware that society is governed in part by
_____ _____
concerning appropriate behavior.

33. The distinction between moral values and social

conventions _____ (is/is not) consistent across different cultures.

34. Most children, _____ (do/do not) cheat, or bend rules, when loyalty to friends is at stake.

35. Most studies have shown that moral reasoning _____ (does/does not) significantly influence moral behavior. Juvenile delinquents generally _____ (do/do not) score lower on tests of moral reasoning than do other children their age.

Family Structure and Child Development (pp. 494–505)

36. Family structures are defined as _____ _____ .

37. At mid-twentieth century the preferred family structure in most industrialized nations consisted of _____ _____ . At the same time, the preferred family structure in most developing countries in Asia and Latin America consisted of _____ _____ , while in _____ and _____ nations a variety of family structures flourished.

38. The "traditional" family structure that predominated during most of America's history is becoming _____ (more/less) common.

39. If current trends continue, about _____ percent of American children born in the 1990s will live with both biological parents from birth to age 18.

40. Longitudinal research studies demonstrate that children can thrive _____ (only in certain family structures/in almost any family structure).

41. In terms of developmental effects on children, specifics of family function, such as _____ _____ _____ , are more crucial than specifics of family structure.

42. Children who have fewer physical, emotional, or learning difficulties are those who live with _____ _____ _____ .

Describe how children reared in this family structure fare at adolescence and early adulthood.

43. Give two reasons for the benefits of this family structure.

    a. _____

    b. _____

44. The advantages of traditional families are often _____ (overstated/understated). Contributing to this is the fact that many studies do not take sufficient account of other factors that affect child development, the most obvious being _____ . Other factors that correlate with family structure and functioning include _____ _____ .

45. In acknowledging that two-parent homes are generally best, the text authors note two important qualifications.

    a. _____

    b. _____

46. Children raised in families with persistently high levels of conflict usually _____ (do/do not) become impervious to the stress and tension.

47. The disruption surrounding divorce almost always adversely affects children for at least _____ . Whether this distress is short-lived or long-lasting depends primarily on three postdivorce factors:

    a. _____ ;

    b. _____ ;

    c. _____ .

48. The aspect of the parents' relationship that seems most critical for the development of children is the _____ .

Cite several sources of instability that make it more difficult for children to adjust to divorce.

49. The immediate disruptions of family life are generally harder on _____ (older/younger) children and children who themselves are in _____ .

50. Because of the other inevitable challenges of this stage of life, _____ is, overall, one of the worst times for children to experience divorce.

51. Until recently, custody of children in a divorce was based almost exclusively on _____ . Early in the nineteenth century, for example, custody nearly always went to the _____ (father/mother), and for most of this century, it nearly always went to the _____ (father/mother).

Explain why joint custody arrangements are not as easy as many parents and children expect.

52. In general, the best situation for a child after a divorce is one in which the child _____
_____ .

53. The number of single-parent households has increased markedly over the past two decades in virtually every major industrialized nation except _____ .

54. When compared to others of the same ethnicity and socioeconomic status, children who live with one biological parent develop _____ (just as well as/more poorly than) those who live with two. This has been demonstrated in three areas of development: _____
_____ , _____
_____ , and _____
_____
_____ . This generality _____ (holds/does not hold) equally for preschoolers, school-age children, and adolescents.

55. One source of stress for single parents is that they often suffer from _____
_____ . Another is that the _____ of such households is substantially lower than that of two-parent households. One factor that is important in helping single parents cope is the presence of

_____   _____ .

56. Generally, children develop quite _____ (similarly/differently) in father-only homes as in mother-only homes.

Give several reasons that children in father-only homes may fare better than children in mother-only homes.

57. Most divorced parents _____ (do/do not) remarry within a few years. The divorce rate for second marriages is _____ (higher than/lower than/the same as) that for first marriages.

58. One study comparing young children in various family structures found that those living with both grandparents had poorer _____ skills and more _____ problems than children in any other kind of home. This effect was not seen for _____ (European-

American/African-American) children, for whom the grandparent-headed household is traditionally less unusual. This indicates that _____ context is an important variable in the functioning of a family.

Poverty in Middle Childhood (pp. 505–511)

59. As SES decreases, the risk of health hazards—including _____ _____ —increases. The toll of poverty on the biosocial domain is blunted for two reasons.

   a. _____
   _____

   b. _____
   _____

60. The U.S. method of supporting education makes poverty a particularly devastating liability because _____ _____ .

61. Poverty during middle childhood may take the greatest toll on development in the _____ domain. One reason this is so is that school-age children are preoccupied with the status conveyed by _____ _____ . School-age children also are compelled to engage in _____ _____ as they check each other out on everything from allowances to grades.

62. Today, poverty affects _____ (fewer/more) children than adults.

63. (Public Policy) On the whole, homeless children are even more disadvantaged than their peers of equal SES, with the result that almost one in three suffers from _____ _____ , a loss of faith in life's possibilities.

Coping with Life (pp. 511–514)

64. Between ages 6 and 11 the overall frequency of various psychological problems _____ (increases/decreases), while the number of evident competencies _____ (increases/decreases).

65. Two factors that combine to buffer school-age children against the stresses they encounter are the development of _____ _____ and an expanding _____ _____ .

66. The impact of a given stress on a child depends on _____ _____ and the degree to which they affect _____ _____ .

67. One reason competence can compensate for life stresses is that if children feel confident, their _____ benefits and they are better able to put the rest of their life in perspective. This explains why older children tend to be _____ (more/less) vulnerable to life stresses than are children who are just beginning middle childhood.

68. In promoting competence in children, the _____ _____ _____ of a school is even more important than the academic quality of its curriculum.

List specific characteristics of schools that are more successful in promoting student competence.

69. Another element that helps children deal with problems is the _____ _____ they receive. This can be obtained from grandparents or siblings, for example, or from _____ _____ and _____ .

70. Most children _____ (do/do not) have an idyllic childhood. Such a childhood _____ (is/is not) necessary for healthy development.

71. The best strategy for helping children who are faced with multiple problems that affect their daily routines is to _____ _____ .

Progress Test 1

Multiple-Choice Questions

Circle your answers to the following questions and check them with the answers on page 218. If your answer is incorrect, read the explanation for why it is incorrect and then consult the appropriate pages of the text (in parentheses following the correct answer).

1. In describing development in middle childhood, the text stresses:
   a. latency.
   b. the society of children.
   c. learned helplessness.
   d. the learning of academic and social skills.

2. According to Kohlberg's longitudinal research, the level of moral reasoning that may *not* be attained even by adults is that in which the individual:
   a. seeks the approval of others.
   b. considers punishment and other personal consequences of behavior.
   c. believes that the right behavior means obeying the laws.
   d. recognizes that the laws one obeys ought to reflect the needs of society.

3. The best strategy for helping children who are at risk of developing serious psychological problems because of multiple stresses generally seems to be:
   a. obtaining assistance from a psychiatrist.
   b. changing the household situation.
   c. reducing the peer group's influence.
   d. increasing competencies within the child or social supports surrounding him or her.

4. In making moral choices, according to Gilligan, females are more likely than males to:
   a. score at a higher level in Kohlberg's system.
   b. emphasize the needs of others.
   c. judge right and wrong in absolute terms.
   d. formulate abstract principles.

5. Compared to preschoolers, older children who disagree with each other are more likely to:
   a. experience emotional distress.
   b. seek retaliation or respond aggressively.
   c. appeal to adult authority.
   d. use humor to resolve the conflict.

6. In promoting the development of student competence, the overall _____ of a particular school is an especially important factor.

   a. competitiveness   c. emotional tone
   b. academic quality   d. size

7. Compared with average or popular children, rejected children tend to be:
   a. brighter and more competitive.
   b. affluent and "stuck-up."
   c. economically disadvantaged.
   d. socially immature.

8. Studies support the general conclusion that children function well in single-parent households when:
   a. feelings of "role overload" are minimal.
   b. the father is the head of the home and major wage-earner.
   c. a network of social support reduces stress on the single parent.
   d. all of the above are true.

9. Divorce and parental remarriage typically prove beneficial to children when they result in less financial stress and:
   a. less loneliness for the parent.
   b. greater role overload.
   c. significant changes in lifestyle.
   d. the inclusion of stepsiblings.

10. Older schoolchildren tend to be _____ vulnerable to the stresses of life than children who are just beginning middle childhood because they _____ .
   a. more; tend to overpersonalize their problems
   b. less; have better developed skills for coping with problems
   c. more; are more likely to compare their well-being with that of their peers
   d. less; are less egocentric

11. Between the ages of 6 and 11, the overall frequency of various psychological problems:
   a. increases in both boys and girls.
   b. decreases in both boys and girls.
   c. increases in boys and decreases in girls.
   d. decreases in boys and increases in girls.

12. Studies of single-parent homes demonstrate that when compared to others of the same ethnicity and SES, children:
   a. fare better in mother-only homes.
   b. fare better in father-only homes, especially if the children are girls.
   c. develop quite similarly in both mother-only and father-only homes.
   d. fare better than children in two-parent homes.

13. During the school years, children become _____ selective about their friends and their friendship groups become _____ .
    a. less; larger
    b. less; smaller
    c. more; larger
    d. more; smaller

14. At mid-twentieth century, the "ideal" family structure:
    a. in most industrialized nations consisted of two biological parents living with their own two or three dependent children.
    b. in Asia and Latin America was the large extended family with grandparents, cousins, aunts, and uncles living within the same household.
    c. in many African and Arab nations included a greater variety of family structures, including the polygamous household.
    d. was all of the above.

15. Erikson sees the crisis of the school years as that of:
    a. industry versus inferiority.
    b. acceptance versus rejection.
    c. initiative versus guilt.
    d. male versus female.

True or False Items

Write *true* or *false* on the line in front of each statement.

_____ 1. As they evaluate themselves according to increasingly complex self-theories, school-age children typically experience a rise in self-esteem.

_____ 2. Research suggests that children tend to be more sensitive to others, and less happy with themselves, as they grow older.

_____ 3. Children in middle childhood develop and transmit their own subculture, complete with vocabulary, dress codes, and rules of behavior.

_____ 4. Nearly one-fourth of all school-age children can be described as "rejected," "neglected," or "controversial."

_____ 5. In the United States, one child in five lives below the poverty line.

_____ 6. Socioeconomic status is less important to children in middle childhood than it is to preschool children.

_____ 7. Households headed by single fathers tend to be better off financially than households headed by single mothers.

_____ 8. Divorce almost always adversely affects the children for at least a year or two, although many eventually benefit.

_____ 9. The quality of family interaction seems to be a more powerful predictor of children's development than the actual structure of the family.

_____ 10. Child custody laws in the fifty states are clear in preferring joint custody over other custody arrangements.

Progress Test 2

Progress Test 2 should be completed during a final chapter review. Answer the following questions after you thoroughly understand the correct answers for the Chapter Review and Progress Test 1.

Multiple-Choice Questions

1. Kohlberg's stage theory of moral development is based on his research on a group of boys, on the writings of various philosophers, and on:
   a. psychoanalytic ideas.
   b. Piaget's theory of cognitive development.
   c. Carol Gilligan's research on moral dilemmas.
   d. questionnaires distributed to a nationwide sample of high school seniors.

2. The main reason for the special vocabulary, dress codes, and behaviors that flourish within the society of children is that they:
   a. lead to clubs and gang behavior.
   b. are unknown to or unapproved by adults.
   c. imitate adult-organized society.
   d. provide an alternative to useful work in society.

3. In the area of social cognition, developmentalists are impressed by the school-age child's increasing ability to:
   a. identify and take into account other people's viewpoints.
   b. develop an increasingly wide network of friends.
   c. relate to the opposite sex.
   d. resist social models.

4. The school-age child's greater understanding of emotions is best illustrated by:
   a. an increased tendency to take everything personally.
   b. more widespread generosity and sharing.
   c. the ability to see through the insincere behavior of others.
   d. a refusal to express unfelt emotions.

5. Typically, children in middle childhood experience a decrease in self-esteem as a result of:
   a. a wavering self-theory.
   b. increased awareness of personal shortcomings and failures.
   c. rejection by peers.
   d. difficulties with members of the opposite sex.

6. A 10-year-old's sense of self-esteem is most strongly influenced by his or her:
   a. peers.   c. mother.
   b. siblings.   d. father.

7. Research by Elliot Turiel reveals that school-age children become increasingly able to distinguish between ethical principles and:
   a. social conventions.
   b. cultural values.
   c. the values of the "society of children."
   d. all of the above.

8. Social competence with peers increases during the school years because:
   a. the ability to evaluate the potential outcomes of social problem-solving strategies improves.
   b. the ability to generate alternative strategies to resolve conflicts improves.
   c. children become increasingly able to redirect conflict, for example, through humor.
   d. of all of the above reasons.

9. If current trends continue, it is estimated that _____ of American children born in the 1990s will live with both biological parents from birth to age 18.
   a. less than 10 percent
   b. about 40 percent
   c. 50 percent
   d. 75 percent

10. Which of the following is true of children who live with both biological parents?
    a. They tend to have fewer physical and emotional problems.
    b. They tend to have fewer learning difficulties.
    c. They are less likely to abuse drugs.
    d. All of the above are true.

11. Two factors that most often help the child cope well with multiple stresses are social support and:
    a. learned helplessness.
    b. competence in a specific area.
    c. remedial education.
    d. referral to mental health professionals.

12. Some developmentalists believe that the advantage that traditional families confer on the psychosocial development of children is overstated because:
    a. many studies do not take sufficient account of other factors that affect child development, such as income.
    b. very little reliable research has been conducted on this issue.
    c. parents often are not honest in reporting their children's problems.
    d. of all of the above reasons.

13. Family _____ is more crucial to children's well-being than family _____ is.
    a. structure; SES
    b. SES; stability
    c. stability; SES
    d. functioning; structure

14. According to Freud, the period between ages 7 and 11 when a child's sexual drives are relatively quiet is the:
    a. phallic stage.
    b. genital stage.
    c. period of latency.
    d. period of industry versus inferiority.

15. What percentage of schoolchildren are unpopular and friendless most of the time?
    a. 1 to 2   c. 10 to 12
    b. 10   d. 12 to 15

True or False Items

Write *true* or *false* on the line in front of each statement.

_____ 1. One common criticism of Kohlberg's stage theory is that it overemphasizes religious faith.

_____ 2. Social cognition refers to a specialized area of study within learning theory.

_____ 3. Children become better able to understand the motives, beliefs, and personality traits of others at about age 7.

_____ 4. Children of low socioeconomic status in middle childhood are more likely than other children to have difficulty mastering basic academic skills.

_____ 5. The income of single-parent households is about the same as that of two-parent households in which only one parent works.

_____ 6. In the majority of divorce cases in which the mother is the custodial parent, the father maintains a close, long-term relationship with the children.

_____ 7. A blended family is one that includes a stepparent and perhaps stepsiblings.

_____ 8. Serious problems between parents and children, as well as severe emotional disturbances, are more common in middle childhood than in early childhood.

_____ 9. The problems of most rejected children nearly always disappear by adolescence.

_____ 10. Friendships become more selective and exclusive as children grow older.

Thinking Critically About Chapter 14

Answer these questions the day before an exam as a final check on your understanding of the chapter's terms and concepts.

1. A child's feelings that numerous failures in a particular area are proof that he or she can do nothing to improve the situation describes:
   a. industry versus inferiority.
   b. learned helplessness.
   c. peer rejection.
   d. positive self-esteem.

2. According to Kohlberg, a child who emphasizes social rules and obeying the law is demonstrating _____ moral reasoning.
   a. preconventional   c. postconventional
   b. conventional   d. ideological

3. (A Closer Look) Bonnie, who is low-achieving, shy, and withdrawn, is rejected by most of her peers. Her teacher, who wants to help Bonnie increase her self-esteem and social acceptance, encourages her parents to:
   a. transfer Bonnie to a different school.
   b. help their daughter improve her motor skills.
   c. help their daughter learn to accept more responsibility for her academic failures.
   d. help their daughter improve her skills in relating to peers.

4. Jorge, who has no children of his own, is worried about his 12-year-old niece because she wears unusual clothes and uses vocabulary unknown to him. What should Jorge do?
   a. Tell his niece's parents they need to discipline their daughter more strictly.
   b. Convince his niece to find a new group of friends.

   c. Recommend that his niece's parents seek professional counseling for their daughter since such behaviors often are the first signs of a lifelong pattern of antisocial behavior.
   d. Jorge need not necessarily be worried since children typically develop their own subculture of speech, dress, and behavior.

5. Compared to her 7-year-old brother Walter, 10-year-old Felicity is more likely to describe their cousin:
   a. in terms of physical attributes.
   b. as feeling exactly the same way she does when they are in the same social situation.
   c. in terms of personality traits.
   d. in terms of their cousin's outward behavior.

6. Seven-year-old Chantal fumes after a friend compliments her new dress, thinking that the comment was intended to be sarcastic. Chantal's reaction is an example of:
   a. egocentrism.
   b. learned helplessness.
   c. the distorted thought processes of an emotionally disturbed child.
   d. immature social cognition.

7. In discussing friendship, 9-year-old children, in contrast to younger children, will:
   a. deny that friends are important.
   b. state that they prefer same-sex playmates.
   c. stress the importance of help and emotional support in friendship.
   d. be less choosy about who they call a friend.

8. Children who have serious difficulties in peer relationships during elementary school:
   a. are at a greater risk of having emotional problems later in life.
   b. usually overcome their difficulties in a year or two.
   c. later are more likely to form an intense friendship with one person than children who did not have difficulties earlier on.
   d. do both b. and c.

9. After years of unhappiness in a marriage characterized by excessive conflict, Brad and Diane file for divorce and move 500 miles apart. In ruling on custody for their 7-year-old daughter, the wise judge decides:
   a. joint custody should be awarded, since this arrangement is nearly always the most beneficial for children.
   b. the mother should have custody, since this

arrangement is nearly always the most beneficial for children in single-parent homes.

c. the father should have custody, since this
arrangement is nearly always the most beneficial for children in single-parent homes.

d. to more fully investigate the competency of
each parent, since whoever was the most competent and most involved parent before the
divorce should continue to be the primary
caregiver.

10. Of the following children, who is likely to have
the lowest overall self-esteem?

a. Karen, age 5   c. Carl, age 9
b. David, age 7   d. Cindy, age 10

11. Ten-year-old Benjamin is less optimistic and self-
confident than his 5-year-old sister. This may be
partly explained by the tendency of older children to:

a. evaluate their abilities by comparing them
with their own competencies a year or two
earlier.

b. evaluate their competencies by comparing
them with those of others.

c. be less realistic about their own abilities.

d. do both b. and c.

12. Based on research on the norms for childhood
aggression, which of the following schoolchildren
is likely to be viewed most favorably by his or her
peers?

a. Eddie, the class bully

b. Luwanda, who is not arrogant but doesn't shy
away from defending herself whenever necessary

c. Daniel, who often suffers attacks from his
peers yet refuses to retaliate

d. Hilary, who often suffers attacks from her
peers yet refuses to retaliate

13. In a study conducted by Turiel, 6- and 10-year-
old children were asked whether it is a more serious transgression for a child to steal an eraser
than to wear pajamas to school. Which of the following summarizes the findings of this study?

a. Both groups of children saw the theft of the
eraser as being more serious.

b. Both groups of children saw wearing pajamas
to school as being more serious.

c. The 10-year-olds, but not the 6-year-olds,
were convinced that the theft was the more
serious transgression.

d. The 6-year-olds, but not the 10-year-olds,
were convinced that the theft was the more
serious transgression.

14. Each of the following children lives in an impoverished family. Which child is likely to have the
greatest difficulty coping with this source of
stress?

a. twelve-year-old Darren, who has an emotionally disturbed father

b. six-year-old Simone, who lives in a single-parent household

c. ten-year-old Brenda, who is an accomplished
dancer

d. It is impossible to predict from the information provided.

15. From which of the following ethnic groups are
children living in grandparent-headed households *least* likely to have behavioral problems?

a. European-American   c. Native American
b. African-American   d. Asian-American

Key Terms

Using your own words, write a brief definition or
explanation of each of the following terms on a separate piece of paper.

1. latency
2. industry versus inferiority
3. social cognition
4. learned helplessness
5. peer group
6. society of children
7. prosocial behaviors
8. preconventional moral reasoning
9. conventional moral reasoning
10. postconventional moral reasoning
11. social conventions
12. family structure

ANSWERS

CHAPTER REVIEW

1. latency; quieter; repressed; submerged
2. industry versus inferiority
3. acquisition; coalesce
4. social cognition; multifaceted
5. underlying motives
6. personality traits
7. increases

Children are likely to become more sensitive to, and empathize with, the emotional experiences of others. They are also able to recognize and rephrase or avoid potentially offensive statements. In general, it helps them to get along better with other people.

8. situation; personality traits; feelings

9. regulation

10. more; dips; more; girls

11. decline steadily

12. learned helplessness; failures

13. a group of individuals of similar age and social status who play, work, and learn together

14. society of children

The society of children typically has a special vocabulary, dress codes, and rules of behavior.

15. aggression; counteraggression; reconciliation; has; social situation

16. prosocial; more

17. less; advance

18. mutual help; self-disclosure

19. smaller; more

20. 10; rejected; neglected; controversial

21. social cognition

Rejected children often misinterpret social situations, considering a compliment as sarcastic, for example.

22. home; rejected; aggressive-rejected; stress; fathers

23. problem solving; attributional retraining; skills training; supportive interventions

24. lifelong

The prominence of peer relationships gives children new opportunities to learn about moral reasoning. In addition, the expanded cognitive skills of middle childhood advance moral reasoning. And, as their awareness of their world expands, school-age children begin to think about moral concerns on a larger scale.

25. Kohlberg; preconventional; conventional; postconventional

26. avoiding punishment and gaining rewards; 1; 2

27. social rules; 4; 3

28. moral principles; social contracts; universal ethical principles

29. less

30. liberal; Western; stagelike; rational; religious faith; males

31. Gilligan; have not; interpersonal issues; moral absolutes

32. social conventions

33. is not

34. do

35. does; do

36. households composed of people connected to each other in various legal and biosocial ways

37. two biological parents living with their own two or three dependent children; a large extended family, with grandparents and great-grandparents, and often cousins, aunts, and uncles, living in the same household; African; Arab

38. less

39. 40

40. in almost any family structure

41. excessive conflict, overly authoritarian parenting, and coldness

42. both biological parents

At adolescence, they are less likely to abuse drugs or be arrested and more likely to graduate from high school; in adulthood, they are more likely to graduate from college and to continue to develop with self-confidence, social acceptance, and career success.

43. a. Two adults generally provide more complete caregiving than one.

    b. Two-parent homes usually have a financial advantage over other forms.

44. overstated; income; race, ethnic background, and religion

45. a. Not every biological parent is a fit parent.

    b. Not every marriage creates a nurturant household.

46. do not

47. a year or two

    a. the harmony of the parents' ongoing relationship

    b. the stability of the child's life

    c. the adequacy of the caregiving arrangement

48. degree of harmony or discord

One source of instability is the child's being separated from a caregiver to whom he or she is highly attached. Another is a reduction in the household income. Still another is the disorientation of the parents.

49. younger; transition

50. puberty

51. gender; father; mother

The logistics of joint custody arrangements are often difficult for parents and disorienting for children, who shuttle between homes with different rules, expectations, and emotional settings.

52. can continue an intimate, positive relationship with each parent

53. Japan

54. just as well as; school achievement; emotional stability; protection from serious injury; holds

55. role overload; income; social support

56. similarly

Children sometimes respond better to a man's authority than to a woman's. In addition, fathers who choose custody are those who are likely to be suited for it, whereas mothers typically have custody whether they prefer it or not. Father-only homes are, on average, more secure financially.

57. do; higher than

58. language; behavior; African-American; social

59. malnutrition, disease, accidents, abuse, and neglect

    a. Schoolchildren's natural immunities, physical strengths, and growth patterns make them relatively unlikely to suffer the most devastating consequences of malnutrition and disease.

    b. Their developing independence and reasoning ability make schoolchildren better able to protect themselves against dangers.

60. public school funding depends primarily on local property taxes, resulting in significant disparities

61. psychosocial; material possessions; social comparison

62. more

63. clinical depression

64. decreases; increases

65. social cognition; social world

66. the number of stresses the child is experiencing concurrently; the overall pattern of the child's daily life

67. self-esteem; less

68. overall emotional tone

Such schools care about students and have high expectations of both students and teachers.

69. social support; religious faith; practice

70. do not; is not

71. increase competencies within the child or the social supports surrounding him or her

PROGRESS TEST 1

Multiple-Choice Questions

1. **d.** is the answer. (p. 471)

    a. This is Freud's term for psychosexual development during middle childhood.

    b. This refers to the schoolchild's subculture of vocabulary, dress codes, and rules of behavior.

    c. This refers to the perception that one can do nothing to improve one's performance in a specific area.

2. **d.** is the answer. (p. 490)

    a. & c. These are examples of conventional morality.

    b. This is an example of preconventional morality.

3. **d.** is the answer. (p. 514)

4. **b.** is the answer. (p. 491)

    a. Gilligan maintains that Kohlberg's scoring system tends to devalue the female perspective.

    c. & d. According to Gilligan, males are more likely to reason from absolute, or abstract, moral principles.

5. **d.** is the answer. (p. 481)

    a., b., & c. As social awareness expands, schoolchildren develop a larger repertoire of social problem-solving skills.

6. **c.** is the answer. (p. 513)

7. **d.** is the answer. (p. 485)

8. **d.** is the answer. (p. 503)

9. **a.** is the answer. (p. 504)

    b., c., & d. These factors are likely to increase, rather than decrease, stress, and therefore to have an adverse effect on children.

10. **b.** is the answer. (p. 512)

11. **b.** is the answer. (p. 511)

12. **c.** is the answer. (p. 503)

13. **d.** is the answer. (p. 483)

14. **d.** is the answer. (pp. 494–495)

15. **a.** is the answer. (p. 472)

True or False Items

1. F   As they develop increasingly complex self-theories, children typically become more self-critical, and their self-esteem drops. (p. 476)

2. T (pp. 474–475)

3. T (pp. 477–478)

4. F   Only 10 percent of school-age children would fall in these categories. (p. 484)

5. T (p. 509)

6. F   Socioeconomic status is more important to older children, who can compare themselves with others in terms of possessions and lifestyle. (p. 508)

7. T (p. 504)

8. T (p. 498)

9. T (pp. 498–499)

10. F   The state legislatures have been cautious in their stand on joint custody, in light of experiences that suggest that joint custody is not the best arrangement for some families—for example, families in which there is continuing hostility between parents. (pp. 500–501)

PROGRESS TEST 2

Multiple-Choice Questions

1. **b.** is the answer. (p. 490)

2. **b.** is the answer. (p. 478)

3. **a.** is the answer. (p. 473)

   b. Friendship circles typically become smaller during middle childhood, as children become more choosy about their friends.

   c. & d. These issues are not discussed in the chapter.

4. **c.** is the answer. (p. 475)

5. **b.** is the answer. (p. 476)

   a. This tends to promote, rather than reduce, self-esteem.

   c. Only 10 percent of schoolchildren experience this.

   d. This issue becomes more important during adolescence.

6. **a.** is the answer. (p. 477)

7. **a.** is the answer. (pp. 492–493)

8. **d.** is the answer. (pp. 481–482)

9. **b.** is the answer. (p. 495)

10. **d.** is the answer. (p. 496)

11. **b.** is the answer. (p. 512)

12. **a.** is the answer. (pp. 496–497)

   b. In fact, a great deal of research has been conducted on this issue.

   c. There is no evidence that this is so.

13. **d.** is the answer. (pp. 495–496)

14. **c.** is the answer. (p. 472)

15. **b.** is the answer. (p. 484)

True or False Items

1. F   The theory has been criticized for *underrating* religious faith. (p. 491)

2. F   Social cognition refers to a person's understanding of people and the dynamics of human interaction. (p. 473)

3. T (pp. 473–474)

4. T (p. 506)

5. F   The income of single-parent households is substantially lower than that of two-parent households in which only one parent works. (p. 503)

6. F   Only a minority of fathers who do not have custody continue to maintain a close relationship with their children. (p. 500)

7. T (p. 504)

8. F   Serious problems between parents and children, and severe emotional disturbances, are less common in middle childhood than earlier or later. (p. 511)

9. F   The problems of rejected children often get worse as they get older. (p. 485)

10. T (p. 483)

THINKING CRITICALLY ABOUT CHAPTER 14

1. **b.** is the answer. (p. 477)

   a. This answer refers to the crisis of middle childhood as described in Erikson's theory.

   c. There is no indication that the child described in this situation is being rejected by his or her peers.

   d. This situation more accurately describes *low* self-esteem.

2. **b.** is the answer. (p. 489)

   a. In this type of moral reasoning, the emphasis is on avoiding punishments and gaining rewards.

   c. In this type of moral reasoning, the emphasis is on moral principles.

   d. This is not one of Kohlberg's stages of moral reasoning.

3. **d.** is the answer. (pp. 486–487)

   a. Because it would seem to involve "running away" from her problems, this approach would likely be more harmful than helpful.

   b. Improving motor skills is not a factor considered in the text and probably has little value in raising self-esteem in such situations.

   c. If Bonnie is like most school-age children, she is quite self-critical and already accepts responsibility for her failures.

4. **d.** is the answer. (p. 478)

5. **c.** is the answer. (p. 474)

   a., b., & d. These are more typical of preschoolers.

6. **d.** is the answer. (p. 485)

   a. Egocentrism is self-centered thinking. In this

example, Chantal is misinterpreting her friend's comment.

b. & c. There is no reason to believe that Chantal is suffering from learned helplessness or an emotional disturbance.

7. **c.** is the answer. (p. 482)

8. **a.** is the answer. (p. 485)

9. **d.** is the answer. (pp. 500–501)

10. **d.** is the answer. Self-esteem decreases throughout middle childhood. (p. 476)

11. **b.** is the answer. (p. 476)

    a. & c. These are more typical of preschoolers than school-age children.

12. **b.** is the answer. (p. 479)

    a. Although a certain amount of aggression is the norm during childhood, children who are perceived as overly arrogant or aggressive are not viewed very favorably.

    c. & d. Both girls and boys are expected to defend themselves when appropriate, and are viewed as weak if they do not.

13. **c.** is the answer. (p. 493)

14. **a.** is the answer. All other things being equal, poverty is likely to have a more adverse effect on children during middle childhood, for whom material possessions are important measures of self-worth, than earlier in life. Furthermore, family functioning is more important to children's well-being than is family structure. Thus living with an emotionally disturbed father is likely to be more damaging than living in a single-parent household. (pp. 495–496, 507–508, 512)

    c. Brenda's success as a dancer is likely to boost her self-esteem, an important buffer to childhood stress.

15. **b.** is the answer. Extended family structures are more common, and more accepted, by African-Americans, with established patterns of interaction serving to ease tensions between generations. (p. 505)

KEY TERMS

1. Freud describes middle childhood as the period of **latency**, when children's emotional drives are quieter, their psychosexual needs are repressed, and their unconscious conflicts are submerged. (p. 472)

   Memory aid: Something that is *latent* exists but is not manifesting itself.

2. According to Erikson, the crisis of middle childhood is that of **industry versus inferiority** as children develop views of themselves as either competent or incompetent. (p. 472)

3. **Social cognition** refers to a person's understanding of other people and groups. (p. 473)

4. **Learned helplessness** develops when children's past failures in a particular area have taught them to believe that they are unable to do anything to improve their performance. (p. 477)

5. A **peer group** is defined as a group of individuals of roughly the same age and social status who play, work, and learn together. (p. 477)

6. Children in middle childhood develop and transmit their own subculture, called the **society of children**, that has its own vocabulary, dress codes, and rules of behavior. (pp. 477–478)

7. **Prosocial behaviors** are acts of sharing and caring that benefit others without the benefactor's expectation of reward. (p. 480)

8. The first of Kohlberg's stages of moral reasoning, **preconventional moral reasoning** emphasizes obedience to authority in order to avoid punishment (stage 1), and being nice to other people so they will be nice to you. (stage 2). (p. 489)

9. The second of Kohlberg's stages, **conventional moral reasoning** emphasizes winning the approval of others (stage 3), and obeying the laws set down by those in power (stage 4). (p. 489)

10. The last of Kohlberg's stages, **postconventional moral reasoning** emphasizes the social and contractual nature of moral principles (stage 5), and the existence of universal ethical principles (stage 6). (p. 489)

11. **Social conventions** are the customs and traditions of a particular society, for example, concerning modes of dress, appropriate ways of eating, and suitable behavior in public places. (p. 492)

12. **Family structure** refers to households composed of people connected to each other in various legal and biosocial ways. (p. 494)

Adolescence: Biosocial Development

Chapter Overview

Between the ages of 10 and 20, young people cross the great divide between childhood and adulthood. This crossing encompasses all three domains of development—biosocial, cognitive, and psychosocial. Chapter 15 focuses on the dramatic changes that occur in the biosocial domain, beginning with puberty and the growth spurt. The biosocial metamorphosis of the adolescent is discussed in detail, with emphasis on sexual maturation, nutrition, and the effects of the timing of puberty, including possible problems arising from early or late maturation.

Although adolescence is, in many ways, a healthy time of life, the text addresses two health hazards that too often affect adolescence: eating disorders and violence.

NOTE: Answer guidelines for all Chapter 15 questions begin on page 232.

Guided Study

The text chapter should be studied one section at a time. Before you read, preview each section by skimming it, noting headings and boldface items. Then read the appropriate section objectives from the following outline. Keep these objectives in mind and, as you read the chapter section, search for the information that will enable you to meet each objective. Once you have finished a section, write out answers for its objectives.

Puberty (pp. 522–532)

1. Describe physical growth in both the male and the female adolescent.

2. Discuss the development of the sex organs and secondary sex characteristics in males and females during puberty.

3. (A Closer Look) Discuss the adolescent's preoccupation with body image and the problems that sometimes arise in the development of a healthy body image.

Health and Survival (pp. 532–539)

4. Discuss the nutritional needs and problems of adolescents.

5. Identify those populations at greatest risk for bulimia and/or anorexia nervosa and discuss possible explanations for these disorders.

6. Discuss the approaches of psychoanalytic and learning theorists in treating these disorders.

7. (text and Research Report) Discuss the biosocial, familial, and cultural factors that may account for the high rate of vioilent death during adolescence.

The Timing of Puberty (pp. 540–544)

8. Discuss the factors that influence the onset of puberty.

9. Discuss adjustment problems of boys and girls who develop earlier or later than their peers, noting any significant short- and long-term consequences.

Chapter Review

When you have finished reading the chapter, work through the material that follows to review it. Complete the sentences and answer the questions. As you proceed, evaluate your performance for each section by consulting the answers on page 232. Do not continue with the next section until you understand each answer. If you need to, review or reread the appropriate section in the textbook before continuing.

Puberty (pp. 522–532)

1. The period of rapid physical growth and sexual maturation that ends childhood and brings the young person to adult size, shape, and sexual potential is called _____ .

   List, in order, the major physical changes of puberty in

   girls: _____

   _____

   boys: _____

   _____

2. Normal children begin to notice pubertal changes between the ages of _____ and

   _____ .

3. Once puberty begins, the sequence of physical changes _____ (varies from child to child/is usually the same in all children). These changes are usually complete approximately _____ years after the first visible signs appear.

4. Puberty begins when hormones from the _____ trigger hormone production in the _____

_____, which in turn triggers increased hormone production by the

_____ _____ and by the _____, which include the _____ in males and the _____ in females.

5. The hormone _____ causes the gonads to dramatically increase production of sex hormones, especially _____ and _____. This, in turn, triggers the hypothalamus and pituitary to increase production of _____.

6. The increase in the hormone _____ is dramatic in boys and slight in girls, while the increase in the hormone _____ is marked in girls and slight in boys. These hormones begin increasing at least _____ year(s) before the first visible signs of puberty.

7. The importance of these hormonal increases in puberty is highlighted by their use in the medical treatment of _____ _____. The emotional impact of puberty, however, depends less on hormonal changes and more on _____ _____.

8. The observable changes in appearance at puberty are grouped into two categories: the _____, and the emergence of _____ _____.

9. The first sign of the growth spurt is increased bone _____ and _____, beginning in the ends of the extremities and working toward the center. At the same time, children begin to _____ (gain/lose) weight at a relatively rapid rate.

10. The change in weight that typically occurs between 10 and 12 years of age is due primarily to the accumulation of _____. The amount of weight gain an individual experiences depends on several factors, including

_____, _____, _____, and _____.

11. During the spurt in height, a greater percentage of fat is retained by _____ (males/females), who naturally have a higher proportion of body fat in adulthood.

12. About a year after these height and weight changes occur, a period of _____ increase occurs, causing the pudginess and clumsiness of an earlier age to disappear. In boys, this increase is particularly notable in the _____ body.

13. Overall, the typical girl gains about _____ in weight and _____ in height between the ages of 10 and 14, while the typical boy gains about _____ in height and about _____ in weight between the ages of 12 and 16.

14. The chronological age for the growth spurt _____ (varies/does not vary) from child to child.

15. One of the last parts of the body to grow into final form is the _____.

16. The two halves of the body _____ (always/do not always) grow at the same rate.

17. Internal organs also grow during puberty. The _____ increase in size and capacity, the _____ doubles in size, heart rate _____ (increases/decreases), and blood volume _____ (increases/decreases). These changes increase the adolescent's physical

_____.

Explain why the physical demands placed on a teenager, as in athletic training, should not be the same as those for a young adult of similar height and weight.

18. During puberty, one organ system, the _____ system, decreases in size, making teenagers _____ (more/less) susceptible to respiratory ailments.

19. The hormones of puberty also cause many relatively minor physical changes that can have significant emotional impact. These include increased activity in _____ , _____ , and _____ glands.

20. Changes in _____ _____ _____ involve the sex organs that are directly involved in reproduction. By the end of puberty, reproduction _____ (is/is still not) possible.

Describe the major changes in primary sex characteristics that occur in both sexes during puberty.

21. The first menstrual period is called _____ . For boys, the comparable indicator of reproductive potential is the first ejaculation of seminal fluid containing sperm, which is called _____ . In both sexes, full reproductive maturity occurs _____ (at this time/several years later).

22. The first menstrual cycles are usually _____ , that is, they occur without ovulation. When pregnancy occurs before a girl's body is fully developed, the combined nutritional demands of her own growth and her fetus's increase the risk of giving birth to a _____-_____ infant.

23. Attitudes toward menarche, menstruation, and spermarche _____ (have/have

not) changed over the past two decades, so that most young people _____ (do/do not) face these events with anxiety, embarrassment, or guilt.

24. Two possible problems associated with menstruation are _____ and _____ in the days before menstruation begins.

25. Sexual features other than those associated with reproduction are referred to as _____ _____ .

Describe the major pubertal changes in the secondary sex characteristics of both sexes.

26. Two secondary sex characteristics that are mistakenly considered signs of womanhood and manliness, respectively, are _____ _____ and _____ _____ .

27. (A Closer Look) Adolescents' mental conception of, and attitude toward, their physical appearance is referred to as their _____ _____ .

(A Closer Look) Identify some common behaviors related to adolescents' preoccupation with their body image.

28. (A Closer Look) Partly because cigarettes are believed to decrease _____ , teenage _____ (boys/girls) are more likely than those of the opposite sex to smoke. For other drugs, the relationship between

gender and drug use is _____ (the same/reversed).

29. (A Closer Look) When asked what traits they look for in the other sex, adolescents list _____ _____ .

30. (A Closer Look) Media images reinforce the cultural ideal that American men should be _____ and women should be _____ .

31. (A Closer Look) Overall, _____ (boys/girls) tend to be more dissatisfied with their appearance than the other sex. In adolescence, feelings of _____ correlate strongly with a negative body image.

Health and Survival (pp. 532–539)

32. Although adolescence is, in many ways, a healthy time of life, adolescents often put themselves at risk for three health hazards: _____ _____ _____ , _____ _____ , and _____ .

33. Due to rapid physical growth, the adolescent needs a higher daily intake of _____ , _____ , and _____ . Specifically, the typical adolescent needs about 50 percent more of the minerals _____ , _____ , and _____ during the growth spurt. Because of menstruation, adolescent females also need additional _____ in their diets and are more likely to suffer _____ -_____ _____ than any other subgroup of the population.

34. Although most adolescents in developed nations are well nourished most of the time, most also experience periods of _____ , _____ , or _____ .

35. Adolescent nutrition can also be adversely affected by _____ use, which alters

the appetite and digestive processes. Another problem, particularly for adolescent girls, is _____ , which can lead to serious undernourishment.

36. Research studies demonstrate that _____ (most/a minority of) adolescent girls wish they were thinner. This finding _____ (varied/did not vary) with the girls' status in terms of physical maturation.

37. Repeated or extensive dieting may alter body _____ , so that the body begins to maintain its weight on _____ (fewer/a greater number of) calories.

38. Adolescents may begin to take _____ until tolerance requires that they quit or get hooked, or use over-the-counter appetite _____ .

39. Dieting may also lead to the eating disorder called _____ , which involves cycles of _____ and _____ . This pattern of eating can damage the _____ system or create an imbalance in _____ sufficient to trigger a _____ .

40. Bulimia is sometimes a precursor of _____ _____ , an eating disorder in which a person restricts eating until her weight is _____ percent or more below normal.

41. Anorexia affects less than _____ percent of young women. Girls who develop this disorder are more likely to do so at the _____ or _____ of adolescence; they are also likely to be _____ (high/low) achievers, of _____ (average/below-average/above-average) intelligence, and from relatively _____ (poor/wealthy) backgrounds.

State the psychoanalytic and learning theory explanations for eating disorders.

42. According to learning theorists, the psychological consequences of excessive dieting often include _____ _____ and _____ , which can trigger an eating disorder and behaviors that act as immediate _____ in relieving distress.

43. Recovery from an eating disorder usually _____ (requires/does not require) outside intervention.

44. Successful treatment for eating disorders may include individual psychotherapy for _____ and a distorted _____ _____ . It may also include _____ or _____ therapy.

45. Generally speaking, boys and adult males _____ (are/are not) susceptible to eating disorders.

46. Stereotypes about "manly" behavior may lead to a problem that afflicts mostly young men—that is, to behavior that leads to _____ _____ from an _____ , _____ , or _____ .

List the biosocial factors that have been suggested as causes of masculine violence.

List cultural and familial factors that may promote masculine violence.

47. (text and Research Report) Researchers agree that _____ _____ are at the root of masculine violence. Within nations, violent death varies by subgroup, largely because of _____ , _____ , and _____ forces.

The Timing of Puberty (pp. 540–544)

48. Although the _____ of pubertal events is very similar for all young people, there is great variation in its _____ . The most typical ages for the beginning of puberty are _____ , _____ , and _____ . Some of the factors that affect the age of onset include the child's ____ _____ _____ .

49. The average American girl reaches menarche at about age _____ , while the average boy first ejaculates at age _____ . The average boy is about _____ years behind the average girl in the appearance of the growth spurt.

50. Genes are an important factor in the timing of menarche, as demonstrated by the fact that _____ and _____ reach menarche at very similar ages.

51. The average age of onset of puberty _____ (does/does not) vary from nation to nation and/or from ethnic group to ethnic group.

52. Stocky individuals tend to experience puberty _____ (earlier/later) than those with taller, thinner builds.

53. Menarche seems to be related to the accumulation of a certain amount of _____ . Consequently, female dancers, runners, and other athletes menstruate _____ (earlier/later) than the average girl, while females who are relatively inactive menstruate _____ (earlier/later).

54. The tendency of successive generations to develop in somewhat different ways as the result of improved nutrition and medical advances is called the _____ _____ . There is evidence that this trend has stopped in recent years in _____ countries.

55. Longitudinal research suggests that family emotional distance and stress may _____ (accelerate/delay) the onset of puberty.

56. Young people who experience puberty at the same time as their friends tend to view the experience more _____ (positively/negatively) than those who experience it early or late. Timing is particularly important for _____ (girls/boys).

57. For girls, _____ (early/late) maturation may be especially troublesome.

Describe several common problems and developmental hazards experienced by early-maturing girls.

58. For boys, _____ (early/late) maturation is usually more difficult.

Describe several characteristics and/or problems of late-maturing boys.

59. Research on the timing of puberty in boys has found that the effects of early puberty are generally _____ (positive/negative/mixed), while the effects of late puberty are _____ (positive/negative/mixed).

60. In general, the more social changes adolescents go through, the _____ (more/less) likely they are to experience problems such as a drop in grades, lowered self-esteem, and difficulties with teachers.

61. The events of puberty typically _____ (increase/decrease/do not affect) the distance between parents and their adolescent children.

62. The effects of early or late maturation are _____ (more/less) apparent among adolescents of lower socioeconomic status than among middle- or upper-SES teenagers.

63. The effects of early or late maturation _____ (vary from culture to culture/are universal).

Progress Test 1

Multiple-Choice Questions

Circle your answers to the following questions and check them with the answers on page 234. If your answer is incorrect, read the explanation for why it is incorrect and then consult the appropriate pages of the text (in parentheses following the correct answer).

1. Which of the following most accurately describes the sequence of pubertal development in girls?
   a. breast buds and pubic hair; growth spurt in which fat is deposited on hips and buttocks; first menstrual period; ovulation

b. growth spurt; breast buds and pubic hair; first menstrual period; ovulation
c. first menstrual period; breast buds and pubic hair; growth spurt; ovulation
d. breast buds and pubic hair; growth spurt; ovulation; first menstrual period

2. Although both sexes grow rapidly during adolescence, boys typically begin their accelerated growth about:
   a. two years later than girls.
   b. a year earlier than girls.
   c. the time they reach sexual maturity.
   d. the time facial hair appears.

3. The first readily observable sign of the onset of puberty is:
   a. the growth spurt.
   b. the appearance of facial, body, and pubic hair.
   c. a change in the shape of the eyes.
   d. a lengthening of the torso.

4. More than any other group in the population, adolescent girls are likely to have:
   a. asthma.
   b. acne.
   c. iron-deficiency anemia.
   d. testosterone deficiency.

5. For most young women, even a year after menarche, ovulation:
   a. cannot result in pregnancy.
   b. occurs regularly.
   c. is irregular.
   d. is in remission.

6. For males, the secondary sex characteristic that usually occurs last is:
   a. breast enlargement.
   b. the appearance of facial hair.
   c. growth of the testes.
   d. the appearance of pubic hair.

7. For girls, the specific event that is taken to indicate fertility is _____ ; for boys, it is _____ .
   a. the growth of breast buds; voice deepening
   b. menarche; spermarche
   c. anovulation; the testosterone surge
   d. the growth spurt; pubic hair

8. The most significant hormonal changes of puberty include an increase of _____ in _____ and an increase of _____ in _____ .
   a. progesterone; boys; estrogen; girls
   b. estrogen; boys; testosterone; girls

c. progesterone; girls; estrogen; boys
   d. estrogen; girls; testosterone; boys

9. (A Closer Look) In general, most adolescents are:
   a. overweight.
   b. satisfied with their appearance.
   c. dissatisfied with their appearance.
   d. unaffected by cultural attitudes about beauty.

10. (A Closer Look) In adolescence, as at other times in the life span, negative body image is most likely to be accompanied by:
    a. feelings of depression.
    b. loss of appetite.
    c. delayed maturation.
    d. overeating.

11. The average American girl reaches menarche at age _____ , while the average boy reaches spermarche at age _____ .
    a. 11; 12   c. 12 1/2; 13
    b. 12; 11   d. 13; 15

12. Early physical growth and sexual maturation:
    a. tends to be equally difficult for girls and boys.
    b. tends to be more difficult for boys than for girls.
    c. tends to be more difficult for girls than for boys.
    d. is easier for both girls and boys than late maturation.

13. (A Closer Look) After puberty, most adolescents:
    a. have a more positive body image.
    b. have a more negative body image.
    c. have the same body image they had prior to puberty.
    d. have a body image that will not change significantly for the rest of their lives.

14. Adolescents who experience many social changes, such as changing schools, moving to a new neighborhood, and so forth:
    a. often experience delayed physical maturation.
    b. are no more likely to have a difficult adolescence than are teenagers who experience few social changes.
    c. are likely to score higher in measures of social competence than teenagers who experience few social changes.
    d. are more likely to experience difficulties, such as a decrease in self-esteem.

15. Eating disorders such as bulimia and anorexia nervosa are most often associated with:
    a. depression.   c. obesity.
    b. alcohol abuse.   d. suicide.

True or False Items

Write *true* or *false* on the line in front of each statement.

_____ 1. More calories are necessary during adolescence than at any other period during the life span.

_____ 2. Ovulation usually does not occur during a girl's first menstrual cycles.

_____ 3. The first indicator of reproductive potential in males is menarche.

_____ 4. Lung capacity, heart size, and total volume of blood increase significantly during adolescence.

_____ 5. Puberty generally begins sometime between ages 8 and 14.

_____ 6. Girls who mature late and are thinner than average tend to be satisfied with their weight.

_____ 7. (A Closer Look) The strong emphasis on physical appearance is unique to adolescents and finds little support from teachers, parents, and the larger culture.

_____ 8. (A Closer Look) Girls are more dissatisfied than boys with their appearance, their weight, and specific body parts.

_____ 9. The problems of the early-maturing girl tend to be temporary.

_____ 10. Both the sequence and timing of pubertal events vary greatly from one young person to another.

Progress Test 2

Progress Test 2 should be completed during a final chapter review. Answer the following questions after you thoroughly understand the correct answers for the Chapter Review and Progress Test 1.

Multiple-Choice Questions

1. Which of the following is the correct sequence of pubertal events in boys?
   a. growth spurt; pubic hair; first ejaculation; lowering of voice
   b. pubic hair; first ejaculation; growth spurt; lowering of voice
   c. lowering of voice; pubic hair; growth spurt; first ejaculation
   d. growth spurt; lowering of voice; pubic hair; first ejaculation

2. Which of the following statements about adolescent physical development is *not* true?
   a. Hands and feet generally lengthen before arms and legs.

   b. Facial features usually grow before the head itself reaches adult size and shape.
   c. Oil, sweat, and odor glands become more active.
   d. The lymphoid system increases slightly in size, and the heart increases by nearly half.

3. In puberty, a hormone that increases markedly in girls (and only somewhat in boys) is:
   a. estrogen.   c. androgen.
   b. testosterone.   d. menarche.

4. Nutritional deficiencies in adolescence are frequently the result of:
   a. eating pizza.
   b. exotic diets or food fads.
   c. anovulatory menstruation.
   d. excessive exercise.

5. In females, puberty is typically marked by a(n):
   a. significant widening of the shoulders.
   b. significant widening of the hips.
   c. enlargement of the torso and upper chest.
   d. decrease in the size of the eyes and nose.

6. Nonreproductive sexual characteristics, such as the deepening of the voice and development of breasts, are called:
   a. gender-typed traits.
   b. primary sex characteristics.
   c. secondary sex characteristics.
   d. pubertal prototypes.

7. Puberty is initiated when hormones are released from the _____ , then from the _____ , and then from the _____ .
   a. hypothalamus; pituitary; gonads
   b. pituitary; gonads; hypothalamus
   c. gonads; pituitary; hypothalamus
   d. pituitary; hypothalamus; gonads

8. (A Closer Look) In forming their own body image, adolescents are *most* strongly influenced by:
   a. their own potential.   c. cultural ideals.
   b. their parents.   d. heredity.

9. (A Closer Look) With regard to appearance, adolescent girls are *most* commonly dissatisfied with:
   a. timing of maturation.   c. weight.
   b. eyes and other facial features. d. legs.

10. Statistically speaking, to predict the age at which a girl first has sexual intercourse, it would be *most* useful to know her:
    a. socioeconomic level.   c. religion.
    b. race or ethnic group. d. age at menarche.

11. Although the _____ of puberty is quite variable, its _____ is largely fixed.
    a. sequence; timing   c. timing; sequence
    b. duration; onset   d. onset; duration

12. Repeated or extensive weight loss may result in:
    a. altered metabolism such that the body begins to maintain its weight on fewer calories.
    b. unusual stress on the heart.
    c. low self-esteem.
    d. all of the above.

13. Puberty is most accurately defined as:
    a. the period of rapid physical growth that occurs during adolescence.
    b. the period during which sexual maturation is attained.
    c. the period of rapid physical growth and sexual maturation that ends childhood.

d. the period during which adolescents establish identities separate from their parents.

14. Which of the following does *not* typically occur during puberty?
    a. The lungs increase in size and capacity.
    b. The heart's size and rate of beating increase.
    c. Blood volume increases.
    d. The lymphoid system decreases in size.

15. Teenagers' susceptibility to respiratory ailments typically _____ during adolescence, due to a(n) _____ in the size of the lymphoid system.
    a. increases; increase
    b. increases; decrease
    c. decreases; increase
    d. decreases; decrease

Matching Items

Match each term or concept with its corresponding description or definition.

Terms or Concepts
_____ 1. puberty
_____ 2. GH
_____ 3. testosterone
_____ 4. estrogen
_____ 5. growth spurt
_____ 6. primary sex characteristics
_____ 7. menarche
_____ 8. spermarche
_____ 9. secondary sex characteristics
_____ 10. body image

Descriptions or Definitions
a. onset of menstruation
b. period of rapid physical growth and sexual maturation that ends childhood
c. hormone that increases dramatically in boys during puberty
d. hormone that increases steadily during puberty in both sexes
e. hormone that increases dramatically in girls during puberty
f. first sign is increased bone length and density
g. attitude toward one's physical appearance
h. physical characteristics not involved in reproduction
i. characteristics of sex organs involved in reproduction
j. first ejaculation containing sperm

Thinking Critically About Chapter 15

Answer these questions the day before an exam as a final check on your understanding of the chapter's terms and concepts.

1. (A Closer Look) Fifteen-year-old Janice is preoccupied with her "disgusting appearance" and seems depressed most of the time. The best thing her parents could do to help her through this difficult time would be to:

a. ignore her self-preoccupation since their attention would only reinforce it.
b. encourage her to "shape up" and not give in to self-pity.
c. kid her about her appearance in the hope that she will see how silly she is acting.
d. offer practical advice, such as clothing suggestions, to improve her body image.

2. Thirteen-year-old Rosa, an avid runner and dancer, is worried because most of her friends

have begun to menstruate regularly. Her doctor tells her:

a. that she should have a complete physical exam, since female athletes usually menstruate earlier than average.

b. not to worry, since female athletes usually menstruate later than average.

c. that she must stop running immediately, since the absence of menstruation is a sign of a serious health problem.

d. that the likely cause of her delayed menarche is an inadequate diet.

3. Twelve-year-old Bradley is worried because his twin sister has suddenly grown taller and more physically mature than he. His parents should:

a. reassure him that the average boy is two years behind the average girl in the onset of the growth spurt.

b. tell him that within a year or less he will grow taller than his sister.

c. tell him that one member of each fraternal twin pair is always shorter.

d. encourage him to exercise more to accelerate the onset of his growth spurt.

4. Calvin, the class braggart, boasts that because his beard has begun to grow, he is more virile than his male classmates. Jacob informs him that:

a. the tendency to grow facial and body hair has nothing to do with virility.

b. beard growth is determined by heredity.

c. facial hair is usually the last secondary sex characteristic to develop, sometimes occurring long after males have become sexually active.

d. all of the above are true.

5. The most likely source of status for a late-maturing, middle-SES boy would be:

a. academic achievement or vocational goal.

b. physical build.

c. athletic prowess.

d. success with the opposite sex.

6. Which of the following students is likely to be the most popular in a sixth-grade class?

a. Vicki, the most sexually mature girl in the class

b. Sandra, the tallest girl in the class

c. Brad, who is at the top of the class scholastically

d. Dan, the tallest boy in the class

7. Regarding the effects of early and late maturation on boys and girls, which of the following is *not* true?

a. Early maturation is usually easier for boys to manage than it is for girls.

b. Late maturation is usually easier for girls to manage than it is for boys.

c. Late-maturing girls may be drawn into older peer groups and may exhibit problem behaviors such as early sexual activity.

d. Late-maturing boys may not "catch up" physically, or in terms of their self-images, for many years.

8. Eleven-year-old Clarice, who matured early, is depressed because she often is teased about her well-developed figure. Her wise mother tells her that early-maturing girls:

a. eventually have more close friends than those who are slower to mature.

b. have fewer emotional problems in the long run than late-maturing girls.

c. often become more popular by seventh or eighth grade.

d. enjoy all of the above benefits.

9. As a psychoanalyst, Dr. Mendoza is most likely to believe that eating disorders are caused by:

a. the reinforcing effects of fasting, binging, and purging.

b. low self-esteem and depression, which act as stimuli for destructive patterns of eating.

c. unresolved conflicts with parents.

d. the desire of working women to project a strong, self-controlled image.

10. (A Closer Look) Thirteen-year-old Darren spends hours examining himself in front of the mirror. His worried parents consult the school psychologist, who tells them that Darren's behavior:

a. is a warning sign of possible emotional trauma.

b. is perfectly normal, since few adolescents are satisfied with their appearance.

c. should be discouraged, since such self-absorption is often followed by depression.

d. is puzzling, since preoccupation with appearance is usually more typical of adolescent girls.

11. Which of the following adolescents is likely to begin puberty at the earliest age?

a. Aretha, an African-American teenager who hates exercise

b. Todd, a football player of European ancestry

c. Kyu, an Asian-American honors student

d. There is too little information to make a prediction.

12. Of the following teenagers, those most likely to be distressed about their physical development are:
    a. late-maturing girls.
    b. late-maturing boys.
    c. early-maturing boys.
    d. girls or boys who masturbate.

13. Thirteen-year-old Kristin seems apathetic and lazy to her parents. You tell them:
    a. that Kristin is showing signs of chronic depression.
    b. that Kristin may be experiencing psychosocial difficulties.
    c. that Kristin has a poor attitude and needs more discipline.
    d. to have Kristin's iron level checked.

14. I am a hormone that rises steadily during puberty in both males and females. What am I?
    a. estrogen   c. GH
    b. testosterone   d. menarche

15. Eleven-year-old Linda, who has just begun to experience the first signs of puberty laments, "When will the agony of puberty be over?" You tell her that the major events of puberty typically end about _____ after the first visible signs appear.
    a. 6 years   c. 2 years
    b. 3 or 4 years   d. 1 year

Key Terms

Using your own words, write a brief definition or explanation of each of the following terms on a separate piece of paper.

1. puberty
2. GnRH (gonad releasing hormone)
3. GH (growth hormone)
4. testosterone
5. estrogen
6. precocious puberty
7. growth spurt
8. primary sex characteristics
9. menarche
10. spermarche
11. secondary sex characteristics
12. body image
13. bulimia
14. anorexia nervosa

15. violent death
16. secular trend

ANSWERS
CHAPTER REVIEW

1. puberty

   Girls: emergence of breast buds, initial appearance of pubic hair, widening of the hips, peak growth spurt, first menstrual period, completion of pubic-hair growth, and final breast development

   Boys: growth of the testes, growth of the penis, initial appearance of pubic hair, first ejaculation, peak growth spurt, voice changes, beard development, and completion of pubic-hair growth

2. 8; 14

3. is usually the same in all children; 3 or 4

4. hypothalamus; pituitary gland; adrenal glands; gonads (sex glands); testes; ovaries

5. GnRH (gonad releasing hormone); estrogen; testosterone; GH (growth hormone)

6. testosterone; estrogen; 1

7. precocious puberty; the psychological impact of the visible signs of puberty

8. rapid increase in size; sexual characteristics

9. length; density; gain

10. fat; gender; heredity; diet; exercise

11. females

12. muscle; upper

13. 38 pounds (17 kilograms); 9 5/8 inches (24 centimeters); 10 inches (25 centimeters); 42 pounds (19 kilograms)

14. varies

15. head

16. do not always

17. lungs; heart; decreases; increases; endurance

    The fact that the more visible spurts of weight and height precede the less visible ones of the muscles and organs means that athletic training and weight-lifting should match the young person's size of a year or so earlier.

18. lymphoid; less

19. oil; sweat; odor

20. primary sex characteristics; is

    Girls: growth of uterus and thickening of the vaginal lining

    Boys: growth of testes and lengthening of penis; also scrotal sac enlarges and becomes pendulous

21. menarche; spermarche; several years later
22. anovulatory; low-birthweight
23. have; do not
24. cramping; moodiness
25. secondary sex characteristics

Males grow taller than females and become wider at the shoulders than at the hips. Females become wider at the hips and their breasts begin to develop. About 65 percent of boys experience some temporary breast enlargement. As the larynx grows, the adolescent's voice (especially in boys) becomes lower. Head and body hair become coarser and darker in both sexes. Facial hair (especially in boys) begins to grow.

26. breast development; facial and body hair
27. body image

Many adolescents spend hours examining themselves in front of the mirror; some exercise or diet with obsessive intensity.

28. appetite; girls; reversed
29. good looks, sexy, fun, and kind and honest
30. tall and muscular; thin and shapely
31. girls; depression
32. risky sexual activity; abusive drug use; suicidal depression
33. calories; vitamins; minerals; calcium; iron; zinc; iron; iron-deficiency anemia
34. overeating; undereating; nutritional imbalance
35. drug; a preoccupation with being thin
36. most; did not vary
37. metabolism; fewer
38. stimulants; suppressants
39. bulimia; binging; purging; gastrointestinal; electrolytes; heart attack
40. anorexia nervosa; 15
41. 5; beginning; end; high; above-average; wealthy

Psychoanalytic therapists believe that anorexics have a severe disturbance of body image. The anorexic is believed to be afraid of becoming a woman and so maintains a childlike form by extreme dieting. Learning theorists see eating disorders as the result of maladaptive behavior (intended as a means of getting parents' attention, for example).

42. low self-esteem; depression; reinforcers
43. requires
44. depression; body image; family; group
45. are
46. violent death; accident; homicide; suicide

Biosocial factors include higher testosterone levels, dyslexia, attention-deficit disorder with hyperactivity, and certain genetic abnormalities.

Cultural and familial factors include child maltreatment, divorce, movie and television violence, the glorification of war, and the lure of drug abuse.

47. social values; cohort; ethnic; socioeconomic
48. sequence; timing; 10; 11; 12; sex, genes, body type, nourishment, metabolism, and emotional and physical health
49. 12 1/2; 13; 2
50. sisters; monozygotic twins
51. does
52. earlier
53. fat; later; earlier
54. secular trend; developed
55. accelerate
56. positively; girls
57. early

Early-maturing girls may be teased about their big feet or developing breasts. Those who date early may begin "adult" activities at an earlier age and suffer a decrease in self-esteem associated with being scrutinized by parents and criticized by friends. They are also likely to have sexual intercourse before high school is over, less likely to use contraception, and thus more likely to become pregnant and to find their plans for educational and career accomplishments deflected.

58. late

Late-maturing boys tend to be less poised, less relaxed, more restless, and more talkative than early-maturing boys. Late-maturing boys are more playful, more creative, and more flexible, qualities that are not usually admired by other adolescents. They also tend to have more conflicts with parents.

59. positive; mixed
60. more
61. increase
62. more
63. vary from culture to culture

PROGRESS TEST 1

Multiple-Choice Questions

1. **a.** is the answer. (p. 522)
2. **a.** is the answer. (p. 540)

3. **a.** is the answer. (p. 524)

4. **c.** is the answer. This is because each menstrual period deletes some iron from the body. (p. 533)

5. **c.** is the answer. (p. 528)

   a. & b. Even a year after menarche, when ovulation is irregular, pregnancy is possible.

   d. Remission means a disappearance of symptoms, such as those of a particular disease; although at first ovulation is irregular, it certainly does not disappear.

6. **b.** is the answer. (pp. 523, 532)

7. **b.** is the answer. (p. 528)

8. **d.** is the answer. (p. 523)

9. **c.** is the answer. (p. 530)

   a. Although some adolescents become overweight, many diet and lose weight in an effort to attain a desired body image.

   d. On the contrary, cultural attitudes about beauty are an extremely influential factor in the formation of a teenager's body image.

10. **a.** is the answer. (p. 531)

11. **c.** is the answer. (p. 540)

12. **c.** is the answer. (p. 541)

13. **a.** is the answer. (p. 531)

14. **d.** is the answer. (p. 544)

15. **a.** is the answer. (p. 535)

True or False Items

1. T (p. 532)

2. T (p. 528)

3. F The first indicator of reproductive potential in males is ejaculation of seminal fluid containing sperm (spermarche). Menarche (the first menstrual period) is the first indication of reproductive potential in females. (p. 528)

4. T (p. 526)

5. T (p. 522)

6. F Studies show that the majority of adolescent girls, even those in the thinnest group, want to lose weight. (p. 534)

7. F The strong emphasis on appearance is reflected in the culture as a whole; for example, teachers (and no doubt prospective employers) tend to judge people who are physically attractive as being more competent than those who are less attractive. (pp. 530–531)

8. T (p. 531)

9. T (p. 542)

10. F Although the sequence of pubertal events is very similar for all young people, there is great variation in its timing. (p. 540)

PROGRESS TEST 2

Multiple-Choice Questions

1. **b.** is the answer. (p. 522)

2. **d.** is the answer. During adolescence, the lymphoid system *decreases* in size and the heart *doubles* in size. (pp. 526–527)

3. **a.** is the answer. (p. 523)

   b. Testosterone increases markedly in boys.

   c. Androgen is another name for testosterone.

   d. Menarche is the first menstrual period.

4. **b.** is the answer. (p. 534)

5. **b.** is the answer. (p. 525)

   a. The shoulders of males tend to widen during puberty.

   c. The torso typically lengthens during puberty.

   d. The eyes and nose *increase* in size during puberty.

6. **c.** is the answer. (p. 529)

   a. Although not a term used in the textbook, a gender-typed trait is one that is typical of one sex but not the other.

   b. Primary sex characteristics are those involving the reproductive organs.

   d. This is not a term used by developmental psychologists.

7. **a.** is the answer. (p. 523)

8. **c.** is the answer. (pp. 530–531)

   a., b., & d. These certainly are factors that influence physical characteristics as well as body image; cultural ideals, however, exert an even stronger influence.

9. **c.** is the answer. (p. 531)

   a. If the timing of maturation differs substantially from that of the peer group, dissatisfaction is likely; however, this is not the most common source of dissatisfaction in teenage girls.

   b. & d. Although teenage girls are more likely than boys to be dissatisfied with certain features, which body parts are troubling varies from girl to girl.

10. **d.** is the answer. (p. 542)

11. **c.** is the answer. (p. 540)

    b. & d. The onset of puberty is quite variable; the text does not suggest that the duration of puberty varies significantly.

12. **d.** is the answer. (pp. 535–536)

13. **c.** is the answer. (p. 522)

14. **b.** is the answer. Although the size of the heart increases during puberty, heart rate *decreases*. (p. 526)

15. **d.** is the answer. (pp. 526–527)

Matching Items

1. b (p. 522)   5. f (p. 524)   8. j (p. 528)
2. d (p. 523)   6. i (p. 527)   9. h (p. 529)
3. c (p. 523)   7. a (p. 528)   10. g (p. 530)
4. e (p. 523)

THINKING CRITICALLY ABOUT CHAPTER 15

1. **d.** is the answer. (p. 531)

   a., b., & c. These would likely make matters worse.

2. **b.** is the answer. (p. 540)

   a. Because they typically have little body fat, female dancers and athletes menstruate *later* than average.

   c. Delayed maturation in a young dancer or athlete is usually quite normal.

   d. The text does not indicate that the age of menarche varies with diet.

3. **a.** is the answer. (p. 540)

   b. It usually takes longer than one year for a prepubescent male to catch up with a female who has begun puberty.

   c. This is not true.

   d. The text does not suggest that exercise has an effect on the timing of the growth spurt.

4. **d.** is the answer. (p. 532)

5. **a.** is the answer. (pp. 542–544)

   b., c., & d. These are more typically sources of status for early-maturing boys.

6. **d.** is the answer. (p. 541)

   a. & b. Early-maturing girls often are teased and criticized by their friends.

   c. During adolescence, physical stature is typically a more prized attribute among peers than is scholastic achievement.

7. **c.** is the answer. It is *early*-maturing girls who often are drawn into older peer groups. (p. 542)

8. **d.** is the answer. (p. 542)

9. **c.** is the answer. (p. 536)

10. **b.** is the answer. (p. 530)

    a. & c. These are untrue.

    d. Preoccupation with appearance is typical of both teenage boys and girls.

11. **a.** is the answer. African-Americans often begin puberty earlier than Asian-Americans or Americans of European ancestry. Furthermore, females who are inactive menstruate earlier than those who are more active. (pp. 540–541)

12. **b.** is the answer. (p. 542)

    a. Late maturation is typically more difficult for boys than for girls.

    c. Early maturation is generally a positive experience for boys.

    d. Adolescent masturbation is no longer the source of guilt or shame that it once was.

13. **d.** Kristin's symptoms are typical of iron-deficiency anemia, which is more common in teenage girls than in any other age group. (p. 533)

14. **c.** is the answer. (p. 523)

    a. Only in girls do estrogen levels rise markedly during puberty.

    b. Only in boys do testosterone levels rise markedly during puberty.

    d. Menarche is the first menstrual period.

15. **b.** is the answer. (p. 523)

KEY TERMS

1. **Puberty** is the period of rapid physical growth and sexual maturation that ends childhood and brings the young person to adult size, shape, and sexual potential. (p. 522)

2. **GnRH (gonad releasing hormone)** is the hormone that causes the gonads to dramatically increase production of sex hormones, chiefly estrogen and testosterone. (p. 523)

3. **GH (growth hormone)**, which is one of about a dozen hormones involved in puberty, rises steadily in both sexes during this period of development. (p. 523)

4. **Testosterone** is a hormone of puberty that increases dramatically in boys and slightly in girls. (p. 523)

5. **Estrogen** is a hormone of puberty that increases markedly in girls and slightly in boys. (p. 523)

   Example: Levels of **testosterone** in boys and **estrogen** in girls begin to increase at least a year before the first perceptible signs of puberty.

6. **Precocious puberty** is the unusually early onset of puberty, whose causes include genetic factors and teratogenic effects. (p. 524)

7. The **growth spurt**, which begins with an increase in bone length and density and includes rapid

weight gain and organ growth, is one of the many observable signs of puberty. (p. 524)

8. During puberty, changes in **primary sex characteristics** involve those sex organs that are directly involved in reproduction. (p. 527)

9. **Menarche,** which refers to the first menstrual period, is the specific event that is taken to indicate fertility in adolescent girls. (p. 528)

10. **Spermarche,** which refers to the first ejaculation of seminal fluid containing sperm, is the specific event that is taken to indicate fertility in adolescent boys. (p. 528)

11. During puberty, changes in **secondary sex characteristics** involve parts of the body other than the sex organs. (p. 529)

12. **Body image** refers to adolescents' mental conception of, and attitude toward, their physical appearance. (p. 530)

13. **Bulimia** is an eating disorder that involves compulsive binge-eating followed by purging through vomiting or taking massive doses of laxatives. (p. 535)

14. **Anorexia nervosa** is an eating disorder characterized by self-starvation that is most common in high-achieving, relatively well-to-do adolescent girls. (p. 536)

15. Stereotypes about "manly" behavior may lead to a problem that afflicts mostly young men—**violent death** from accident, homicide, or suicide. (p. 537)

16. The **secular trend** is the tendency of successive generations to develop in somewhat different ways as the result of improved nutrition and medical advances. (p. 540)

CHAPTER 16

Adolescence: Cognitive Development

Chapter Overview

Chapter 16 begins by describing the cognitive advances of adolescence. With the attainment of formal operational thought, the developing person becomes able to think in an adult way, that is, to be logical, to think in terms of possibilities, to reason scientifically and abstractly.

Not everyone reaches the stage of formal operational thought, however, and even those who do so spend much of their time thinking at less advanced levels. The discussion of adolescent egocentrism supports this generalization in showing that adolescents have difficulty thinking rationally about themselves and their immediate experiences. Adolescent egocentrism makes them see themselves as psychologically unique and more socially significant than they really are.

The second section addresses the question, "What kind of school best fosters adolescent intellectual growth?" Many adolescents enter secondary school feeling less motivated and more vulnerable to self-doubt than they did in elementary school. The rigid behavioral demands and intensified competition of most secondary schools do not, unfortunately, provide a supportive learning environment for adolescents. Schools can be more effectively organized by setting clear, attainable educational goals that are supported by the entire staff.

The chapter concludes with an example of adolescent cognition at work: decision making in the area of sexual behavior. The discussion relates choices made by adolescents to their cognitive abilities and typical shortcomings, and it suggests ways in which adolescents may be helped to make healthy choices.

NOTE: Answer guidelines for all Chapter 16 questions begin on page 247.

Guided Study

The text chapter should be studied one section at a time. Before you read, preview each section by skimming it, noting headings and boldface items. Then read the appropriate section objectives from the following outline. Keep these objectives in mind and, as you read the chapter section, search for the information that will enable you to meet each objective. Once you have finished a section, write out answers for its objectives.

Adolescent Thought (pp. 548–557)

1. Describe adolescent thinking, including its gains and limitations.

2. Describe evidence of formal operational thinking during adolescence and provide examples of adolescents' emerging theory-building ability.

3. Discuss adolescent egocentrism and give two examples of egocentric fantasies or fables.

7. Explain how schools can be organized to more effectively meet adolescents' cognitive needs and discuss the role of parents in adolescent intellectual growth.

Schools, Learning, and the Adolescent Mind
(pp. 557–564)

4. Evaluate the typical secondary school's ability to meet the cognitive needs of the typical adolescent.

Adolescent Decision Making (pp. 564–576)

8. Explain how adolescent thinking contributes to the high incidence of adolescent pregnancy and sexually transmitted disease.

5. Discuss the impact of ego- and task-involvement learning on the typical adolescent.

9. (Public Policy) Discuss the risk-taking behaviors of adolescents, including their frequency and their "logic" and public-policy implications.

6. (A Closer Look) Discuss the impact of academic tracking on students.

10. Discuss and evaluate the new approach to sex education.

Chapter Review

When you have finished reading the chapter, work through the material that follows to review it. Complete the sentences and answer the questions. As you proceed, evaluate your performance for each section by consulting the answers on page 247. Do not continue with the next section until you understand each answer. If you need to, review or reread the appropriate section in the textbook before continuing.

Adolescent Thought (pp. 548–557)

1. The basic skills of thinking, learning, and remembering that advance during the school-age years _____ (continue to progress/stabilize) during adolescence.

2. Advances in _____ deepens adolescents' ability to play at what Flavell calls "the _____ _____ _____ ." These advances also make adolescents more scrutinizing of their own _____ _____ .

3. Piaget's term for the fourth stage of cognitive development is _____ _____ thought. Other theorists may explain adolescent advances differently, but virtually all theorists agree that adolescent thought _____ (is/is not) qualitatively different from children's thought. For many developmentalists, including _____ and the _____-_____ researchers, the single most distinguishing feature of adolescent thought is the capacity to think in terms of _____ . One specific example of this type of thinking is the development of _____ thought.

4. Compared to younger individuals, adolescents have _____ (more/less) difficulty arguing against their personal beliefs and self-interest.

5. During the school years, children make great strides in _____ (inductive/deductive) reasoning.

6. Along with their developing ability to think hypothetically, adolescents become more capable of _____ reasoning—that is, they can begin with a general _____ or _____

and draw logical _____ from it. This type of reasoning is a hallmark of formal operational thought.

7. Piaget devised a number of famous tasks involving principles of _____ and _____ to study how children of various ages reasoned hypothetically and deductively.

8. Experiments by information-processing researcher Robert Siegler demonstrate that adolescents, but not younger children, are able to solve the "balance-beam" problem by generating _____ relationships between different aspects of the problem, and then systematically testing various alternatives to derive the solution.

9. Whereas younger children tend to generalize from their _____ _____ , adolescents attempt to create more comprehensive, inclusive _____ that are broader and more generalizable.

10. Adolescents and even most adults often confuse theory and _____ . They also often have difficulty thinking of _____ _____ to the ones they hold, or imagining what _____ evidence would be.

11. The adolescent's belief that he or she is uniquely significant and that the social world revolves around him or her is a psychological phenomenon called _____ _____ . David Elkind has argued that this form of thinking occurs because adolescents fail to differentiate between the _____ and the _____ .

Give an example of this flawed thinking in adolescents.

12. An adolescent's tendency to feel that he or she is somehow immune to the consequences of dangerous or illegal behavior is expressed in the _____ _____ .

13. An adolescent's tendency to imagine that her or his own life is unique, heroic, or even mythical, and that she or he is destined for great accomplishments, is expressed in the _____ _____ .

14. Adolescents, who believe that they are under constant scrutiny from nearly everyone, create for themselves an _____ _____ . Their acute self-consciousness reveals that young people are often not at ease with the broader _____ _____ .

15. Adolescent egocentrism enables them to reflect more thoughtfully on their lives, but often at the cost of greater _____ .

16. Many adolescents develop hypothetical thinking and deductive reasoning _____ (earlier/later) than Piaget predicted. This type of thinking _____ (is/is not) eventually demonstrated by all adults.

Schools, Learning, and the Adolescent Mind
(pp. 557–564)

17. The best setting for personal growth, called the optimum _____- _____ _____ , depends on several factors, including _____ _____ _____ .

18. The goals of the American education system _____ (have/have not) changed significantly over the generations.

19. The emergence of hypothetical, abstract thought makes adolescents _____ (more/less) interested in the opinions of others. At the same time, they are _____ (more/less) vulnerable to criticism than their behaviors imply. One outcome of the relatively common mismatch between student needs and the school environment is a widespread dip in

academic _____ as young people enter secondary school.

Cite several ways in which educational settings tend not to be supportive of adolescents' self-confidence.

20. Many teachers have _____ (lower/higher) expectations of adolescent students than they do of younger students. As a result, most students experience a(n) _____ (increase/drop) in motivation and achievement as they move from the sixth to the seventh grade.

21. Developmentalists generally agree that _____ (cooperation/competition) in the classroom is healthy for adolescents.

22. In _____- _____ learning, academic grades are based solely on individual test performance, and students are ranked against each other. In such situations, many students, especially _____ , find it psychologically safer not to work very hard. Curricular areas in which girls suddenly score lower in high school than in elementary school are those areas in which _____ achievement scores are widely used—for example, _____ and _____ .

23. The tendency to avoid advanced math and science is also seen in many _____ students, especially those from cultures that stress _____ and _____ .

24. In _____- _____ learning, grades are based on cooperatively acquiring certain competencies and knowledge that everyone is expected to attain.

25. Cooperative learning is _____ (more/less) likely to lead to rivalry among various ethnic, religious, and racial groups.

26. (A Closer Look) The separation of students into distinct groups based on standardized tests of ability and achievement is called _____ . This practice is often instituted for the first time at about age _____ .

27. (A Closer Look) The impact of tracking on student motivation, pace of learning, and achievement is most deleterious for _____ (lower/middle/upper)-track students.

(A Closer Look) Explain why this is so.

28. (A Closer Look) Studies have found that the precipitating reason for dropping out is usually _____ _____ _____ .

29. Schools that are most effective in educating students share the central characteristic of _____ _____ .

30. To promote student learning, it is important that the expectations and incentives of _____ and _____ be in sync.

31. Generally speaking, parents' values _____ (do/do not) have a significant influence on their children's academic goals and motivation.

32. Parents tend to expect their sons to excel at _____ and _____ , and their daughters to excel at _____ and _____ .

Adolescent Decision Making (pp. 564–576)

33. Developmentalists are divided on the question of whether the _____ advances that adolescents experience help them make sound decisions.

34. Supporting those who believe that adolescents are prone to poor decision making are statistics on the high rates of adolescent

_____ _____ .

35. Supporting the other side of the debate is evidence that adolescents are comparable to adults in their ability to obtain _____ _____ , to evaluate and compare _____ and _____ , to anticipate _____ , and to _____ their decisions. However, this maturity is *not* shown by adolescents who are under age _____ , have less _____ , and have fewer _____ to talk to.

36. (Public Policy) Most adolescents _____ (are/are not) aware of the consequences of their risky behavior. This has led developmentalists to question the _____ and _____ of adolescent reasoning. One researcher, however, believes that adolescent thinking is entirely rational, that they generally weigh the _____ and _____ of their actions. that often accompanies egocentric thinking.

37. Generally, research reveals that adolescent beliefs, values, and reasoning processes _____ (do/do not) significantly affect their sexual behavior.

38. Teenage pregnancy _____ (is/is not) a worldwide problem. The country with the highest teenage pregnancy rate in the industrialized world is the _____ .

Describe the likely consequences to all concerned of an American adolescent giving birth.

39. Diseases that are spread by sexual contact are called _____ _____ _____ .

40. The highest rates of the most prevalent STDs occur in sexually active people between the ages of _____ and
_____ .

41. The most common transmission of the
_____ _____
_____ , which causes AIDS, is
through _____ contact. It is presently estimated that one in every _____
teenagers is at high risk for AIDS because of unsafe practices, such as _____
_____ .

42. Ignorance about sex and unavailability of contraception _____ (do/do not) explain the high rates of adolescent pregnancy and STD.

43. Knowing facts about sex has so little effect on adolescent sexual behavior because _____
_____ ;
_____ ;
and, because adolescents' thinking tends to be
_____ , they reason in terms of their own immediate needs, rather than considering the consequences of their behavior for their sexual partner or for a possible child.

44. Because of their sense of personal
_____ , many adolescents seriously underestimate the chances of pregnancy or of contracting a disease.

45. The first step in encouraging adolescents to make more rational decisions about their sexuality requires adults to be more _____
in their thinking about adolescent sexuality.

46. Some research suggests that _____
(sons/daughters) listen more to their parents on the topic of sex because the underlying message is somewhat more accepting of sexuality.

Briefly explain why traditional sex education is often irrelevant or ineffective.

47. A new form of sex education involves a
_____ _____
procedure in which, through role-playing and discussions, adolescents are taught reasoning skills for dealing with sexual pressures.

48. Collectively, research indicates that effective sex education must _____
_____ .

Progress Test 1

Multiple-Choice Questions

Circle your answers to the following questions and check them with the answers on page 248. If your answer is incorrect, read the explanation for why it is incorrect and then consult the appropriate pages of the text (in parentheses following the correct answer).

1. Many psychologists consider the distinguishing feature of adolescent thought to be the ability to think in terms of:
   a. moral issues.
   b. concrete operations.
   c. possibility, not just reality.
   d. logical principles.

2. Piaget's last stage of cognitive development is:
   a. formal operational thought.
   b. concrete operational thought.
   c. universal ethical principles.
   d. symbolic thought.

3. Advances in metacognition deepen adolescents' abilities in:
   a. concrete operational thought.
   b. "the game of thinking."
   c. the personal fable.
   d. the scientific method.

4. The adolescent who takes risks and feels immune to the laws of mortality is evidencing the:
   a. invincibility fable.   c. imaginary audience.
   b. personal fable.   d. death instinct.

5. Imaginary audiences, invincibility fables, and personal fables are expressions of adolescent:
   a. morality.   c. decision making.
   b. thinking games.   d. egocentrism.

6. The typical adolescent is:
   a. tough-minded.
   b. indifferent to public opinion.

c. self-absorbed and hypersensitive to criticism.

d. all of the above.

7. When adolescents enter secondary school, many:

a. experience a drop in academic self-confidence.

b. are less motivated than they were in elementary school.

c. are less conscientious than they were in elementary school.

d. experience all of the above.

8. In _____ , academic grades are based solely on individual test performance, and students are ranked against each other.

a. task-involvement learning

b. ego-involvement learning

c. academic tracking

d. preconventional classroom environments

9. Thinking that begins with a general premise and then draws logical inferences from it is called:

a. inductive reasoning.

b. deductive reasoning.

c. "the game of thinking."

d. hypothetical reasoning.

10. Serious reflection on important issues is a wrenching process for many adolescents because of their newfound ability to reason:

a. inductively.   c. hypothetically.

b. deductively.   d. symbolically.

11. The main reason for high rates of STD and pregnancy during adolescence is cognitive immaturity, as evidenced by:

a. the decline of the "good girl" morality.

b. increased sexual activity.

c. the inability to think logically about the consequences of sexual activity.

d. a lack of information about sexual matters.

12. Many adolescents seem to believe that *their* lovemaking will not lead to pregnancy. This belief is an expression of the:

a. personal fable.   c. imaginary audience.

b. invincibility fable.   d. "game of thinking."

13. One reason that AIDS statistics do not show a high rate of infection among today's adolescents is that:

a. adolescents are less likely than others to be infected by exposure to HIV.

b. most adolescents use condoms.

c. adolescents are more likely to receive medical care for STDs in general.

d. AIDS takes about 10 years to develop in an infected individual.

14. In the social inoculation method of sex education, adolescents:

a. develop reasoning skills to build up a "cognitive immunity" to sexual pressures.

b. are exposed to scare tactics designed to discourage sexual activity.

c. are taught by teenagers who have contracted a sexually transmitted disease.

d. experience all of the above.

15. To estimate the risk of a behavior, such as unprotected sexual intercourse, it is most important that the adolescent be able to think clearly about:

a. universal ethical principles.

b. personal beliefs and self-interest.

c. probability.

d. peer pressure.

True or False Items

Write *true* or *false* on the line in front of each statement.

_____ 1. By the time they reach adolescence, most children have outgrown "the game of thinking."

_____ 2. Adolescents are generally better able than 8-year-olds to recognize the validity of arguments that clash with their own beliefs.

_____ 3. Everyone attains the stage of formal operational thought by adulthood.

_____ 4. (Public Policy) Most adolescents who engage in risky behavior are unaware of the consequences, and potential costs, of their actions.

_____ 5. Adolescents often create an imaginary audience as they envision how others will react to their appearance and behavior.

_____ 6. Most developmentalists feel that competitive classroom environments are a healthy cognitive influence on adolescents.

_____ 7. (A Closer Look) The separation of students into different groups based on standardized tests of ability and achievement is especially beneficial for low-achieving students.

_____ 8. Inductive reasoning is a hallmark of formal operational thought.

_____ 9. Adolescents are the group with the highest rates of the most prevalent sexually transmitted diseases (STDs).

_____ 10. The new wave of sex education tries to take into account adolescent thinking patterns, often involving role-playing, discussions, and specific exercises designed to help adolescents weigh alternatives and analyze risks.

Progress Test 2

Progress Test 2 should be completed during a final chapter review. Answer the following questions after you thoroughly understand the correct answers for the Chapter Review and Progress Test 1.

Multiple-Choice Questions

1. Adolescents who fall prey to the invincibility fable may be more likely to:
   a. engage in risky behaviors.
   b. suffer from depression.
   c. have low self-esteem.
   d. drop out of school.

2. In one experiment, the investigator held a red chip so it could be seen and said, "Either the chip in my hand is green or it is not yellow." The results demonstrated that _____ accurately evaluate the logic of this kind of statement.
   a. most preadolescents and adolescents were unable to
   b. adolescents were more likely to be able to
   c. most of the girls, but few of the boys, could
   d. most of the boys, but few of the girls, could

3. Recent research regarding Piaget's theory has found that:
   a. many adolescents arrive at formal operational thinking later than Piaget predicted.
   b. formal operational thinking is more likely to be demonstrated in certain domains than in others.
   c. whether formal operational thinking is demonstrated depends in part on an individual's experiences, talents, and interests.
   d. all of the above are true.

4. When young people overestimate their significance to others, they are displaying:
   a. concrete operational thought.
   b. adolescent egocentrism.
   c. a lack of cognitive growth.
   d. immoral development.

5. The personal fable refers to adolescents imagining that:
   a. they are immune to the dangers of risky behaviors.
   b. they are always being scrutinized by others.
   c. their own lives are unique, heroic, or even mythical.
   d. the world revolves around their actions.

6. The typical secondary school environment:
   a. has more rigid behavioral demands than the average elementary school.
   b. does not meet the cognitive needs of the typical adolescent.
   c. emphasizes ego-involvement learning.
   d. is described by all of the above.

7. The most likely reason high school girls suddenly tend to score lower on standardized math and science tests is that:
   a. girls are socialized to be nurturant and non-competitive.
   b. they have weaker elementary school backgrounds in these subjects.
   c. they too often have been the victims of task-involvement learning.
   d. they simply dislike these subjects.

8. In _____ , grades are not assigned competitively, but are based on acquiring competencies that *everyone* is expected to attain.
   a. ego-involvement learning
   b. task-involvement learning
   c. academic tracking
   d. preconventional classroom environments

9. (A Closer Look) The precipitating reason for an adolescent dropping out of school is usually:
   a. lack of ability.
   b. irrelevance of curriculum.
   c. lack of achievement.
   d. lack of encouragement, acceptance, and intellectual excitement from teachers and classmates.

10. Educational settings that emphasize individual competition and tracking:
    a. may be destructive to adolescent development if not used properly.
    b. tend to be the most effective in educating students.
    c. are more effective in large schools than small schools.
    d. have proven very effective in educating minority students.

11. One of the hallmarks of formal operational thought is:
    a. egocentrism.   c. symbolic thinking.
    b. deductive thinking.   d. all of the above.

12. In explaining adolescent advances in thinking, sociocultural theorists emphasize:
   a. the accumulated improvement in specific skills.
   b. mental advances resulting from the transition from primary school to secondary school.
   c. the completion of the myelination process in cortical neurons.
   d. advances in metacognition.

13. Compared to their peers, adolescents who score highest on tests that measure knowledge of sexual matters are:
   a. more likely to be sexually active.
   b. less likely to be sexually active.
   c. more likely to use contraception.
   d. not significantly different.

14. In the social inoculation method of sex education, the group or class leaders are:
   a. eighth-graders.
   b. older teenagers.
   c. teachers and medical authorities.
   d. attractive celebrities.

15. Compared with elementary school teachers, junior high teachers:
   a. are more likely to regard their students as unmotivated.
   b. tend to expect less of themselves.
   c. are more likely to feel that students need to be "kept in their place."
   d. are described by all of the above.

Matching Items

Match each term or concept with its corresponding description or definition.

Terms or Concepts

_____ 1. invincibility fable
_____ 2. imaginary audience
_____ 3. person-environment fit
_____ 4. hypothetical thought
_____ 5. deductive reasoning
_____ 6. social inoculation
_____ 7. tracking
_____ 8. ego-involvement learning
_____ 9. task-involvement learning
_____ 10. "game of thinking"

Descriptions or Definitions

a. the ability to suspend knowledge of reality and think about possibilities
b. adolescents feel immune to the consequences of dangerous behavior
c. grading is based solely on individual test performance
d. a creation of adolescents who are preoccupied with how others react to their appearance and behavior
e. the match or mismatch between an adolescent's needs and the educational setting
f. grading does not foster competition among students
g. involves reasoning about propositions that may or may not reflect reality
h. the separation of students into groups based on standardized tests of ability and achievement
i. thinking that moves from premise to conclusion
j. procedure at the heart of a new form of sex education

Thinking Critically About Chapter 16

Answer these questions the day before an exam as a final check on your understanding of the chapter's terms and concepts.

1. A 13-year-old can create and solve logical problems on the computer but is not usually reasonable, mature, or consistent in his or her thinking when it comes to people and social relationships. This supports the finding that:
   a. some children reach the stage of formal operational thought earlier than others.
   b. the stage of formal operational thought is not attained by age 13.
   c. formal operational thinking may be demonstrated in certain domains and not in other domains.
   d. older adolescents and adults often do poorly on standard tests of formal operational thought.

2. An experimenter hides a ball in her hand and says, "Either the ball in my hand is red or it is not red." Most preadolescent children say:
   a. the statement is true.
   b. the statement is false.
   c. they cannot tell if the statement is true or false.
   d. they do not understand what the experimenter means.

3. Fourteen-year-old Monica is very idealistic, and often develops crushes on people she doesn't even know. This reflects her newly developed cognitive ability to:
   a. deal simultaneously with two sides of an issue.
   b. take another person's viewpoint.
   c. imagine possible worlds and people.
   d. see herself as others see her.

4. Which of the following is the *best* example of a personal fable?
   a. Adriana imagines that she is destined for a life of fame and fortune.
   b. Ben makes up stories about his experiences to impress his friends.
   c. Kalil questions his religious beliefs when they seem to offer little help for a problem he faces.
   d. Julio believes that every girl he meets is attracted to him.

5. Which of the following is the *best* example of "the game of thinking"?

a. Twelve-year-old Stanley feels that people are always watching him.
b. Fourteen-year-old Mindy engages in many risky behaviors, reasoning that, "nothing bad will happen to me."
c. Fifteen-year-old Philip feels that no one understands his problems.
d. Thirteen-year-old Josh delights in finding logical flaws in virtually everything his teachers and parents say.

6. Frustrated because of the dating curfew her parents have set, Melinda exclaims, "You just don't know how it feels to be in love!" Melinda's thinking demonstrates:
   a. the invincibility fable.
   b. the personal fable.
   c. the imaginary audience.
   d. adolescent egocentrism.

7. Compared to her 13-year-old brother, 17-year-old Yolanda is likely to:
   a. be more critical about herself.
   b. be more egocentric.
   c. have less confidence in her abilities.
   d. be more capable of reasoning hypothetically.

8. Nathan's fear that his friends will ridicule him because of a pimple that has appeared on his nose reflects a preoccupation with:
   a. his personal fable.
   b. the invincibility fable.
   c. an imaginary audience.
   d. preconventional reasoning.

9. Thirteen-year-old Malcolm, who lately is very sensitive to the criticism of others, feels significantly less motivated and capable than when he was in elementary school. Malcolm is probably:
   a. experiencing a sense of vulnerability that is common in adolescents.
   b. a lower-track student.
   c. a student in a task-involvement classroom.
   d. all of the above.

10. A high school principal who wished to increase the interest level and achievement of minority and female students in math and science would be well advised to:
    a. create classroom environments in these subjects that are not based on competitive grading procedures.
    b. encourage greater use of standardized testing in the elementary schools that feed students to the high school.

c. separate students into academic tracks based on achievement.

d. do all of the above.

11. (A Closer Look) A new high school principal states that remedial math classes will be eliminated because, "Students will perform as well as they are expected to perform." Research reveals that the principal's attitude is:

a. contradicted by evidence that setting high academic goals usually *lowers* the academic performance of lower-track students.

b. supported by evidence that lower-track teachers are more likely to provide repetitive and uninteresting classwork, leading to low morale and a slower rate of student achievement.

c. contradicted by evidence that the precipitating reason for truancy and dropping out of school is usually fear of failure when academic expectations are set too high.

d. both b. and c.

12. Who is the *least* likely to display mature decision making?

a. Brenda, an outgoing 17-year-old art student

b. Fifteen-year-old Kenny, who has few adults in whom he confides

c. Monique, a well-educated 15-year-old

d. Damon, an 18-year-old high school graduate who lives alone

13. If Sheila's parents are typical, they probably expect their daughter to excel at _____ and her brother to excel at _____ .

a. math; science   c. English; math

b. science; math   d. math; English

14. Cindy, a sexually active teenager who does not practice contraception, is likely to think that:

a. having a child might not be so bad.

b. she will be perceived as being "easy" if she carries a contraceptive with her on a date.

c. she is less likely to become pregnant, or contract a STD, than others.

d. all of the above are true.

15. Dr. Malone, who wants to improve the effectiveness of her adolescent sex education class, would be well advised to:

a. focus on the biological facts of reproduction and disease, since teenage misinformation is largely responsible for the high rates of unwanted pregnancy and STD.

b. personalize the instruction, in order to make the possible consequences of sexual activity more immediate to students.

c. teach boys and girls in separate classes, so that discussion can be more frank and open.

d. use all of the above strategies.

Key Terms

Using your own words, write a brief definition or explanation of each of the following terms on a separate piece of paper.

1. formal operational thought
2. hypothetical thought
3. deductive reasoning
4. adolescent egocentrism
5. invincibility fable
6. personal fable
7. imaginary audience
8. person-environment fit
9. ego-involvement learning
10. task-involvement learning
11. tracking
12. sexually transmitted disease (STD)
13. social inoculation

ANSWERS

CHAPTER REVIEW

1. continue to progress
2. metacognition; game of thinking; mental processes
3. formal operational; is; Piaget; information-processing; possibility; hypothetical
4. less
5. inductive
6. deductive; premise; theory; inferences
7. chemistry; physics
8. hypothetical
9. immediate experience; theories
10. evidence; alternative theories; disconfirming
11. adolescent egocentrism; unique; universal

One example of adolescent egocentrism is the young person who believes that no one else has ever had the particular emotional experiences he or she is having (feeling sad and lonely or being in love, for example).

12. invincibility fable

13. personal fable

14. imaginary audience; social world

15. self-criticism

16. later; is not

17. person-environment fit; the individual's developmental stage, cognitive strengths and weaknesses, and learning style, and the traditions, educational objectives, and future needs of society

18. have

19. more; more; self-confidence

Compared to elementary schools, most secondary schools have more rigid behavioral demands, intensified competition, more punitive grading practices, as well as less individualized attention and procedures.

20. lower; drop

21. cooperation

22. ego-involvement; girls; standardized; math; science

23. minority; cooperation; collaboration

24. task-involvement

25. less

26. tracking; 12

27. lower

Lower-track teachers are likely to provide repetitive, uninteresting classwork, leading to more boredom, distraction, and disturbances and, consequently, to disciplinarian instruction rather than to creative attempts to foster intellectual growth.

28. the overall lack of encouragement, acceptance, and intellectual excitement from teachers and classmates

29. having educational goals that are high, clear, and attainable, and supported by the entire staff

30. home; school

31. do

32. math; science; English; reading

33. cognitive

34. risk taking

35. pertinent information; risks; benefits; consequences; justify; 16; education; adults

36. are; maturity; rationality; costs; benefits

37. do

38. is; United States

For the mother, the consequences include interference with education and social and vocational growth; for the couple if they marry, greater risk of abuse and divorce; for the child, greater risk of prenatal and birth complications, of lower academic achievement, and, at adolescence, of drug abuse, arrest, and early parenthood.

39. sexually transmitted diseases

40. 10; 19

41. human immunodeficiency virus (HIV); sexual; 5; having several sexual partners and failing to use condoms

42. do not

43. young people have difficulty envisioning and evaluating alternatives; they tend to focus on immediate considerations rather than on future ones; egocentric

44. invincibility

45. rational

46. sons

Adolescents are often put off by traditional sex eduction courses that focus on biological facts, rather than deal with their actual sexual dilemmas and pressures.

47. social inoculation

48. begin early and have curricula geared to the cognitive abilities of the participants

PROGRESS TEST 1

Multiple-Choice Questions

1. c. is the answer. (p. 549)

   a. Although moral reasoning becomes much deeper during adolescence, it is not limited to this stage of development.

   b. & d. Concrete operational thought, which *is* logical, is the distinguishing feature of childhood thinking.

2. a. is the answer. (p. 549)

   b. In Piaget's theory, this stage precedes formal operational thought.

   c. & d. These are not stages in Piaget's theory.

3. b. is the answer. (p. 548)

4. a. is the answer. (p. 555)

   b. This refers to adolescents' tendency to imagine their own lives as unique, heroic, or even mythical.

   c. This refers to adolescents' tendency to fantasize about how others will react to their appearance and behavior.

   d. This is a concept in Freud's theory.

5. d. is the answer. These thought processes are manifestations of adolescents' tendency to see themselves as being much more central and im-

portant to the social scene than they really are. (pp. 555–556)

6. **c.** is the answer. (pp. 547, 558)

7. **d.** is the answer. (p. 559)

8. **b.** is the answer. (p. 559)

   a. In task-involvement learning, grades are based on acquiring certain competencies and knowledge that everyone, with enough time and effort, is expected to attain.

   c. Tracking refers to the separation of students into distinct groups based on standardized tests of ability and achievement.

   d. This is not a type of classroom environment discussed in the text.

9. **b.** is the answer. (p. 551)

   a. Inductive reasoning moves from specific facts to a general conclusion.

   b. & c. The "game of thinking," which is an example of hypothetical reasoning, involves the ability to think creatively about possibilities.

10. **c.** is the answer. (p. 551)

11. **c.** is the answer. (p. 570)

    a. The text does not suggest that declining moral standards are responsible for the increased rate of STD.

    b. Although this may be true, in itself it is not necessarily a result of adolescent cognitive immaturity.

    d. Various studies have found that merely understanding the facts of sexuality does not correlate with more responsible and cautious sexual behavior.

12. **b.** is the answer. (p. 572)

    a. This refers to adolescents' tendency to imagine their own lives as unique, heroic, or even mythical.

    c. This refers to adolescents' tendency to fantasize about how others will react to their appearance and behavior.

    d. This is the adolescent ability to suspend knowledge of reality in order to think playfully about possibilities.

13. **d.** is the answer. (p. 569)

14. **a.** is the answer. (p. 574)

15. **c.** is the answer. (p. 572)

True or False Items

1. F   Only with the advances in metacognition experienced by adolescents are they better able to play "the game of thinking." (p. 548)

2. T (pp. 550–551)

3. F   Some people never reach the stage of formal operational thought. (p. 557)

4. F   According to William Gardner, adolescent behavior is guided by assumptions about costs and benefits. (p. 566)

5. T (p. 556)

6. F   In such competitive situations, many students find it easier and psychologically safer not to try, thereby avoiding the potential gains and pains of both success and failure. (p. 559)

7. F   Lower-track students' pace of learning actually slows, as the curriculum generally repeats basic skills that should have been mastered years before. (p. 561)

8. F   Deductive reasoning is a hallmark of formal operational thought. (p. 552)

9. T (p. 568)

10. T (p. 574)

PROGRESS TEST 2

Multiple-Choice Questions

1. **a.** is the answer. (pp. 555, 566)

   b., c., & d. The invincibility fable leads some teens to believe that they are immune to the dangers of risky behaviors; it is not necessarily linked to depression, low self-esteem, or the likelihood that an individual will drop out of school.

2. **b.** is the answer. (p. 550)

3. **d.** is the answer. (p. 557)

4. **b.** is the answer. (p. 555)

5. **c.** is the answer. (p. 555)

   a. This describes the invincibility fable.

   b. This describes the imaginary audience.

   d. This describes adolescent egocentrism in general.

6. **d.** is the answer. (pp. 558–559)

7. **a.** is the answer. (p. 560)

   b. The elementary school backgrounds of boys and girls in math and science are usually very similar.

   c. Both girls and boys are usually exposed to ego- rather than task-involvement learning. Furthermore, task-involvement learning is *more* likely than ego-involvement learning to promote cognitive growth and learning for all students.

   d. There is no evidence that this is so.

8. **b.** is the answer. (p. 560)

a. In ego-involvement learning, grades *are* assigned competitively.

c. Tracking refers to the separation of students into distinct groups based on standardized tests of ability and achievement.

d. This is not a type of classroom environment discussed in the text.

9. **d.** is the answer. (p. 561)

10. **a.** is the answer. (pp. 558–559)

11. **b.** is the answer. (p. 552)

12. **b.** is the answer. (p. 549)

   a. & d. These are more likely to be emphasized by information-processing theorists.

   c. This reflects the biological perspective on development.

13. **d.** is the answer. (p. 570)

14. **b.** is the answer. (p. 574)

15. **d.** is the answer. (p. 559)

Matching Items

1. b (p. 555)	5. i (p. 551)	8. c (p. 559)
2. d (p. 556)	6. j (p. 574)	9. f (p. 560)
3. e (p. 557)	7. h (p. 561)	10. a (p. 548)
4. g (p. 550)		

THINKING CRITICALLY ABOUT CHAPTER 16

1. **c.** is the answer. (p. 557)

2. **c.** is the answer. Although this statement is logically verifiable, preadolescents who lack formal operational thought cannot prove or disprove it. (p. 550)

3. **c.** is the answer. pp. 555–556)

4. **a.** is the answer. (pp. 555–556)

   b. & d. These behaviors are more indicative of a preoccupation with the imaginary audience.

   c. Kalil's questioning attitude is a normal adolescent tendency that helps foster moral reasoning.

5. **d.** is the answer. (p. 548)

   a. This is an example of the imaginary audience.

   b. This is an example of the invincibility fable.

   c. This is an example of adolescent egocentrism.

6. **d.** is the answer. (p. 555)

7. **d.** is the answer. (pp. 549–550)

8. **c.** is the answer. (p. 556)

   a. In this fable adolescents see themselves destined for fame and fortune.

   b. In this fable young people feel that they are

somehow immune to the consequences of common dangers.

   d. This is a stage of moral reasoning in Kohlberg's theory.

9. **a.** is the answer. (pp. 558–559)

10. **a.** is the answer. (p. 560)

11. **b.** is the answer. (p. 561)

12. **b.** is the answer. Mature decision making is least likely to be displayed by adolescents who are under age 16, who have less education, and who have few adults to talk with. (p. 565)

13. **c.** is the answer. (p. 564)

14. **d.** is the answer. (pp. 570–572)

15. **b.** is the answer. (p. 573)

KEY TERMS

1. In Piaget's theory, the last stage of cognitive development is called **formal operational thought**. A hallmark of formal operational thinking is the capacity to reason in terms of possibility rather than merely concrete reality. (p. 549)

2. **Hypothetical thought** involves reasoning about propositions that may or may not reflect reality. (p. 550)

3. **Deductive reasoning** is thinking that moves from the general to the specific, or from a premise to a logical conclusion. (p. 551)

4. **Adolescent egocentrism** refers to the tendency of adolescents to see themselves as much more central and significant on the social stage than they actually are. (p. 555)

5. Adolescents who experience the **invincibility fable** feel that they are immune to the dangers of risky behaviors. (p. 555)

6. Another example of adolescent egocentrism is the **personal fable**, through which adolescents imagine their own lives as unique, heroic, or even mythical. (p. 555)

   Memory aid: A *fable* is a mythical story.

7. Adolescents often create an **imaginary audience** for themselves, as they fantasize about how others will react to their appearance and behavior. (p. 556)

8. The term **person-environment fit** refers to the best setting for an individual's development, as in the optimum educational setting. (p. 557)

9. In **ego-involvement learning**, academic grading is based solely on individual test performance,

and students are ranked against each other. (p. 559)

Memory aid: In **ego-involvement learning,** one's ego is on the line as one is placed in competition with other students.

10. In **task-involvement learning,** grades are based on mastery of knowledge that everyone is expected to attain. (p. 560)

11. **Tracking** is the separation of students into academic groups based on standardized tests of ability and achievement. (p. 561)

12. **Sexually transmitted disease (STD)** includes all diseases that are spread by sexual contact. (p. 568)

13. **Social inoculation** is a new form of sex education in which role-playing and discussion are used to help adolescents develop a cognitive immunity to the various kinds of sexual pressures they might face in the future. (p. 574)

Memory aid: An *inoculation* is an injection of a disease agent into a person, usually to cause a mild form of the disease in order to help a person develop an immunity to it.

CHAPTER 17

Adolescence: Psychosocial Development

Chapter Overview

Chapter 17 focuses on the psychosocial development, particularly the formation of identity, that is required for the attainment of adult status and maturity. The influences of family, friends, and society on this development are examined in some detail. The special problems posed by drug use, delinquency, and adolescent maltreatment are discussed, and suggestions for alleviating or treating these problems are given. Suicide—one of the most perplexing problems of adolescence—is then explored. The chapter concludes with the message that, while no other period of life is characterized by so many changes in the three domains of development, for most young people the teenage years are happy ones. Furthermore, serious problems in adolescence do not necessarily lead to lifelong problems.

NOTE: Answer guidelines for all Chapter 17 questions begin on page 263.

Guided Study

The text chapter should be studied one section at a time. Before you read, preview each section by skimming it, noting headings and boldface items. Then read the appropriate section objectives from the following outline. Keep these objectives in mind and, as you read the chapter section, search for the information that will enable you to meet each objective. Once you have finished a section, write out answers for its objectives.

The Self and Identity (pp. 580–584, 585–586)

1. Discuss several factors that contribute to the dip in self-esteem during adolescence.

2. Describe the development of identity during adolescence, including the importance of social influences on identity formation.

3. Describe the characteristics and give examples of each of the four major identity statuses.

4. (A Closer Look) Discuss the problems of identity formation encountered by minority adolescents.

Family and Friends (pp. 584, 587–600)

5. Discuss parental influence on identity formation, including the effect of parent-child conflict and the factors that affect its frequency and severity.

6. Discuss the role of peers and friends in identity formation and in the development of male-female relationships.

7. Examine the oftentimes complementary, sometimes conflicting, influences of parents and peers on adolescents.

Special Problems (pp. 600–612)

8. Discuss drug use and delinquency among adolescents today, noting their prevalence, significance for later development, and best approaches for prevention or treatment.

9. Discuss adolescent maltreatment, including sexual abuse, noting its prevalence, long-term consequences, and best approaches for prevention or treatment.

10. (text and A Closer Look) Discuss adolescent suicide, noting its prevalence, contributing factors, and warning signs.

Chapter Review

When you have finished reading the chapter, work through the material that follows to review it. Complete the sentences and answer the questions. As you proceed, evaluate your performance for each section by consulting the answers on page 263. Do not continue with the next section until you understand each answer. If you need to, review or reread the appropriate section in the textbook before continuing.

The Self and Identity (pp. 580–584, 585–586)

1. In the process of trying to find their "true self," many adolescents experience the emergence of

_____ _____ .

2. Awareness of the conflicts between one's true self and one's _____

_____ is one of several factors that contribute to a gradual _____ (improvement/decline) in self-esteem during early adolescence. This change in self-esteem begins at about age _____ and reaches its _____ (high/low) point by about age _____ .

3. Another factor that contributes to the change in

self-esteem during adolescence is the transition from _____ _____ to _____ _____ . Two others are the increased size and diversity of _____ _____ and the impact that puberty can have on _____ _____ , perceived _____ , and physical _____ .

4. A teenager's evaluation of his or her _____ _____ is the most important determinant of self-esteem.

5. According to Erikson, the challenge of adolescence is _____ _____ _____ _____ .

6. The specific task of this challenge is to integrate the various aspects of one's self-understanding into a coherent _____ .

7. The ultimate goal of adolescence is to establish a new identity that involves both repudiation and assimilation of childhood values; this is called _____ _____ .

8. The young person who prematurely accepts earlier roles and parental values without exploring alternatives or truly forging a unique identity is experiencing identity _____ .

9. An adolescent who adopts an identity that is the opposite of the one he or she is expected to adopt has taken on a _____ _____ .

10. The young person who has few commitments to goals or values and is apathetic about defining his or her identity is experiencing _____ _____ .

11. A "time-out" period during which a young person experiments with different identities, postponing important choices, is called a _____ .

12. A developmentalist who has extensively compared adolescents' identity statuses with various measures of their cognitive and psychological development is _____ .

13. In terms of their attitudes toward parents, the diffused adolescent is often _____ , the moratorium adolescent is more _____ , the forecloser shows more _____ and _____ , and the achiever treats parents with more _____ .

14. Adolescents who have _____ _____ and those who have prematurely _____ tend to have a strong sense of ethnic identification. Those who have _____ tend to be high in prejudice, while those who are _____ _____ tend to be relatively low in prejudice.

15. The process of identity formation can take _____ or longer.

16. Societies aid the identity formation of adolescents in two ways: by providing _____ , and by providing _____ _____ and _____ that ease the transition from childhood to adulthood.

17. In a culture where most people hold the same moral, political, religious and sexual values, identity is _____ (easier/more difficult) to achieve.

18. (A Closer Look) School staff and curricula typically _____ (are/are not) very helpful to the minority adolescent in finding the right balance between his or her heritage and the majority culture.

19. (A Closer Look) For members of minority ethnic groups, identity achievement is often _____ (more/less) difficult than it is for other adolescents. This may cause them to embrace a _____ identity or, as is more often the case, to _____ on identity prematurely.

20. (A Closer Look) Relationships with parents and other relatives _____ (are/are not) particularly stressful for minority adolescents in the United States. Members of minority groups are often criticized by their

_____ if they make an effort to join the majority culture.

21. (A Closer Look) Over the past forty years in America, the emphasis on the individual's racial and ethnic heritage has once again _____ (increased/decreased).

Family and Friends (pp. 584, 587–600)

22. People who focus on differences between the younger and older generations speak of a

_____ _____ .

Numerous studies have shown that parents and adolescents substantially _____ (agree/disagree) in their political, religious, educational, and vocational opinions. One notable exception concerns attitudes about _____ . Parents tend to estimate the size of the generation gap as _____ (smaller/larger) than adolescents do.

23. The idea that family members in different developmental stages have a natural tendency to see the family in different ways is called the

_____ _____ .

24. In terms of the adolescent's achievement and self-esteem, _____ parenting is better than either _____ or _____ parenting. Especially harmful are parents who are

_____-_____ :

Their teenagers are likely to lack _____ and to be

_____ , _____- _____ , and _____ .

Briefly describe the relationship between the likelihood of adolescent rebellion and family socioeconomic status.

25. Parental watchfulness about where one's child is and what he or she is doing and with whom is called parental _____ . The higher a family's SES, the _____ (greater/less) the need for stringent curfews, restrictions on friends, and other seemingly authoritarian measures.

26. Parent-child conflict is most common in _____ (early/late) adolescence, and is more likely to involve _____ (mothers/fathers) and their _____- (early/late) maturing offspring.

27. Greater family conflict is also often associated with the _____ _____ of puberty, as well as the teenager's changing perceptions of his or her parents' _____ and _____ .

28. First-born children tend to have _____ (more/fewer) conflicts with parents than later-borns do.

29. By late adolescence, parent-child relations in all family types and nations, and among children of both sexes, tend to be _____ (more/less) harmonious. If there is a "generation gap," then, it is more likely to occur in _____ (early/late) adolescence, and to center on issues of _____ and _____ . Approximately _____ percent of all families find that conflict continues throughout adolescence.

30. According to B. Bradford Brown, during adolescence the peer group serves four important functions.

a. _____

b. _____
_____

c. _____
_____

d. _____

31. The largely constructive role of peers runs counter to the notion of _____

_____ . Social pressure to conform _____ (falls/rises) dramatically in early adolescence, until about age _____ , when it begins to _____ (fall/rise).

32. Usually, the first sign of heterosexual attraction is a seeming _____ of members of the other sex. The pattern by which adolescents "warm up" to the other sex _____ (is similar/varies greatly) from nation to nation.

33. The typical adolescent friendship circle is _____ (large/small) and _____ (stable/fluid).

34. Generally, feeling at ease with one's sexual identity takes _____ (less time/longer) if one's preferences are for one's own sex.

35. Anthropological research reveals _____ (very little variation/wide variations) in the pace and character of the emergence of true intimacy. Peers _____ (do/do not) play an important role in this process in most cultures.

36. Despite the _____ and _____ influences of parents and peers, there are distinct differences between them as sources of social support.

37. In conversations, _____ (parents/peers) are more likely to offer and justify their own thoughts than to try to understand an adolescent's ideas. This is one reason that adolescents are more likely to share personal information with _____ (parents/peers).

38. Generally speaking, parent and peer influences are usually _____ (compatible/opposing). Adolescents who experience extreme or overpowering influences in either their parent or peer relationships _____ (are/are not) more vulnerable to problems, such as drug use or delinquency.

39. (Research Report) Although to many teens part-time jobs provide an important social network and contribute to _____ and

_____ , some developmentalists believe that part-time jobs detract from _____ opportunities. In addition, the unskilled jobs teens often perform _____ (usually/rarely) provide opportunities for advancement.

40. (Research Report) Even more worrisome is that students who work long hours are more likely than those who work fewer hours or not at all to use _____ and _____ and to engage in _____ behaviors.

Special Problems (pp. 600–612)

41. When serious adolescent problems occur, they usually are a consequence of long-standing problems in the _____ and persistent vulnerabilities in the adolescent's _____ , as well as the special strains of adolescence.

42. Confidential surveys reveal that most high school seniors today _____ (have/have not) tried alcohol and tobacco. Approximately _____ percent have tried at least one illegal drug, most commonly _____ .

43. After a long period of _____ (decline/increase) dating back to the late 1970s, drug use by adolescents has begun to _____ (increase/decrease) in the 1990s.

44. Regular users of alcohol are more vulnerable to virtually every serious problem of adolescence, including _____ _____ , which is the leading cause of adolescent mortality.

45. A serious concern is the finding that attitudes toward drug use _____ (are/are not) liberalizing among adolescents and the age of first use is _____ (earlier/later) than it had been.

46. Those individuals who use more drugs, more often, at younger ages, than their classmates are _____ (more/no more) likely to

have multiple drug- and alcohol-abuse problems later.

Describe the typical adolescent who is a frequent user of illegal drugs.

47. Researchers have found that patterns of drug use—whether one is a frequent user, abstainer, or experimenter—reflect preexisting _____ _____ .

48. The findings of the fifteen-year longitudinal study of adolescent drug use indicate that, for adolescents who are _____ vulnerable, abstinence from drugs is the best choice.

Identify the two problems of adolescent drug abuse.

49. Arrests are far more likely to occur during _____ and _____ than during any other period of life.

Briefly describe data on gender, class, and ethnic differences in adolescent arrests.

50. Arrest statistics have been questioned because, at least in some jurisdictions, police are more inclined to arrest _____ teenagers than others.

51. If all illegal acts—including minor infractions—are included, most adolescents _____ (do at one time or another/do not) engage in law-breaking that could lead to arrest.

52. The period of greatest increase in criminal activity appears to be age _____ . By age 20, the rate of criminal activity is about _____ the rate at age 17.

53. Adolescents whose law-breaking ends as adulthood approaches usually cite _____ , rather than _____ , as their reason for stopping their criminal behavior.

54. A number of studies have revealed that children who by age 10 have _____ _____ and significant _____ at home are more likely to become delinquent. This is especially true if, as early as age 6, they show signs of _____-_____ _____ and _____ behavior.

55. Most experts agree that those adolescents whose crimes include _____ acts need intensive intervention.

56. The best response to adolescent crime is to encourage the teenager to understand the _____ _____ of his or her offense.

Identify several promising approaches to preventing adolescent delinquency.

57. It is estimated that more than half of all children who leave or are thrown out of their homes between the ages of 10 and 16 were victims of _____ .

58. Children are at the greatest risk of being sexually abused between the ages of _____ and _____ .

59. Adolescents may react to maltreatment in ways

that younger children rarely do, with

_____ , or by _____ .

60. Adolescent problems, such as pregnancy, often are tied to _____ .

61. Two important issues, in terms of the developmental consequences of sexual abuse, are whether the abuse is _____ , and whether it _____ .

62. Although _____ (boys/girls) are the most common victims of sexual abuse, increasingly it is recognized that the other sex is also often sexually abused.

63. Sexual molestation of _____ (girls/boys) occurs more often outside the home and is committed by someone, most often a _____ (male/female), who is not a family member.

64. Mothers and other female relatives seem to be _____ (more/less) often the perpetrators of obvious sexual abuse.

65. Parents who are in _____ with each other, _____ , _____ _____ , _____ , or _____ - _____ are much more likely to be sexually abusive. Income and education level _____ (do/do not) predict who is likely to be sexually abusive.

66. The psychological effects of sexual abuse depend on the _____ and _____ of the abuse, the age of the child, and the _____ _____ once the abuse is known.

67. Adolescent victims of abuse tend to become anxious, angry, and fearful, and they are likely to become _____ . They also tend to become involved again in _____ _____ .

68. Prevention of sexual abuse requires recognizing factors that begin in the community, such as _____ values, community _____ and _____ , and the family's _____ status and _____ isolation.

69. Another recommended preventive measure involves sex education programs that focus not just on biology but also on values concerning

_____ _____ between adults and children, and between men and women.

70. The suicide rate between ages 15 and 19 is _____ (higher/lower) than half that for any subsequent age group. The rate of adolescent suicide has _____ (increased/decreased) over the past twenty-five years.

71. Suicidal adolescents tend to be more _____ than normal adolescents, and show a greater tendency to be _____ _____ .

72. One of the most prominent problems associated with adolescent suicide attempts is long-standing _____ _____ .

73. (A Closer Look) List five warning signs of suicide.

    a. _____
    b. _____
    c. _____
    d. _____
    e. _____

Conclusion (pp. 612–613)

74. For most young people, the teenage years overall are _____ (happy/unhappy) ones.

Progress Test 1

Multiple-Choice Questions

Circle your answers to the following questions and check them with the answers on page 265. If your answer is incorrect, read the explanation for why it is incorrect and then consult the appropriate pages of the text (in parentheses following the correct answer).

1. According to Erikson, the primary task of adolescence is that of establishing:
   a. basic trust.   c. intimacy.
   b. identity.   d. integrity.

2. According to developmentalists who study identity formation, foreclosure involves:
   a. accepting an identity prematurely, without exploration.
   b. taking time off from school, work, and other commitments.
   c. opposing parental values.
   d. failing to commit oneself to a vocational goal.

3. When adolescents adopt an identity that is the opposite of the one they are expected to adopt, they are considered to be taking on a:
   a. foreclosed identity.   c. negative identity.
   b. diffused identity.   d. reverse identity.

4. The main sources of emotional support for most young people who are establishing independence from their parents are:
   a. older adolescents of the opposite sex.
   b. older siblings.
   c. teachers.
   d. peer groups.

5. (A Closer Look) For members of minority ethnic groups, identity achievement may be particularly complicated because:
   a. school staff are often ignorant of very real differences among members of minority groups.
   b. democratic ideology espouses a color-blind, multiethnic society in which background is irrelevant.
   c. parents and other relatives are often unsure about how much to encourage their children to adapt to the majority culture and how much to preserve past tradition.
   d. of all of the above reasons.

6. In a crime-ridden neighborhood, parents can protect their adolescents by keeping close watch over activities, friends, and so on. This practice is called:
   a. generational stake.   c. peer screening.
   b. foreclosure.   d. parental monitoring.

7. Drug use by adolescents:
   a. peaked in the 1970s.
   b. peaked in the 1980s.
   c. has began to increase in the 1990s.
   d. continues to decline in the 1990s.

8. If there is a "generation gap," it is likely to occur in _____ adolescence and to center on issues of _____ .
   a. early; morality   c. early; self-control
   b. late; self-discipline   d. late; politics

9. (A Closer Look) Because of the conflict between their ethnic background and the larger culture, minority adolescents will *most often*:
   a. reject the traditional values of both their ethnic culture and the majority culture.
   b. foreclose on identity prematurely.
   c. declare a moratorium.
   d. experience identity diffusion.

10. In the long run, the most effective programs for preventing juvenile delinquency would include all of the following except:
    a. helping parents discipline in an authoritative manner.
    b. strengthening the schools.
    c. increasing police presence in the area.
    d. shoring up neighborhood networks.

11. Compounding the problem of sexual abuse of boys, abused boys:
    a. feel shame at the idea of being weak.
    b. have fewer sources of social support.
    c. are more likely to be abused by fathers.
    d. have all of the above problems.

12. Compared with normal adolescents, suicidal adolescents are:
    a. more concerned about the future.
    b. less accomplished academically.
    c. more solitary, self-punishing, and depressed.
    d. less likely to have attempted suicide.

13. Most experts feel that the adolescent law-breaker who is most in need of intensive intervention is the one who:
    a. has attention-deficit disorder and other learning problems.
    b. comes from a low-income or single-parent family.
    c. commits antisocial crimes, such as muggings.
    d. has been arrested more than once for playing hookey and disorderly conduct.

14. When a young girl is a victim of long-standing sexual abuse, the most likely perpetrator is a:
    a. mentally disturbed stranger.
    b. boyfriend.
    c. father or close family friend.
    d. brother or younger male relative.

15. Conflict between parents and adolescent offspring:
    a. is most likely to involve fathers and their early-maturing offspring.
    b. is more frequent in single-parent homes.

c. is more likely between first-borns and their parents than between later-borns and their parents.

d. is likely in all of the above situations.

True or False Items

Write *true* or *false* on the line in front of each statement.

_____ 1. In cultures where everyone's values are similar and social change is slight, identity is relatively easy to achieve.

_____ 2. Most adolescents have political views and educational values that are markedly different from those of their parents.

_____ 3. Peer pressure is inherently destructive to the adolescent seeking an identity.

_____ 4. For most adolescents, group socializing and dating precede the establishment of true intimacy with one member of the opposite sex.

_____ 5. The drug most likely to have been tried by a high school senior is alcohol.

_____ 6. A study cited in the text found that, among adolescents, frequent drug users did not differ psychologically from infrequent users, or experimenters.

_____ 7. The vast majority of adolescent boys report that they have at some time engaged in law-breaking that might have led to arrest.

_____ 8. Self-evaluation of physical appearance is the most important determinant of an adolescent's self-esteem.

_____ 9. Parents who are authoritative have the most destructive effect on their teenage offspring.

_____ 10. (A Closer Look) Warning signs of suicide include a sudden decline in school attendance and achievement, and withdrawal from social relationships.

Progress Test 2

Progress Test 2 should be completed during a final chapter review. Answer the following questions after you thoroughly understand the correct answers for the Chapter Review and Progress Test 1.

Multiple-Choice Questions

1. The best way to limit adolescent law-breaking in general would be to:
   a. strengthen the family, school, and community fabric.
   b. increase the number of police officers in the community.
   c. improve the criminal justice system.
   d. establish rehabilitative facilities for law-breakers.

2. (A Closer Look) Which of the following was *not* identified as a warning sign of suicide in an adolescent?
   a. a sudden decline in school achievement
   b. an attempted suicide
   c. a break in a love relationship
   d. a sudden interest in friends and family

3. Research has found that one of the best predictors of later delinquent behavior is _____ during childhood.
   a. quarrels with brothers and sisters
   b. authoritative parenting
   c. learning difficulties in school
   d. a submissive attitude toward peers

4. Adolescents who get along well with peers probably:
   a. are experiencing unusually severe conflict with their parents.
   b. are simply "caving in" to peer pressure and not thinking for themselves.
   c. also have good relationships with their parents.
   d. are first-borns.

5. Which style of parenting do most psychologists recommend?
   a. authoritarian   c. very strict
   b. permissive   d. authoritative

6. Which of the following is the *most* accurate description of the typical friendship circle of young adolescents?
   a. a small and stable group of friends
   b. a small and fluid group of friends
   c. a large and stable group of friends
   d. a large and fluid group of friends

7. The adolescent experiencing identity diffusion is typically:
   a. very apathetic.
   b. a risk-taker anxious to experiment with alternative identities.
   c. willing to accept parental values wholesale, without exploring alternatives.
   d. one who rebels against all forms of authority.

8. Adolescents help each other in many ways, including:
   a. identity formation.   c. social skills.
   b. independence.   d. all of the above.

9. Crime statistics show that during adolescence:
   a. males and females are equally likely to be arrested.
   b. males are more likely to be arrested than females.
   c. females are more likely to be arrested than males.
   d. males commit more crimes than females, but are less likely to be arrested.

10. Which of the following is the most common problem behavior among adolescents?
   a. pregnancy
   b. daily use of illegal drugs
   c. minor law-breaking
   d. attempts at suicide

11. A "time-out" period during which a young person experiments with different identities, postponing important choices, is called a(n):
   a. identity foreclosure.   c. identity diffusion.
   b. negative identity.   d. moratorium.

12. When adolescents' political, religious, educational, and vocational opinions are compared with their parents', the so-called "generation gap":
   a. is much smaller than when the younger and older generations are compared overall.
   b. is much wider than when the younger and older generations are compared overall.

c. is wider between parents and sons than between parents and daughters.
d. is wider between parents and daughters than between parents and sons.

13. Which of the following was *not* cited as a reason for the decline in self-esteem that often accompanies adolescence?
   a. conflicts between one's true and ideal selves
   b. the transition from elementary school to middle school
   c. increasing peer pressure
   d. threats to body image that accompany puberty

14. Individuals who experiment with drugs early are:
   a. typically affluent teenagers who are experiencing an identity moratorium.
   b. more likely to have multiple drug-abuse problems later on.
   c. less likely to have alcohol-abuse problems later on.
   d. usually able to resist later peer pressure leading to long-term addiction.

15. Parents who are _____ are much more likely to abuse or neglect their adolescent children.
   a. immature   c. alcoholic
   b. socially isolated d. all of the above

Matching Items

Match each term or concept with its corresponding description or definition.

Terms or Concepts
_____ 1. identity
_____ 2. identity achievement
_____ 3. foreclosure
_____ 4. negative identity
_____ 5. identity diffusion
_____ 6. moratorium
_____ 7. generation gap
_____ 8. generational stake
_____ 9. parental monitoring

Descriptions or Definitions
a. premature identity formation
b. family members in different developmental stages see the family in different ways
c. the adolescent has few commitments to goals or values
d. differences between the younger and older generations
e. an identity opposite of the one an adolescent is expected to adopt
f. awareness of where children are and what they are doing
g. an individual's self-definition
h. a time-out period during which adolescents experiment with alternative identities
i. the adolescent establishes his or her own goals and values

Thinking Critically About Chapter 17

Answer these questions the day before an exam as a final check on your understanding of the chapter's terms and concepts.

1. From childhood, Sharon thought she wanted to follow in her mother's footsteps and be a homemaker. Now, at age 40 with a home and family, she admits to herself that what she really wanted to be was a medical researcher. Erik Erikson would probably say that Sharon:
   a. adopted a negative identity when she was a child.
   b. experienced identity foreclosure at an early age.
   c. never progressed beyond the obvious identity diffusion she experienced as a child.
   d. took a moratorium from identity formation.

2. Fifteen-year-old David is rebelling against his devoutly religious parents by taking drugs, stealing, and engaging in other antisocial behaviors. Evidently, David has:
   a. foreclosed on his identity.
   b. declared an identity moratorium.
   c. adopted a negative identity.
   d. experienced identity diffusion.

3. Fourteen-year-old Sean, who is fiercely proud of his Irish heritage, is prejudiced against members of several other ethnic groups. It is likely that, in forming his identity, Sean:
   a. attained identity achievement.
   b. foreclosed on his identity.
   c. declared a lengthy moratorium.
   d. experienced identity diffusion.

4. (A Closer Look) In 1957, 6-year-old Raisel and her parents emigrated from Poland to the United States. Compared to her parents, who grew up in a culture in which virtually everyone held the same religious, moral, political, and sexual values, Raisel is likely to have:
   a. an easier time achieving her own unique identity.
   b. a more difficult time forging her identity.
   c. a greater span of time in which to forge her own identity.
   d. a shorter span of time in which to forge her identity.

5. An adolescent tends to exaggerate the importance of differences in her values and those of her parents. Her parents see these differences as smaller and less important. This phenomenon is called the:
   a. generation gap.
   c. family enigma.
   b. generational stake.
   d. parental imperative.

6. In our society, the most obvious examples of institutionalized moratoria on identity formation are:
   a. the Boy Scouts and the Girl Scouts.
   b. college and the peacetime military.
   c. marriage and divorce.
   d. Bar Mitzvahs and baptisms.

7. First-time parents Norma and Norman are worried that, during adolescence, their healthy parental influence will be undone as their children are encouraged by peers to become sexually promiscuous, drug-addicted, or delinquent. Their wise neighbor, who is a developmental psychologist, tells them that:
   a. during adolescence, peers are generally more likely to complement the influence of parents than they are to pull their friends in the opposite direction.
   b. research suggests that peers provide a negative influence in every major task of adolescence.
   c. only through authoritarian parenting can parents give children the skills they need to resist peer pressure.
   d. unless their children show early signs of learning difficulties or antisocial behavior, parental monitoring is unnecessary.

8. Regarding experimentation with psychoactive drugs, the *best* choice for the young adolescent who tends to be emotionally vulnerable or unstable is:
   a. avoiding drugs that are socially disinhibiting, such as alcohol.
   b. occasional experimentation with marijuana and no more than one other drug.
   c. occasional use of mood-elevating drugs, such as cocaine.
   d. complete abstinence from psychoactive drugs.

9. In forming an identity, the young person seeks to make meaningful connections with his or her past. This seeking is described by Erikson as an unconscious striving for:
   a. individual uniqueness.
   b. peer group membership.
   c. continuity of experience.
   d. vocational identity.

10. (A Closer Look) A friend tells you that he doesn't want to live any more because his girlfriend has left him. The most helpful response would be:
    a. "Don't be ridiculous. You have plenty to live for."
    b. "Everyone has these experiences; you'll get over it."
    c. "She wasn't right for you. You're certain to find someone else."
    d. "When did this happen? Let's talk about it."

11. Statistically, the person least likely to commit a crime is a(n):
    a. African-American or Latino adolescent.
    b. middle-class white boy.
    c. white adolescent of any socioeconomic background.
    d. Asian-American.

12. In longitudinal studies, many adults report law-breaking that ended in adulthood. The reason they most often give for having stopped their criminal behavior is:
    a. incarceration or other severe punishment.
    b. peer influence.
    c. intervention, such as psychotherapy.
    d. maturity, or simply growing up.

13. Adolescents who lack confidence or who rebel by leaving home, taking drugs, or becoming sexually active too early are more likely to come from:
    a. authoritative low-income families.
    b. authoritative high-income families.
    c. very strict, or very permissive, lower-income families.
    d. average-income families in which disciplinary measures are moderate.

14. When he was a teenager, Dwayne used various psychoactive drugs regularly. As a result, it is *most* likely that at age 30 Dwayne is:
    a. an avid activist against drug use.
    b. a more mature and happier individual.
    c. not very good at relating to people.
    d. all of the above.

15. Twenty-four-year-old Connie, who has a distorted view of sexuality, has gone from one abusive relationship with a man to another. It is likely that Connie:
    a. has been abusing drugs all her life.
    b. was sexually abused as a child.
    c. will eventually become a normal, nurturing mother.
    d. had attention-deficit disorder as a child.

Key Terms

Using your own words, write a brief definition or explanation of each of the following terms on a separate piece of paper.

1. identity versus role confusion
2. identity
3. identity achievement
4. foreclosure
5. negative identity
6. identity diffusion
7. moratorium
8. generational stake
9. parental monitoring
10. peer pressure

ANSWERS
CHAPTER REVIEW

1. possible (or multiple) selves
2. ideal self; decline; 11; low; 13
3. elementary school; junior high (or middle school); peer networks; body image; attractiveness; self-confidence
4. physical appearance
5. identity versus role confusion
6. identity
7. identity achievement
8. foreclosure
9. negative identity
10. identity diffusion
11. moratorium
12. James Marcia
13. withdrawn; independent; respect; deference; concern
14. achieved identity; foreclosed; foreclosed; identity achievers
15. ten years
16. values; social structures; customs
17. easier
18. are not
19. more; negative; foreclose
20. are; peers
21. increased

22. generation gap; agree; sex; smaller

23. generational stake

24. authoritative; authoritarian; permissive; rejecting-neglecting; confidence; depressed; low-achieving; delinquent

Adolescents who lack confidence or who rebel by leaving home, taking drugs, or becoming sexually active too early are more likely to come from very strict, or very permissive, lower-income families than from homes that are more moderate in discipline and average in SES.

25. monitoring; less

26. early; mothers; early

27. physical changes; wisdom; authority

28. more

29. more; early; self-discipline; self-control; 20

30. a. a source of information and a self-help group

    b. a source of support for the adolescent who is adjusting to changes in the social ecology of adolescence

    c. a kind of mirror in which to check one's reflection

    d. a sounding board for experimenting and discovering which of one's personality characteristics and possible behaviors will be accepted and admired

31. peer pressure; rises; 14; fall

32. dislike; is similar

33. large; fluid

34. longer

35. wide variations; do

36. overlapping; complementary

37. parents; peers

38. compatible; are

39. independence; self-esteem; educational; rarely

40. drugs; alcohol; delinquent

41. home; temperament

42. have; 40; marijuana

43. decline; increase

44. violent death

45. are; earlier

46. more

The typical user is a "troubled adolescent" who is interpersonally alienated, emotionally withdrawn, and manifestly unhappy, and who expresses his or her maladjustment through undercontrolled, overtly antisocial behavior.

47. personality characteristics

48. emotionally

One problem applies to all adolescents, whose poor judgment about when and how to experiment with drugs, and whose behavior when "under the influence," might lead to fatal accidents or other serious consequences. The second applies to those adolescents who use drugs as an attempt to solve or forget long-standing problems.

49. adolescence; young adulthood

Boys are four times as likely to be arrested as girls, lower-SES adolescents are almost twice as likely to be arrested as middle-SES adolescents, and African-American and Latino youth are close to twice as likely to be arrested as European-Americans, who are more than twice as likely to be arrested as Asian-Americans.

50. lower-SES or dark-skinned

51. do at one time or another

52. 15 or 16; half

53. maturity; contact with the criminal justice system

54. learning difficulties; stresses; attention-deficit disorder; antisocial

55. antisocial

56. social consequences

Helping parents discipline their children authoritatively, strengthening schools so that fewer young people have learning problems, and shoring up neighborhood networks so that community institutions provide constructive challenges for youths are all promising ways of preventing delinquency.

57. maltreatment

58. 7; 13

59. self-destruction; counterattack

60. maltreatment

61. persistent; interferes with normal development

62. girls

63. boys; male

64. less

65. conflict; immature; socially isolated; alcoholic; drug-abusing; do not

66. extent; duration; reaction of other people

67. depressed; abusive relationships

68. cultural; stress; support; economic; social

69. appropriate relationships

70. lower; increased

71. solitary; depressed, anxious, or to have other psychiatric problems, to feel hopeless and self-

punishing, and to believe they lack support and understanding from others

72. family conflict

73. **a.** a sudden decline in school attendance and achievement

   b. a break in a love relationship

   c. withdrawal from social relationships

   d. an attempted suicide

   e. cluster suicides

74. happy

PROGRESS TEST 1

Multiple-Choice Questions

1. **b.** is the answer. (p. 581)

   a. According to Erikson, this is the crisis of infancy.

   c. & d. In Erikson's theory, these crises occur later in life.

2. **a.** is the answer. (p. 582)

   b. This describes an identity moratorium.

   c. This describes negative identity.

   d. This describes identity diffusion.

3. **c.** is the answer. (p. 582)

4. **d.** is the answer. (p. 591)

5. **d.** is the answer. (p. 585)

6. **d.** is the answer. (p. 589)

   a. The generational stake refers to differences in how family members from different generations view the family.

   b. Foreclosure refers to the premature establishment of identity.

   c. Peer screening is an aspect of parental monitoring, but was not specifically discussed in the text.

7. **c.** is the answer. (p. 600)

8. **c.** is the answer. (p. 591)

9. **b.** is the answer. (p. 585)

   a. This occurs in some cases, but not in *most* cases.

   c. Moratorium is a "time-out" in identity formation in order to allow the adolescent to try out alternative identities. It is generally not a solution in such cases.

   d. Young people who experience identity diffusion are often apathetic, which is not the case here.

10. **c.** is the answer. (p. 606)

11. **a.** is the answer. (p. 608)

b. This was not discussed in the text.

c. This is true of girls.

12. **c.** is the answer. (p. 611)

13. **c.** is the answer. (p. 606)

14. **c.** is the answer. (p. 608)

15. **c.** is the answer. (p. 590)

   a. In fact, parent-child conflict is more likely to involve mothers and their early-maturing offspring.

   b. The text did not compare the rate of conflict in two-parent and single-parent homes.

True or False Items

1. T (p. 584)

2. F Numerous studies have shown substantial agreement between parents and their adolescent children on political opinions and educational values. (p. 587)

3. F (p. 593)

4. T (p. 594)

5. T (p. 600)

6. F Frequent drug users were more troubled, alienated, and likely to have unsatisfactory interpersonal relationships than experimenters, who were outgoing and cheerful. (p. 603)

7. T (p. 605)

8. T (p. 581)

9. F Authoritative parenting is the style most likely to *foster* the adolescent's achievement and self-esteem. (p. 588)

10. T (p. 612)

PROGRESS TEST 2

Multiple-Choice Questions

1. **a.** is the answer. (p. 606)

2. **d.** is the answer. In fact, just the opposite is true: a sudden loss of interest in friends and family may be a warning sign of suicide. (p. 612)

3. **c.** is the answer. (p. 605)

4. **c.** is the answer. (p. 597)

   d. The text does not discuss the relationship between birth order and peer relationships.

5. **d.** is the answer. (p. 588)

6. **d.** is the answer. (p. 594)

7. **a.** is the answer. (p. 582)

b. This describes an adolescent undergoing an identity moratorium.

c. This describes identity foreclosure.

d. This describes an adolescent who is adopting a negative identity.

8. **d.** is the answer. (p. 592)

9. **b.** is the answer. (p. 604)

10. **c.** is the answer. (p. 605)

11. **d.** is the answer. (p. 582)

a. Identity foreclosure occurs when the adolescent prematurely adopts an identity, without fully exploring alternatives.

b. Adolescents who adopt an identity that is opposite to the one they are expected to develop have taken on a negative identity.

c. Identity diffusion occurs when the adolescent is apathetic and has few commitments to goals or values.

12. **a.** is the answer. (p. 587)

c. & d. The text does not suggest that the size of the generation gap varies with the offspring's sex.

13. **c.** is the answer. (pp. 580–581)

14. **b.** is the answer. (p. 602)

15. **d.** is the answer. (p. 608)

Matching Items

1. g (p. 581)	4. e (p. 582)	7. d (p. 587)
2. i (p. 582)	5. c (p. 582)	8. b (p. 588)
3. a (p. 582)	6. h (p. 582)	9. f (p. 589)

THINKING CRITICALLY ABOUT CHAPTER 17

1. **b.** is the answer. Apparently, Sharon never explored alternatives or truly forged a unique personal identity. (p. 582)

a. Individuals who rebel by adopting an identity that is the opposite of the one they are expected to adopt have taken on a negative identity.

c. Individuals who experience identity diffusion have few commitments to goals or values. This was not Sharon's problem.

d. Had she taken a moratorium on identity formation, Sharon would have experimented with alternative identities and perhaps would have chosen that of a medical researcher.

2. **c.** is the answer. (p. 582)

3. **b.** is the answer. (pp. 582–583)

a. Identity achievers often have a strong sense of ethnic identification, but usually are low in prejudice.

c. & d. The text does not present research that links ethnic pride and prejudice with either identity diffusion or moratorium.

4. **b.** is the answer. Minority adolescents struggle with finding the right balance between transcending their background and becoming immersed in it. (pp. 585–586)

c. & d. The text does not suggest that the amount of time adolescents have to forge their identities varies from one ethnic group to another, or has changed over historical time.

5. **b.** is the answer. (p. 588)

a. The generation gap refers to actual differences in attitudes and values between the younger and older generations. This example is concerned with how large these differences are perceived to be.

c. & d. These terms are not used in the text in discussing family conflict.

6. **b.** is the answer. (p. 582)

7. **a.** is the answer. (p. 597)

b. In fact, just the opposite is true.

c. Developmentalists recommend authoritative, rather than authoritarian, parenting.

d. Parental monitoring is important for all adolescents.

8. **d.** is the answer. (p. 603)

9. **c.** is the answer. (p. 581)

10. **d.** is the answer. A break in a love relationship is a warning sign of suicide, and this person is obviously thinking about it. This attempt to communicate should be acted upon immediately; one way is to get the person to talk about it . (p. 612)

11. **d.** is the answer. (p. 604)

12. **d.** is the answer. (p. 605)

13. **c.** is the answer. (p. 589)

a., b., & d. Adolescents from authoritative families (in which disciplinary measures typically are moderate), regardless of SES, tend to be better adjusted and more confident than those from very strict or very permissive families.

14. **c.** is the answer. (pp. 603–604)

15. **b.** is the answer. (pp. 608–609)

KEY TERMS

1. Erikson's term for the psychosocial crisis of adolescence, **identity versus role confusion** refers to the adolescent's need to form a coherent identity. (p. 581)

2. **Identity**, as used by Erikson, refers to a person's self-definition as a separate individual in terms of roles, attitudes, beliefs, and aspirations. (p. 581)

3. In Erikson's theory, **identity achievement** occurs when adolescents attain their new identity by establishing their own goals and values, and abandoning some of those set by parents and society. (p. 582)

4. In identity **foreclosure**, the adolescent forms an identity prematurely, accepting earlier roles and parental values wholesale, without truly forging a unique personal identity. (p. 582)

5. Adolescents who take on a **negative identity** adopt an identity that is the opposite of the one they are expected to adopt. (p. 582)

6. Adolescents who experience **identity diffusion** have few commitments to goals or values and are often apathetic about trying to find an identity. (p. 582)

7. In the process of finding a mature identity, many young people seem to declare a **moratorium**, a kind of time-out during which they experiment with alternative identities without trying to settle on any one. (p. 582)

8. The **generational stake** refers to the tendency of each family member, because of that person's different developmental stage, to see the family in a certain way. (p. 588)

9. **Parental monitoring** is parental watchfulness about where one's child is and what he or she is doing, and with whom. (p. 589)

10. **Peer pressure** refers to the idea that the norms of the peer group force adolescents to act in ways that they otherwise would not. (p. 593)